Once More
Around the Park

Once More Around the Park

A BASEBALL READER

by Roger Angell

IVAN R. DEE, PUBLISHER
CHICAGO

Grateful acknowledgment is made to the following for permission to reprint previously published material:

HOUGHTON MIFFLIN COMPANY: "In the Fire," "Quis," "Not So, Boston," "La Vida," and "The Arms Talks" reprinted from *Season Ticket* by Roger Angell. Copyright © 1988 by Roger Angell. Reprinted by permission of Houghton Mifflin Company.

SIMON & SCHUSTER, INC.: "Three for the Tigers," "Gone for Good," "Agincourt and After," and "On the Ball" reprinted from *Five Seasons* by Roger Angell. Copyright © 1972, 1973, 1974, 1975, 1976 by Roger Angell. "Several Stories with Sudden Endings," "Wilver's Way," "So Long at the Fair," "Distance," "The Web of the Game," and "In the Country" reprinted from *Late Innings* by Roger Angell. Copyright © 1972, 1973, 1974, 1975, 1976 by Roger Angell. Reprinted by permission of Simon & Schuster, Inc.

VIKING PENGUIN: "Box Scores," copyright © 1963 by Roger Angell, "The 'Go!' Shouters," copyright © 1962 by Roger Angell, "Days and Nights with the Unbored," copyright © 1969 by Roger Angell, "The Interior Stadium," copyright © 1972 by Roger Angell. Reprinted from *The Summer Game* by Roger Angell, by permission of Viking Penguin, a division of Penguin Books USA Inc.

"Box Scores" first appeared in 1963 as a Comment in *The New Yorker*. "Life in the Pen" first appeared as a "Profile" in *The New Yorker*. Seventeen of this book's selections first appeared as "Sporting Scene" articles in *The New Yorker*.

Library of Congress Cataloging-in-Publication Data:
Angell, Roger.
    Once more around the park : a baseball reader / Roger Angell.—1st Ivan R. Dee paperback ed.
        p. cm.
    Reprint. Originally published: New York : Ballantine Books, 1991.
    ISBN 1-56663-371-0 (alk. paper)
        1. Baseball. I. Title.

GV867 .A538 2001
796.357—dc21

00-050436

Contents

CONTENTS

Preface

This is a selection of baseball pieces of mine previously published in four books—*The Summer Game, Five Seasons, Late Innings,* and *Season Ticket*—along with a few chapters not previously booked: a re-collection, one might say. Baseball and memory come together so naturally—the silky leather of an old mitt slipping into place around the warm hand it has come to replicate—that I feel no trepidation in presenting a book that encompasses almost thirty years of writing about the game. Anyone who has spent only a dozen hours at the park comes to understand that baseball's slow innings and noisy evenings accrue oddly in mind, and constitute not just an entertainment but an elegant way of marking the years. It is the pastime: no other sport owns so sweet a monicker or qualifies for this one. This book concludes with some early observations of mine about time and the river of baseball, but I was often aware of the conjunction while I reread (often for the first time in many years) articles and chapters of mine about the game and began to select among them for this reader. I had half-expected that the earlier stuff—about Casey Stengel's Mets, or the Big Red Machine, or the dashing, mustachioed early Oaklands, or Willy Stargell at full flower, or a younger Tom Seaver—would sadden me a little or tarnish my feelings about today's stars and champions, but that didn't happen. I would hate it if this book made anyone yearn for baseball time gone by, or otherwise tainted our pleasures in the game. The scarcity of landmarks like Mount Ted Williams, Lac DiMaggio, or Gibson Gulch in our present baseball landscape does not alter my conviction that the game is faster and more difficult today, and in many respects better played, than it ever was, and its regulars more talented. I never go to an Old Timers' Day if I can help it.

Dan Quisenberry, the dandy side-arming reliever, announced his retirement from baseball this spring, and my feelings at the news again made me think about the mystery of baseball's continuity. It was hard to see him go, for he was an original: a gentle spirit, a comic sensibility, and a fierce competitor, all rolled into one (there is a glimpse of him, just for flavor, in a very short chapter here). My regret came also from my knowledge of Quis's appreciation of some secondary aspects of big-league ball—the cameraderie of the clubhouse, the proper study of restaurants and museums and shops and walks in cities around the league, a fondness for the quiet hours between games—which he would now of necessity forgo. But along with this I felt an odd pleasure that I had noticed and wondered about before when other favorites of mine had hung up their spikes at last. Quisenberry had struggled in recent years, moving from the Royals to the Cardinals and then to the Giants in a space of less than three seasons, while encountering some hard innings and diminished appearances, but now all that was over. He had closed the book, and in that moment had become fresh and young again, and wonderfully clear in my mind. He was complete. More vividly now, I could see his angular, unthreatening appearance on the mound as he went about his work; the little staggering hop that finished off his odd, upsweeping delivery; and the round-eyed attention he gave to the adventurous passage of each pitch. This fixitive power of baseball memory is known to every fan, I believe, and each of us retains an album of sharp miniatures—the glitter of Reggie's glasses under his deep helmet as he turns his dangerous gaze toward the pitcher; Willie Mays going down in the box in a splatter, with the bat flying, after still another knockdown, and then bouncing up again, happy at the thought of what he will do with the next pitch; Pete Rose galloping around first base, watching the batted ball loose in the outfield once again; Catfish Hunter resettling his cap out there; Carl Yastrzemski hitching at his pants with his right hand and tapping the plate, gloom-stricken at the weight of the moment and the game and the season; Johnny Mize, melon-cheeked and immobile in the batter's box, unfurling his sweet stroke and lining the ball into left field; and so on, right back to the little twirl of the bat, up behind his head, as Lou Gehrig starts his weight forward toward the pitch. Sometimes I wish I had private portraits, of friends or loves gone by, that stayed as clear as these.

This is a linear sport. Something happens and then something else happens, and then the next man comes up and digs in at the plate. Here's the pitch, and here, after a pause, is the next. There's time to write it down in your scorecard or notebook, and then perhaps to look about and reflect on what's starting to happen out there now. It's not much like the swirl and blur of hockey and basketball, or the highway crashes of the NFL. Baseball is the writer's game (there were three hundred and fifty baseball books published in the past year), and its train of thought, we come to sense, is a shuttle, carrying us constantly forward to the next pitch or inning, or to the sudden double into the left-field corner, but we keep hold of the other half of our ticket, for the return trip on the same line. We anticipate happily, and, coming home, reenter an old landscape brightened with fresh colors. Baseball games and plays and mannerisms (even the angle of a cap) fade stubbornly and come to mind unbidden, putting us back in some particular park on that special October afternoon or June evening. The players are as young as ever, and we, perhaps, not yet entirely old.

○

One more ride on the local brings back for me the precise tone of voice—at once polite and venturesome, weighing and inviting—with which William Shawn, my editor at the *New Yorker*, first suggests that I might want to try my hand at some sort of baseball piece for the magazine. It is the winter of 1962, and in time we decide that I should head down to the spring training camps in Florida and see what I find there. The assignment is vague and I am apprehensive. It has not occurred to me that I am beginning what will turn out to be a longish journey, but for Shawn, I later came to realize, every piece contained boundless possibilities. He never put limits on what one of his reporters might discover out there, or how the subject should be attacked, or what length or tone or turn the article would take in the end, or what its writer might wish to look into next. His patience had no boundaries, and his curiosity and passion for facts always seemed to exceed my own. Everyone who was lucky enough to write for Shawn had this same exhilarating and sustaining experience, and came to count on it across the years. He was not a baseball fan, I discovered, but that didn't matter. One afternoon after I'd handed in that first piece, or perhaps the one that came next, there was a polite tap at my door and he walked in, with some galleys of mine in his hand. He apologized and then came forward and pointed out a place on the proof. "What's this?" he asked.

I looked and said, "Oh, that's a double play."

"I'm sorry," he said, "but what's a double play?"

I explained, and I can still see the look of barely suppressed excitement in his eyes and the pinkish flush on his cheeks as the news sank home.

"Really?" he whispered. *"Really?"*

I laughed a little when he'd left, but then I stopped and thought about the D.P. again, almost for the first time in years, and saw the wonder of it. He'd set me on my way.

○

This is not a "Best of————" anthology; All-Star lineups promise much but tend to be fatuous once they take the field. It is a private selection of baseball stories (or parts of stories) of mine that still gave me pleasure when I went back and read them again. The pieces are presented in rough but not absolute chronological order, but this is not a history of baseball from 1962 to 1990, or even a balanced presentation of my work in that period. Only five World Series out of the twenty-nine I have covered are dealt with in any sustained fashion, and my happily repeated working vacations of spring training have been trimmed as well. The later pieces, I notice, are longer than the earlier ones, but I learned more about baseball as I went along and had more that I wanted to pass on. I have not rewritten, or supplied any catch-up material about the hundreds of players and other baseball figures, seen here at their best or worst but not often at rest.

—R.A.

Once More
Around the Park

Box Scores

Today the *Times* reported the arrival of the first pitchers and catchers at the spring training camps, and the morning was abruptly brightened, as if by the delivery of a seed catalogue. The view from my city window still yields only frozen tundras of trash, but now spring is guaranteed and one of my favorite urban flowers, the baseball box score, will burgeon and flourish through the warm, languid, information-packed weeks and months just ahead. I can remember a spring, not too many years ago, when a prolonged New York newspaper strike threatened to extend itself into the baseball season, and my obsessively fannish mind tried to contemplate the desert prospect of a summer without daily box scores. The thought was impossible; it was like trying to think about infinity. Had I been deprived of those tiny lists of sporting personae and accompanying columns of runs batted in, strikeouts, double plays, assists, earned runs, and the like, all served up in neat three-inch packages from Pittsburgh, Milwaukee, Baltimore, Houston, and points east and west, only the most aggressive kind of blind faith would have convinced me that the season had begun at all or that its distant, invisible events had any more reality than the silent collision of molecules. This year, thank heaven, no such crisis of belief impends; summer will be admitted to our breakfast table as usual, and in the space of half a cup of coffee I will be able to discover, say, that Ferguson Jenkins went eight innings in Montreal and won his fourth game of the season while giving up five hits, that Al Kaline was horse-collared by Fritz Peterson at the Stadium, that Tony Oliva hit a double and a single off Mickey Lolich in Detroit, that Juan Marichal was bombed by the Reds in the top of the sixth at Candlestick Park, and that similar disasters and triumphs befell a couple of dozen-odd of the other ballplayers—favorites and knaves—whose fortunes I follow from April to October.

3

The box score, being modestly arcane, is a matter of intense indifference, if not irritation, to the non-fan. To the baseball-bitten, it is not only informative, pictorial, and gossipy but lovely in aesthetic structure. It represents happenstance and physical flight exactly translated into figures and history. Its totals—batters' credit vs. pitchers' debit—balance as exactly as those in an accountant's ledger. And a box score is more than a capsule archive. It is a precisely etched miniature of the sport itself, for baseball, in spite of its grassy spaciousness and apparent unpredictability, is the most intensely and satisfyingly mathematical of all our outdoor sports. Every player in every game is subjected to a cold and ceaseless accounting; no ball is thrown and no base is gained without an instant responding judgment—ball or strike, hit or error, yea or nay—and an ensuing statistic. This encompassing neatness permits the baseball fan, aided by experience and memory, to extract from a box score the same joy, the same hallucinatory reality, that prickles the scalp of a musician when he glances at a page of his score of *Don Giovanni* and actually hears bassos and sopranos, woodwinds and violins.

The small magic of the box score is cognominal as well as mathematical. Down the years, the rosters of the big-league teams have echoed and twangled with evocative, hilarious, ominous, impossible, and exactly appropriate names. The daily, breathing reality of the ballplayers' names in box scores accounts in part, it seems to me, for the rarity of convincing baseball fiction. No novelist has yet been able to concoct a baseball hero with as tonic a name as Willie Mays or Duke Snider or Vida Blue. No contemporary novelist would dare a supporting cast of characters with Dickensian names like those that have stuck with me ever since I deciphered my first box scores and began peopling the lively landscape of baseball in my mind—Ossee Schreckengost, Smead Jolley, Slim Sallee, Elon Hogsett, Urban Shocker, Burleigh Grimes, Hazen Shirley Cuyler, Heinie Manush, Cletus Elwood Poffenberger, Virgil Trucks, Enos Slaughter, Luscious Easter, and Eli Grba. And not even a latter-day O. Henry would risk a tale like the true, electrifying history of a pitcher named Pete Jablonowski, who disappeared from the Yankees in 1933 after several seasons of inept relief work with various clubs. Presumably disheartened by seeing the losing pitcher listed as "J'bl'n's'i" in the box scores of his day, he changed his name to Pete Appleton in the semi-privacy of the minors, and came back to win fourteen games for the Senators in 1936 and to continue in the majors for another decade.

The "Go!" Shouters

—JUNE 1962

Through April and May, I resisted frequent invitations, delivered via radio and television, to come up to the Polo Grounds and see "those amazin' Mets." I even resisted a particularly soft blandishment, extended by one of the Mets' announcers on a Saturday afternoon, to "bring the wife and come on up tomorrow after church and brunch." My nonattendance was not caused by any unwillingness to attach my loyalty to New York's new National League team. The only amazement generated by the Mets had been their terrifying departure from the runway in a full nosedive—the team lost the first nine games of its regular season—and I had decided it would be wiser, and perhaps kinder, to postpone my initial visit until the novice crew had grasped the first principles of powered flight. By the middle of May, however, the Mets had developed a pleasing habit of coming from behind in late innings, and when they won both ends of a doubleheader in Milwaukee on May 20, I knew it was time to climb aboard. In the five days from Memorial Day through June 3, the Los Angeles Dodgers and the San Francisco Giants were scheduled to play seven games at the Polo Grounds, and, impelled by sentiment for the returning exiles, who would be revisiting the city for the first time since 1957, and by guilt over my delayed enthusiasm for the Mets, I impulsively bought seats for all five days. The resulting experience was amazin', all right, but not quite in the manner expected by the Mets or by me or by any of the other 197,428 fans who saw those games.

I took my fourteen-year-old daughter to the opening doubleheader, against the Dodgers, and even before we arrived at the park it was clear that neither the city subway system nor the Mets themselves had really believed we were coming. By game time, there were standees three-deep behind the lower-deck stands, sitting-standees peering through the rafters from the ramps behind the upper deck, and opportunist-standees perched on telephone booths and lining the runways behind the bleachers. The shouts, the cheers, and the deep, steady roar made by 56,000-odd fans in excited conversation were comical and astonishing, and a cause for self-congratulation; just by coming out in such ridiculous numbers (ours was the biggest baseball crowd of the 1962 season, the biggest Polo Grounds crowd since September 6, 1942), we had heightened our own occasion, building a considerable phenomenon out of the attention and passion each of us had brought along for the games and for the players we were to see.

It must have been no more than an hour later when it first occurred to me that the crowds, rather than the baseball, might be the real news of the two series. The Dodgers ran up twelve runs between the second and the sixth innings. I was keeping score, and after I had jotted down the symbols for their seven singles, two doubles, one triple, three home runs, three bases on balls, and two stolen bases in that span, the Dodgers half of my scorecard looked as if a cloud of gnats had settled on it. I was pained for the Mets, and embarrassed as a fan.

"Baseball isn't usually like this," I explained to my daughter.

"Sometimes it is," she said. "This is like the fifth grade against the sixth grade at school."

For a time, the long, low "Oooh!" sound and the accompanying thunderclap of applause that greeted the cannon shots by Ron Fairly, Willie Davis, Frank Howard, and the other visitors convinced me that I was in an audience made up mostly of veteran Dodger loyalists. The Mets' pitchers came and went in silence, and there were derisive cheers when the home team finally got the third out in the top of the fourth and came in to bat trailing 10–0. I didn't change my mind even when I heard the explosive roar for the pop-fly homer by Gil Hodges that led off the home half; Hodges, after all, is an ex-Dodger and perhaps the most popular ballplayer in the major leagues today. Instantly, however, I learned how wrong I had been. Gil's homer pulled the cork, and now there arose from all over the park a full, furious, happy shout of "Let's go, *Mets*! Let's go, *Mets*!" There were wild cries of encouragement before every pitch, boos for every called strike. This was no Dodger crowd, but a huge gathering of sentimental home-towners. Nine runs to the bad, doomed, insanely hopeful, they pleaded raucously for the impossible. When Hickman and Mantilla hit a double and a single for one run, and Christopher singled for another, the Mets fans screeched, yawped, pounded their palms, leaped up and down, and raised such a din that players in both dugouts ducked forward and peered nervously back over the dugout roofs at the vast assemblage that had suddenly gone daft behind them.

The fans' hopes, of course, *were* insane. The Dodgers got two runs back almost instantly in the fifth, and in the top of the ninth their lead was 13–4.

Undiscouraged, the spectators staged another screaming fit in the bottom half, and the Mets responded with four singles, good for two more runs, before Sandy Koufax, the Dodger pitcher, grinning with embarrassment and disbelief, got the last man out. It was the ninth successive victory for the Dodgers, the ninth successive defeat for the Mets, and the Mets had never been in the game, yet Koufax looked a little shaken.

The second game was better baseball, but the fans, wearied by their own exercise or made fearful by legitimate tension, were noticeably more repressed. A close, sensible game seemed to make them more aware of reality and more afraid of defeat. The Mets spotted the Dodgers three runs in the first on Ron Fairly's second homer of the afternoon, and then tied it in the third on homers by Hodges and Hickman. It was nearly seven o'clock and the lights had been turned on when Hodges, who was having a memorable day, put the Mets in the lead with still another home run. Suddenly convinced that this was the only moment in the day (and perhaps in the entire remainder of the season) when the Mets would find themselves ahead, I took my fellow fan reluctantly away to home and supper. This was the right decision in one respect (the game, tied at 4–4 and then at 5–5, was won by the Dodgers when Willie Davis hit a homer in the ninth) but the wrong one in another. A few minutes after we left the park, the Mets pulled off a triple play— something I have never seen in more than thirty years of watching big-league baseball. Sandy Koufax and I had learned the same odd lesson: It is safe to assume that the Mets are going to lose, but dangerous to assume that they won't startle you in the process.

o

In the following four days, the Mets lost five ball games—one more to the Dodgers and all four to the Giants—to run their losing streak to fifteen. Some of the scores were close, some lopsided. In three of the games, the Mets displayed their perverse, enchanting habit of handing over clusters of runs to the enemy and then, always a little too late, clawing and scratching their way back into contention. Between these rallies, during the long, Gobi stretches of home-team fatuity, I gave myself over to admiration of the visiting stars. Both the Dodgers and the Giants, who are currently running away from the rest of the league, are stocked with large numbers of stimulating, astonishingly good ballplayers, and, along with the rest of their old admirers here, I was grateful for the chance to collect and store away views of the new West Coast sluggers and pitchers. Now I have them all: Frank Howard, the six-foot-seven Dodger monster, striding the outfield like a farmer stepping through a plowed field; Ron Fairly, a chunky, redheaded first baseman, exultantly carrying his hot bat up to the plate and flattening everything thrown at him; Maury Wills, a skinny, lizard-quick base-runner. In the

Thursday-night game, Wills stole second base twice in the span of three minutes. He was called back after the first clean steal, because Jim Gilliam, the batter, had interfered with the catcher; two pitches later, he took off again, as everyone knew he would, and beat the throw by yards. Willie Davis, the Dodger center fielder, is the first player I am tempted to compare to Willie Mays. Speed, sureness, a fine arm, power, a picture swing—he lacks nothing, and he shares with Mays the knack of shifting directly from lazy, loose-wristed relaxation into top gear with an explosion of energy.

I don't understand how Orlando Cepeda, the Giants' slugger, ever hits a pitch. At the plate, he stands with his hands and the bat twisted back almost behind his right shoulder blade, and his vast riffles look wild and looping. Only remarkable strength can control such a swing. In one game, he hit a line drive that was caught in front of the center-field screen, 425 feet away; in another, he took a checked half-swing at an outside pitch and lined it into the upper right-field stands. Harvey Kuenn, by contrast, has the level, intelligent swing of the self-made hitter. He is all concentration, right down to the clamped wad of tobacco in his left cheek; he runs with heavy, pounding determination, his big head jouncing with every step. Mays, it is a pleasure to say, is just the same—the best ballplayer anywhere. He hit a homer each day at the Polo Grounds, made a simple, hilarious error on a ground single to center, and caught flies in front of his belt buckle like a grocer catching a box of breakfast food pulled from a shelf. All in all, I most enjoy watching him run bases. He runs low to the ground, his shoulders swinging to his huge strides, his spikes digging up great chunks of infield dirt; the cap flies off at second, he cuts the base like a racing car, looking back over his shoulder at the ball, and lopes grandly into third, and everyone who has watched him finds himself laughing with excitement and shared delight.

The Mets' "Go!" shouters enjoyed their finest hour on Friday night, after the Giants had hit four homers and moved inexorably to a seventh-inning lead of 9–1. At this point, when most sensible baseball fans would be edging toward the exits, a man sitting in Section 14, behind first base, produced a long, battered foghorn and blew mournful, encouraging blasts into the hot night air. Within minutes, the Mets fans were shouting in counterpoint—*Tooot!* "Go!" *Tooot!* "Go!" *Toooooot!* "GO!"—and the team, defeated and relaxed, came up with five hits and five runs that sent Billy Pierce to the showers. It was too late again, even though in the ninth the Mets put two base-runners on and had the tying run at the plate. During this exciting foolishness, I scrutinized the screamers around me and tried to puzzle out the cause of their unique affliction. It seemed statistically unlikely that there could be, even in New York, a forty- or fifty-thousand-man audience made up exclusively of born losers—leftover Landon voters, collectors of mongrel puppies, owners of stock in played-out gold mines—who had been waiting

8

years for a suitably hopeless cause. Nor was it conceivable that they were all ex-Dodgers or ex-Giant rooters who had been embittered by the callous snatching away of their old teams; no one can stay *that* bitter for five years. And they were not all home-town sentimentalists, for this is a city known for its cool and its successful teams.

The answer, or part of the answer, came to me in the lull during the eighth inning, while the Giants were bringing in a relief pitcher. Two men just to my right were talking about the Mets.

"I tell you, there isn't one of 'em—not one—that could make the Yankee club," one of them said. "I never saw such a collection of dogs."

"Well, what about Frank Thomas?" said the other. "What about him? What's he batting now? .315? .320? He's got thirteen homers, don't he?"

"Yeah, and who's he going to push out of the Yankee outfield? Mantle? Maris? Blanchard? You can't call these characters *ball*players. They all belong back in the minors—the *low* minors."

I recognized the tone. It was knowing, cold, full of the contempt that the calculator feels for those who don't play the odds. It was the voice of the Yankee fan. The Yankees have won the American League pennant twenty times in the past thirty years; they have been world champions sixteen times in that period. Over the years, many of their followers have come to watch them with the smugness and arrogance of holders of large blocks of blue-chip stocks. These fans expect no less than perfection. They coolly accept the late-inning rally, the winning homer, as only their due. They are apt to take defeat with ill grace, and they treat their stars as though they were executives hired to protect their interests. During a slump or a losing streak, these capitalists are quick and shrill with their complaints: "They ought to damn well do better than *this*, considering what they're being paid!"

Suddenly the Mets fans made sense to me. What we were witnessing was precisely the opposite of the kind of rooting that goes on across the river. This was the losing cheer, the gallant yell for a good try—antimatter to the sounds of Yankee Stadium. This was a new recognition that perfection is admirable but a trifle inhuman, and that a stumbling kind of semi-success can be much more warming. Most of all, perhaps, these exultant yells for the Mets were also yells for ourselves, and came from a wry, half-understood recognition that there is more Met than Yankee in every one of us. I knew for whom that foghorn blew; it blew for me.

Days and Nights
with the Unbored

The Series and the season are over—four days done at this writing—and the Mets are still Champions of the World. Below midtown office windows, scraps and streamers of torn paper still litter the surrounding rooftops, sometimes rising and rearranging themselves in an autumn breeze. I just looked out, and they're still there. It's still true. The Mets won the National League's Eastern divisional title, and won it easily; they won the playoffs, beating the Atlanta Braves in three straight; they took the World Series—one of the finest short Series of all—beating the Orioles in five games. The Mets. The New York *Mets?* . . . This kind of disbelief, this surrendering to the idea of a plain miracle, is tempting but derogatory. If in the end we remember only a marvelous, game-saving outfield catch, a key hit dropped in, an enemy batter fanned in the clutch, and then the ridiculous, exalting joy of it all—the smoke bombs going off in the infield, the paper storm coming down and the turf coming up, and the clubhouse baptisms—we will have belittled the makers of this astonishment. To understand the achievement of these Mets, it is necessary to mount an expedition that will push beyond the games themselves, beyond the skill and the luck. The journey will end in failure, for no victorious team is entirely understandable, even to itself, but the attempt must always be made, for winning is the ultimate sports mystery. On the night of September 24, when the Mets clinched their divisional title, Manager Gil Hodges sat in his clubhouse office after the game and tried to explain the season. He mentioned good pitching, fine defense, self-reliance, momentum, and a sense of team confidence. The reporters around his desk nodded and made notes, but they all waited for something more. From the locker room next door came a sharp, heady whiff of sloshed champagne and the cries of exultant young athletes. Then someone said, "Gil, how did it all happen? Tell us what it all *proves*."

Hodges leaned back in his chair, looked at the ceiling, and then spread his large hands wide. "Can't be done," he said, and he laughed.

Disbelief persists, then, and one can see now that disbelief itself was one of the Mets' most powerful assets all through the season. Again and again this summer, fans or friends, sitting next to me in the stands at Shea Stadium would fill out their scorecards just before game time, and then turn and shake their heads and say, "There's no way—just *no* way—the Mets can take this team tonight." I would compare the two lineups and agree. And then, later in the evening or at breakfast the next morning, I would think back on the game—another game won by the Mets, and perhaps another series swept— and find it hard to recall just how they *had* won it, for there was still no way, *no* way, it could have happened. Finally, it began to occur to me that if my friends and I, partisans all, felt like this, then how much more profoundly those other National League teams, deeper in talent and power and reputation than the Mets, must have felt it. For these were still the Mets—the famous and comical losers, ninth-place finishers last year, a team that had built a fortune and a following out of defeat and perversity, a team that had lost seven hundred and thirty-seven games in seven years and had finished a total of two hundred and eighty-eight and a half games away from first place. No way, and yet it happened and went on happening, and the only team, interestingly, that did not disbelieve in the Mets this summer was the Houston Astros, a club born in the same year as the Mets and the owners of a record almost as dismal; the Astros, who also came to competence and pride this summer, won ten out of twelve games from the Mets and were the only rivals to take a season series from them.

The Amazin's amazed us so often that almost every one of the 2,175,373 fans who saw them at home this year (an attendance record that topped all clubs in both leagues) must be convinced that he was there on that one special afternoon or crucial evening when the Mets won *the* big game that fused them as contenders and future champions. Many claim it was that afternoon of July 8, when the Mets, five games behind the Cubs in the standings and two runs behind the Cubs in the game, came up with ninth-inning pinch doubles by Ken Boswell and Donn Clendenon that were both misplayed by a rookie Chicago center fielder; a tying double by Cleon Jones; and a bloop two-out single by Ed Kranepool that won it. Some think it was the next day, when the Mets' shining leader, Tom Seaver, came within two outs of a perfect game, shutting out the Cubs, 4–0, and cutting their lead to three. Some hold out for the televised game at Wrigley Field the following week when Al Weis, the weak-hitting spare infielder, bashed his first homer

11

of the year to drive in three runs in a 5–4 victory. Or the next game there, when Weis hit *another* homer and Tommie Agee delivered a lead-off double and a lead-off homer in the first two innings, as the Mets won again. Others remember the doubleheader against San Diego at Shea on August 16 (four-hit shutout by Seaver in the first; winning pinch single by Grote in the nightcap) that started the Mets back from their midsummer nadir, nine and a half games behind. After that day, the team won twelve of its next fourteen games, all against Western teams, and Seaver and Koosman embarked on a joint record of sixteen wins in their last seventeen decisions. My own choice of *the* game is a much earlier wonder—a fifteen-inning, 1–0 bleeder against the Dodgers on the night of June 4. In the top of the fifteenth, with a Dodger on third, Al Weis, playing second base, darted to his left for a hard grounder that was deflected in midflight by pitcher Ron Taylor's glove; Weis had to leap the other way, to his right, for the carom, but came up with the ball and an instant off-balance throw that nailed the runner at the plate and saved the tie. Moments later, Tommie Agee scored the winning run all the way from first on an error. The victory sustained what came to be an eleven-game winning streak and completed successive series sweeps against the Dodgers and the Giants. Manager Hodges said later that Weis's double reverse and peg was one of the greatest infield plays he had ever seen.

What matters here is not the selection of one winning game (there were many others as close and perhaps as important) but the perception of a pattern in them all. Ten separate players, many of them part-timers or pinch-hitters, figure significantly in these brief accounts of seven key games. This happened all year, and in time the Mets began to recognize the pattern as their main source of strength. This is a phenomenon unique in baseball. The Mets were the first team in the history of the game to enter a World Series with only two players (Cleon Jones and Tommie Agee) who had over four hundred official at-bats in the course of the regular season. From the beginning, successful big-league clubs have won with set lineups, which has usually meant sending at least five or six hitters to the plate four or five hundred times a year. The 1967 Cardinals had eight players with more than four hundred ABs; the 1964 Yankees had six with more than *five* hundred. Even Casey Stengel's famous Yankee platoons of the nineteen-fifties, even those constantly reshuffled castoffs who played for the Mets in their first season presented more stable lineups than the new champions. Hodges' Irregulars, to be sure, were a creation of pure necessity. Cold bats, injuries, and call-ups to Army Reserve duty required improvisation all through the season, but every substitution seemed to work. Young Wayne Garrett niftily spelled old Ed Charles at third; rookie Bobby Pfeil and backup glove Al Weis filled in for Bud Harrelson and Ken Boswell; Ed Kranepool and Donn Clendenon (who was acquired from Montreal just before the trading deadline in June) together added up to a switch-hitting first baseman who delivered twenty-three home runs; Art Shamsky and Ron Swoboda became a switch-hitting right fielder who hit twenty-three more homers; Rod Gaspar, mostly played as a pair of fast wheels in late innings, led the outfielders in assists, which means enemy runners cut down in key situations. No professional ballplayer likes to sit out even one game, but in time all the Mets, sensing that no one on the bench had actually lost his job, were infected with a guerrilla spirit. Ed Charles, who has played pro ball for eighteen years, talked about it one day near the end of the season. "I've never seen it or heard of it before," Charles said. "Every one of us knew when it was time to pick the other guy up. The bottom of the order, a pinch-hitter, a man who'd just fanned three times— everybody figured, 'What the hell, what am I waiting for? Do it now, baby, because there's no big man going to do it for you.' Give No. 14 a lot of credit." No. 14 is Gil Hodges.

Other components of the new-Metsian physiology are more traditional. They include:

PITCHING—Tom Seaver and Jerry Koosman, who appeared and flowered in succession in the past two seasons, are now the best one-two starting pair on any team in the majors. This year's freshman was Gary Gentry, up from Arizona State (the Notre Dame of college baseball) and only two years in the minors, who won thirteen games and invariably proved obdurate in the tough, close ones. A veteran, Don Cardwell, and two more youngsters, Nolan Ryan and Jim McAndrew, together provided the fourth and fifth starters, and Ron Taylor and Tug McGraw were the stoppers from the bullpen. Ryan throws pure smoke (in the minors he once fanned eighteen batters in seven innings), but there are those who think that McAndrew may be an even better pitcher in the end. Young hurlers' arms are as delicate as African violets, and Hodges and the Mets' pitching coach, Rube Walker, stuck to a five-day rotation through the most crowded weekends of the schedule, arriving at September with a pitching staff that was in splendid fettle. Rube has been known to glare at a pitcher whom he finds playing catch on the sidelines without his permission.

DEFENSE—Gil Hodges, trying to put to rest the notion that his winners were somehow spawned out of sunshine, recently pointed out that last year's team, which finished twenty-four games back, was almost never beaten badly. I looked it up: the 1968 club lost only ten times by six runs or more. Give No. 14 a lot of credit. Even while losing, the young Mets were taught the essentials of winning baseball—hitting the cutoff man, throwing to the right base, holding the runner close. The new Mets do not beat themselves, which is a failing far more common in baseball than one would suspect.

HITTING—Batting is very nearly unteachable, but it thrives on confidence. The Mets' two most talented swingers, Cleon Jones and Tommie Agee, are lifelong friends from Mobile, Alabama; both, curiously, are subject to self-doubt and depression. Hodges has stuck with them for two seasons, patiently playing them in the top of the order and ignoring slumps and glooms. Agee, always a fine center fielder, came back from a terrible .217 season to a solid .271 this year, with twenty-six homers, while Jones, down to .223 at one point last year, was in the thick of the fight for the National League batting title this summer, finishing in third place, with .340. Shamsky, Boswell, Harrelson, and Grote all had surprising years at the plate (Shamsky's .300 was sixty-nine points above his lifetime average), which may be due to example, or to the exuberance of winning, or to just plain

GOOD LUCK—Always, this is the identifying mark of a pennant winner. You can see it beginning to happen: Key hits start to drop in, fair by inches, while the enemy's line shots seem to be hit straight into a waiting glove or to carom off the wall to produce an overstretched hit-and-out. These Mets, however, have been the recipients of several extra kisses of providence. This spring, Commissioner Bowie Kuhn persuaded Donn Clendenon to come out of a month's retirement after he had been traded from Atlanta to Montreal, thus keeping him available for a trade to the Mets in June. Tom Seaver was illegally signed to a bonus by the Braves in 1966, thus making him available for a lucky draw from a hat by the Mets. The son of a Shea Stadium usher happened to write his father that there was a pretty fair sort of pitcher at his Army camp, thus bringing the name of Jerry Koosman to the attention of Met scouts.

YOUTH AND CHARACTER—The Mets' locker room was a pleasant place to visit this summer—for once, a true clubhouse. These ballplayers are younger than most, the great majority in their mid-twenties, and their lack of super-stars and supersalaries accounted for an absence of the cliques, feuds, and barracks irritability to be found on many ball teams. The Mets are articulate and educated (twenty-two of the twenty-six have attended college), and they seem to take pride in their varying life styles and interests, which include love beads and business suits, rock music and reading, the stock market, practical jokes, alligator shoes, and sometimes even world affairs. Donn Clendenon owns a night club in Atlanta and is a vice-president for industrial relations of Scripto, the pen company; Ron Taylor is an electrical engineer, who has been known to say, "Doubleheader tomorrow, barring nuclear holocaust"; Jim McAndrew is a psychologist; Ed Charles sends his inspirational poems to kids who write for autographs; Ron Swoboda talks of entering politics someday, because he wants to do something about racial tensions. Ed Kranepool is the only original Met still with the team, but Swoboda, to my

14

mind, most typifies the change from the old Mets to the new. He arrived in 1965, at the age of twenty—an enormous young man with an enormous, eager smile. He hit prodigious homers and had appalling difficulties with outside curves and high flies. He fell down in the outfield, threw to the wrong base, lost his temper, and was involved in Metsian misadventures. Once, in Candlestick Park, he popped up with men on base, returned to the bench, and stamped so hard on his batting helmet that it could not be pulled off his spikes in time for him to return to the field for the next inning. The Shea fans have stuck with him through sulks and slumps and strikeouts ("RON SWOBODA IS STRONGER THAN DIRT," one banner read), because he is *never* unsurprising—as the Baltimore Orioles will forever remember.

Tom Seaver, still only twenty-four, was the biggest winner in baseball this year (he finished at 25–7) and the undisputed leader of the Mets' upsurge. Arriving two years ago to join a hopeless collection of habitual cellar mice, he made it clear at once that losing was unacceptable to him. His positive qualities—good looks, enthusiasm, seriousness, lack of affectation, good humor, intelligence—are so evident that any ball team would try to keep him on the roster even if he could only pitch batting practice. This is unlikely to happen. In his first three years, he has won fifty-seven games and has been voted onto three All Star teams, and he is now a prime favorite to win both the Cy Young and the Most Valuable Player awards for 1969. Such a combination of Galahad-like virtues has caused some baseball old-timers to compare him with Christy Mathewson. Others, a minority, see an unpleasantly planned aspect to this golden image—planned, that is, by Tom Seaver, who is a student of public relations. However, his impact on his teammates can be suggested by something that happened to Bud Harrelson back in July. Harrelson was away on Army Reserve duty during that big home series with the Cubs, and he watched Seaver's near-no-hitter (which Seaver calls "my imperfect game") on a television set in a restaurant in Watertown, New York. "I was there with a couple of Army buddies who also play in the majors," Harrelson said later, "and we all got steamed up watching Tom work. Then—it was the strangest thing—I began feeling more and more like a little kid watching that game and that great performance, and I wanted to turn to the others and say, 'I *know* Tom Seaver. Tom Seaver is a friend of mine.'"

Most of the other Mets, it seems to me, are equally susceptible to enthusiasm. Young and alert and open, they are above all suggestible, and this quality—the lead-off hit just after a brilliant inning-ending catch; the valiant but exhausted starting pitcher taken off the hook by a sudden cluster of singles—is what made the Mets' late innings so much worth waiting for this year. It is also possible that these intuitive, self-aware athletes sensed, however vaguely, that they might be among the few to achieve splendor in a profession that is so often disappointing, tedious, and degrading. Their immense good fortune was to find themselves together at the same moment of sudden maturity, combined skills, and high spirits. Perhaps they won only because they didn't want this ended. Perhaps they won because they were unbored.

Something else—a sense of unreality, some persistent note of recognition of difference—stayed with me after all my visits to the Mets' clubhouse this year. Only in the end did I realize what it was. Instead of resembling a real ball team, the new Mets reminded me most of a Hollywood cast assembled to play in still another unlikely baseball movie. They seemed smaller and younger and more theatrical than a real team, and their drama was hopelessly overwritten. Certainly the cast was right—Harrelson and Boswell (Bud and Ken), the eager, sharp-faced infielders; Wayne Garrett, the freckle-faced rookie with the sweet smile; Jerry Grote, the broken-nosed, scrappy catcher; Agee and Jones, the silent, brooding big busters; Jerry Koosman, the cheerful hayseed; Ed Charles, the philosophical black elder; Art Shamsky, the Jewish character actor with persistent back pains; Hodges and Berra, the seamy-faced, famous old-timers (neither, unfortunately, called Pop); and Tom Seaver, of course, the hero. And who can say that the Mets didn't sense this, too—that they didn't know all along that this year at Shea life was imitating not just art but a United Artists production?

O

The only bad luck suffered by the Mets this year was the collapse of their opposition. A few cynics will insist (I have heard them already) that the Mets did not win their divisional title but had it handed to them. They somehow overlook the fact that the Mets won thirty-eight of their last forty-nine regular-season games (twenty-nine of thirty-six when it really mattered), and point instead to the Cubs' loss of ten out of eleven games in early September, to the Cubs' blowing a nine-and-a-half-game lead in less than a month, and to the failure of the powerful Pirates and the pennant-holding Cardinals ever to mount a consistent assault on the leaders. We all wanted that culminating explosion of open warfare similar to the famous Trafalgar staged by the American League in 1967, but the major fleets seemed only to glide past each other in the night. One brief skirmish—a pair of evening games at Shea on September 8 and 9—sufficed to convince me, however, that the Mets would have won just as surely if the issue had come down to the last afternoon of the season. The Cubs by then were a badly rattled club, exhausted by the silences and rages of their manager, Leo Durocher, and apprehensive about the impending loss of their lead, which they had held too long (a hundred and forty-two days) and too easily. Cub pitcher Bill Hands opened the first game by decking Tommie Agee with an inside fast ball—a mistake against the Suggestibles. Jerry Koosman responded classically by hitting the next

16

Cub batter, Ron Santo, on the wrist, and an inning later Agee banged a two-run homer. The Cubs tied it in the sixth, but Agee scored the winning run in the bottom half, sliding in ahead of a sweeping tag by catcher Randy Hundley, who then suggested that the umpire had blown the call. (I was watching at home, and Hundley's enraged leap took him right off the top of my TV screen, leaving only his shoes in view, like Santa's boots disappearing up the chimney.) The next night, Seaver threw a five-hitter, the Mets racked up ten hits and seven runs, and Durocher was treated to several dozen touching renditions of the new anthem, "Good-by, Leo!" The Mets took over first place the next day.

They went on winning—sometimes implacably, sometimes improbably. They won a doubleheader from Pittsburgh in which the only run in each game was driven in by the Met pitcher. They won again from the Pirates the next day, when Ron Swoboda hit the first grand-slam home run of his career. Against the Cardinals, they set an all-time mark by striking out nineteen times in one game, but beat the brand-new record-holder, Steve Carlton, on two two-run homers by Swoboda. Against the Pirates, a Pittsburgh pop single was converted into a sudden out when Swoboda scooped up the ball and fired it to catcher Jerry Grote, who had raced up the line to take the throw at first base just as the base-runner turned the corner. Had we but seen it, these games contained all the market indications of a brilliant investment coup in the coming playoff and Series.

Fittingly, the game that clinched the Mets' half-pennant was against the old league champs, the Cardinals. Thoughtfully, the Cubs had won that afternoon, thus keeping the Mets from backing in. Appropriately, it was the last home game at Shea, and 54,928 of us had turned out. Undramatically, the Mets won it in the very first inning, bombing out Steve Carlton with two homers—a three-run shot by a new favorite, Donn Clendenon, and a two-run poke by an old favorite, Ed Charles, who clapped his hands delightedly as he circled the bases. It was a slow, humid, comical evening, presided over by a festive orange moon. Plenty of time to read the fans' banners ("QUEENS LITHO LOVES THE METS," "YOU GUYS ARE TOO MUCH!"), to read the scoreboard ("METS WELCOME THE GOODTIME CHARLIE PHYSICAL FITNESS GROUP"; "METS WELCOME THE PASSIONIST RETREATISTS"), to fly paper airplanes, to grin idiotically at each other, to tear programs into confetti, and to join in a last, loud "Good-by, Leo!" rendered *a cappella*, with the right-field tenors in especially good voice. Then, in a rush, came the game-ending double play, the hero-hugging (Gary Gentry had pitched a 6–0 shutout), the sprint for life (Met fans are not the most excited pennant locusts I have ever seen, but they are the quickest off the mark and the most thorough), and the clubhouse water sports (Great Western, Yoo-Hoo, Rise lather, beer, cameras, interviews, music, platitudes, disbelief). Ed Charles sat in front of his locker, away from the television lights and the screeching, and said, "Beautiful, baby. Nine years in the minors for me, then nine more with the Athletics and Mets. Never, *never* thought I'd make it. These kids will be back next year, but I'm thirty-six and time is running out. It's better for me than for them."

A few minutes later, I saw George Weiss, the Mets' first general manager, trying to push his way through the mob outside Gil Hodges' office. He got to the door at last and then peered in and waved to Hodges, who had played for the Mets in their terrible first season.

"Nineteen sixty-two!" Weiss called.

"Nineteen sixty-two!" Hodges replied.

Rod Kanehl and Craig Anderson, two other Original Mets, met in the middle of the clubhouse, cried "Hey!" in unison, and fell into each other's arms. Soon they became silent, however, and stood there watching the party—two heavy men in business suits, smoking cigars.

○

The playoffs—the television-enriching new autumn adjunct known officially as the Championship Series—matched up the Orioles and the Minnesota Twins, and the Mets and the Atlanta Braves, who had barely escaped the horrid possibility of three-way or four-way pre-playoff with the Dodgers, Giants, and Cincinnati Reds in the National League West. Atlanta filled its handsome white stadium to capacity for its two weekend games against New York, but to judge from the local headlines, the transistor-holders in the stands, the television interviews with Georgia coaches, and the high-school band and majorettes that performed each morning in the lobby of the Regency Hyatt House hotel, autumn baseball was merely a side attraction to another good old Deep South football weekend. Georgia beat South Carolina, 41–16; Clemson beat Georgia Tech, 21–10; the Colts beat the Falcons, 21–14; and the Mets beat the Braves, 9–5 and 11–6. The cover of the official program for the baseball games displayed a photograph of the uniformed leg of an Atlanta Brave descending from a LEM onto a home plate resting on the moon, with the legend "One Step for the Braves, One Giant Leap for the Southeast," but Manager Hodges saw to it that the astronaut never got his other foot off the ladder. Not wanting to lose his ace in the significant first game, he kept Tom Seaver on the mound for seven innings, while Seaver absorbed an uncharacteristic eight-hit, five-run pounding. Tom plugged away, giving up homers and doubles, and resolutely insisting in the dugout that the Mets were going to win it. The lead changed hands three times before this finally happened, in the eighth, when the Mets scored five times off Phil Niekro on three successive hits, a gift stolen base, a fearful throwing error by Orlando Cepeda, and a three-run pinch single by J.C. Martin. The next day's match was just as sloppy. The Braves scored five runs with two out in

18

the fifth, all off Koosman and all too late, since the Mets had already run up a 9–1 lead. Hank Aaron hit his second homer in two days, Agee and Jones and Boswell hit homers for the Mets, and the Braves left for Shea Stadium with the almost occult accomplishment of having scored eleven runs off Seaver and Koosman without winning either game.

Hodges, having demonstrated slow managing in the first game, showed how to manage fast in the last one. His starter, Gary Gentry, who had given up a two-run homer to the unquenchable Aaron in the first inning, surrendered a single and a double (this also by Aaron) in the third, and then threw a pitch to Rico Carty that the Atlanta outfielder bombed off the left-field wall on a line but about two feet foul. Hodges, instantly taking the new ball away from Gentry, gave it to Nolan Ryan, in from the bullpen, who thereupon struck out Carty with one pitch, walked Cepeda intentionally, fanned Clete Boyer, and retired Bob Didier on a fly. Agee responded in obligatory fashion, smashing the first pitch to him in the same inning for a homer, and Ken Boswell came through with a two-run job in the fourth, to give the Mets the lead. Cepeda, who so far had spent the series lunging slowly and unhappily at Met singles and doubles buzzing past him at first, then hit a home run well beyond the temporary stands behind the left-center-field fence, making it 4–3, Braves. Even he must have sensed by then what would happen next: Ryan, a .103 hitter, singled to lead off the home half; Garrett, who had hit but one home run all year, hit another into the right-field loges, for two runs; Jones and Boswell and Grote and Harrelson and Agee combined to fashion two insurance runs; Ryan fanned seven Braves in all, and won by 7–4. Just about everybody got into the act in the end—the turf-moles onto the field again, Nolan Ryan and Garrett under the kliegs, and Mayor Lindsay under the champagne. Forehandedly, he had worn a drip-dry.

○

After a season of such length and so many surprises, reason suggested that we would now be given a flat and perhaps one-sided World Series, won by the Orioles, who had swept their three playoff games with the Minnesota Twins, and whom reporters were calling the finest club of the decade. There would be honor enough for the Mets if they managed only to keep it close. None of this happened, of course, and the best news—the one *true* miracle— was not the Mets' victory but the quality of those five games—an assemblage of brilliant parables illustrating every varied aspect of the beautiful game.

The Baltimore fans expected neither of these possibilities, for there were still plenty of tickets on sale before the opener at Memorial Stadium, and the first two Series games were played to less than capacity crowds. This is explicable only when one recalls that two other league champions from Baltimore—the football Colts and the basketball Bullets—had been humiliated by New York teams in postseason championships this year. Baltimore, in fact, is a city that no longer expects *any* good news. In the press box, however, the announcement of the opening lineups was received in predictable fashion ("Just *no* way . . ."), and I could only agree. The Orioles, who had won a hundred and nine games in the regular season, finishing nineteen games ahead of the next team and clinching their divisional title on September 13, were a poised and powerful veteran team that topped the Mets in every statistic and, man for man, at almost every position. Their three sluggers—Frank Robinson, Boog Powell, and Paul Blair—had hit a total of ninety-five homers, as against the Mets' *team* total of a hundred and nine. Their pitching staff owned a lower earned-run average than the Mets' sterling corps. Their ace, screwballer Mike Cuellar, had won twenty-three games and led the staff in strikeouts; their second starter, Dave McNally, had won fifteen games in a row this year; the third man, Jim Palmer, had a record of 16–4, including a no-hitter. Since Cuellar and McNally are left-handers, Hodges was forced to start his righty specialists (Clendenon, Charles, Swoboda, and Weis) and bench the hot left-handed hitters (Kranepool, Garrett, Shamsky, and Boswell) who had so badly damaged the Braves. Just *no* way.

Confirmation seemed instantaneous when Don Buford, the miniature Baltimore left fielder, hit Seaver's second pitch of the game over the right-field fence, just above Swoboda's leap. (Swoboda said later that his glove just ticked the ball "at my apogee.") For a while after that, Seaver did better—pitched much more strongly than he had in Atlanta, in fact—but with two out in the Baltimore fourth the steam suddenly went out of his fastball, and the Orioles racked up three more runs. The game, however, belonged not to Buford, or to the other Oriole hitters, or to Cuellar, but to Brooks Robinson, the perennial All-Star Baltimore third baseman, who was giving us all a continuous lesson in how the position can be played. Almost from the beginning, I became aware of the pressure he puts on a right-handed batter with his aggressive stance (the hands are cocked up almost under his chin), his closeness to the plate, his eager appetite for the ball. His almost supernaturally quick reactions are helped by the fact that he is ambidextrous; he bats and throws right-handed, but eats, writes, plays ping-pong, and fields blue darters with his left. In the fifth, he retired Al Weis on a tough, deep chance that leaped up and into his ribs. In the seventh, after the Mets had scored once on a pair of singles and a fly, he crushed the rally when he sprinted in toward Rod Gaspar's topped roller, snatched it up barehanded, and got off the throw, overhand, that retired Gaspar by yards. The Orioles won, 4–1, and Brooks had made it look easy for them.

The Mets were grim the next day (Frank Robinson had baited them after their loss, commenting on the silence in their dugout), and they played a grim, taut, riveting game. Brooks Robinson went on making fine plays, but he had plenty of company—an extraordinary catch and falling throw to second by Baltimore shortstop Mark Belanger, a base-robbing grab by gaunt little Bud Harrelson. (The tensions of the season had burned Harrelson down from a hundred and sixty-eight to a hundred and forty-five pounds.) The Mets led, 1–0, on Donn Clendenon's wrong-field homer off McNally in the fourth, and Baltimore had no hits at all off Koosman until the bottom of the seventh, when Paul Blair led off with a single. Two outs later, Blair stole second on a change-up curve, and Brooks Robinson scored him with a single up the middle. The tie seemed only to make the crowd more apprehensive, and the Baltimore partisans seemed unamused when a large "LET'S GO, METS!" banner appeared in the aisle behind home plate; it was carried by four Met wives—Mesdames Pfeil, Dyer, Ryan, and Seaver, smashers all, who had made it the night before out of a Sheraton bedsheet. There were two out in the top of the ninth before the Mets could act on this RSVP, winning the game on successive singles by Charles and Grote and a first-pitch hit to left by the .215 terror, Al Weis. Koosman, throwing mostly curves in the late going, walked two Orioles in the bottom half, but Ron Taylor came in to get the last out and save Jerry's two-hit, 2–1, essential victory. It was a game that would have delighted John McGraw.

Back at Shea Stadium, before an uncharacteristically elegant but absolutely jam-packed audience, Tommie Agee rocked Jim Palmer with a lead-off first-inning homer—Agee's fifth such discouragement this year. Gary Gentry, who had taken such a pounding from the Braves, was in fine form this time, challenging the big Baltimore sluggers with his hummer and comforted by a 3–0 lead after the second inning. He was further comforted in the fourth, when Tommie Agee, with two Orioles aboard, ran for several minutes toward deep left and finally, cross-handed, pulled down Elrod Hendricks' drive just before colliding with the fence. Agee held on to the ball, though, and carried it all the way back to the infield like a trophy, still stuck in the topmost webbing of his glove. It was 4–0 for the home side by the seventh, when Gentry walked the bases full with two out and was succeeded by Nolan Ryan. Paul Blair hit his 0–2 pitch on a line to distant right. Three Orioles took wing for the plate, but Agee, running to his left this time, made a skidding dive just at the warning track and again came up with the ball. The entire crowd—all 56,335 of us—jumped to its feet in shouting tribute as he trotted off the field. The final score was 5–0, or, more accurately, 5–5—five runs for the Mets, five runs saved by Tommie Agee. Almost incidentally, it seemed, the Orioles were suddenly in deep trouble in the Series.

It was Cuellar and Seaver again the next day, and this time the early homer was provided by Donn Clendenon—a lead-off shot to the visitors' bullpen in the second. Seaver, who had not pitched well in two weeks, was at last back in form, and Baltimore manager Earl Weaver, trying to rattle him and to arouse his own dormant warriors, who had scored only one run in the past twenty-four innings, got himself ejected from the game in the third for coming onto the field to protest a called strike. Weaver had a longish wait in his office before his sacrifice took effect, but in the top of the ninth, with the score still 1–0 and the tension at Shea nearly insupportable, Frank Robinson and Boog Powell singled in succession. Brooks Robinson then lined into an out that tied the game but simultaneously won the World Series for the Mets. It was a low, sinking drive, apparently hit cleanly through between Agee and right fielder Ron Swoboda. Ron, who was cheating in close, hoping for a play at the plate, took three or four lunging steps to his right, dived onto his chest, stuck out his glove, caught the ball, and then skidded on his face and rolled completely over; Robinson scored, but that was all. This marvel settled a lengthy discussion held in Gil Hodges' office the day before, when Gil and several writers had tried to decide whether Agee's first or second feat was the finest Series catch of all time. Swoboda's was. Oh, yes—the Mets won the game in the tenth, 2–1, when Grote doubled and his runner, Rod Gaspar, scored from second on J.C. Martin's perfect pinch bunt, which relief pitcher Pete Richert picked up and threw on a collision course with Martin's left wrist. My wife, sitting in the upper left-field stands, could not see the ball roll free in the glazy late-afternoon dimness and thought that Martin's leaping dance of joy on the base path meant that he had suddenly lost his mind.

So, at last, we came to the final game, and I don't suppose many of us who had watched the Mets through this long and memorable season much doubted that they would win it, even when they fell behind, 0–3, on home runs hit by Dave McNally and Frank Robinson off Koosman in the third inning. Jerry steadied instantly, allowing one single the rest of the way, and the Orioles' badly frayed nerves began to show when they protested long and ineffectually about a pitch in the top of the sixth that they claimed had hit Frank Robinson on the leg, and just as long and as ineffectually about a pitch in the bottom of the sixth that they claimed had *not* hit Cleon Jones on the foot. Hodges produced this second ball from his dugout and invited plate umpire Lou DiMuro to inspect a black scuff on it. DiMuro examined the mark with the air of a Maigret and proclaimed it the true Shinola, and a minute later Donn Clendenon damaged another ball by hitting it against the left-field façade for a two-run homer. Al Weis, again displaying his gift for modest but perfect contingency, hit his very first Shea Stadium homer to lead off the seventh and tie up the game, and the Mets won it in the eighth on doubles by Jones and Swoboda and a despairing but perfectly understandable Oriole double error at first base, all good for two runs and the famous 5–3 final victory.

I had no answer for the question posed by that youngster in the infield who held up—amid the crazily leaping crowds, the showers of noise and paper, the vermilion smoke-bomb clouds, and the vanishing lawns—a sign that said "WHAT NEXT?" What was past was good enough, and on my way down to the clubhouses it occurred to me that the Mets had won this great Series with just the same weapons they had employed all summer—with the Irregulars (Weis, Clendenon, and Swoboda had combined for four homers, eight runs batted in, and an average of .400); with fine pitching (Frank Robinson, Powell, and Paul Blair had been held to one homer, one RBI, and an average of .163); with defensive plays that some of us would remember for the rest of our lives; and with the very evident conviction that the year should not be permitted to end in boredom. Nothing was lost on this team, not even an awareness of the accompanying sadness of the victory—the knowledge that adulation and money and the winter disbanding of this true club would mean that the young Mets were now gone forever. In the clubhouse (Moët et Chandon this time), Ron Swoboda said it precisely for the TV cameras: "This is the first time. Nothing can ever be as sweet again."

Later, in his quiet office, Earl Weaver was asked by a reporter if he hadn't thought that the Orioles would hold on to their late lead in the last game and thus bring the Series back to Baltimore and maybe win it there. Weaver took a sip of beer and smiled and said, "No, that's what you can never do in baseball. You can't sit on a lead and run a few plays into the line and just kill the clock. You've got to throw the ball over the goddam plate and give the other man his chance. That's why baseball is the greatest game of them all."

Three for the Tigers

—SEPTEMBER 1973

Max. It is lunchtime at Gene & Georgetti's Restaurant, on North Franklin Street in downtown Chicago. It is the middle of the week, and the place is pretty full. A lot of businessmen eat here: Bloody Marys, chopped sirloin or the veal scallopini, salad, coffee, shop-talk. At one table—a party of three—somebody mentions the St. Louis Browns, the old American League baseball club that moved to Baltimore in 1954 and became the Orioles. A man rises from a nearby table, approaches the threesome, and bows. "Excuse me, gentlemen," he says. They look up. He is a sandy-haired, bright-eyed man—still a bit below middle age, one would guess—with a small cigar in his hand; his eyeglasses are in the new aviator-goggle style. "Excuse me," he says again, smiling cheerfully. "I just overheard one of you mention the old St. Louis Browns, and I'm sure you would all like to be reminded of the lineup of the 1944 Brownies, which, as you will recall, was the only Browns team ever to win the AL pennant, and which lost that World Series, of course, to their hometown rivals, the Cardinals, in six games. It was one of the two World Series, in fact, in which both participating teams came from west of the Mississippi River. The Browns' regular lineup in 1944 went: catcher, Frank Mancuso; first base, George McQuinn; second base, Don Gutteridge; third base, Mark Christman . . ." He runs through the eight names (one of the least celebrated lineups in the history of the game), adds starting pitchers Jack Kramer, Sig Jakucki, Bob Muncrief, and Denny Galehouse and, for good measure, throws in a second-string catcher named Red Hayworth. "You probably remember," he says, still smiling, "that Red Hayworth and the regular catcher, Frank Mancuso, both had brothers who were also major-league catchers and, in both cases, *better* catchers. Thank you." He bows and departs.

The three men at the table look at one another, and then one of them

24

calls after their informant. "Hey!" he says. "Do you come from St. Louis?"
"No," says the stranger. "Detroit."

He sits down at his table again, but he has stopped smiling. He has just remembered that he lives in Chicago now—away from Detroit, away from the Tigers.

○

Bert. A little after nine-thirty on a Monday morning in June, Bert walks into his ground-floor office in Oak Park, Michigan, which is a suburb on the north side of Detroit. His name is on the door: "Bert Gordon, Realty." He says good morning to his secretary and to his assistant, Barbara Rosenthal, and goes on into his own office, which looks out on a parking strip and, beyond that, onto Greenfield Road. He sits down at his desk, leans forward and takes off his shoes, and slides his feet into a pair of faded blue espadrilles. Then he swings his swivel chair to the right, so that he is facing a desk-model calculator on a side table, and punches out on it the numbers "2922" and "1596." The first figure is the total number of days of President Nixon's two terms in the White House; the second is the number of days the President has served to date. He hits another button, and the answer slot at the top of the machine offers up "54.62" in illuminated green numbers. Bert is a member of the Michigan Democratic State Central Committee, and he has just figured (as he figures every weekday morning) the expired percentage of President Nixon's two terms of office. Now Bert clears the machine and punches out the numbers "9345" and "2806." (Since Friday morning, the first number has gone up by seven and the second by one: Al Kaline, the veteran star outfielder for the Detroit Tigers, hit one single in seven official times at bat against the Minnesota Twins over the weekend.) The machine silently presents another set of green numbers; today Kaline's lifetime major-league batting average stands at .3000267. Bert sighs, erases the figure, and picks up his telephone. He is ready to start his day.

○

Don. Don and his wife, Susan, are attending a performance of *The Marriage of Figaro* by the touring Metropolitan Opera company at the Masonic Temple Auditorium in Detroit. They are both very fond of the theater, and they go to a play or an opera whenever they can manage it. As usual, Don has bought seats near the back of the balcony, where he knows the radio reception is better. The two of them are following the opera attentively, but Don is also holding a small transistor radio up to his left ear. (He is left-eared all the way.) Through long training, he is able to hear both the opera and (because of the good reception) the voice of Ernie Harwell, the sports broadcaster for Station WJR, who is at this moment describing the action at Tiger

Stadium, where the Brewers are leading the Tigers 1–0 in the top of the fourth. A woman sitting directly behind Don and Susan is unable to restrain her curiosity, and during a recitative she leans forward and taps Don on the shoulder.

"Excuse me," she whispers. "I was just wondering what you're listening to on that little radio."

Don half turns in his seat. "Simultaneous translation," he whispers.

○

In this country's long love affair with professional sports, the athlete has more and more come to resemble the inamorata—an object of unceasing scrutiny, rapturous adoration, and expensive adornment—while the suitor, or fan, remains forever loyal, shabby, and unknown. Sports fans are thought of as a mass—statistics that are noticed only when they do not fall within their predicted norms—but the individual fan (except for a few self-made celebrities, like Hilda Chester, the Ebbets Field bell ringer, or the Knicks' Dancing Harry, or the Mets' folding-sign man) is a loner, a transient cipher, whose streaks and slumps go unrecorded in the annals of his game. Every sport, however, has its great fans as well as its great athletes—classic performers whose exceptional powers set them apart from the journeyman spectator. They are veterans who deserve notice if only for the fact that their record of attachment and service to their game and their club often exceeds that of any player down on the field. The home team, in their belief, belongs to them more than to this passing manager or to that arriviste owner, and they are often cranky possessors, trembling with memory and pride and frustration, as ridiculous and touching as any lovers. These rare ones make up a fraction of every sporting audience, but they seem to cluster more thickly in the homes of the older, well-entrenched franchises. The three Detroit nonpareils are a vivid constellation of contemporary baseball fandom: Maxwell H. Lapides, a businessman who went to work last spring as a vice-president of a national collection agency in Chicago, thus painfully exiling himself from his friends and his ball team; Bertram Gordon, whose real-estate agency specializes in finding and leasing business and shopping-center locations in the areas of thickening population outside the central city; and Dr. Donald N. Shapiro, a distinguished oral surgeon. They are intimate friends, united by their ages (middle to upper forties), their similar backgrounds and styles of life, their neighboring families, their Jewishness, and their wit and intelligence, but most of all by their consuming passion for the Detroit Tigers. None of the three is willing to accept the cheerfully patronizing tone that nonsporting friends and relatives usually direct toward the baseball-bitten; none of the three, for that matter, regards himself as a baseball fan at all. "Right from the beginning, I have been a Tiger fan and nothing else," Max Lapides said this summer. "Other men can happily go to ball games wherever they happen to find themselves—not me. My interest is the Tigers. They are the sun, and all the twenty-three other teams are satellites. You can't begin to understand or appreciate this game unless you have an intense involvement."

Dr. Donald Shapiro, in spite of the demands imposed by his successful and extensive practice, by his family (he is married and has three children), by his writing for medical and dental journals, by his sideline in theatricals (he played a small part in a Hollywood gangster film shot in Detroit last winter), by his weekend career as a highly competitive Class A tennis player, and by his voluminous, wide-ranging reading, manages to keep abreast of the Tigers' news almost inning by inning throughout their 162-game season. Evenings, friends at his house or at their own have taught themselves to ignore the fact that his left ear, like van Gogh's, is of no immediate social use; in the spring, when a good many ball games are played in the afternoon, Shapiro tries to schedule his surgical appointments in hospital operating rooms that he knows to have an acceptable interior Harwell-level. (Sinai Hospital has the worst reception in Detroit.) When all else fails, he calls his baseball friends, and Bert Gordon has come to recognize the sound of Don's telephone voice, blurred with haste and a surgical mask, asking, "How're we doing?" One afternoon in 1970, Bert answered his phone and heard Don whisper, "This is probably a violation of every professional canon, but I can't help it. Guess who I've got in the chair!"

"Who?" said Bert.

"Chet Laabs!"

"Chet Laabs!"

"Chet Laabs!"

They hung up. (Chet Laabs, a chunky, unremarkable outfielder, played for the Tigers from 1937 to 1939.)

This kind of belonging brooks no alternatives. "When I'm listening to a game, there is nothing that annoys me as much as somebody who clearly doesn't care coming up to me and smiling and saying 'How's it going?' " Don says, *"How's it going!* Why, don't they understand that for a real fan it's always a matter of suffering and ecstasy? What we're involved with here is exaltation!"

Bert Gordon, in turn, detected a crucial slight in the midst of a recent bridge-table conversation, and demanded, "How come you're a bridge authority and your partner's an art aficionado but I'm a baseball nut?"

Bert and Don are lifelong friends who grew up in the near-northwest section of Detroit and graduated from Central High together in the class of 1942. Max Lapides, who is forty-five years old—three and a half years younger than the others—did not live in the same neighborhood, and thus the triumvirate was not completed until early in the nineteen sixties, although they have subsequently established the fact that they were fellow witnesses, usually in person, of innumerable famous moments in Tiger history: Goose Goslin's championship-winning single in the ninth inning of the sixth game in the 1935 Series; an unknown thirty-year-old rookie named Floyd Giebell outpitching Bob Feller in Cleveland on the second-to-last day of the 1940 season to nail down the pennant for Detroit; Rudy York and Pinky Higgins hitting two-run homers in the same inning against the Reds in the Series that fall; Earl Torgeson stealing home in the bottom of the tenth inning to defeat the hated Yanks in 1955; Joe DiMaggio hammering a grounder that broke George Kell's jaw—and Kell picking up the ball and stepping on the bag to force the runner from second before collapsing in front of third base. Don and Max met at last in 1960, when a friend in common brought them together at a dinner party, having assured each one beforehand that the other was a Tiger fan of surpassing tenacity and knowledge. Both of them, of course, utterly ignored the proffered *bona fides*, and the marriage very nearly expired on the spot. Late in the evening, however, the two chanced to arrive at the drinks table together. Don Shapiro, regarding Max with evident distrust, ventured a minute opening. "R.L.," he said.

"R.L.?" returned Max.

Don nodded, watching his man.

"Why, Roxie Lawson," said Max. (Roxie Lawson was a right-handed pitcher for the Tigers in the mid-thirties.) "Of course."

They fell into each other's arms.

In recent years, the three-way entente has deepened in complexity, ritual, and affection. Max Lapides, who has regularly attended about thirty or thirty-five Tiger home games every year, often to the extent of going to the park alone ("He even likes a night game against the Texas Rangers in the last week of September," says Bert Gordon), has been an energizing catalyst for the three, organizing baseball dates and tickets, nudging baseball memories, berating the Tiger management, comparing active and erstwhile ballplayers, inventing bets and interior games, finding causes for contention and laughter. Since each of the three friends sustains an almost permanent state of transcendental baseball meditation, they are forever making and sharing new discoveries. Last year, for instance, Bert startled Max with the sudden announcement that Aurelio Rodriguez, the present Tiger third baseman, is the only major-league infielder with all five vowels in his first name.

Max and Bert are telephone addicts, and have made several thousand calls to each other in the past four or five years (Bert: "Think how many if we *liked* each other!"), mostly to exchange baseball talk. In a recent call, Max baited Bert for having inexplicably forgotten that Don Heffner had played in six games for the Tigers in 1944, long before beginning his tenure as a Detroit coach. "Now we're even for Milt Bolling, right?" he said. "It must be a *year* you haven't let me up because I forgot Milt and Frank Bolling played together that once for us in the fifties." In time, they went on to bubble-gum cards. "I never saw the Waners, because they were in the wrong league, but I know how they each looked up at the plate," Max said. "Both were lefty hitters, of course, but Lloyd held the bat sort of out in front of him when he was up, and Paul's bat was tipped sideways and back. That's the way it was on my cards, anyway. Listen, what were the worst baseball cards you used to have—you know, the ones you always had so many of you couldn't get rid of them? . . . Harlond Clift? Oh, yes, my God, you're right, Bert! I'd absolutely forgotten. But with me it was always too many Hudlins. Willis Hudlin, the old Cleveland twirler—right? I think I had a hundred Willis Hudlins. . . . What were the *best* baseball cards? You mean like the Gehringers and . . . Oh, the rarest ones. Let me see. . . . I guess they were so rare I never got one. I mean, I can't remember. Probably some good ballplayer on a terrible team. Somebody on the old Athletics who'd get overlooked there. Like—oh, like Bob Johnson. You remember him—Indian Bob. He used to *kill* us. . . . I think we talked about this once already, but let's talk about it some more, OK?"

By agreement among the three, Max holds the post of official historian, Don is entrusted with tactics, and Bert is the statistician, though none of them is reticent about intruding upon another's turf of expertise. Like most long-term fans, they are absolutely opposed to the American League's new designated-hitter rule, but Bert Gordon may be the first classicist to point out that the addition of the tenth man means that the pregame public announcement of the team lineups now takes 11.1 percent longer to complete than it did last year. His avidity for figures seems to remove him a little from the day-to-day adventures of his team, but he keeps his Kaline statistics warm, and this summer he spent a good many hours extrapolating the day on which Kaline would pass Charlie Gehringer as the player with the third-highest number of base hits (behind Ty Cobb and Sam Crawford) in Tiger history. Early in June, Bert settled on August 17 as the likely date for the event, but later revised it to August 9; the epochal Kaline hit actually came on August 8—a single against Oakland that was probably appreciated more quickly and more deeply by Bert Gordon than by the man who struck it. Bert polishes such Tiger events and figures in his mind—the unmatched Ty Cobb records; Harry Heilmann's odd-year batting championships, in 1921, '23, '25, and '27; Denny McLain's startling 31–6 year in 1968—but the one Tiger record he believes to be absolutely unassailable was made in an afternoon game on June 21, 1970, when a modestly talented Tiger infielder named Cesar Gutierrez hit safely in seven consecutive times at bat. "For one thing, you have to send fifty-five men to the plate in the game before the thing even becomes statistically possible," Bert said recently. "Why, only two men in the entire history of this game, out of all the thousands and thousands that have played big-league ball, have ever gone seven for seven. Just think about that for a minute." He lit a Lucky Strike and thought about it for a minute, humming happily under his breath. "You know something about that Gutierrez?" he said, and an enormous laugh convulsed him. "Oh, boy, was he ever *lucky!*"*

Max Lapides, by his own careful, historian's estimate, has attended at least twelve hundred Tiger games. Looking back from this Everest over a baseball landscape of almost forty years, he still has no difficulty in selecting the greatest Tiger games of his time; in the spring of 1967, acting out of a pure, Thucydidean sense of duty, he wrote a considerable monograph on the two—or, in strict fact, three—battles that remained brightest in his memory. (Today, he has said, he might have to add either the fifth or the seventh game of the 1968 World Series, when the Tigers came back from an almost hopeless disadvantage to defeat the Cardinals for the World Championship.) On the night of June 23, 1950, playing at home, the Tigers gave up four home runs to the Yankees in the first four innings, to fall behind by 6–0; in their half of the fourth they hit four home runs of their own, including a grand slam by pitcher Dizzy Trout, altogether good for eight runs. Homers by Joe DiMaggio and Tommy Henrich again put the visitors ahead, by 9–8, but Hoot Evers won the thing with a two-run inside-the-park homer in the bottom of the ninth. This Waterloo—eleven homers, sixty-two total bases, all nineteen runs the result of home runs—still holds a number of all-time baseball records (perhaps including "Frightened Pitchers, Most"), but Max's true fanly preference falls upon quite a different game, a two-part event of almost total austerity that began on July 21, 1945, when the Tigers and the Athletics played a twenty-four-inning, 1–1 standoff in Philadelphia. (Max Lapides happened to see this afternoon of mime because he had just begun his freshman year at the University of Pennsylvania. He also happened to see every game played by the Tigers at Shibe Park during his undergraduate years. Later in the summer of 1945, he and a college friend took a train to Washington to see a significant series between the Tigers and the Senators, who were then neck and neck in the pennant race; the students slept on park benches, subsisted

*Bert Gordon's pleasure in the Gutierrez miracle was expunged on September 16, 1975, when Rennie Stennett, second baseman for the Pittsburgh Pirates, went seven for seven against the Chicago Cubs, in a game at Wrigley Field that the Pirates won by the score of 22–0. Gutierrez had set his mark in a twelve-inning game, but Stennett's seven straight hits—four singles, two doubles, and a triple—came in the regulation distance; actually, Stennett wrapped up his day's work in *eight* innings, and then was allowed to sit out the ninth. The next day, Stennett singled on his first two trips to the plate and then at last popped out, after nine straight safeties. The first (and only other) seven-for-seven performance was achieved in 1892 by Wilbert Robinson, of the Baltimore Orioles, which was at that time a National League club. Gutierrez—as Bert now sometimes murmurs to himself—still holds the American League consecutive-hit record for one game.

on hot dogs and cornflakes, and saw five games in three days.) That 1–1 game was rescheduled for September 12, 1945, and again the Tigers and Athletics froze at 1–1 after nine innings, and then at 2–2 after eleven. The A's won at last, in the sixteenth inning, and Max's precise and admirable account—his prose style may owe something to a press-box titan of his boyhood, H. G. Salsinger, of the Detroit *News*—concludes ringingly:

> It was a fatal move. The exhausted Dazzler [Dizzy Trout] had nothing left—even in the dark shadows of Shibe Park. . . . Next came the troublesome Estalella, always a thorn in the Tiger paw. . . . Roberto and Diz battled to a full count and then, swinging late in the murky dusk, the Cuban sliced a sharp line drive to the right-field corner. Cullenbine, shading center field for the righthanded batter, never had a chance as Smith raced around to score the winning run and wrap up the "longest game" in baseball history after forty innings of play.
>
> Two days later, whatever justice there was for the Tigers came when Leslie Mueller defeated the Athletics 1–0 in a five-inning game, while allowing only two hits.

On a Saturday morning late last May, Bert Gordon and Don Shapiro drove to the Detroit Metropolitan Airport to meet Max Lapides, who was returning from Chicago to attend his first Tiger game of the year with his old friends. Max's wife and their two young daughters were staying in their Detroit home, in the suburban Birmingham section, until the end of the school year, so Max's exile was still leavened by weekend paroles. On the way to the airport, Bert and Don considered the awful possibility that Max might someday be converted to the White Sox, but the subject died of unlikelihood, and in time the two began comparing some Tiger managers. Red Rolfe (1949–52), it was agreed, had been decent; Fred Hutchinson (1952–54) had been sound but touched with temper; Charlie Dressen (1963–66) had been deep in knowledge but past his prime. Surprisingly, the vote for the best manager since Mickey Cochrane (1934–38) went to the incumbent, Billy Martin, who had taken an aged Tiger team into the playoffs the previous fall, and who had the same seniors currently, if barely, at the top of their division again. "He's winning ball games," said Don, "and that's absolutely all that counts."

"Plus he's exciting," said Bert. "This is the first time since I was eleven years old that you see a Tiger base runner go from second to third on a fly ball."

Another passenger inquired about Mayo Smith, the pilot who brought the Tigers to within one game of a pennant in 1967, and who won it all the following year. There was a painful pause, and then Don Shapiro, the resident strategist, said, "Listen, there were times when Mayo Smith was managing, and he would call in somebody from the bullpen, and I would know who he had chosen and I knew that he was going to be wrong. I knew the game was down the drain, and so did everybody else in the ball park. Why, that sense of impending disaster was so strong you could almost chart it. It was palpable. And then the disaster would happen. Mayo Smith absolutely lacked that mystical foreknowledge of baseball events, and as a manager you *have* to have that. Oh, this man was a monkey on my back for so long, and the worst part of it was that everybody loved Mayo Smith, because he was such a nice guy and such a charming guy. Mayo the nice poker companion, Mayo the great drinking companion—nobody had anything bad to say about him, and it was all absolutely true except for one thing: the man was overwhelmingly inept. Oh, boy, I hated that man, and I hated myself for hating him. I probably would have *killed* him if I'd run into him in '67 after he blew the pennant for us." The Tigers lost a famous three-way race on the last day of the 1967 season, when the Red Sox won the pennant by beating the Minnesota Twins while the Tigers lost the second game of a doubleheader to the California Angels at home. "That last game, he did everything wrong," Don went on. "He let our pitcher stay in, and I was standing up on my seat screaming, 'Take him out! Take him out!' I was blind with rage. I can still see what happened next—that pitch coming in to the Angels' Fregosi, and Fregosi getting ready to hit it—and I can see the ball going through the hole between short and third, and I can see the man coming around third to put them ahead. And then, like everybody else in this town, I can still see Dick McAuliffe, in the ninth, hitting into only his second double play of the entire season, to end it all. Listen, I'm like a dying man; I can see that whole game flashing before my eyes. It was like a scene out of Fellini, because right in back of me this guy is sitting there and listening to a *football* game—it was a Sunday, and football was on—and his radio is blaring football as the runner is rounding third base, and Mayo Smith is standing there, riveted to that post of his, holding up the dugout." He shook his head and laughed hollowly. "That was the day I came home and went down in the basement and broke all our flowerpots."

Bert, from the front seat, said, "Think about something happier. Think about 1968."

"The trouble with you is you don't suffer enough," Don said.

"I don't *suffer* enough!" said Bert, shouting with laughter. "I'm Jewish, I'm short, I'm fat, I'm poor, I'm ugly—what else do you want me to suffer?"

"That's all true," Don said, looking at his friend affectionately. "A man like you probably can't bear the necessary onus of suffering. After all, this isn't just a game of ours. It isn't just a preoccupation. It isn't an obsession. It's a—well, it's a—"

They said it together: "It's an obsession."

At the airport, Max was met and hugged, and the car aimed back toward the ball park. Suddenly, it was a party.

"Everything is fine, I guess," Max said. "Only, I miss my friends, now I'm with them again. I like this so much I may do it every week. But things are not fine back there, really. Listen, the other night when we beat the Yanks I turned on the TV in Chicago and the guy forgot to give the Tigers' score. He absolutely forgot. I couldn't get to sleep until four in the morning. Nobody knew. You pick up the morning paper in Chicago, and it says, 'N.Y. at Detroit (n.).' I mean, doesn't a man have a Constitutional right to the box scores?" He said that he was sometimes able to pick up Ernie Harwell on his car radio. "It only happens a little bit outside the city, on the north side," he added. "Sometimes it's only a snatch of the game broadcast, with a lot of static, but I can always tell from Ernie's voice how we're doing. Anyway, that's how come we bought the new house in Highland Park—so I can get the broadcasts and be closer to drive to all the Tiger games in Milwaukee. Fortunately, my wife likes the area."

At the ball park, the three friends sat in their accustomed place, in Section 24, between first and home; Tiger Stadium is an ancient, squared-off green pleasance, and the view was splendid. None of the three bought scorecards. ("The thing to do," Bert said, "is *remember*.") The World Champion Oakland A's, who had barely beaten out the Tigers in a violent five-game playoff the previous fall, were the opposition, and a modest but enthusiastic audience was filling up the nearby seats. Don Shapiro has a dark, vivid face—a downturned mustache, some lines of pain, some lines of hope—and he now looked about with satisfaction and clapped his hands. "Well!" he said. "Well, well. What could be nicer than this? I mean that. I really mean it. I'm supremely happy. I like this park even better than my Eames chair." He caught sight of the Oakland starting pitcher, Ken Holtzman, warming up, and his face fell. "*Uh*-oh," he said. "A very tough man, and now I've got some ethnic problems, too. A Jewish pitcher against our guys."

The game was a quiet, almost eventless affair for the first few innings, but Don was a restless spectator, twisting and bending in his seat, grimacing, groaning occasionally, leaping up for almost every enemy out. In the fifth, Gene Tenace, the Oakland first baseman, hit a home run into the left-field stands, and Shapiro fell back into his seat. He stared at the concrete floor in silence. "God damn it," he muttered at last. "This is *serious*." The A's added two more runs off the Detroit starter, Woodie Fryman, but in the bottom half the Tigers put together two singles, a walk, and a third single, by Bill Freehan, the Detroit catcher, to tie it up, and the party was delighted.

"That was a good little rally," Max said. "Just right. Lots of running, and we have a tie."

"Yes, I don't like that *one* big blow," Bert said.

Don, watching the game and his emotions simultaneously, announced, "I'm elated. I'm back to my original state of anxiety. But listen, Max, we're lucky they decided to pitch to Freehan."

"Yes," Max said. "First of all, I would walk him. But then I absolutely don't throw him any kind of up pitch like that."

Jim Northrup, the Tiger right fielder, came up to the plate in the sixth, and Bert said, "I still don't see why this guy doesn't hit about .380."

"We've been saying that for ten years," Don said.

Northrup flied out, and Rodriguez stood in. Bert cried, "Au-reeli-*oh!*"

"See, here's another one," Max said. "This guy hit nineteen homers one year, and everybody called him a home-run hitter. They've been waiting ever since."

"He hit *nineteen*?" said Bert.

"Yes, for the Angels."

"Not for us, of course."

"Aurelio has a lazy bat," Don said. "He doesn't whip that bat."

"Frank Bolling had a lazy bat, too," Max said.

"You can't remember Milt Bolling?" Bert said.

Rodriguez hit a two-run home run to left, and Max, waving his arms and laughing, cried, "Exactly what I said! He's a great home-run hitter. I always knew it. Anyway, Williams should have taken out Holtzman. The man was dying out there—anybody could see it."

In the eighth, however, the Oakland designated hitter, Deron Johnson, jumped on a pitch by a Detroit reliever named Tom Timmerman and drove it high into the left-field seats. The game was tied. There was an enormous silence, and Don Shapiro, holding his head, stood up and turned his back on the field. "I knew it," he said. "I *knew* it!" He swayed slightly. "Oh, listen to that damned organ, will you? They're playing funeral selections." (Another bitter cause: In 1966, Don and Max directed a barrage of letters at the Tigers' general manager, Jim Campbell, protesting the installation of an organ at the stadium. Max wrote, "Baseball games are baseball games, and vesper services are vesper services." Don wrote, "Who in hell wants to hear 'Funiculi Funicula' in the middle of a Tiger rally?" Max wrote, "The object of a ball game for the fan is not to be entertained. It is to win." The organ was not removed.)

Rich Reese, leading off the bottom of the eighth, was walked, and hopes revived noisily. Dick Sharon stood in, and Max said, "He should bunt, but we have the worst bunting team in history."

"It's an absolute must-bunt situation," Don agreed. Last year, Don mailed a lengthy letter to Billy Martin outlining a new defense for the must-bunt, which involved sending the second baseman to charge the plate on the right side of the diamond, instead of the traditional move by the first baseman.

Don's plan quoted from his correspondence with the Michigan State baseball coach, Danny Litwhiler, who had devised the new play. No answer came from Martin, but his response, relayed later to Don, was "I don't go for that funny stuff."

Here, in any case, Sharon did bunt, and was safe when first baseman Tenace muffed the ball. A moment later, Northrup smacked a triple for the go-ahead runs—good enough, it turned out, for the game. The Tigers won, 8–5, and Don, on his feet and clapping, had brightened perceptibly. "I was never worried for an instant," he said. A moment later, he added, "Well, that's a lie. My trouble is I tend to view these games viscerally. Baseball gives me that endogenous epinephrine. I'm hooked on my own adrenaline."

○

Detroit in the nineteen-thirties had few visible civic or economic virtues, but it just may have been the best baseball town in the country. The Tigers—a dangerous and contentious team built around the power hitting of the enormous Hank Greenberg, and around Charlie Gehringer and Mickey Cochrane and, later, Rudy York, and around the pitching of Schoolboy Rowe, Tommy Bridges, and, later, Bobo Newsom—did not win nearly as often as the lordly Yankees, but victory, when it came, was treasured. There was a pennant in 1934 (the first since 1909), a championship in 1935 (the first ever for Detroit), and another pennant in 1940. At his home on Tuxedo Avenue, young Don Shapiro, listening to games over Station WWJ in the afternoon, tried to work magic spells to make the Tigers win: twenty-eight baby steps across his bedroom without losing his balance could bring Gehringer a hit (not quite pure magic, since Gehringer's batting average between 1933 and 1940 was .336). The Ernie Harwell of those Piltdown days was Ty Tyson, for Mobil Oil and "The Sign of the Flying Red . . . Horse!," who called Greenberg "Hankus-Pankus" and Schoolboy Rowe "Schoolhouse" or "Schoolie." ("For a pitcher, Schoolie is sure pickin' 'em up and layin' 'em down.") Whenever they could, Don and Bert and their friends took the Trumbull Avenue streetcar at noontime to the ball park, then called Navin Field, and stood beside an iron gate on the corner of National Street, behind home plate. In time, the gate rolled up, to a great clattering of chains, and a Tigers' supervisor would conduct a mini-shape-up ("You and you and you and *you* over there") for the job of assistant ushers. The designees took up their posts in the outer reaches of the upper deck, beyond the uniformed regulars, and returned batting-practice fly balls and dusted seats and, between times, eyed the Olympians on the field: not just Greenberg and Gehringer and Rowe but the others—Marv Owen and Gee Walker and Elon Hogsett and Pete Fox, and batboy Whitey Willis and trainer Denny Carroll and groundskeeper Neil Conway. A lot of the players lived in apartment houses out on Chicago and Dexter Boulevards, or Boston and Dexter, and if you walked out there and waited long enough, you could sometimes pick up an autograph. The game and the players must have seemed very near in those days. Once, in 1936, when Don Shapiro was twelve years old, he played catch with Tiger first baseman Jack Burns, who split Don's left thumb with a throw; the wonderful stigma—a white cicatrix on the first knuckle—is still visible.

Bert Gordon's father, a rabbi, was a passionate fan who sometimes got his tickets through the Detroit Council of Churches, which provided free seats for the clergy. "I'd be sitting beside him at the park, and I'd say 'Father—' and the whole section would turn around," Bert said recently. He laughed, and went on, "My father was a city man—like all our fathers, I guess. He never went fishing, or anything. It was baseball that was the bond between us. Baseball was the whole thing. I don't think anybody can imagine the terrific importance of Hank Greenberg to the whole Jewish community then. He was a god, a true folk hero. That made baseball acceptable to our parents, so for once they didn't mind if we took a little time off from the big process of getting into college. And then, of course, Hank Greenberg was so big and so handsome—a handsome giant. Plus he didn't change his name. I can remember Rosh Hashanah, or some day like that, in 1938, when Hank was going after Babe Ruth's record of sixty home runs in a season. Of course, nobody in the synagogue could go near a radio that day, but somebody came in late from the parking lot with a report about the game, and the news went through the congregation like a *wind*."

Don kept a scrapbook that summer, pasting up Greenberg's pictures and box scores and headlines ("HANK'S NINE DAYS AHEAD!"). Under one photograph of Greenberg swinging a bat, he penciled "There she goes!" and under the headline "HANK NEEDS FOUR HOMERS IN NINE GAMES TO TIE" he wrote "Two bits he does it!" He was wrong; Hank hit fifty-eight, falling shy of the record by two. A year or two earlier, Greenberg had accepted an invitation to dinner with some friends of his who had a house in Max Lapides' part of town, and word was sent out that he would shake hands with the neighborhood kids. The excited juniors lined up (in their sweatshirts with Greenberg's number 5 inked on the back, and carrying, nearly all of them, first basemen's mitts), but Max was not among them, for he had broken a leg a few days before and was forbidden to get out of bed. He cried himself to sleep that night, but he was awakened by his father turning on the light and ushering Hank Greenberg into the room. The sudden visitor was so enormous, Max recalls, that he had to duck his head to get through the door. Greenberg sat on Max's bed and talked to him for half an hour. Before he left, he took out a pen and signed Max's cast and then, seeing a copy of Max's favorite baseball book—*Safe!*, by Harold Sherman—on the bedside table, he signed that, too.

"In our household, we used to talk about only three things—current events, the Jewish holidays, and baseball," Max has said. "You have to try to remember how much easier it was to keep up with all the baseball news back then. For us, there were just the Tigers and the seven other teams in the American League, so we knew them by heart. All the games were played in the afternoon, and none of the teams was in a time zone more than an hour away from Detroit, so you got just about all the scores when the late-afternoon papers came. You could talk about that at supper, and then there were the stories in the morning papers to read and think about the next day. Why, in those days we knew more about the farms than I know about some of the West Coast teams right now. By the time a Hoot Evers or a Fred Hutchinson was ready to come up from Beaumont, we knew all about him."

Max's father, Jack, did not need Hank Greenberg to introduce him to baseball. *His* father, in turn, had been a butcher in Rochester, New York, and young Jack Lapides had often made the morning rounds in the family cart and then sat next to his father in a saloon and studied the pictures of the baseball players of the day—with their turtleneck uniforms and handlebar mustaches—up above the big, cool bar mirror. Jack Lapides had a laundry business in Detroit, and by the nineteen thirties he had arranged things well enough so that in the stirring seasons of 1934 and 1935 he was able to attend every single Tiger home game and many on the road. "My father used to take me to fifty or sixty games a year," Max recalled this summer, "and I recently became aware that between us we encompassed just about the entire history of big-league ball in this century. He went to most of the games every year right up to the end of his life, in 1967. I'd met Don by then, and in those last few years he would come along with us, too."

Don Shapiro's father, a tallow merchant, knew nothing about baseball, but one of Don's uncles was a junk dealer who owned a semipro team in Lapeer, Michigan; and even as a very young boy, Don was sometimes allowed to sit on the bench with the players. That was enough—more than enough—to start it all for him. Don has a vivid and affectionate memory of Jack Lapides. "He was a very formal man, a reserved sort of man," he said not long ago, "and I can still see him sitting up there in the stands, in his coat and collar and tie, with one hand on the railing in front of him. He kept me and Max on our toes. 'Pay attention, boys,' he always said. 'This is a serious business.' "

○

It is another Saturday, the last day in June, and Max is back from Chicago again, to be with his family and his Tigers and his Tiger friends. This time, it has been decided, the game will be watched on television, and the three meet for lunch at Bert's big, comfortable house in Huntington Woods. Before lunch, Max and Don throw a baseball back and forth in Bert's backyard;

according to custom, each is wearing the top half of a gray Tiger road uniform. The name on Don's back, above the number 42, is SZOTKIEWICZ; Max is 21, ZEPP. The shirts, which are both beautifully pressed, were gifts from Ernie Harwell, who extracted them from the Tiger clubhouse after the brief, almost unnoticed careers of two Tiger foot soldiers—Kenny Szotkiewicz and Bill Zepp—had come to a close. (Harwell, who is a friend and admirer of Don Shapiro, telephoned Don from Cleveland one afternoon late in the 1966 season, and asked if he would care to work out with the Tigers before their game with the Indians that evening. Don canceled his appointments, flew to Cleveland and suited up, was introduced to Tiger manager Frank Skaff—who may have been a trifle surprised to find that the "prospect" Harwell had promised him was a slight, forty-two-year-old oral surgeon—and then warmed up with Don Wert, Ray Oyler, Willie Horton, and the rest. In photographs of the event, which hang on the wall of Don's living room, the ballplayers look bemused, but the prospect is ecstatic.) Max begins throwing harder now, and Don, who has a catcher's mitt and is wearing a Tiger cap on backward, goes into a crouch. Max's motion is a little stiff, but you can see in it the evidences of a fair high-school ballplayer. Don handles his glove elegantly, coming up smoothly and in one motion after each pitch and snapping the throw back from behind his shoulder. He is smiling. He caught briefly for the University of Michigan varsity and, later, on a Sixth Service Command team in Chicago. The ball is beginning to pop in the gloves, and Bert, umpiring from behind the invisible mound, expresses concern for his wife's borders. Max pauses for breath and reminds everyone of a similar pregame workout some years ago when a small protective sponge fell out of Don's glove. "All he could say was 'These hands. These golden hands.' From catcher to surgeon in one second."

"Throw the ball," says the catcher-surgeon.

"Knuckler," says Max.

"Hey!" says Don. "Not bad. Again."

The next knuckleball sails over Don's head and through the hedge.

"OK, that's it," Bert declares, calling the game. "Zena will kill me."

"Listen," Don says as they troop toward Bert's sun porch. "I think my arm is coming back. I really mean that. Wouldn't that be *something*, to get my arm back after all this time?" He notices that a lacing on his mitt has come loose, and he stops to tie it up. "Goddam dog," he murmurs.

The Tigers, who have recently lost eight straight and have slipped to fifth place, are playing the rising Orioles, but they score two unearned runs off Mike Cuellar in the first inning, and in the second Mickey Stanley hits a home run. The Tiger pitcher is a big, strong-looking young right-hander named Mike Strahler. The friends sit in easy chairs in Bert's study, with plates of sandwiches and salad in their laps. Zena Gordon, Bert's wife, brings around seconds. Brian Gordon, Bert's younger son, who is sixteen, comes in and watches for an inning or two and then wanders out again. The Gordons' other son, Merrill, is away at his summer job. He is a Michigan State sophomore, who wants to become a forester; he does not care about baseball. "He thinks it's a lot of men running around in funny suits," Bert explains. Bert used to take Merrill to games, but the summer Merrill was eleven years old he finally got up the nerve to tell his father that baseball meant nothing to him. "Everything you do in life, you do so that your son will go to ball games with you, and then he doesn't want to," Bert says now. He makes a joke of it, but at the time the news shook him so severely that he himself hardly went to the ball park for two years. "If my family wanted to be home, I wanted to be home with them," he says. Max Lapides has two daughters, who are seven and eleven; he says he can't tell yet about them and baseball. Don's son, Alan, who is fifteen, is crazy about baseball. He catches for a team called the Rangers in his suburban Colt League, and he watches the Tigers with something of his father's unhappy intensity. Still, there are no streetcars that run from his house to the ball park, and it is almost certain that he will never discover a baseball world that is as rich and wide as his father's "You know what I really wish?" Alan said to Don one day last spring. "I wish I had friends like yours."

The wives of the three friends apparently accept their husbands' zealotry and their arcane closed company; indeed, they have no choice, since they cannot enter it on anything like even terms, and none of them, in truth, is much of a fan. Max and Sissi Lapides used to go to several games together each year, but then during one Yankee game, with the score tied at 6–6 in the eighth inning, Max noticed that his wife was quietly reading a book under her program, and it was thenceforth agreed that their interests in the pastime were not really comparable. Sue Shapiro is an admitted front-runner, who gets excited about the Tigers only when they are doing well. "Don is a fan," she said recently. "It's a fact of his life, so I have no trouble with it at all."

The game at Bert's house glides along, with the Tigers leading the Orioles by 4–1 after the fifth, and everything apparently in hand; the lighted figures move distantly on the screen, the room deepens in shadow, and the men lean back in their big chairs and let the baseball lull them. There is nothing to be concerned about except Kaline's average (computed today by Bert on a pocket calculator), and now, after his second unsuccessful trip to the plate, the figures slip at last to .2994788, and Al Kaline is no longer a lifetime .300 man. It is sad; this may be Kaline's last year. Then, a bit later, Eddie Brinkman singles, and Tiger first-base coach Dick Tracewski slaps him on the rump as he stands on the bag. Max Lapides says, "I wonder who holds the lifetime record for handing out most pats on the ass."

"It has to be Crosetti," Bert says instantly. "All those years he stood there in the third-base box for the Yankees and slapped all those big guys as they came around. He must be ahead by thousands."

"A true piece of baseball trivia!" Max shouts.

"You can't *say* 'baseball trivia,' " Don says. "It's a contradiction in terms. It's antithetical. We don't use the word 'trivia.' "

"OK, then," Max says. "OK—how about 'A Compendium of Little-Known Facts'?"

○

We cannot quite leave these friends here—three aging men, laughing together still, but too comfortable with their indoor, secondhand sport, and too much like the rest of us. Perhaps this sort of unremarkable fandom is what is ahead for them now; perhaps not. Bert Gordon, who worries about his health, goes to fewer and fewer night games. "You get older," he says. "It gets colder." Max Lapides, much happier in his Chicago job than he was in the old one in Detroit, has less time to call Bert with a baseball stumper in the middle of the morning. "I'm beginning to change a little," he confessed recently. "Sometimes I even put an old player on the wrong team by a year or two. I sometimes think that after the big years of '67 and '68 I couldn't really stay intense *all* summer about the Tigers if they were playing under-.500 ball again. I'm looking at it all from farther off, I guess." The Lapides family now lives in Highland Park, Illinois, where the new school year is just beginning; by next April the late Tiger scores will bother Max a little less. The Tigers, in any case, have just about slipped from contention for this year; now in third place, behind Baltimore and Boston, they trail the division-leading Orioles by seven games—a margin that, according to Bert's calculator, will require them to play at an .864 clip throughout September (plus a helpful Baltimore slump to a .500 level) in order to bring about another miracle. The friends have also lost Billy Martin, who, despite their stamp of approval, was recently fired as the manager of the Tigers. It's been a hard season. No matter; these three men should be remembered in full summer, and at their home ball park, for it is there that they, like a few other great fans in other cities, made their game into something resembling a private work of art. It is a modest genre, to be sure, and terribly dated now, but still perhaps not one to be put aside too quickly. At the very least, these gentle prodigals have used their sport to connect themselves to their fathers and to their boyhood and to their city—the inner city that they long since lost and left—and also to connect themselves to friends with whom they could share a passion, a special language, and an immense private history. Baseball has been a family to them.

Don Shapiro, perhaps the most intricate of the three, may be the only one who will not change—the last to give up that mad, splendid hope of one absolutely perfect season: one hundred and sixty-two straight wins for his Tigers. Late last May, Don went to a night game against the Oakland A's, and after eight and a half innings the score still stood at 0–0. Mickey Stanley led off the ninth for the Tigers with a single, and Gates Brown came up to bat. "He's got to bunt. He's *got* to!" Don said, watching the field intently. "He's got to bunt, but he can't. Just wait and see." He was right; Brown swung away and singled to right, sending Stanley to third, as vast sounds of joy rose in the night. Oakland changed pitchers, and Duke Sims struck out. Tony Taylor batted for Cash, and on the one-and-two count Stanley set sail for the plate at full career, and Taylor, bunting on the suicide squeeze, fouled the ball off and was out.

"I don't *believe* it!" Don cried hoarsely. "They've lost their minds down there! They're trying to kill me. They're doing it on purpose. If they don't do it, I'll have to kill myself."

Dick McAuliffe then struck out, taking the called third strike without moving his bat from his shoulder, and the rally and the inning ended. Don, who had been standing and clutching his temples, now sat down and buried his head in his arms. He shuddered, and at last forced himself to look out at the emerald field. "If we lose, this is the worst game I ever saw," he announced.

○

Following the Tigers has not become any easier since this report was written. Kaline and Cash and Northrup and McAuliffe and other stalwarts have departed; the team finished third in its division in 1973, and dead last in 1974 and 1975. Thanks to some new stars like Ron LeFlore and Mark Fidrych, they moved up to fifth place in 1976 but finished twenty-four games behind the division-winning Yankees. The three great fans, it is comforting to report, have changed much less than their team. Max Lapides, now entirely at home in Chicago, has not turned to the White Sox or the Cubs for solace. He follows the Tigers as best he can, sometimes calling Bert for a good long catch-up on the team, and he goes to every Tiger game within reach. Two years ago, in June, he arranged things so that he was able to drive to Milwaukee and back on three successive days—a total of more than five hundred miles—to watch a Tigers-Brewers series. The Tigers lost the first game, 8–4; on the second day, they dropped a doubleheader, 5–0 and 4–2; they also lost the last game, 5–4.

President Nixon resigned from office on August 9, 1974, thus relieving Bert Gordon of one of his self-imposed morning tasks; the last reading on Bert's calculator showed that Mr. Nixon had surrendered 30.62970 percent of his White House tenancy. Bert's other vigil ended in October 1974, when Al Kaline retired. Shortly before game-time on the afternoon of the Tigers' final home game that year, Bert suddenly realized that he was missing his last chance to see Kaline in action. He jumped in his car and raced for Tiger Stadium. He turned on the car radio and heard Ernie Harwell describe Kaline's first turn at bat in the game; he parked in his regular lot and was hurrying across Michigan Avenue to the ball park when he heard the crowd roar that greeted Kaline's second appearance. Bert went in and happily took his seat, and for an inning or two he did not notice that Kaline had left the lineup after that second time up—left it for good. "I got up and went home," Bert said later. "There wasn't even anybody there I could *tell* about it. It was the story of my life." The next morning, in his office, he punched out the final Kaline numbers: 10,116 at-bats, 3007 hits, for a lifetime batting average of .2972518.

Since then, Bert has suffered the diminution of Cesar Gutierrez at the hands of Rennie Stennett, and one day last summer, when he was idly skimming the box scores, it suddenly came to him that Ed Figueroa, the Yankee pitcher, has all five vowels in his *last* name. "Goodbye, Aurelio," Bert wrote in a letter to Max. "I still can't believe the whole thing."

Don Shapiro gave up on the Tigers in the terrible season of 1975, when they lost 102 games and finished 37½ games behind the division-leading Red Sox. "I hated myself," he says, "but I couldn't help it. They were literally killing me." Last year, when the young Tigers suddenly began knocking off the Yankees and the champion Red Sox in surprising fashion, Don allowed himself to be won back. He called me late in the summer and told me that he and Bert were going to Tiger Stadium that night. "This Mark Fidrych is pitching," he said, "and he's got a little color, you know. At least, I think he does—we're not used to that sort of thing here in Detroit, so it's hard to tell. And Ralph Houk [the incumbent Detroit manager] is so lackluster that it has this deadening effect on everybody, especially me. But I'm getting optimistic again, I think. I really am. The fires are being stoked."

Gone for Good

—JUNE 1975

The photograph shows a perfectly arrested moment of joy. On one side—the left, as you look at the picture—the catcher is running toward the camera at full speed, with his upraised arms spread wide. His body is tilting toward the center of the picture, his mask is held in his right hand, his big glove is still on his left hand, and his mouth is open in a gigantic shout of pleasure. Over on the right, another player, the pitcher, is just past the apex of an astonishing leap that has brought his knees up to his chest and his feet well up off the ground. Both of *his* arms are flung wide, and he, too, is shouting. His hunched, airborne posture makes him look like a man who just made a running jump over a sizable object—a kitchen table, say. By luck, two of the outreaching hands have overlapped exactly in the middle of the photograph, so that the pitcher's bare right palm and fingers are silhouetted against the catcher's glove, and as a result the two men are linked and seem to be executing a figure in a manic and difficult dance. There is a further marvel—a touch of pure fortune—in the background, where a spectator in dark glasses, wearing a dark suit, has risen from his seat in the grandstand and is lifting his arms in triumph. This, the third and central Y in the picture, is immobile. It is directly behind the overlapping hand and glove of the dancers, and it binds and recapitulates the lines of force and the movements and the theme of the work, creating a composition as serene and well ordered as a Giotto. The subject of the picture, of course, is classical— the celebration of the last out of the seventh game of the World Series.

This famous photograph (by Rusty Kennedy, of the Associated Press) does not require captioning for most baseball fans or for almost anyone within the Greater Pittsburgh area, where it is still prominently featured in the art collections of several hundred taverns. It may also be seen, in a much enlarged version, on one wall of the office of Joe L. Brown, the general

43

manager of the Pittsburgh Pirates, in Three Rivers Stadium. The date of the photograph is October 17, 1971; the place is Memorial Stadium, in Baltimore. The catcher is Manny Sanguillen, of the Pirates, and his leaping teammate is pitcher Steve Blass, who has just defeated the defending (and suddenly former) World Champion Baltimore Orioles by a score of 2–1, giving up four hits.

I am not a Pittsburgher, but looking at this photograph never fails to give me pleasure, not just because of its aesthetic qualities but because its high-bounding happiness so perfectly brings back that eventful World Series and that particular gray autumn afternoon in Baltimore and the wonderful and inexpungible expression of joy that remained on Steve Blass's face after the game ended. His was, to be sure, a famous victory—a close and bitterly fought pitchers' battle against the Orioles' Mike Cuellar, in which the only score for seven innings had been a solo home run by the celebrated Pirate outfielder Roberto Clemente. The Pirates had scored again in the eighth, but the Orioles had responded with a run of their own and had brought the tying run around to third base before Blass shut them off once and for all. The win was the culmination of a stirring uphill fight by the Pirates, who had fallen into difficulties by losing the first two games to the Orioles; Steve Blass had begun their comeback with a wonderfully pitched three-hit, 5–1 victory in the third game. It was an outstanding Series, made memorable above all by the play of Roberto Clemente, who batted .414 over the seven games and fielded his position with extraordinary zeal. He was awarded the sports car as the most valuable player of the Series, but Steve Blass was not far out of the running for the prize. After that last game, Baltimore manager Earl Weaver said, "Clemente was great, all right, but if it hadn't been for Mr. Blass, *we* might be popping the corks right now."

I remember the vivid contrast in styles between the two stars in the noisy, floodlit, champagne-drenched Pirate clubhouse that afternoon. Clemente, at last the recipient of the kind of national attention he had always deserved but had rarely been given for his years of brilliant play, remained erect and removed, regarding the swarming photographers with a haughty, incandescent pride. Blass was a less obvious hero—a competent but far from overpowering right-hander who had won fifteen games for the Pirates that year, with a most respectable 2.85 earned-run average, but who had absorbed a terrible pounding by the San Francisco Giants in the two games he pitched in the National League playoffs, just before the Series. His two Series victories, by contrast, were momentous by any standard—and, indeed, were among the very best pitching performances of his entire seven years in the majors. Blass, in any case, celebrated the Pirates' championship more exuberantly than Clemente, exchanging hugs and shouts with his teammates, alternately smoking a cigar and swigging from a champagne bottle. Later, I saw him in front of his locker with his arm around his father, Bob Blass, a plumber from Falls Village, Connecticut, who had once been a semipro pitcher; the two Blasses, I saw, were wearing identical delighted, nonstop smiles.

Near the end of an article I wrote about that 1971 World Series, I mentioned watching Steve Blass in batting practice just before the all-important seventh game and suddenly noticing that, in spite of his impending responsibilities, he was amusing himself with a comical parody of Clemente at the plate: "Blass . . . then arched his back, cricked his neck oddly, rolled his head a few times, took up a stance in the back corner of the batter's box, with his bat held high, and glared out at the pitcher imperiously—Clemente, to the life." I had never seen such a spirited gesture in a serious baseball setting, and since then I have come to realize that Steve Blass's informality and boyish play constituted an essential private style, as original and as significant as Clemente's eaglelike pride, and that each of them was merely responding in his own way to the challenges of an extremely difficult public profession. Which of the two, I keep wondering, was happier that afternoon about the Pirates' championship and his part in it? Roberto Clemente, of course, is dead; he was killed on December 31, 1972, in Puerto Rico, in the crash of a plane he had chartered to carry emergency relief supplies to the victims of an earthquake in Nicaragua. Steve Blass, who is now thirty-three, is out of baseball, having been recently driven into retirement by two years of pitching wildness—a sudden, near-total inability to throw strikes. No one, including Blass himself, can cure or explain it.

○

The summer of 1972, the year after his splendid World Series, was in most respects the best season that Steve Blass ever had. He won nineteen games for the Pirates and lost only eight, posting an earned-run average of 2.48—sixth-best in the National League—and being selected for the NL All-Star team. What pleased him most that year was his consistency. He went the full distance in eleven of the thirty-two games he started, and averaged better than seven and a half innings per start—not dazzling figures (Steve Carlton, of the Phillies, had thirty complete games that year, and Bob Gibson, of the Cards, had twenty-three) but satisfying ones for a man who had once had inordinate difficulty in finishing games. Blass, it should be understood, was not the same kind of pitcher as a Carlton or a Gibson. He was never a blazer. When standing on the mound, he somehow looked more like a journeyman pitcher left over from the nineteen thirties or forties than like one of the hulking, hairy young flingers of today. (He is six feet tall, and weighs about one hundred and eighty pounds.) Watching him work, you sometimes wondered how he was getting all those batters out. The word on him among the other clubs in his league was something like: Good but not overpowering stuff, excellent slider, good curve, good change-up curve. A pattern pitcher, whose slider works because of its location. No control problems. Intelligent, knows how to win.

I'm not certain that I saw Blass work in the regular season of 1972, but I did see him pitch the opening game of the National League playoffs that fall against the Cincinnati Reds, in Pittsburgh. After giving up a home run to the Reds' second batter of the day, Joe Morgan, which was hit off a first-pitch fastball, Blass readjusted his plans and went mostly to a big, slow curve, causing the Reds to hit innumerable rainmaking outfield flies, and won by 5–1. I can still recall how Blass looked that afternoon—his characteristic, feet-together stance at the outermost, first-base edge of the pitching rubber, and then the pitch, delivered with a swastikalike scattering of arms and legs and a final lurch to the left—and I also remember how I kept thinking that at any moment the sluggers of the Big Red Machine would stop overstriding and overswinging against such unintimidating deliveries and drive Blass to cover. But it never happened—Blass saw to it that it didn't. Then, in the fifth and deciding game, he returned and threw seven and one-third more innings of thoughtful and precise patterns, allowing only four hits, and departed with his team ahead by 3–2—a pennant-winning outing, except for the fact that the Pirate bullpen gave up the ghost in the bottom of the ninth, when a homer, two singles, and a wild pitch entitled the Reds to meet the Oakland A's in the 1972 World Series. It was a horrendous disappointment for the Pittsburgh Pirates and their fans, for which no blame at all could be attached to Blass.

My next view of Steve Blass on a baseball diamond came on a cool afternoon at the end of April this year. The game—the White Sox vs. the Orioles—was a close, 3–1 affair, in which the winning White Sox pitcher, John McKenzie, struck out seventeen batters in six innings. A lot of the Sox struck out, too, and a lot of players on both teams walked—more than I could count, in fact. The big hit of the game was a triple to left center by the White Sox catcher, David Blass, who is ten years old. His eight-year-old brother, Chris, played second, and their father, Steve Blass, in old green slacks and a green T-shirt, coached at third. This was a late-afternoon date in the Upper St. Clair (Pennsylvania) Recreation League schedule, played between the White Sox and the Orioles on a field behind the Dwight D. Eisenhower Elementary School—Little League baseball, but at a junior and highly informal level. The low, *low* minors. Most of the action, or inaction, took place around home plate, since there was not much bat-on-ball contact, but there was a shrill nonstop piping of encouragement from the fielders, and disappointed batters were complimented on their overswings by a small, chilly assemblage of mothers, coaches, and dads. When Chris Blass went down swinging in the fourth, his father came over and said, "The sinker down and away is *tough*." Steve Blass has a longish, lightly freckled face, a tilted nose, and an alert and engaging expression. At this ball game, he looked like any young suburban father who had caught an early train home from the office in order to see his kids in action. He looked much more like a commuter than like a professional athlete.

Blass coached quietly, moving the fielders in or over a few steps, asking the shortstop if he knew how many outs there were, reminding someone to take his hands out of his pockets. "Learning the names of all the kids is the hard part," he said to me. It was his second game of the spring as a White Sox coach, and between innings one of the young outfielders said to him, "Hey, Mr. Blass, how come you're not playing with the Pirates at Three Rivers today?"

"Well," Blass said equably, "I'm not *in* baseball anymore."

"Oh," said the boy.

Twilight and the end of the game approached at about the same speed, and I kept losing track of the count on the batters. Steve Blass, noticing my confusion, explained that, in order to avert a parade of walked batters in these games, any strike thrown by a pitcher was considered to have wiped out the balls he had already delivered to the same batter; a strike on the 3–0 count reconverted things to 0–1. He suddenly laughed. "Why didn't they have that rule in the NL?" he said. "I'd have lasted until I was fifty."

Then it was over. The winning (and undefeated) White Sox and the losing Orioles exchanged cheers, and Karen Blass, a winning and clearly undefeated mother, came over and introduced me to the winning catcher and the winning second baseman. The Blasses and I walked slowly along together over the thick new grass, toting gloves and helmets and Karen's fold-up lawn chair, and at the parking lot the party divided into two cars— Karen and the boys homeward bound, and Steve Blass and I off to a nearby shopping center to order one large cheese-and-peppers-and-sausage victory pizza, to go.

o

Blass and I sat in his car at the pizza place, drinking beer and waiting for our order, and he talked about his baseball beginnings. I said I had admired the relaxed, low-key tenor of the game we had just seen, and he told me that his own Little League coach, back in Connecticut—a man named Jerry Fallon— had always seen to it that playing baseball on his club was a pleasure. "On any level, baseball is a tough game if it isn't really fun," Blass said. "I think most progress in baseball comes from enjoying it and then wanting to extend yourself a little, wanting it to become more. There should be a feeling of 'Let's go! Let's keep on with this!' "

He kept on with it, in all seasons and circumstances. The Blasses' place in Falls Village included an old barn with an interestingly angled roof, against which young Steve Blass played hundreds of one-man games (his four brothers and sisters were considerably younger) with a tennis ball. "I had all kinds of games, with different, very complicated ground rules," he said. "I'd throw the ball up, and then I'd be diving into the weeds for pop-ups or running back and calling for the long fly balls, and all. I'd always play a full game—a made-up game, with two big-league teams—and I'd write down the line score as I went along, and keep the results. One of the teams always had to be the Indians. I was a *total* Indians fan, completely buggy. In the summer of '54, when they won that record one hundred and eleven games, I managed to find every single Indians box score in the newspapers and clip it, which took some doing up where we lived. I guess Herb Score was my real hero—I actually pitched against him once in Indianapolis, in '63, when he was trying to make a comeback—but I knew the whole team by heart. Not just the stars but all the guys on the bench, like George Strickland and Wally Westlake and Hank Majeski and the backup third baseman, Rudy Regalado. My first big-league autograph was Hank Majeski."

Blass grew up into an athlete—a good sandlot football player, a second-team All-State Class B basketball star, but most of all a pitcher, like his father. ("He was wilder than hell," Blass said. "Once, in a Canaan game, he actually threw a pitch over the backstop.") Steve Blass pitched two no-hitters in his junior year at Housatonic Regional High School, and three more as a senior, but there were so many fine pitchers on the team that he did not get to be a starter until his final year. (One of the stars just behind him was John Lamb, who later pitched for the Pirates; Lamb's older sister, Karen, was a classmate of Steve's, and in time she found herself doubly affiliated with the Pirate mound staff.)

The Pittsburgh organization signed Steve Blass right out of Housatonic High in 1960, and he began moving up through the minors. He and Karen Lamb were married in the fall of 1963, and they went to the Dominican Republic that winter, where Steve played for the Cibaeñas Eagles and began working on a slider. He didn't quite make the big club when training ended in the spring, and was sent down to the Pirates' Triple A club in Columbus, but the call came three weeks later. Blass said, "We got in the car, and I floored it all the way across Ohio. I remember it was raining as we came out of the tunnel in Pittsburgh, and I drove straight to Forbes Field and went in and found the attendant and put my uniform on, at two in the afternoon. There was no *game* there, or anything—I just had to see how it looked."

We had moved along by now to the Blasses' house, a medium-sized brick structure on a hillside in Upper St. Clair, which is a suburb about twelve miles southeast of Pittsburgh. The pizza disappeared rapidly, and then David and

Chris went off upstairs to do their homework or watch TV. The Blass family room was trophied and comfortable. On a wall opposite a long sofa there was, among other things, a plaque representing the J. Roy Stockton Award for Outstanding Baseball Achievement, a Dapper Dan Award for meritorious service to Pittsburgh, a shiny metal bat with the engraved signatures of the National League All-Stars of 1972, a 1971 Pittsburgh Pirates World Champions bat, a signed photograph of President Nixon, and a framed, decorated proclamation announcing Steve Blass Day in Falls Village, Connecticut: "Be it known that this twenty-second day of October in the year of our Lord 1971, the citizens of Falls Village do set aside and do honor with pride Steve Blass, the tall skinny kid from Falls Village, who is now the hero of baseball and will be our hero always." It was signed by the town's three selectmen. The biggest picture in the room hung over the sofa—an enlarged color photograph of the Blass family at the Father-and-Sons Day at Three Rivers Stadium in 1971. In the photo, Karen Blass looks extremely pretty in a large straw hat, and all three male Blasses are wearing Pirate uniforms; the boys' uniforms look a little funny, because in their excitement each boy had put on the other's pants. Great picture.

Karen and Steve pointed this out to me, and then they went back to their arrival in the big time on that rainy long-ago first day in Pittsburgh and Steve's insisting on trying on his Pirate uniform, and they leaned back in their chairs and laughed about it again.

"With Steve, everything is right out in the open," Karen said. "Every accomplishment, every stage of the game—you have no idea how much he loved it, how he enjoyed the game."

That year, in his first outing, Blass pitched five scoreless innings in relief against the Braves, facing, among others, Hank Aaron. In his first start, against the Dodgers in Los Angeles, he pitched against Don Drysdale and won, 4–2. "I thought I'd died and gone to Heaven," Blass said to me.

He lit a cigar and blew out a little smoke. "You know, this thing that's happened has been painted so bad, so tragic," he said. "Well, I don't go along with that. I know what I've done in baseball, and I give myself all the credit in the world for it. I'm not bitter about this. I've had the greatest moments a person could ever want. When I was a boy, I used to make up those fictitious games where I was always pitching in the bottom of the ninth in the World Series. Well, I really *did* it. It went on and happened to me. Nobody's ever enjoyed winning a big-league game more than I have. All I've ever wanted to do since I was six years old was to keep on playing baseball. It didn't even have to be major-league ball. I've never been a goal-planner— I've never said I'm going to do this or that. With me, everything was just a continuation of what had come before. I think that's why I enjoyed it all so much when it did come along, when the good things did happen."

All this was said with an air of summing up, of finality, but at other times that evening I noticed that it seemed difficult for Blass to talk about his baseball career as a thing of the past; now and then he slipped into the present tense—as if it were still going on. This was understandable, for he was in limbo. The Pirates had finally released him late in March ("outrighted" him, in baseball parlance), near the end of the spring-training season, and he had subsequently decided not to continue his attempts to salvage his pitching form in the minor leagues. Earlier in the week of my visit, he had accepted a promising job with Josten's, Inc., a large jewelry concern that makes, among other things, World Series rings and high-school graduation rings, and he would go to work for them shortly as a traveling representative in the Pittsburgh area. He was out of baseball for good.

○

Pitching consistency is probably the ingredient that separates major-league baseball from the lesser levels of the game. A big-league fastball comes in on the batter at about eighty-five or ninety miles an hour, completing its prescribed journey of sixty feet six inches in less than half a second, and, if it is a strike, generally intersects no more than an inch or two of the seventeen-inch-wide plate, usually near the upper or lower limits of the strike zone; curves and sliders arrive a bit later but with intense rotation, and must likewise slice off only a thin piece of the black if they are to be effective. Sustaining this kind of control over a stretch of, say, one hundred and thirty pitches in a seven- or eight-inning appearance places such excruciating demands on a hurler's body and psyche that even the most successful pitchers regularly have games when they simply can't get the job done. Their fastball comes in high, their curves hang, the rest of their prime weapons desert them. The pitcher is knocked about, often by an inferior rival team, and leaves within a few innings; asked about it later, he shrugs and says, "I didn't have it today." He seems unsurprised. Pitching, it sometimes appears, is too hard for *anyone*. Occasionally, the poor performance is repeated, then extended. The pitcher goes into a slump. He sulks or rages, according to his nature; he asks for help; he works long hours on his motion. Still he cannot win. He worries about his arm, which almost always hurts to some degree. Has it gone dead? He worries about his stuff. Has he lost his velocity? He wonders whether he will ever win again or whether he will now join the long, long list—the list that awaits him, almost surely, in the end—of suddenly slow, suddenly sore-armed pitchers who have abruptly vanished from the big time, down the drain to oblivion. Then, unexpectedly, the slump ends—most of the time, that is—and he is back where he was: a winning pitcher. There is rarely an explanation for this, whether the slump has lasted for two games or a dozen, and managers and coaches, when pressed for one, will usually mutter that "pitching is a delicate thing," or—as if it explained anything—"he got back in the groove."

In spite of such hovering and inexplicable hazards, every big-league pitcher knows exactly what is expected of him. As with the other aspects of the game, statistics define his work and—day by day, inning by inning— whether he is getting it done. Thus, it may be posited as a rule that a major-league hurler who gives up an average of just over three and a half runs per game is about at the middle of his profession—an average pitcher. (Last year, the National League and the American League both wound up with a per-game earned-run average of 3.62.) At contract-renewal time, earned-run averages below 3.30 are invariably mentioned by pitchers; an ERA close to or above the 4.00 level will always be brought up by management. The select levels of pitching proficiency (and salary) begin below the 3.00 line; in fact, an ERA of less than 3.00 certifies true quality in almost exactly the same fashion as an over-.300 batting average for hitters. Last year, both leagues had ten pitchers who finished below 3.00, led by Buzz Capra's NL mark of 2.28 and Catfish Hunter's 2.49 in the AL. The best season-long earned-run average of the modern baseball era was Bob Gibson's 1.12 mark, set in 1968.

Strikeouts are of no particular use in defining pitching effectiveness, since there are other, less vivid ways of retiring batters, but bases on balls matter. To put it in simple terms, a good, middling pitcher should not surrender more than three or four walks per game—unless he is also striking out batters in considerable clusters. Last year, Ferguson Jenkins, of the Texas Rangers, gave up only 45 walks in 328 innings pitched, or an average of 1.19 per game. Nolan Ryan, of the Angels, walked 202 men in 333 innings, or 5.4 per game; however, he helped himself considerably by fanning 367, or just under ten men per game. The fastball is a great healer.

At the beginning of the 1973 season, Steve Blass had a lifetime earned-run average of 3.25 and was averaging 1.9 walks per game. He was, in short, an extremely successful and useful big-league pitcher, and was understandably enjoying his work. Early that season, however, baseball suddenly stopped being fun for him. He pitched well in spring training in Bradenton, which was unusual, for he has always been a very slow starter. He pitched on opening day, against the Cards, but threw poorly and was relieved, although the Pirates eventually won the game. For a time, his performance was borderline, but his few wins were in sloppy, high-scoring contests, and his bad outings were marked by streaks of uncharacteristic wildness and ineffectuality. On April 22, against the Cubs, he gave up a walk, two singles, a homer, and a double in the first inning, sailed through the second inning, and then walked a man and hit two batsmen in the third. He won a complete game against the Padres, but in his next two appearances, against the Dodgers and the Expos, he survived for barely half the distance; in the Expos game, he threw three scoreless innings, and then suddenly gave up two singles, a double, and two walks. By early June, his record was three wins and three losses, but his earned-run average suggested that his difficulties were serious. Bill Virdon, the Pirate manager, was patient and told Blass to take all the time he needed to find himself; he reminded Blass that once—in 1970—he had had an early record of two and eight but had then come back to finish the season with a mark of ten and twelve.

What was mystifying about the whole thing was that Blass still had his stuff, especially when he warmed up or threw on the sidelines. He was in great physical shape, as usual, and his arm felt fine; in his entire pitching career, Blass never experienced a sore arm. Virdon remained calm, although he was clearly puzzled. Some pitching mechanics were discussed and worked on: Blass was sometimes dropping his elbow as he threw; often he seemed to be hurrying his motion, so that his arm was not in synchronization with his body; perhaps he had exaggerated his peculiar swoop toward first base and thus was losing his power. These are routine pitching mistakes, which almost all pitchers are guilty of from time to time, and Blass worked on them assiduously. He started again against the Braves on June 11, in Atlanta; after three and one-third innings he was gone, having given up seven singles, a home run, two walks, and a total of five runs. Virdon and Blass agreed that a spell in the bullpen seemed called for; at least he could work on his problems there every day.

Two days later, the roof fell in. The team was still in Atlanta, and Virdon called Blass into the game in the fifth inning, with the Pirates trailing by 8–3. Blass walked the first two men he faced, and gave up a stolen base and a wild pitch and a run-scoring single before retiring the side. In the sixth, Blass walked Darrell Evans. He walked Mike Lum, throwing one pitch behind him in the process, which allowed Evans to move down to second. Dusty Baker singled, driving in a run. Ralph Garr grounded out. Davey Johnson singled, scoring another run. Marty Perez walked. Pitcher Ron Reed singled, driving in two more runs, and was wild-pitched to second. Johnny Oates walked. Frank Tepedino singled, driving in two runs, and Steve Blass was finally relieved. His totals for the one and one-third innings were seven runs, five hits, six bases on balls, and three wild pitches.

"It was the worst experience of my baseball life," Blass told me. "I don't think I'll ever forget it. I was embarrassed and disgusted. I was totally unnerved. You can't imagine the feeling that you suddenly have no *idea* what you're doing out there, performing that way as a major-league pitcher. It was kind of scary."

None of Blass's appearances during the rest of the '73 season were as dreadful as the Atlanta game, but none of them were truly successful. On August 1, he started against the Mets and Tom Seaver at Shea Stadium and gave up three runs and five walks in one and two-thirds innings. A little later, Virdon gave him a start in the Hall of Fame game at Cooperstown; this is a meaningless annual exhibition, played that year between the Pirates and the Texas Rangers, but Blass was as wild as ever and had to be relieved after two and one-third innings. After that, Bill Virdon announced that Blass would probably not start another game; the Pirates were in a pennant race, and the time for patience had run out.

Blass retired to the bullpen and worked on fundamentals. He threw a lot, once pitching a phantom nine-inning game while his catcher, Dave Ricketts, called the balls and strikes. At another point, he decided to throw every single day in the bullpen, to see if he could recapture his groove. "All it did was to get me very, very tired," Blass told me. He knew that Virdon was not going to use him, but whenever the Pirates fell behind in a game, he felt jumpy about the possibility of being called upon. "I knew I wasn't capable of going in there," he said. "I was afraid of embarrassing myself again, and letting down the club."

On September 6, the Pirate front office announced that Danny Murtaugh, who had served two previous terms as the Pirates' manager, was replacing Bill Virdon at the helm; the Pirates were caught up in a close, four-team division race, and it was felt that Murtaugh's experience might bring them home. One of Murtaugh's first acts was to announce that Steve Blass would be given a start. The game he picked was against the Cubs, in Chicago, on September 11. Blass, who had not pitched in six weeks, was extremely anxious about this test; he walked the streets of Chicago on the night before the game, and could not get to sleep until after five in the morning. The game went well for him. The Cubs won, 2–0, but Steve gave up only two hits and one earned run in the five innings he worked. He pitched with extreme care, throwing mostly sliders. He had another pretty good outing against the Cardinals, for no decision, and then started against the Mets, in New York, on September 21, but got only two men out, giving up four instant runs on a walk and four hits. The Mets won, 10–2, dropping the Pirates out of first place, but Blass, although unhappy about his showing, found some hope in the fact that he had at least been able to get the ball over the plate. "At that point," he said, "I was looking for even a little bit of success—one good inning, a few real fastballs, anything to hold on to that might halt my negative momentum. I wanted to feel I had at least got things turned around and facing in the right direction."

The Mets game was his last of the year. His statistics for the 1973 season were three wins and nine defeats, and an earned-run average of 9.81. That figure and his record of eighty-four walks in eighty-nine innings pitched were the worst in the National League.

○

I went to another ball game with Steve Blass on the night after the Little League affair—this time at Three Rivers Stadium, where the Pirates were meeting the Cardinals. We sat behind home plate, down near the screen, and during the first few innings a lot of young fans came clustering down the aisle to get Steve's autograph. People in the sections near us kept calling and waving to him. "Everybody has been great to me, all through this thing," Blass said. "I don't think there are too many here who are thinking, 'Look, there's the wild man.' I've had hundreds and hundreds of letters—I don't know how many—and not one of them was down on me."

In the game, Bob Gibson pitched against the Pirates' Jerry Reuss. When Ted Simmons stood in for the visitors, Blass said, "He's always hit me pretty good. He's really developed as a hitter." Then there was an error by Richie Hebner, at third, on a grounder hit by Ken Reitz, and Blass said, "Did you notice the batter take that big swing and then hit it off his hands? It was the swing that put Richie back on his heels like that." Later on, Richie Zisk hit a homer off Gibson, on a three-and-two count, and Blass murmured, "The high slider is one of *the* hittable pitches when it isn't just right. I should know."

The game rushed along, as games always do when Gibson is pitching. "You know," Blass said, "before we faced him we'd always have a team meeting and we'd say, 'Stay out of the batter's box, clean your spikes—anything to make him slow up.' But it never lasted more than an inning or two. He makes you play his game."

A little later, however, Willie Stargell hit a homer, and then Manny Sanguillen drove in another run with a double off the left-field wall ("*Get* out of here!" Steve said while the ball was in flight), and it was clear that this was not to be a Gibson night. Blass was enjoying himself, and it seemed to me that the familiarities and surprises of the game had restored something in him. At one point, he leaned forward a little and peered into the Pirate dugout and murmured, "Is Dock Ellis over in his regular corner there?" but for the most part he kept his eyes on the field. I tried to imagine what it felt like for him not to be down in the dugout.

I had talked that day to a number of Blass's old teammates, and all of them had mentioned his cheerfulness and his jokes, and what they had meant to the team over the years. "Steve's humor in the clubhouse was unmatched," relief pitcher Dave Giusti said. "He was a terrific mimic. Perfect. He could do Robert Kennedy. He could do Manny Sanguillen. He could do Roberto Clemente—not just the way he moved but the way he talked. Clemente loved it. He could do rat sounds—the noise a rat makes running. Lots of other stuff. It all made for looseness and togetherness. Because of Steve, the clubhouse was never completely silent, even after a loss." Another Pirate said, "Steve was about ninety percent of the good feeling on this club. He was always up, always agitating. If a player made a mistake, Steve knew how to say something about it that would let the guy know it was OK. Especially the young guys—he really understood them, and they put their confidence in him because of that. He picked us all up. Of course, there was a hell of a lot less of that from him in the last couple of years. We sure missed it."

For the final three innings of the game, Blass and I moved upstairs to general manager Joe Brown's box. Steve was startled by the unfamiliar view. "Hey, you can really see how it works from here, can't you?" he said. "Down there, you've got to look at it all in pieces. No wonder it's so hard to play this game right."

In the Pirates' seventh, Bill Robinson pinch-hit for Ed Kirkpatrick, and Blass said, "Well, *that* still makes me wince a little." It was a moment or two before I realized that Robinson was wearing Blass's old uniform number. Robinson fanned, and Blass said, "Same old twenty-eight."

The Pirates won easily, 5–0, with Jerry Reuss going all the way for the shutout, and just before the end Steve said, "I always had trouble sleeping after pitching a real good game. And if we were home, I'd get up about seven in the morning, before anybody else was up, and go downstairs and make myself a cup of coffee, and then I'd get the newspaper and open it to the sports section and just—just soak it all in."

We thanked Joe Brown and said good night, and as we went down in the elevator I asked Steve Blass if he wanted to stop off in the clubhouse for a minute and see his old friends. "Oh, no," he said. "No, I couldn't do that."

○

After the end of the 1973 season, Blass joined the Pirates' team in the Florida Instructional League (an autumn institution that exists mostly to permit the clubs to look over their prime minor-league prospects), where he worked intensively with a longtime pitching coach, Don Osborn, and appeared in three games. He came home feeling a little hopeful (he was almost living on such minimal nourishments), but when he forced himself to think about it he had to admit that he had been too tense to throw the fastball much, even against rookies. Then, in late February, 1974, Blass reported to Bradenton with the other Pirate pitchers and catchers. "We have a custom in the early spring that calls for all the pitchers to throw five minutes of batting practice every day," he told me. "This is before the rest of the squad arrives, you understand, so you're just pitching to the other pitchers. Well, the day before that first workout I woke up at four-thirty in the morning. I was so worried that I couldn't get back to sleep—and all this was just over going out and throwing to *pitchers*. I don't remember what happened that first day, but I went out there very tense and anxious every time. As you can imagine, there's very little good work or improvement you can do under those circumstances."

The training period made it clear that nothing had altered with him (he walked twenty-five men in fourteen innings in exhibition play), and when the club went north he was left in Bradenton for further work. He joined the team in Chicago on April 16, and entered a game against the Cubs the next afternoon, taking over in the fourth inning, with the Pirates down by 10–4. He pitched five innings, and gave up eight runs (three of them unearned), five hits, and seven bases on balls. The Cubs batted around against him in the first inning he pitched, and in the sixth he gave up back-to-back home runs. His statistics for the game, including an ERA of 9.00, were also his major-league figures for the year, because late in April the Pirates sent him down to the Charleston (West Virginia) Charlies, their farm team in the Class AAA International League. Blass did not argue about the decision; in fact, as a veteran with more than eight years' service in the majors, he had to agree to the demotion before the parent club could send him down. He felt that the Pirates and Joe Brown had been extraordinarily patient and sympathetic in dealing with a baffling and apparently irremediable problem. They had also been generous, refusing to cut his salary by the full twenty percent permissible in extending a major-league contract. (His pay, which had been ninety thousand dollars in 1973, was cut to seventy-five thousand for the next season, and then to sixty-three thousand this spring.) In any case, Blass wanted to go. He needed continuous game experience if he was ever to break out of it, and he knew he no longer belonged with a big-league club.

The distance between the minors and the majors, always measurable in light-years, is probably greater today than ever before, and for a man making the leap in the wrong direction the feeling must be sickening. Blass tries to pass off the experience lightly (he is apparently incapable of self-pity), but one can guess what must have been required of him to summon up even a scrap of the kind of hope and aggressive self-confidence that are prerequisites, at every level, of a successful athletic performance. He and Karen rented an apartment in Charleston, and the whole family moved down when the school year ended; David and Chris enjoyed the informal atmosphere around the ball park, where they were permitted to shag flies in batting practice. "It wasn't so bad," Blass told me.

But it was. The manager of the Charlies, Steve Demeter, put Blass in the regular starting rotation, but he fared no better against minor-leaguers than he had in the big time. In a very brief time, his earned-run average and his bases-on-balls record were the worst in the league. Blass got along well with his teammates, but there were other problems. The mystery of Steve Blass's decline was old stuff by now in most big-league-city newspapers, but as soon as he was sent down, there was a fresh wave of attention from the national press and the networks; and sportswriters for newspapers in Memphis and Rochester and Richmond and the other International League cities looked on his arrival in town as a God-given feature story. Invariably, they asked him how much money he was earning as a player; then they asked if he thought he was worth it.

The Charlies did a lot of traveling by bus. One day, the team made an eight-hour trip from Charleston to Toledo, where they played a night game. At eleven that same night, they reboarded the bus and drove to Pawtucket, Rhode Island, for their next date, arriving at about nine in the morning. Blass had started the game in Toledo, and he was so disgusted with his perform-ance that he got back on the bus without having showered or taken off his uniform. "We'd stop at an all-night restaurant every now and then, and I'd walk in with a two-day beard and my old Charleston Charlies uniform on, looking like go-to-hell," Blass said. "It was pretty funny to see people looking at me. I had some books along, and we had plenty of wine and beer on the bus, so the time went by somehow." He paused and then shook his head. "*God*, that was an awful trip," he said.

By early August, Blass's record with Charleston was two and nine, and 9.74. He had had enough. With Joe Brown's permission, he left the Charlies and flew West to consult Dr. Bill Harrison, of Davis, California. Dr. Harrison is an optometrist who has helped develop a system of "optometherapy," designed to encourage athletes to concentrate on the immediate physical task at hand—hitting a ball, throwing a strike—by visualizing the act in advance; his firm was once retained by the Kansas City Royals baseball team, and his patients have included a number of professional golfers and football players. Blass spent four days with him, and then rejoined the Pirates, this time as a batting-practice pitcher. He says now that he was very interested in Dr. Harrison's theories but that they just didn't seem to help him much.

In truth, nothing helped. Blass knew that his case was desperate. He was almost alone now with his problem—a baseball castaway—and he had reached the point where he was willing to try practically anything. Under the guidance of pitching coach Don Osborn, he attempted some unusual experi-ments. He tried pitching from the outfield, with the sweeping motion of a fielder making a long peg. He tried pitching while kneeling on the mound. He tried pitching with his left foot tucked up behind his right knee until the last possible second of his delivery. Slow-motion films of his delivery were stud-ied and compared with films taken during some of his best games of the past;

much of his motion, it was noticed, seemed extraneous, but he had thrown exactly the same way at his peak. Blass went back and corrected minute details, to no avail.

The frustrating, bewildering part of it all was that while working alone with a catcher Blass continued to throw as well as he ever had; his fastball was alive, and his slider and curve shaved the corners of the plate. But the moment a batter stood in against him he became a different pitcher, especially when throwing a fastball—a pitcher apparently afraid of seriously injuring somebody. As a result, he was of very little use to the Pirates even in batting practice.

Don Osborn, a gentle man in his mid-sixties, says, "Steve's problem was mental. He had mechanical difficulties, with some underlying mental cause. I don't think anybody will ever understand his decline. We tried everything—I didn't know anything else to do. I feel real bad about it. Steve had a lot of guts to stay out there as long as he did. You know, old men don't dream much, but just the other night I had this dream that Steve Blass was all over his troubles and could pitch again. I said, 'He's ready, we can use him!' Funny . . ."

It was probably at this time that Blass consulted a psychiatrist. He does not talk about it—in part out of a natural reticence but also because the Pirate front office, in an effort to protect his privacy, turned away inquiries into this area by Pittsburgh writers and persistently refused to comment on whether any such therapy was undertaken. It is clear, however, that Blass does not believe he gained any profound insights into possible unconscious causes of his difficulties. Earlier in the same summer, he also experimented briefly with transcendental meditation. He entered the program at the suggestion of Joe Brown, who also enrolled Dave Giusti, Willie Stargell, pitcher Bruce Kison, and himself in the group. Blass repeated mantras and meditated twice a day for about two months; he found that it relaxed him, but it did not seem to have much application to his pitching. Innumerable other remedies were proposed by friends and strangers. Like anyone in hard straits, he was deluged with unsolicited therapies, overnight cures, naturopathies, exorcisms, theologies, and amulets, many of which arrived by mail. Blass refuses to make jokes about these nostrums. "Anyone who takes the trouble to write a man who is suffering deserves to be thanked," he told me.

Most painful of all, perhaps, was the fact that the men who most sympathized with his incurable professional difficulties were least able to help. The Pirates were again engaged in a close and exhausting pennant race fought out over the last six weeks of the season; they moved into first place for good only two days before the end, won their half-pennant, and then were eliminated by the Dodgers in a four-game championship playoff. Steve Blass was with the team through this stretch, but he took no part in the campaign, and by now he was almost silent in the clubhouse. He had become an extra wheel. "It must have been hell for him," Dave Giusti says. "I mean *real* hell. I never could have stood it."

When Blass is asked about this last summer of his baseball career, he will only say that it was "kind of a difficult time" or "not the most fun I've had." In extended conversations about himself, he often gives an impression of an armored blandness that suggests a failure of emotion; this apparent insensitivity about himself contrasts almost shockingly with his subtle concern for the feelings of his teammates and his friends and his family, and even of strangers. "My overriding philosophy is to have a regard for others," he once told me. "I don't want to put myself over other people." He takes pride in the fact that his outward, day-to-day demeanor altered very little through his long ordeal. "A person lives on," he said more than once, smiling. "The sun will come up tomorrow." Most of all, perhaps, he sustained his self-regard by not taking out his terrible frustrations on Karen and the boys. "A ballplayer learns very early that he can't bring the game home with him every night," he said once. "Especially when there are young people growing up there. I'm real proud of the fact that this thing hasn't bothered us at home. David and Chris have come through it all in fine shape. I think Karen and I are closer than ever because of this."

Karen once said to me, "Day to day, he hasn't changed. Just the other morning, he was out working on the lawn, and a couple of the neighbors' children came over to see him. Young kids—maybe three or four years old. Then I looked out a few minutes later, and there was a whole bunch of them yelling and rolling around on the grass with him, like puppies. He's always been that way. Steve has worked at being a man and being a father and a husband. It's something he has always felt very strongly about, and I have to give him all the credit in the world. Sometimes I think I got to hate the frustration and pain of this more than he did. He always found something to hold on to—a couple of good pitches that day, some little thing he had noticed. But I couldn't always share that, and I didn't have his ability to keep things under control."

I asked if maintaining this superhuman calm might not have damaged Steve in some way, or even added to his problems.

"I don't know," she said. "Sometimes in the evening—once in a great while—we'd be sitting together, and we'd have a couple of drinks and he would relax enough to start to talk. He would tell me about it, and get angry and hurt. Then he'd let it come out, and yell and scream and pound on things. And I felt that even this might not be enough for him. He would never do such a thing outside. Never." She paused, and then she said, "I think he directed his anger toward making the situation livable here at home. I've had my own ideas about Steve's pitching, about the mystery, but they haven't made much difference. You can't force your ideas on somebody, especially when he is doing what he thinks he has to do. Steve's a very private person."

O

Steve Blass stayed home last winter. He tried not to think much about baseball, and he didn't work on his pitching. He and Karen had agreed that the family would go back to Bradenton for spring training, and that he would give it one more try. One day in January, he went over to the field house at the University of Pittsburgh and joined some other Pirates there for a workout. He threw well. Tony Bartirome, the Pirate trainer, who is a close friend of Steve's thought he was pitching as well as he ever had. He told Joe Brown that Steve's problems might be over. When spring training came, however, nothing had altered. Blass threw adequately in brief streaks, but very badly against most batters. He hit Willie Stargell and Manny Sanguillen in batting practice; both players told him to forget it. They urged him to cut loose with the fastball.

Joe Brown had told Blass that the end of the line might be approaching. Blass agreed. The Pirate organization had been extraordinarily patient, but it was, after all, in the business of baseball.

On March 24, Steve Blass started the second game of a doubleheader against the White Sox at Bradenton. For three innings, he escaped serious difficulty. He gave up two runs in the second, but he seemed to throw without much tension, and he even struck out Bill Melton, the Chicago third baseman, with a fastball. Like the other Pirates, Dave Giusti was watching with apprehensive interest. "I really thought he was on his way," he told me. "I was encouraged. Then, in the fourth, there were a couple of bases on balls and maybe a bad call by the ump on a close pitch, and suddenly there was a complete reversal. He was a different man out there."

Blass walked eight men in the fourth inning and gave up eight runs. He threw fifty-one pitches, but only seventeen of them were strikes. Some of his pitches were close to the strike zone, but most were not. He worked the count to 3–2 on Carlos May, and then threw the next pitch behind him. The booing from the fans, at first scattered and uncomfortable, grew louder. Danny Murtaugh waited, but Blass could not get the third out. Finally, Murtaugh came out very slowly to the mound and told Blass that he was taking him out of the game; Dave Giusti came in to relieve his old roommate. Murtaugh, a peaceable man, then charged the home-plate umpire and cursed him for the bad call, and was thrown out of the game. Play resumed. Blass put on his warm-up jacket and trotted to the outfield to run his wind sprints. Roland Hemond, the general manager of the White Sox, was at Bradenton that day, and he said, "It was the most heartbreaking thing I have ever seen in baseball."

60

Three days later, the Pirates held a press conference to announce that they had requested waivers from the other National League clubs, with the purpose of giving Blass his unconditional release. Blass flew out to California to see Dr. Bill Harrison once more, and also to visit a hypnotist, Arthur Ellen, who has worked with several major-league players, and has apparently helped some of them, including Dodger pitcher Don Sutton, remarkably. Blass made the trip mostly because he had promised Maury Wills, who is now a base-running consultant to several teams, that he would not quit the game until he had seen Mr. Ellen.

Blass then returned to Bradenton and worked for several days with the Pirates' minor-league pitching coach, Larry Sherry, on some pitching mechanics. He made brief appearances in two games against Pirate farmhands, and threw well. He struck out some players with his fastball. After the second game, he showered and got into his Volkswagen and started north to join his family, who had returned to Pittsburgh. It was a good trip, because it gave him time to sort things out, and somewhere along the way he decided to give it up. The six-day waiver period had expired, and none of the other clubs had claimed him. He was encouraged about his pitching, but he had been encouraged before. This time, the fastball had been much better, and at least he could hold on to that; maybe the problem had been mechanical all along. If he came back now, however, it would have to be at the minor-league level, and even if he made it back to the majors, he could expect only three or four more years before his effectiveness would decline because of age and he would have to start thinking about retirement. At least *that* problem could be solved now. He didn't want to subject Karen to more of the struggle. It was time to get out.

○

Of all the mysteries that surround the Steve Blass story, perhaps the most mysterious is the fact that his collapse is unique. There is no other player in recent baseball history—at least none with Blass's record and credentials—who has lost his form in such a sudden and devastating fashion and been totally unable to recover. The players and coaches and fans I talked to about Steve Blass brought up a few other names, but then they quickly realized that the cases were not really the same. Some of them mentioned Rex Barney, a Dodger fastball pitcher of the nineteen-forties, who quit baseball while still a young man because of his uncontrollable wildness; Barney, however, had only one good year, and it is fair to say he never did have his great stuff under control. Dick Radatz, a very tall relief pitcher with the Red Sox a decade ago, had four good years, and then grew increasingly wild and ineffective. (He is said to have once thrown twenty-seven consecutive balls in a spring-training game.) His decline, however, was partially attributable to his failure to stay in shape. Von McDaniel, a younger brother of Lindy McDaniel, arrived suddenly as a pitcher with the Cardinals, and disappeared just as quickly, but two years' pitching hardly qualifies as a record. There have been hundreds of shiningly promising rookie pitchers and sluggers who, for one reason or another, could not do their thing once they got up to the big time. Blass's story is different. It should also be understood that this was not at all the somewhat commonplace experience of an established and well-paid major-league star who suffers through one or two mediocre seasons. Tom Seaver went through such a slump last summer. But Seaver's problems were only relatively serious (his record for 1974 was 11–11), and were at least partly explicable (he had a sore hip), and he has now returned to form. Blass, once his difficulties commenced, was helpless. Finally, of course, one must accept the possibility that a great many players may have suffered exactly the same sort of falling off as Blass for exactly the same reasons (whatever they may be) but were able to solve the problem and continue their athletic careers. Sudden and terrible batting and pitching slumps are mysterious while they last; the moment they end, they tend to be forgotten.

What happened to Steve Blass? Nobody knows, but some speculation is permissible—indeed, is perhaps demanded of anyone who is even faintly aware of the qualities of the man and the depths of his suffering. Professional sports have a powerful hold on us because they display and glorify remarkable physical capacities, and because the artificial demands of games played for very high rewards produce vivid responses. But sometimes, of course, what is happening on the field seems to speak to something deeper within us; we stop cheering and look on in uneasy silence, for the man out there is no longer just another great athlete, an idealized hero, but only a man—only ourself. We are no longer at a game. The enormous alterations of professional sport in the past three decades, especially the prodigious inflation of franchises and salaries, have made it evident even to the most thoughtless fan that the play he has come to see is serious indeed, and that the heart of the game is not physical but financial. Sport is no longer a release from the harsh everyday American business world but its continuation and apotheosis. Those of us (fans and players alike) who return to the ball park in the belief that the game and the rules are unchanged—merely a continuation of what we have known and loved in the past—are deluding ourselves, perhaps foolishly, perhaps tragically.

Blass once told me that there were "at least seventeen" theories about the reason for his failure. A few of them are bromides: He was too nice a guy. He became smug and was no longer hungry. He lost the will to win. His pitching motion, so jittery and unclassical, at last let him down for good. His eyesight went bad. (Blass is myopic, and wears glasses while watching television and driving. He has never worn glasses when pitching, which meant that Pirate catchers had to flash him signals with hand gestures rather than with finger waggles; however, he saw well enough to win when he was winning, and his vision has not altered in recent years.) The other, more serious theories are sometimes presented alone, sometimes in conjunction with others. Answers here become more gingerly.

He was afraid of injury—afraid of being struck by a line drive.

Blass was injured three times while on the mound. He cracked a thumb while fielding a grounder in 1966. He was struck on the right forearm by a ball hit by Joe Torre in 1970, and spent a month on the disabled list. While trying for his twentieth victory in his last start in 1972, he was hit on the point of the elbow of his pitching arm by a line drive struck by the Mets' John Milner; he had to leave the game, but a few days later he pitched that first playoff game for the Pirates and won it handily. (Blass's brother-in-law, John Lamb, suffered a fractured skull when hit by a line drive in spring training in 1971, and it was more than a year before he recovered, but Blass's real pitching triumphs all came after that.)

He was afraid of injuring someone—hitting a batter with a fastball.

Blass did hit a number of players in his career, of course, but he never caused anyone to go on the disabled list or, for that matter, to miss even one day's work. He told me he did not enjoy brushing back hitters but had done so when it was obviously called for. The only real criticism of Blass I ever heard from his teammates was that he would not always "protect" them by retaliating against enemy hitters after somebody had been knocked down. During his decline, he was plainly unable to throw the fastball effectively to batters—especially to Pirate batters in practice. He says he hated the idea of hitting and possibly sidelining one of his teammates, but he is convinced that this anxiety was the result of his control problems rather than the cause.

He was seriously affected by the death of Roberto Clemente.

There is no doubt but that the sudden taking away of their most famous and vivid star affected all the Pirates, including Steve Blass. He and Clemente had not been particularly close, but Blass was among the members of the team who flew at once to Puerto Rico for the funeral services, where Blass delivered a eulogy in behalf of the club. The departure of a superstar leaves an almost visible empty place on a successful team, and the leaders next in line—who in this case would certainly include Steve Blass—feel the inescapable burden of trying to fill the gap. A Clemente, however, can never be replaced. Blass never pitched well in the majors after Clemente's death. This argument is a difficult one, and is probably impossible to resolve. There are Oedipal elements here, of course, that are attractive to those who incline in such a direction.

He fell into a slump, which led to an irreparable loss of confidence.

This is circular, and perhaps more a description of symptoms than of the disability itself. However, it is a fact that a professional athlete—and most especially a baseball player—faces a much more difficult task in attempting to regain lost form than an ailing businessman, say, or even a troubled artist; no matter how painful his case has been, the good will of his associates or the vagaries of critical judgment matter not at all when he tries to return. All that matters is his performance, which will be measured, with utter coldness, by the stats. This is one reason that athletes are paid so well, and one reason that fear of failure—the unspeakable "choking"—is their deepest and most private anxiety. Steve Blass passed over my questions about whether he had ever felt this kind of fear when on the mound. "I don't think pitchers, by their nature, allow themselves to think that way," he said. "To be successful, you turn that kind of thought away." On the other hand, he often said that two or three successive well-pitched games probably would have been all he needed to dissipate the severe tension that affected his performances once things began to go badly for him. They never came.

The remaining pieces of evidence (if, indeed, they have any part in the mystery) have been recounted here. Blass is a modest man, both in temperament and in background, and his success and fame were quite sudden and, to some degree, unexpected. His salary at the beginning of 1971—the year of his two great Series wins—was forty thousand dollars; two years later it was ninety thousand, and there were World Series and playoff checks on top of that. Blass was never thought of as one of the great pitchers of his time, but in the late sixties and early seventies he was probably the most consistent starter on the Pirate staff; it was, in fact, a staff without stars. On many other teams, he would have been no more than the second- or third-best starter, and his responsibilities, real and imagined, would have been less acute.

I took some of these hard questions to Blass's colleagues. Danny Murtaugh and Bill Virdon (who is now the Yankees' pilot) both expressed their admiration for Blass but said they had no idea what had happened to him. They seemed a bit brusque about it, but then I realized, of course, that ballplayers are forever disappearing from big-league dugouts; the manager's concern is with those who remain—with today's lineup. "I don't know the answer," Bill Virdon told me in the Yankee clubhouse. "If I did, I'd go get Steve to pitch for me. He sure won a lot of big games for us on the Pirates."

Joe Brown said, "I've tried to keep my distance and not to guess too much about what happened. I'm not a student of pitching and I'm not a psychologist. You can tell a man what to do, but you can't *make* him do it. Steve is an outstanding man, and you hate to quit on him. In this business, you bet on character. Big-league baseball isn't easy, yet you can stand it when things are going your way. But Steve Blass never had a good day in baseball after this thing hit him."

Blass's best friends in baseball are Tony Bartirome, Dave Giusti, and Nelson King (who, along with Bob Prince, was part of the highly regarded radio-and-television team that covered the Pirate games).

Tony Bartirome *(He is forty-three years old, dark-haired, extremely neat in appearance. He was an infielder before he became a trainer, and played one season in the majors—with the Pirates, in 1952):* "Steve is unique physically. He has the arm of a twenty-year-old. Not only did he never have a sore arm but he never had any of the stiffness and pain that most pitchers feel on the day after a game. He was always the same, day after day. You know, it's very important for a trainer to know the state of mind and the feelings of his players. What a player is thinking is about eighty percent of it. The really strange thing is that after this trouble started, Steve never showed any feelings about his pitching. In the old days, he used to get mad at himself after a bad showing, and sometimes he threw things around in the clubhouse. But after this began, when he was taken out of a game he only gave the impression that he was happy to be out of there—relieved that he no longer had to face it that day. Somehow, he didn't show any emotion at *all*. Maybe it was like his never having a sore arm. He never talked in any detail about his different treatments—the psychiatry and all. I think he felt he didn't need any of that—that at any moment he'd be back where he was, the Blass of old, and that it all was up to him to make that happen."

Dave Giusti *(He is one of the great relief pitchers in baseball. He earned a BA and an MA in physical education at Syracuse. He is thirty-five—dark hair, piercing brown eyes, and a quiet manner):* "Steve has the perfect build for a pitcher—lean and strong. He is remarkably open to all kinds of people, but I think he has closed his mind to his inner self. There are central areas you can't infringe on with him. There is no doubt that during the past two years he didn't react to a bad performance the way he used to, and you have to wonder why he couldn't apply his competitiveness to his problem. Karen used to bawl out me and Tony for not being tougher on him, for not doing more. Maybe I should have come right out and said he seemed to have lost his will to fight, but it's hard to shock somebody, to keep bearing in on him. You're afraid to lose a friend, and you want to go easy on him because he is your friend.

"Last year, I went through something like Steve's crisis. The first half of the season, I was atrocious, and I lost all my confidence, especially in my fastball. The fastball is my best pitch, but I'd get right to the top of my delivery and then something would take over, and I'd know even before I released the ball that it wasn't going to be in the strike zone. I began worrying about making big money and not performing. I worried about not contributing to the team. I worried about being traded. I thought it might be the end for me. I didn't know how to solve my problem, but I knew I *had* to solve it. In the end, it was talking to people that did it. I talked to everybody, but mostly to Joe Brown and Danny and my wife. Then, at some point, I turned the corner. But it was talking that did it, and my point is that Steve can't talk to people that way. Or won't.

"Listen, it's tough out there. It's hard. Once you start maintaining a plateau, you've got to be absolutely sure what your goals are."

Nellie King (*A former pitcher with the Pirates. He is friendly and informal, with an attractive smile. He is very tall—six-six. Forty-seven years old*): "Right after that terrible game in Atlanta, Steve told me that it had felt as if the whole world was pressing down on him while he was out there. But then he suddenly shut up about it, and he never talked that way again. He covered it all up. I think there *are* things weighing on him, and I think he may be so angry inside that he's afraid to throw the ball. He's afraid he might kill somebody. It's only nickel psychology, but I think there's a lost kid in Steve. I remembered that after the '71 Series he said, 'I didn't think I was as good as this.' He seemed truly surprised at what he'd done. The child in him is a great thing—we've all loved it—and maybe he was suddenly afraid he was losing it. It was being forced out of him.

"Being good up here is *so* tough—people have no idea. It gets much worse when you have to repeat it: 'We know you're great. Now go and do that again for me.' So much money and so many people depend on you. Pretty soon you're trying so hard that you can't function."

I ventured to repeat Nellie King's guesses about the mystery to Steve Blass and asked him what he thought.

"That's pretty heavy," he said after a moment. "I guess I don't have a tendency to go into things in much depth. I'm a surface reactor. I tend to take things not too seriously. I really think that's one of the things that *helped* me in baseball."

A smile suddenly burst from him.

"There's one possibility nobody has brought up," he said. "I don't think anybody's ever said that maybe I just lost my control. Maybe your control is something that can just go. It's no big thing, but suddenly it's gone." He paused, and then he laughed in a self-deprecating way. "Maybe that's what I'd like to believe," he said.

○

On my last morning with Steve Blass, we sat in his family room and played an imaginary ball game together—half an inning of baseball. It had occurred to me that in spite of his enforced and now permanent exile from the game, he still possessed a rare body of precise and hard-won pitching information. He still knew most of the hitters in his league, and probably as well as any other pitcher around, he knew what to pitch to them in a given situation. I had always wanted to hear a pitcher say exactly what he would throw next and why, and now I invited Blass to throw against the Cincinnati Reds, the toughest lineup of hitters anywhere. I would call the balls and strikes and hits. I promised he would have no control problems.

He agreed at once. He poured himself another cup of coffee and lit up a Garcia y Vega. He was wearing slacks and a T-shirt and an old sweater (he had a golfing date later that day), and he looked very young.

"OK," he said. "Pete Rose is leading off—right? First of all, I'm going to try to keep him off base if I can, because they have so many tough hitters coming up. They can bury you before you even get started. I'm going to try to throw strikes and not get too fine. I'll start him off with a slider away. He has a tendency to go up the middle and I'll try to keep it a bit away."

Rose, I decided, didn't offer. It was ball one.

"Now I'll throw him a sinking fastball, and still try to work him out that way. The sinking fastball tends to tail off just a little."

Rose fouled it into the dirt.

"Well, now we come back with another slider, and I'll try to throw it inside. That's just to set up another slider *outside*."

Rose fouled that one as well.

"We're ahead one and two now—right?" Blass said. "Well, this early in the game I wouldn't try to throw him that slow curve—that big slop off-speed pitch. I'd like to work on that a couple of times first, because it's early and he swings so well. So as long as I'm ahead of him, I'll keep on throwing him sliders—keep going that way."

Rose took another ball, and then grounded out on a medium-speed curveball.

Joe Morgan stood in, and Blass puffed on his cigar and looked at the ceiling.

"Joe Morgan is strictly a fastball hitter, so I want to throw him a *bad* fastball to start him off," he said. "I'll throw it in the dirt to show it to him—get him geared to that kind of speed. Now, after ball one, I'll give him a medium-to-slow curveball and try to get it over the plate—just throw it for a strike."

Morgan took: one and one.

"Now I throw him a *real* slow curveball—a regular rainbow. I've had good luck against him with that sort of stuff."

And so it went. Morgan, I decided, eventually singled to right on a curve in on the handle—a lucky hit—but then Blass retired his next Cincinnati hitter, Dan Driessen, who popped out on a slider. Blass laid off slow pitches here, so Sanguillen would have a chance to throw out Morgan if he was stealing.

Johnny Bench stood in, with two out.

"Morgan won't be stealing, probably," Blass said. "He won't want to take the bat out of Bench's hands." He released another cloud of cigar smoke, thinking hard. "Well, I'll start him out with a good, tough fastball outside. I've got to work very carefully to him, because when he's hot he's capable of hitting it out anytime."

Ball one.

"Well, the slider's only been fair today. . . . I'll give him a slider, but away—off the outside."

Swinging strike. Blass threw another slider, and Bench hit a line single to left, moving Morgan to second. Tony Perez was the next batter.

"Perez is not a good high, hard fastball hitter," Blass said. "I'll begin him with that pitch, because I don't want to get into any more trouble with the slider and have him dunk one in. A letter-high fastball, with good mustard on it."

Perez took a strike.

"Now I'll do it again, until I miss—bust him up and in. He has a tendency to go after that kind of pitch. He's an exceptional offspeed hitter, and will give himself up with men on base—give up a little power to get that run in."

Perez took, for a ball, and then Blass threw him an intentional ball—a very bad slider inside. Perez had shortened up on the bat a little, but he took the pitch. He then fouled off a fastball, and Blass threw him another good fastball, high and inside, and Perez struck out, swinging, to end the inning.

"Pretty good inning," I said. "Way to go." We both laughed.

"Yes, you know that *exact* sequence has happened to Perez many times," Blass said. "He shortens up and then chases the pitch up here."

He was animated. "You know, I can almost *see* that fastball to Perez, and I can see his bat going through it, swinging through the pitch and missing," he said. "That's a good feeling. That's one of the concepts of Dr. Harrison's program, you know—visualization. When I was pitching well, I was doing that very thing. You get so locked in, you see yourself doing things before they happen. That's what people mean when they say you're in the groove. That's what happened in that World Series game, when I kept throwing that big slop curveball to Boog Powell, and it really ruined him. I must have thrown it three out of four pitches to him, and I just *knew* it was going to be there. There's no doubt about it—no information needed. The crowd is there, this is the World Series, and all of a sudden you're locked into something. It's like being plugged into a computer. It's 'Gimme the ball, *boom!* Click, click, click . . . *shoom!*' It's that good feeling. You're just flowing easy."

Agincourt and After

Tarry, delight, so seldom met. . . . The games have ended, the heroes are dispersed, and another summer has died late in Boston, but still one yearns for them and wishes them back, so great was their pleasure. The adventures and discoveries and reversals of last month's World Series, which was ultimately won by the Cincinnati Reds in the final inning of the seventh and final game, were of such brilliance and unlikelihood that, even as they happened, those of us who were there in the stands and those who were there on the field were driven again and again not just to cries of excitement but to exclamations of wonder about what we were watching and sharing. Pete Rose, coming up to bat for the Reds in the tenth inning of the tied and retied sixth game, turned to Carlton Fisk, the Red Sox catcher, and said, "Say, this is some kind of game, isn't it?" And when that evening ended at last, after further abrupt and remarkable events, everyone—winners and losers and watchers—left the Fens in exaltation and disarray. "I went home," the Reds' manager, Sparky Anderson, said later, "and I was stunned."

The next day, during the last batting practice of the year, there was extended debate among the writers and players on the Fenway sidelines as to whether game six had been the greatest in Series history and whether we were not, in fact, in on the best Series of them all. Grizzled coaches and senior scribes recalled other famous Octobers—1929, when the Athletics, trailing the Cubs by eight runs in the fourth game, scored ten runs in the seventh inning and won; 1947, when Cookie Lavagetto's double with two out in the ninth ended Yankee pitcher Bill Bevens' bid for a no-hitter and won the fourth game for the Dodgers; 1960, when Bill Mazeroski's ninth-inning homer for the Pirates threw down the lordly Yankees. There is no answer to these barroom syllogisms, of course, but any recapitulation and reexamination of the 1975 Series suggests that at the very least we may conclude that there has never been a better one. Much is expected of the World Series, and in recent years much has been received. In the past decade, we have had the memorable and abrading seven-game struggles between the Red Sox and the Cardinals in 1967, the Cardinals and the Tigers in 1968, and the Orioles and the Pirates in 1971, and the astounding five-game upset of the Orioles by the Mets in 1969. Until this year, my own solid favorite—because of the Pirates' comeback and the effulgent play of Roberto Clemente—was the 1971 classic, but now I am no longer certain. Comebacks and late rallies are actually extremely scarce in baseball, and an excellent guaranteed cash-producing long-term investment is to wager that the winning team in any game will score more runs in a single inning than the losing team scores in nine. In this Series, however, the line scores alone reveal the rarity of what we saw:

In six of the seven games, the winning team came from behind.

In one of the games, the winning team came from behind twice.

In five games, the winning margin was one run.

There were two extra-inning games, and two games were settled in the ninth inning.

Overall, the games were retied or saw the lead reversed thirteen times.

No other Series—not even the celebrated Giants–Red Sox thriller of 1912—can match these figures.

It is best, however, not to press this search for the greatest Series any farther. There is something sterile and diminishing about our need for these superlatives, and the game of baseball, of course, is so rich and various that it cannot begin to be encompassed in any set of seven games. This Series, for example, produced not one low-hit, low-score pitching duel—the classic and agonizing parade of double zeros that strains teams and managers and true fans to their limits as the inevitable crack in the porcelain is searched out and the game at last broken open. This year, too, the Reds batted poorly through most of the early play and offered indifferent front-line pitching, while the Red Sox made too many mistakes on the base paths, were unable to defend against Cincinnati's team speed, and committed some significant (and in the end fatal) errors in the infield. One of the games was seriously marred by a highly debatable umpire's decision, which may have altered its outcome. It was not a perfect Series. Let us conclude then—before we take a swift look at the season and the playoffs; before we return to Morgan leading away and stealing, to Yaz catching and whirling and throwing, to Eastwick blazing a fastball and Tiant turning his back and offering up a fluttering outside curve, to Evans' catch and Lynn's leap and fall, to Perez's bombs and Pete Rose's defiant, exuberant glare—and say only that this year the splendid autumn affair rose to our utmost expectations and then surpassed them, attaining at last such a level of excellence and emotional reward that it seems likely that the participants—the members of the deservedly winning, champion Reds and of the sorely disappointed, almost-champion Red Sox—will in time remember this Series not for its outcome but for the honor of having played in it, for having made it happen.

○

By September 16, the Pirates and the A's were enjoying comfortable leads in their divisions, the Reds had long since won their demi-pennant (they clinched on September 7—a new record), and the only serious baseball was to be found at Fenway Park, where the Orioles, down by four and a half games and running out of time, had at the Red Sox. The game was a pippin—a head-to-head encounter between Jim Palmer and Luis Tiant. Each of the great pitchers struck out eight batters, and the game was won by the Red Sox, 2–0, on two small mistakes by Palmer—fastballs to Rico Petrocelli and Carlton Fisk in successive innings, which were each lofted into the left-field screen. Tiant, who had suffered through almost a month of ineffectiveness brought on by a bad back, was in top form, wheeling and rotating on the mound like a figure in a Bavarian clock tower, and in the fourth he fanned Lee May with a super-curve that seemed to glance off some invisible obstruction in midflight. The hoarse, grateful late-inning cries of "Lu-is! Lu-is! Lu-is!" from 34,724 Beantowners suggested that the oppressive, Calvinist cloud of self-doubt that afflicts Red Sox fans in all weathers and seasons was beginning to lift at last. The fabulous Sox rookies, Jim Rice and Fred Lynn, did nothing much (in fact, they fanned five times between them), but Boston friends of mine encouraged my belief with some of the shiny new legends—the home run that Rice hammered past the Fenway Park center-field flagpole in July; the time Rice checked a full swing and snapped his bat in half just above his hands; Lynn's arm, Lynn's range, Lynn's game against the Tigers in June, when he hit three homers and batted in ten runs and the Sox began their pennant drive. The night before my visit, in fact, against the Brewers, Lynn and Rice had each accounted for his one hundredth run batted in *with the same ball*—a run-forcing walk to Lynn and then a sacrifice fly by Rice. I believed.

Baltimore came right back, winning the next game by 5–2, on some cool and useful hitting by Tommy Davis and Brooks Robinson, and the Sox' cushion was back to four and a half. The Orioles' move, we know now, came a little too late this year, but I think one should not forget what a loose and deadly and marvelously confident September team they have been over the last decade. Before this, their last game at Fenway Park this year, they were enjoying themselves in their dugout while the Sox took batting practice and while Clif Keane, the Boston *Globe*'s veteran baseball writer (who is also the league's senior and most admired insult artist), took them apart. Brooks

Robinson hefted a bat, and Keane, sitting next to manager Earl Weaver, said, "Forget it, Brooksie. They pay you a hundred and twenty-four thousand for your glove, and a thousand for the bat. Put that back in your valise." He spotted Doug DeCinces, the rookie who will someday take over for Robinson in the Oriole infield, and said, "Hey, kid, I was just talkin' to Brooks, here. He says he'll be back again. You'll be a *hundred* before you get in there. Looks like 1981 for you." Tommy Davis picked out some bats and went slowly up the dugout steps; his Baltimore teammates sometimes call him "Uncle Tired." Keane leaned forward suddenly. "Look at that," he said. "Tom's wearin' *new shoes*—he's planning on being around another twenty years. Listen, with Brooks and Davis, Northrup, May, and Muser, you guys can play an Old Timers' Game every day." Davis wandered off, smiling, and Keane changed his tone for a moment. "Did you ever see him when he could play?" he said, nodding at Davis. "He got about two hundred and fifty hits that year with LA, and they were all line drives. He could *hit*." His eye fell on the first group of Oriole batters around the batting cage. "See them all lookin' over here?" he said to Weaver. "They're talking about you again. If you could only hear them—they're really fricasseein' you today, Earl. Now you know how Marie Antoinette felt. . . ." The laughter in the dugout was nice and easy. The men sat back, with their legs crossed and their arms stretched along the back of the bench, and watched the players on the ball field. The summer was running out.

The Sox just about wrapped it up the next week, when they beat the Yankees, 6–4, at Shea, in a game that was played in a steadily deepening downpour—the beginning of the tropical storm that washed away most of the last week of the season. By the ninth inning, the mound and the batters' boxes looked like trenches on the Somme, and the stadium was filled with a wild gray light made by millions of illuminated falling raindrops. The Yankees got the tying runs aboard in the ninth, with two out, and then Dick Drago struck out Bobby Bonds, swinging, on three successive pitches, and the Boston outfielders came leaping and splashing in through the rain like kids home from a picnic. The winning Boston margin, a few days later, was still four and a half games.

○

The playoffs, it will be remembered, were brief. Over in the National League, the Reds embarrassed the Pittsburgh Pirates, winners of the Eastern Division title, by stealing ten bases in their first two games, which they won by 8–3 and 6–1. Young John Candelaria pitched stoutly for the Pirates when the teams moved on to Three Rivers Stadium, fanning fourteen Cincinnati batters, but Pete Rose broke his heart with a two-run homer in the eighth, and the Reds won the game, 5–3, and the pennant, 3–0, in the tenth inning. I had deliberated for perhaps seven seconds before choosing to follow the American League championship games—partly because the Red Sox were the only new faces available (the Reds, the Pirates, and the A's have among them qualified for the playoffs fourteen times in the past six years), but mostly because I know that the best place in the world to watch baseball is at Fenway Park. The unique dimensions and properties of the Palazzo Yawkey (the left-field wall is 37 feet high and begins a bare 315 feet down the foul line from home plate—or perhaps, according to a startling new computation made by the Boston *Globe* this fall, *304* feet) vivify ball games and excite the imagination. On the afternoon of the first A's–Sox set-to, the deep green of the grass and light green of the wall, the variously angled blocks and planes and triangles and wedges of the entirely occupied stands, and the multiple seams and nooks and corners of the outfield fences, which encompass eleven different angles off which a ball or a ballplayer can ricochet, suddenly showed me that I was inside the ultimate origami.

There were two significant absentees—Jim Rice, who had suffered a fractured hand late in the campaign and would not play again this year, and Catfish Hunter, the erstwhile Oakland meal ticket, whose brisk work had been so useful to the A's in recent Octobers. Boston manager Darrell Johnson solved his problem brilliantly, moving Carl Yastrzemski from first base to Rice's spot under the left-field wall—a land grant that Yaz had occupied and prospected for many years. Oakland manager Alvin Dark found no comparable answer to his dilemma, but the startling comparative levels of baseball that were now demonstrated by the defending three-time champion A's and the untested Red Sox soon indicated that perhaps not even the Cat would have made much difference. In the bottom of the very first inning, Yastrzemski singled off Ken Holtzman, and then Carlton Fisk hit a hopper down the third-base line that was butchered by Sal Bando and further mutilated by Claudell Washington, in left. Lynn then hit an undemanding ground ball to second baseman Phil Garner, who muffed it. Two runs were in, and in the seventh the Sox added five more, with help from Oakland center fielder Bill North, who dropped a fly, and Washington, who somehow played Lynn's fly to the base of the wall into a double. Tiant, meanwhile, was enjoying himself. The Oakland scouting report on him warned he had six pitches—fastball, slider, curve, change-up curve, palm ball, and knuckler—all of which he could serve up from the sidearm, three-quarter, or overhand sectors, and points in between, but on this particular afternoon his fastball was so lively that he eschewed the upper ranges of virtuosity. He did not give up his first hit until the fifth inning or, incredibly, his first ground ball until the eighth. The Sox won, 7–1. "Tiant," Reggie Jackson declared in the clubhouse, "is the Fred Astaire of baseball."

The second game, which Alvin Dark had singled out as the crucial one in any three-of-five series, was much better. Oakland jumped away to a 3–0 lead, after a first-inning homer by Jackson, and Sal Bando whacked four successive hits—*bong! whang! bing! thwong!*—off the left-field wall during the afternoon. The second of these, a single, was converted into a killing out by Yastrzemski, who seized the carom off the wall and whirled and threw to Petrocelli to erase the eagerly advancing Campaneris at third—a play that Yaz and Rico first perfected during the Garfield Administration. The same two elders subsequently hit home runs—Yaz off Vida Blue, Rico off Rollie Fingers—and Lynn contributed a run-scoring single and a terrific diving cutoff of a Joe Rudi double to center field that saved at least one run. The Sox won by 6–3. The A's complained after the game that two of Bando's shots would have been home runs in any other park, and that both Yastrzemski's and Petrocelli's homers probably would have been outs in any other park. Absolutely true: the Wall giveth and the Wall taketh away.

Not quite believing what was happening, I followed the two teams to Oakland, where I watched the Bosox wrap up their easy pennant with a 5–3 victory. Yastrzemski, who is thirty-six years old and who had suffered through a long summer of injuries and ineffectuality, continued to play like the Yaz of 1967, when he almost single-handedly carried the Red Sox to their last pennant and down to the seventh game of that World Series. This time, he came up with two hits, and twice astonished Jackson in the field—first with a whirling throw from the deep left-field corner that cleanly excised Reggie at second base, and then, in the eighth, with a sprinting, diving, skidding, flat-on-the-belly stop of Jackson's low line shot to left that was headed for the wall and a sure triple. The play came in the midst of the old champions' courageous two-run rally in the eighth, and it destroyed them. Even though it fell short, I was glad about that rally, for I did not want to see the splendid old green-and-yallers go down meekly or sadly in the end. The Oakland fans, who have not always been known for the depths of their constancy or appreciation, also distinguished themselves, sustaining an earsplitting cacophony of hope and encouragement to the utter end. I sensed they were saying goodbye to their proud and vivid and infinitely entertaining old lineup—to Sal Bando and Campy Campaneris, to Joe Rudi and Reggie Jackson and Gene Tenace and Rollie Fingers and the rest, who will almost surely be broken up now and traded away, as great teams must be when they come to the end of their time in the sun.

○

The finalists, coming together for the Series opener at Fenway Park, were heavily motivated. The Reds had not won a World Series since 1940, the Sox since 1918. Cincinnati's Big Red Machine had stalled badly in its recent October outings, having failed in the World Series of 1970 and '72 and in the playoffs of 1973. The Red Sox had a record of shocking late-season collapses, the latest coming in 1974, when they fizzled away a seven-game lead in the last six weeks of the season. Both teams, however, were much stronger than in recent years—the Reds because of their much improved pitching (most of it relief pitching) and the maturing of a second generation of outstanding players (Ken Griffey, Dave Concepcion, George Foster) to join with the celebrated Rose, Morgan, Perez, and Bench. The Red Sox infield had at last found itself, with Rick Burleson at short and Denny Doyle (a midseason acquisition from the Angels) at second, and there was a new depth in hitting and defense—Beniquez, Cooper, Carbo, and the remarkable Dwight Evans. This was a far better Boston team than the 1967 miracle workers. The advantage, however, seemed to belong to Cincinnati, because of the Reds' combination of speed and power (168 stolen bases, 124 homers) and their implacable habit of winning ball games. Their total of 108 games won had been fashioned, in part, out of an early-season streak of 41 wins in 50 games, and a nearly unbelievable record of 64–17 in their home park. The Red Sox, on the other hand, had Lynn and Tiant. . . .

Conjecture thickened through most of the opening game, which was absolutely close for most of the distance, and then suddenly not close at all. Don Gullett, a powerful left-hander, kept the Red Sox in check for six innings, but was slightly outpitched and vastly outacted over the same distance by Tiant. The venerable stopper (Tiant is listed as being thirty-four and rumored as being a little or a great deal older) did not have much of a fastball on this particular afternoon, so we were treated to the splendid full range of Tiantic mime. His repertoire begins with an exaggerated mid-windup pivot, during which he turns his back on the batter and seems to examine the infield directly behind the mound for signs of crabgrass. With men on bases, his stretch consists of a succession of minute downward waggles and pauses of the glove, and a menacing sidewise, slit-eyed, Valentino-like gaze over his shoulder at the base runner. The full flower of his art, however, comes during the actual delivery, which is executed with a perfect variety show of accompanying gestures and impersonations. I had begun to take notes during my recent observations of the Cuban Garrick, and now, as he set down the Reds with only minimal interruptions (including one balk call, in the fourth), I arrived at some tentative codifications. The basic Tiant repertoire seems to include:

(1) Call the Osteopath: In midpitch, the man suffers an agonizing seizure in the central cervical region, which he attempts to fight off with a sharp backward twist of the head.

(2) Out of the Woodshed: Just before releasing the ball, he steps over a raised sill and simultaneously ducks his head to avoid conking it on the low doorframe.

(3) The Runaway Taxi: Before the pivot, he sees a vehicle bearing down on him at top speed, and pulls back his entire upper body just in time to avoid a nasty accident.

(4) Falling Off the Fence: An attack of vertigo nearly causes him to topple over backward on the mound. Strongly suggests a careless dude on the top rung of the corral.

(5) The Slipper-Kick: In the midpitch, he surprisingly decides to get rid of his left shoe.

(6) The Low-Flying Plane (a subtle development and amalgam of 1, 3, and 4, above): While he is pivoting, an F-105 buzzes the ball park, passing over the infield from the third-base to the first-base side at a height of eighty feet. He follows it all the way with his eyes.

All this, of course, was vastly appreciated by the Back Bay multitudes, including a nonpaying claque perched like seagulls atop three adjacent roof-top billboards (WHDH Radio, Windsor Canadian Whiskey, Buck Printing), who banged on the tin hoardings in accompaniment to the park's deepening chorus of "Lu-is! Lu-is! Lu-is!" The Reds, of course, were unmoved, and only three superior defensive plays by the Sox (including another diving, rolling catch by Yastrzemski) kept them from scoring in the top of the seventh. Defensive sparks often light an offensive flareup in close games, and Tiant now started the Sox off with a single. Evans bunted, and Gullett pounced on the ball and steamed a peg to second a hair too late to nail Tiant—the day's first mistake. Doyle singled, to load the bases, and Yaz singled for the first run. Fisk walked for another run, and then Petrocelli and Burleson singled, too. (Gullett had vanished.) Suddenly six runs were in, and the game—a five-hit shutout for Tiant—was safely put away very soon after.

The next afternoon, a gray and drizzly Sunday, began happily and ended agonizingly for the Sox, who put six men aboard in the first two innings and scored only one of them, thanks to some slovenly base running. In the fourth inning, the Reds finally registered their first run of the Series, but the Sox moved out ahead again, 2–1, and there the game stuck, a little too tight for anyone's comfort. There was a long delay for rain in the seventh. Matters inched along at last, with each club clinging to its best pitching: Boston with its starter, Bill Lee, and Cincinnati with its bullpen—Borbon and McEnaney and Eastwick, each one better, it seemed, than the last. Lee, a southpaw, had thrown a ragbag of pitches—slow curves, sliders, screwballs, and semi-fast-balls—all to the very outside corners, and by the top of the ninth he had surrendered but four hits. Now, facing the heaviest part of the Reds' order, he started Bench off with a pretty good but perhaps predictable outside fastball, which Bench whacked on a low line to the right-field corner for a double. Right-hander Dick Drago came on and grimly retired Perez and then Foster. One more out was required, and the crowd cried for it on every pitch.

Concepcion ran the count to one and one and then hit a high-bouncing, unplayable chop over second that tied things up. Now the steal was on, of course, and Concepcion flashed away to second and barely slipped under Fisk's waist-high peg; Griffey doubled to the wall, and the Reds, for the twenty-fifth time this year, had snatched back a victory in their last licks. Bench's leadoff double had been a parable of winning baseball. He has great power in every direction, but most of all, of course, to left, where the Fenway wall murmurs so alluringly to a right-handed slugger whose team is down a run. Hitting Lee's outside pitch to right—going with it—was the act of a disciplined man.

Bill Lee is a talkative and engaging fellow who will discourse in lively fashion on almost any subject, including zero population growth, Zen Buddhism, compulsory busing, urban planning, acupuncture, and baseball. During the formal postgame press interview, a reporter put up his hand and said, "Bill, how would you, uh, characterize the World Series so far?"

Two hundred pencils poised.

"Tied," Lee said.

○

The action now repaired to the cheerless, circular, Monsantoed close of Riverfront Stadium. The press box there is glassed-in and air-conditioned, utterly cut off from the sounds of baseball action and baseball cheering. After an inning or two of this, I began to feel as if I were suffering from the effects of a mild stroke, and so gave up my privileged niche and moved outdoors to a less favored spot in an auxiliary press section in the stands, where I was surrounded by the short-haired but vociferous multitudes of the Cincinnati. The game was a noisy one, for the Reds, back in their own yard, were sprinting around the Astro Turf and whanging out long hits. They stole three bases and hit three home runs (Bench, Concepcion, and Geronimo—the latter two back-to-back) in the course of moving to a 5-1 lead. Boston responded with a will. The second Red Sox homer of the evening (Fisk had hit the first) was a pinch-hit blow by Bernie Carbo, and the third, by Dwight Evans, came with one out and one on in the ninth and tied the score, astonishingly, at 5-5. The pattern of the game to this point, we can see in retrospect, bears a close resemblance to the classic sixth, and an extravagant dénouement now seemed certain. Instead, we were given the deadening business of the disputed, umpired play—the collision at home plate in the bottom of the tenth between Carlton Fisk and Cincinnati pinch-hitter Ed Armbrister, who, with a man on first, bounced a sacrifice bunt high in the air just in front of the plate and then somehow entangled himself with Fisk's left side as the catcher stepped forward to make his play. Fisk caught the ball, pushed free of Armbrister (without trying to tag him), and then, hurrying things, threw to second in an attempt to force the base runner, Geronimo, and, in all likelihood, begin a crucial double play. The throw, however, was a horrible sailer that glanced off Burleson's glove and went on into center field; Geronimo steamed down to third, from where he was scored, a few minutes later, by Joe Morgan for the winning run. Red Sox manager Darrell Johnson protested, but the complaint was swiftly dismissed by home-plate umpire Larry Barnett and, on an appeal, by first-base umpire Dick Stello.

The curious thing about the whole dismal tort is that there is no dispute whatever about the events (the play was perfectly visible, and was confirmed by a thousand subsequent replayings on television), just as there is no doubt but that the umpires, in disallowing an interference call, cited apparently nonexistent or inapplicable rules. Barnett said, "It was simply a collision," and he and Stello both ruled that only an intentional attempt by Armbrister to obstruct Fisk could have been called interference. There is no rule in baseball that exempts simple collisions, and no one on either team ever claimed that Armbrister's awkward brush-block on Fisk was anything but accidental. This leaves the rules, notably Rule 2.00 (a): "Offensive interference is an act . . . which interferes with, obstructs, impedes, hinders, or confuses any fielder attempting to make a play." Rule 6.06 (c) says much the same thing (the baseball rule book is almost as thick as Blackstone), and so does 7.09: "It is interference by a batter or a runner when (1) He fails to avoid a fielder who is attempting to field a batted ball. . . ." Armbrister failed to avoid. Fisk, it is true, did not make either of the crucial plays then open to him—the tag and the peg—although he seemed to have plenty of time and room for both, but this does not in any way alter the fact of the previous interference. Armbrister should have been called out, and Geronimo returned to first base—or, if a double play had in fact been turned, *both* runners could have been called out by the umps, according to a subclause of 6.06.*

---

*I have truncated this mind-calcifying detour into legal semantics, because time proved it to be both incomplete and misleading. Shortly after the publication of this account, the news filtered out of the league offices that the Series umpires had been operating under a prior "supplemental instruction" to the interference rules, which stated: "When a catcher and a batter-runner going to first have contact when the catcher is fielding the ball, there is generally no violation and nothing should be called." This clearly exonerates Larry Barnett and explains his mystifying "It was simply a collision." What has never been explained is why the existence of this codicil was not immediately divulged to the fans and to the writers covering the Series, thus relieving the umpires of a barrage of undeserved obloquy. We should also ask whether the blanket exculpation of the supplemental instructions really does fit the crucial details of *Armbrister v. Fisk*. Subsequent pondering of the landmark case and several viewings of the Series film have led me to conclude that fairness and good sense would have been best served if Armbrister had been

There were curses and hot looks in the Red Sox clubhouse that night, along with an undercurrent of feeling that Manager Johnson had not complained with much vigor. "If it had been me out there," Bill Lee said, "I'd have bitten Barnett's ear off. I'd have van Goghed him!"

○

Untidiness continued the next night, in game four, but in more likely places. The Reds did themselves out of a run with some overambitious base running, and handed over a run to the Sox on an error by Tony Perez; Sparky Anderson was fatally slow in calling on his great relief corps in the midst of a five-run Red Sox rally; the Boston outfield allowed a short fly ball to drop untouched, and two Cincinnati runs instantly followed. The Sox led, 5–4, after four innings, and they won it, 5–4, after some excruciating adventures and anxieties. Tiant was again at center stage, but on this night, working on short rest, he did not have full command of his breaking stuff and was forced to underplay. The Reds' pitcher over the last three innings was Rawlins J. Eastwick III, the tall, pale, and utterly expressionless rookie fireballer, who was blowing down the Red Sox hitters and seemed perfectly likely to pick up his third straight win in relief. Tiant worked slowly and painfully, running up long counts, giving up line-drive outs, surrendering bases on balls and singles, but somehow struggling free. He was still in there by the ninth, hanging on by his toenails, but he now gave up a leadoff single to Geronimo. Armbrister sacrificed (this time without litigation), and Pete Rose, who had previously hit two ropes for unlucky outs, walked. Johnson came to the mound and, to my surprise, left Tiant in. Ken Griffey ran the count to three and one, fouled off the next pitch, and bombed an enormous drive to the wall in deepest center field, four hundred feet away, where Fred Lynn pulled it down after a long run. Two outs. Joe Morgan, perhaps the most dangerous hitter in baseball in such circumstances, took a ball (I was holding my breath; everyone in the vast stadium was holding his breath) and then popped straight up to Yastrzemski, to end it. Geronimo had broken for third base on the pitch, undoubtedly distracting Morgan for a fraction of a second—an infinitesimal and perhaps telling mistake by the Reds.

Tiant, it turned out, had thrown a total of 163 pitches, and Sparky Anderson selected Pitch No. 160 as the key to the game. This was not the delivery that Griffey whacked and Lynn caught but its immediate predecessor—the three-and-one pitch that Griffey had fouled off. Tiant had thrown a screwball

called out and the base runner, Geronimo, returned to first. It is still plain, however, that Carlton Fisk had the best and quickest opportunity to clarify this passionate affair, with a good, everyday sort of peg down to second; irreversibly, he blew it.

there—"turned it over," in baseball talk—which required the kind of courage that baseball men most respect. "Never mind his age," Joe Morgan said. "Being smart, having an idea—that's what makes a pitcher."

○

Morgan himself has the conviction that he should affect the outcome of every game he plays in every time he comes up to bat and every time he gets on base. (He was bitterly self-critical for that game-ending out.) Like several of the other Cincinnati stars, he talks about his own capabilities with a dispassionate confidence that sounds immodest and almost arrogant—until one studies him in action and understands that this is only another form of the cold concentration he applies to ball games. This year, he batted .327, led the National League in bases on balls, and fielded his position in the manner that has won him a Gold Glove award in each of the past two years. In more than half of his trips to the plate, he ended up on first base, and once there he stole sixty-seven bases in seventy-seven attempts. A short (five foot seven), precise man, with strikingly carved features, he talks in quick, short bursts of words. "I think I can steal off any pitcher," he said to me. "A good base stealer should make the whole infield jumpy. Whether you steal or not, you're changing the rhythm of the game. If the pitcher is concerned about you, he isn't concentrating enough on the batter. You're doing something without doing anything. You're out there to make a difference."

With the Reds leading, 2–1, in the sixth inning of the fifth game, Morgan led off and drew a walk. (He had singled in the first inning and instantly stolen second.) The Boston pitcher, Reggie Cleveland, now threw over to first base seven times before delivering his first pitch to the next Cincinnati hitter, Johnny Bench—a strike. Apparently determining to fight it out along these lines if it took all winter, Cleveland went to first four more times, pitched a foul, threw to first five more times, and delivered a ball. Only one of the throws came close to picking off Morgan, who got up each time and quickly resumed his lead about eleven feet down the line. Each time Cleveland made a pitch, Morgan made a flurrying little bluff toward second. Now Cleveland pitched again and Bench hit a grounder to right—a single, it turned out, because second baseman Denny Doyle was in motion toward the base and the ball skipped through, untouched, behind him. Morgan flew around to third, and an instant later Tony Perez hit a three-run homer—his second homer of the day—and the game was gone, 6–2. Doyle said later that he had somehow lost sight of Bench's hit for an instant, and the box score said later that Perez had won the game with his hitting and that Don Gullett, who allowed only two Boston batters to reach first base between the first and the ninth innings, had won it with his pitching, but I think we all knew better. Morgan had made the difference.

○

Game Six, Game Six . . . what can we say of it without seeming to diminish it by recapitulation or dull it with detail? Those of us who were there will remember it, surely, as long as we have any baseball memory, and those who wanted to be there and were not will be sorry always. Crispin Crispian: for Red Sox fans, this was Agincourt. The game also went out to sixty-two million television viewers, a good many millions of whom missed their bedtime. Three days of heavy rains had postponed things; the outfield grass was a lush, Amazon green, but there was a clear sky at last and a welcoming moon—a giant autumn squash that rose above the right-field Fenway bleachers during batting practice.

In silhouette, the game suggests a well-packed but dangerously over-loaded canoe—with the high bulge of the Red Sox' three first-inning runs in the bow, then the much bulkier hump of six Cincinnati runs amidships, then the counterbalancing three Boston runs astern, and then, *way* aft, one more shape. But this picture needs colors: Fred Lynn clapping his hands once, quickly and happily, as his three-run opening shot flies over the Boston bullpen and into the bleachers . . . Luis Tiant fanning Perez with a curve and the Low-Flying Plane, then dispatching Foster with a Fall Off the Fence. Luis does not have his fastball, however. . . .

Pete Rose singles in the third. Perez singles in the fourth—his first real contact off Tiant in three games. Rose, up again in the fifth, with a man on base, fights off Tiant for seven pitches, then singles hard to center. Ken Griffey triples off the wall, exactly at the seam of the left-field and center-field angles; Fred Lynn, leaping up for the ball and missing it, falls backward into the wall and comes down heavily. He lies there, inert, in a terrible, awkwardly twisted position, and for an instant all of us think that he has been killed. He is up at last, though, and even stays in the lineup, but the noise and joy are gone out of the crowd, and the game is turned around. Tiant, tired and old and, in the end, bereft even of mannerisms, is rocked again and again—eight hits in three innings—and Johnson removes him, far too late, after Geronimo's first-pitch home run in the eighth has run the score to 6–3 for the visitors.

By now, I had begun to think sadly of distant friends of mine—faithful lifelong Red Sox fans all over New England, all over the East, whom I could almost see sitting silently at home and slowly shaking their heads as winter began to fall on them out of their sets. I scarcely noticed when Lynn led off the eighth with a single and Petrocelli walked. Sparky Anderson, flicking levers like a master back-hoe operator, now called in Eastwick, his sixth pitcher of the night, who fanned Evans and retired Burleson on a fly. Bernie Carbo, pinch-hitting, looked wholly overmatched against Eastwick, flailing at one inside fastball like someone fighting off a wasp with a croquet mallet. One more fastball arrived, high and over the middle of the plate, and Carbo smashed it in a gigantic, flattened parabola into the center-field bleachers, tying the game. Everyone out there—and everyone in the stands, too, I suppose—leaped to his feet and waved both arms exultantly, and the bleachers looked like the dark surface of a lake lashed with a sudden night squall.

The Sox, it will be recalled, nearly won it right away, when they loaded the bases in the ninth with none out, but an ill-advised dash home by Denny Doyle after a fly, and a cool, perfect peg to the plate by George Foster, snipped the chance. The balance of the game now swung back, as it so often does when opportunities are wasted. Drago pitched out of a jam in the tenth, but he flicked Pete Rose's uniform with a pitch to start the eleventh. Griffey bunted, and Fisk snatched up the ball and, risking all, fired to second for the force on Rose. Morgan was next, and I had very little hope left. He struck a drive on a quick, deadly rising line—you could still hear the loud *whock!* in the stands as the white blur went out over the infield—and for a moment I thought the ball would land ten or fifteen rows back in the right-field bleachers. But it wasn't hit quite that hard—it was traveling too fast, and there was no sail to it—and Dwight Evans, sprinting backward and watching the flight of it over his shoulder, made a last-second, half-staggering turn to his left, almost facing away from the plate at the end, and pulled the ball in over his head at the fence. The great catch made for two outs in the end, for Griffey had never stopped running and was easily doubled off first.

And so the swing of things was won back again. Carlton Fisk, leading off the bottom of the twelfth against Pat Darcy, the eighth Reds pitcher of the night—it was well into morning now, in fact—socked the second pitch up and out, farther and farther into the darkness above the lights, and when it came down at last, reilluminated, it struck the topmost, innermost edge of the screen inside the yellow left-field foul pole and glanced sharply down and bounced on the grass: a fair ball, fair all the way. I was watching the ball, of course, so I missed what everyone on television saw—Fisk waving wildly, weaving and writhing and gyrating along the first-base line, as he wished the ball fair, *forced* it fair with his entire body. He circled the bases in triumph, in sudden company with several hundred fans, and jumped on home plate with both feet, and John Kiley, the Fenway Park organist, played Handel's "Hallelujah Chorus," *fortissimo*, and then followed with other appropriately exuberant classical selections, and for the second time that evening I suddenly remembered all my old absent and distant Sox-afflicted friends (and all the other Red Sox fans, all over New England), and I thought of them—in Brookline, Mass., and Brooklin, Maine; in Beverly Farms and Mashpee and Presque Isle and North Conway and Damariscotta; in Pomfret, Connecticut, and Pomfret, Vermont; in Wayland and Providence and Revere and Nashua, and in both the Concords and all five Manchesters; and in Raymond, New Hampshire (where Carlton Fisk lives), and Bellows Falls, Vermont (where Carlton Fisk was *born*), and I saw all of them dancing and shouting and kissing and leaping about like the fans at Fenway—jumping up and down in their bedrooms and kitchens and living rooms, and in bars and trailers, and even in some boats here and there, I suppose, and on back-country roads (a lone driver getting the news over the radio and blowing his horn over and over, and finally pulling up and getting out and leaping up and down on the cold macadam, yelling into the night), and all of them, for once at least, utterly joyful and believing in that joy—alight with it.

It should be added, of course, that very much the same sort of celebration probably took place the following night in the midlands towns and vicinities of the Reds' supporters—in Otterbein and Scioto; in Frankfort, Sardinia, and Summer Shade; in Zanesville and Louisville and Akron and French Lick and Loveland. I am not enough of a social geographer to know if the faith of the Red Sox fan is deeper or hardier than that of a Reds rooter (although I secretly believe that it may be, because of his longer and more bitter disappointments down the years). What I do know is that this belonging and caring is what our games are all about; this is what we come for. It is foolish and childish, on the face of it, to affiliate ourselves with anything so insignificant and patently contrived and commercially exploitative as a professional sports team, and the amused superiority and icy scorn that the non-fan directs at the sports nut (I know this look—I know it by heart) is understandable and almost unanswerable. Almost. What is left out of this calculation, it seems to me, is the business of caring—caring deeply and passionately, really *caring*—which is a capacity or an emotion that has almost gone out of our lives. And so it seems possible that we have come to a time when it no longer matters so much what the caring is about, how frail or foolish is the object of that concern, as long as the feeling itself can be saved. Naïveté—the infantile and ignoble joy that sends a grown man or woman to dancing and shouting with joy in the middle of the night over the haphazardous flight of a distant ball—seems a small price to pay for such a gift.

○

The seventh game, which settled the championship in the very last inning and was watched by a television audience of seventy-five million people, probably would have been a famous thriller in some other Series, but in 1975 it was outclassed. It was a good play that opened on the night after the opening night of *King Lear*. The Red Sox sprang away to an easy 3–0 lead in the third inning—easy because Don Gullett was overthrowing and walked in two runs in the course of striking out the side. By the fifth inning, the Sox had also left nine runners aboard, and a gnawing conviction settled on me that this was not going to be their day after all. It occurred to me simultaneously that this lack of confidence probably meant that I had finally qualified as a Red Sox fan, a lifelong doubter (I am *sort* of a Red Sox fan, which barely counts at all in the great company of afflicted true believers), but subsequent study of the pattern of this Series shows that my doubts were perfectly realistic. The Red Sox had led in all seven games, but in every game after the opener the Reds either tied or reversed the lead by the ninth inning or (once) put the tying and winning runs aboard in the ninth. This is called pressure baseball, and it is the absolute distinguishing mark of a championship team.

Here, working against Bill Lee, the Reds nudged and shouldered at the lead, putting their first batter aboard in the third, fourth, and fifth innings but never quite bringing him around. Rose led off with a single in the sixth. (He got on base eleven times in his last fifteen appearances in the Series.) With one out, Bench hit a sure double-play ball to Burleson, but Rose, barreling down toward second, slid high and hard into Doyle just as he was firing on to first, and the ball went wildly into the Boston dugout. Lee, now facing Perez, essayed a looping, quarter-speed, spinning curve, and Perez, timing his full swing exactly, hit the ball over the wall and over the screen and perhaps over the Massachusetts Turnpike. The Reds then tied the game in the seventh (when Lee was permitted to start his winter vacation), with Rose driving in the run.

The Cincinnati bullpen had matters in their charge by now, and almost the only sounds still to be heard were the continuous cries and clappings and shouts of hope from the Reds' dugout. Fenway Park was like a waiting accident ward early on a Saturday night. Ken Griffey led off the ninth and walked, and was sacrificed to second. Willoughby, who had pitched well in relief, had been lost for a pinch-hitter in the bottom of the eighth, and the new Boston pitcher was a thin, tall left-handed rookie named Jim Burton, who now retired a pinch-hitter, Dan Driessen, and then (showing superb intelligence, I thought) walked Pete Rose. Joe Morgan was the next batter, and Burton—staring in intently for his sign, checking the runners, burning with concentration—gave it his best. He ran the count to one and two and then threw an excellent pitch—a slider down and away, off the outer sliver of the plate. Morgan, almost beaten by it, caught it with the outer nub of his bat and lofted a little lob out to very short center field that rose slightly and then lost its hold, dropping in well in front of the onrushing, despairing Lynn, as the last runner of the year came across the plate. That was all; Boston went down in order.

I left soon, walking through the trash and old beer cans and torn-up newspapers on Jersey Street in company with hundreds of murmuring and tired Boston fans. They did not look bitter, and perhaps they felt, as I did, that no team in our time had more distinguished itself in the World Series than the Red Sox—no team, that is, but the Cincinnati Reds.

○

This Series, of course, was replayed everywhere in memory and conversation through the ensuing winter, and even now its colors still light up the sky. In the middle of November that fall, a Boston friend of mine dropped into a tavern in Cambridge—in the workingman's, or non-Harvard, end of Cambridge—and found a place at the bar. "It was a Monday night," he told me later, "and everybody was watching the NFL game on the TV set up at the other end of the bar. There wasn't a sound in the place, and after I'd been there about ten minutes the old guy next to me put down his beer glass and sort of shook his head and whispered to himself, 'We never should have taken out Willoughby.'"

On the Ball

— S U M M E R   1 9 7 6

I t weighs just over five ounces and measures between 2.86 and 2.94 inches in diameter. It is made of a composition-cork nucleus encased in two thin layers of rubber, one black and one red, surrounded by 121 yards of tightly wrapped blue-gray wool yarn, 45 yards of white wool yarn, 53 more yards of blue-gray wool yarn, 150 yards of fine cotton yarn, a coat of rubber cement, and a cowhide (formerly horsehide) exterior, which is held together with 216 slightly raised red cotton stitches. Printed certifications, endorsements, and outdoor advertising spherically attest to its authenticity. Like most institutions, it is considered inferior in its present form to its ancient archetypes, and in this case the complaint is probably justified; on occasion in recent years it has actually been known to come apart under the demands of its brief but rigorous active career. Baseballs are assembled and hand-stitched in Taiwan (before this year the work was done in Haiti, and before 1973 in Chicopee, Massachusetts), and contemporary pitchers claim that there is a tangible variation in the size and feel of the balls that now come into play in a single game; a true peewee is treasured by hurlers, and its departure from the premises, by fair means or foul, is secretly mourned. But never mind: any baseball is beautiful. No other small package comes as close to the ideal in design and utility. It is a perfect object for a man's hand. Pick it up and it instantly suggests its purpose; it is meant to be thrown a considerable distance—thrown hard and with precision. Its feel and heft are the beginning of the sport's critical dimensions; if it were a fraction of an inch larger or smaller, a few centigrams heavier or lighter, the game of baseball would be utterly different. Hold a baseball in your hand. As it happens, this one is not brand-new. Here, just to one side of the curved surgical welt of stitches, there is a pale-green grass smudge, darkening on one edge almost to black—the mark of an old infield play, a tough grounder now lost in memory. Feel the ball, turn it over in your hand; hold it across the seam or the other way, with the seam just to the side of your middle finger. Speculation stirs. You want to get outdoors and throw this spare and sensual object to somebody or, at the very least, watch somebody else throw it. The game has begun.

Thinking about the ball and its attributes seems to refresh our appreciation of this game. A couple of years ago, I began to wonder why it was that pitchers, taken as a group, seemed to be so much livelier and more garrulous than hitters. I considered the possibility of some obscure physiological linkage (the discobologlottal syndrome) and the more obvious occupational discrepancies (pitchers have a lot more spare time than other players), but then it came to me that a pitcher is the only man in baseball who can properly look on the ball as being his instrument, his accomplice. He is the only player who is granted the privilege of making offensive plans, and once the game begins he is (in concert with his catcher) the only man on the field who knows what is meant to happen next. Everything in baseball begins with the pitch, and every other part of the game—hitting, fielding, and throwing—is reflexive and defensive. (The hitters on a ball team are referred to as the "offense," but almost three quarters of the time this is an absolute misnomer.) The batter tapping the dirt off his spikes and now stepping into the box looks sour and glum, and who can blame him, for the ball has somehow been granted in perpetuity to the wrong people. It is already an object of suspicion and hatred, and the reflex that allows him occasionally to deflect that tiny onrushing dot with his bat, and sometimes even to relaunch it violently in the opposite direction, is such a miraculous response of eye and body as to remain virtually inexplicable, even to him. There are a few dugout flannel-mouths (Ted Williams, Harry Walker, Pete Rose) who can talk convincingly about the art of hitting, but, like most arts, it does not in the end seem communicable. Pitching is different. It is a craft ("the crafty portsider . . .") and is thus within reach.

The smiling pitcher begins not only with the advantage of holding his fate in his own hands, or hand, but with the knowledge that every advantage of physics and psychology seems to be on his side. A great number of surprising and unpleasant things can be done to the ball as it is delivered from the grasp of a two-hundred-pound optimist, and the first of these is simply to transform it into a projectile. Most pitchers seem hesitant to say so, but if you press them a little they will admit that the prime ingredient in their intense personal struggle with the batter is probably fear. A few pitchers in the majors have thrived without a real fastball—junk men like Eddie Lopat and Mike Cuellar, superior control artists like Bobby Shantz and Randy Jones, knuckleballers like Hoyt Wilhelm and Charlie Hough—but almost everyone else has had to hump up and throw at least an occasional no-

nonsense hard one, which crosses the plate at eighty-five miles per hour or better, and thus causes the hitter to—well, to *think* a little. The fastball sets up all the other pitches in the hurler's repertoire—the curve, the slider, the sinker, and so on—but its other purpose is to intimidate. Great fastballers like Bob Gibson, Jim Bunning, Sandy Koufax, and Nolan Ryan have always run up high strikeout figures because their money pitch was almost untouchable, but their deeper measures of success—twenty-victory seasons and low earned-run averages—were due to the fact that none of the hitters they faced, not even the best of them, was immune to the thought of what a 90-mph missile could do to a man if it struck him. They had been ever so slightly distracted, and distraction is bad for hitting. The intention of the pitcher has almost nothing to do with this; very few pitches are delivered with intent to maim. The bad dream, however, will not go away. Walter Johnson, the greatest fireballer of them all, had almost absolute control, but he is said to have worried constantly about what might happen if one of his pitches got away from him. Good hitters know all this and resolutely don't think about it (a good hitter is a man who can keep his back foot firmly planted in the box even while the rest of him is pulling back or bailing out on an inside fastball), but even these icy customers are less settled in their minds than they would like to be, just because the man out there on the mound is hiding that cannon behind his hip. Hitters, of course, do not call this fear. The word is "respect."

It should not be inferred, of course, that major-league pitchers are wholly averse to hitting batters, or *almost* hitting batters. A fastball up around the Adam's apple not only is a first-class distracter, as noted, but also discourages a hitter from habitually leaning forward in order to put more of his bat on a dipping curve or a slider over the outer rim of the plate. The truth of the matter is that pitchers and batters are engaged in a permanent private duel over their property rights to the plate, and a tough, proud hurler who senses that the man now in the batter's box has recently had the better of things will often respond in the most direct manner possible, with a hummer to the ribs. Allie Reynolds, Sal Maglie, Don Drysdale, Early Wynn, and Bob Gibson were cold-eyed lawmen of this stripe, and the practice has by no means vanished, in spite of strictures and deplorings from the high chambers of baseball. Early this year, Lynn McGlothen, of the Cards, routinely plunked the Mets' Del Unser, who had lately been feasting on his pitches, and then violated the ancient protocol in these matters by admitting intent. Dock Ellis, now a Yankee but then a Pirate, decided early in the 1974 season that the Cincinnati Reds had somehow established dominance over his club, and he determined to set things right in his own way. (This incident is described at length in a lively new baseball book, *Dock Ellis in the Country of Baseball*, by Donald Hall.) The first Cincinnati batter of the game was Pete Rose, and the first pitch from Ellis was at his head—"not actually to *hit* him," Ellis said later, but as a "*message* to let him know that he was going to be hit." He then hit Rose in the side. The next pitch hit the next Red batter, Joe Morgan, in the kidney. The third batter was Dan Driessen, who took Ellis's second pitch in the back. With the bases loaded, Dock now threw four pitches at Tony Perez (one behind his back), but missed with all of them, walking in a run. He then missed Johnny Bench (and the plate) twice, whereupon Pirate manager Danny Murtaugh came out to the mound, stared at Ellis with silent surmise, and beckoned for a new pitcher.

Hitters can accept this sort of fugue, even if they don't exactly enjoy it, but what they do admittedly detest is a young and scatter-armed smoke-thrower, the true wild man. One famous aborigine was Steve Dalkowski, an Oriole farmhand of the late nineteen fifties and early sixties who set records for strikeouts and jumpy batters wherever he played. In one typical stay with a Class D league, he threw 121 strikeouts and gave up 129 walks and 39 wild pitches, all in the span of 62 innings. Dalkowski never made it to the majors, but, being a legend, he is secure for the ages. "Once I saw him work a game in the Appalachian League," a gravel-voiced retired coach said to me not long ago, "and nothing was hit *forward* for seven innings—not even a foul ball." An attempt was once made to clock Dalkowski on a recording device, but his eventual mark of 93.5 mph was discounted, since he threw for forty minutes before steering a pitch into the machine's recording zone.

Better-known names in these annals of anxiety are Rex Barney, a briefly flaring Brooklyn nova of the nineteen forties, who once threw a no-hit game but eventually walked and wild-pitched his way out of baseball; Ryne Duren, the extremely fast and extremely nearsighted reliever for the Yankees and other American League clubs in the fifties and sixties, whose traditional initial warm-up pitch on his being summoned to the mound was a twelve-foot-high fastball to the foul screen; and a pair of rookies named Sandy Koufax and Bob Feller. Koufax, to be sure, eventually became a superb control artist, but it took him seven years before he got his great stuff entirely together, and there were times when it seemed certain that he would be known only as another Rex Barney. Sandy recalls that when he first brought his boyish assortment of fiery sailers and bouncing rockets to spring-training camp he had difficulty getting in any mound work, because whenever he picked up his glove all the available catchers would suddenly remember pressing appointments in some distant part of the compound. Feller had almost a career-long struggle with *his* control, and four times managed to lead his league simultaneously in walks and in strikeouts. His first appearance against another major-league club came in an exhibition game against the Cardinals in the summer of 1936, when he was seventeen years old; he entered the game in the fourth inning, and eventually struck out eight batters in three innings, but when his searing fastball missed the plate it had the batters jumping around in the box like roasting popcorn. Frank Frisch, the St. Louis player-manager, carefully observed Feller's first three or four deliveries and then walked down to the end of the dugout, picked up a pencil, and removed himself from the Cardinal lineup.

○

The chronically depressed outlook of major-league batters was pushed to the edge of paranoia in the nineteen-fifties by the sudden and utterly unexpected arrival of the slider, or the Pitcher's Friend. The slider is an easy pitch to throw and a hard one to hit. It is delivered with the same motion as the fastball, but with the pitcher's wrist rotated approximately ninety degrees (to the right for a right-hander, to the left for a southpaw), which has the effect of placing the delivering forefinger and middle finger slightly off center on the ball. The positions of hand, wrist, and arm are almost identical with those that produce a good spiral forward pass with a football. The result is an apparent three-quarter-speed fastball that suddenly changes its mind and direction. It doesn't break much—in its early days it was slightingly known as the "nickel curve"—but a couple of inches of lateral movement at the plateward end of the ball's brief sixty-foot-six-inch journey can make for an epidemic of pop-ups, foul balls, and harmless grounders. "Epidemic" is not an exaggeration. The slider was the prime agent responsible for the sickening decline of major-league batting averages in the two decades after the Second World War, which culminated in a combined average of .237 for the two leagues in 1968. A subsequent crash program of immunization and prevention by the authorities produced from the laboratory a smaller strike zone and a lowering of the pitcher's mound by five inches, but the hitters, while saved from extermination, have never regained their state of rosy-cheeked, pre-slider good health.

For me, the true mystery of the slider is not its flight path but the circumstances of its discovery. Professional baseball got under way in the eighteen-seventies, and during all the ensuing summers uncounted thousands of young would-be Mathewsons and Seavers spent their afternoons flinging the ball in every conceivable fashion as they searched for magic fadeaways and flutter balls that would take them to Cooperstown. Why did eighty years pass before anybody noticed that a slight cocking of the wrist would be sufficient to usher in the pitchers' Golden Age? Where were Tom Swift and Frank Merriwell? What happened to American Know-How? This is almost a national disgrace. The mystery is deepened by the fact that—to my knowledge, at least—no particular pitcher or pitching coach is given credit for the discovery and propagation of the slider. Bob Lemon, who may be the first man to have pitched his way into the Hall of Fame with a slider, says he learned the pitch from Mel Harder, who was an elder mound statesman with the Indians when Lemon came up to that club, in 1946. I have also heard some old-timers say that George Blaeholder was throwing a pretty fair slider for the St. Louis Browns way back in the nineteen-twenties. But none of these worthies ever claimed to be the Johnny Appleseed of the pitch. The thing seemed to generate itself—a weed in the bullpen that overran the field.

The slider has made baseball more difficult for the fan as well as for the batter. Since its action is late and minimal, and since its delivery does not require the easily recognizable armsnap by the pitcher that heralds the true curve, the slider can be spotted only by an attentive spectator seated very close to home plate. A curve thrown by famous old pretzel-benders like Tommy Bridges and Sal Maglie really used to *curve*; you could see the thing break even if you were way out in the top deck of Section 31. Most fans, however, do not admit the loss. The contemporary bleacher critic, having watched a doll-size distant slugger swing mightily and tap the ball down to second on four bounces, smiles and enters the out in his scorecard. "Slider," he announces, and everybody nods wisely in agreement.

○

The mystery of the knuckleball is ancient and honored. Its practitioners cheerfully admit that they do not understand why the pitch behaves the way it does; nor do they know, or care much, which particular lepidopteran path it will follow on its way past the batter's infuriated swipe. They merely prop the ball on their fingertips (not, in actual fact, on the knuckles) and launch it more or less in the fashion of a paper airplane, and then, most of the time, finish the delivery with a faceward motion of the glove, thus hiding a grin. Now science has confirmed the phenomenon. Writing in *The American Journal of Physics*, Eric Sawyer and Robert G. Watts, of Tulane University, recently reported that wind-tunnel tests showed that a slowly spinning baseball is subject to forces capable of making it swerve a foot or more between the pitcher's mound and the plate. The secret, they say, appears to be the raised seams of the ball, which cause a "roughness pattern" and an uneven flow of air, resulting in a "nonsymmetric lateral force distribution and . . . a net force in one direction or another."

Like many other backyard baseball stars, I have taught myself to throw a knuckleball that moves with so little rotation that one can almost pick out the signature of Charles S. Feeney in midair; the pitch, however, has shown disappointingly few symptoms of last-minute fluttering and has so far proved to be wonderfully catchable or hittable, mostly by my wife. Now, at last, I understand the problem. In their researches, Sawyer and Watts learned that an entirely spinless knuckler is *not* subject to varying forces, and thus does not dive or veer. The ideal knuckler, they say, completes about a quarter of a revolution on its way to the plate. The speed of the pitch, moreover, is not critical, because "the magnitude of the lateral force increases approximately as the square of the velocity," which means that the total lateral movement is "independent of the speed of the pitch."

All this has been perfectly understood (if less politely defined) by any catcher who has been the battery mate of a star knuckleballer, and has thus spent six or seven innings groveling in the dirt in imitation of a bulldog cornering a nest of field mice. Modern catchers have the assistance of out-sized gloves (which lately have begun to approach the diameter of tea trays), and so enjoy a considerable advantage over some of their ancient predecessors in capturing the knuckler. In the middle nineteen-forties, the receivers for the Washington Senators had to deal with a pitching staff that included *four* knuckleball specialists—Dutch Leonard, Johnny Niggeling, Mickey Haefner, and Roger Wolff. Among the ill-equipped Washington catchers who tried to fend off almost daily mid-afternoon clouds of deranged butterflies were Rick Ferrell and Jake Early; Early eventually was called up to serve in the armed forces—perhaps the most willing inductee of his day.

O

The spitball was once again officially outlawed from baseball in 1974, and maybe this time the prohibition will work. This was the third, and by far the most severe, edict directed at the unsanitary and extremely effective delivery, for it permits an umpire to call an instantaneous ball on any pitch that even looks like a spitter as it crosses the plate. No evidence is required; no appeal by the pitcher to higher powers is permissible. A subsequent spitball or imitation thereof results in the expulsion of the pitcher from the premises, *instanter*, and an ensuing fine. Harsh measures indeed, but surely sufficient, we may suppose, to keep this repellent and unfair practice out of baseball's shining mansion forever. Surely, and yet . . . Professional pitchers have an abiding fondness for any down-breaking delivery, legal or illegal, that will get the job done, and nothing, they tell me, does the job more effectively or more entertainingly than a dollop of saliva or slippery-elm juice, or a little bitty dab of lubricating jelly, applied to the pitching fingers. The ball, which is sent off half wet and half dry, like a dilatory schoolboy, hurries innocently toward the gate and its grim-faced guardians, and at the last second darts under the turnstile. Pitchers, moreover, have before them the inspiring recent example of Gaylord Perry, whose rumored but unverified Faginesque machinations with K-Y Jelly won him a Cy Young Award in 1972 and led inevitably to the demand for harsher methods of law enforcement. Rumor has similarly indicted other highly successful performers, like Don Drysdale, Whitey Ford, and Bill Singer. Preacher Roe, upon retiring from the Dodgers, in 1954, after an extended useful tenure on the mound at Ebbets Field, published a splendidly unrepentant confession, in which he gave away a number of trade secrets. His favorite undryer, as I recall, was a full pack of Juicy Fruit gum, and he loaded up by straightening the bill of his cap between pitches and passing his fingers momentarily in front of his face—now also illegal, alas.

It may be perceived that my sympathies, which lately seemed to lie so rightly on the side of the poor overmatched hitters, have unaccountably swung the other way. I admit this indefensible lapse simply because I find the spitter so enjoyable for its deviousness and skulking disrespect. I don't suppose we should again make it a fully legal pitch (it was first placed outside the pale in 1920), but I would enjoy a return to the era when the spitter was treated simply as a misdemeanor and we could all laugh ourselves silly at the sight of a large, outraged umpire suddenly calling in a suspected wetback for inspection (and the pitcher, of course, *rolling* the ball to him across the grass) and then glaring impotently out at the innocent ("Who—*me*?") perpetrator on the mound. Baseball is a hard, rules-dominated game, and it should have more room in it for a little cheerful cheating.

○

All these speculations, and we have not yet taken the ball out of the hands of its first friend, the pitcher. And yet there is always something more. We might suddenly realize, for instance, that baseball is the only team sport in which the scoring is not done with the ball. In hockey, football, soccer, basketball, lacrosse, and the rest of them, the ball or its equivalent actually scores or is responsible for the points that determine the winner. In baseball, the score is made by the base runner—by the man down there, just crossing the plate—while the ball, in most cases, is a long way off, doing something quite different. It's a strange business, this unique double life going on in front of us, and it tells us a lot about this unique game. A few years ago, there was a suddenly popular thesis put forward in some sports columns and light-heavyweight editorial pages which proposed that the immense recent popularity of professional football could be explained by the fact that the computerlike complexity of its plays, the clotted and anonymous masses of its players, and the intense violence of its action constituted a perfect Sunday parable of contemporary urban society. It is a pretty argument, and perhaps even true, especially since it is hard not to notice that so many professional football games, in spite of their noise and chaos, are deadeningly repetitious, predictable, and banal. I prefer the emotions and suggestions to be found in the other sport. I don't think anyone can watch many baseball games without becoming aware of the fact that the ball, for all its immense energy and unpredictability, very rarely escapes the control of the players. It is released again and again—pitched and caught, struck along the ground or sent high in the air—but almost always, almost instantly, it is recaptured and returned to control and safety and harmlessness. Nothing is altered, nothing has been allowed to happen. This orderliness and constraint are among the prime attractions of the sport; a handful of men, we discover, can police a great green country, forestalling unimaginable disasters. A slovenly, error-filled game can sometimes be exciting, but it never seems serious, and is thus never truly satisfying, for the metaphor of safety—of danger subdued by skill and courage—has been lost. Too much civilization, however, is deadly—in this game, a deadly bore. A deeper need is stifled. The ball looks impetuous and dangerous, but we perceive that in fact it lives in a slow, guarded world of order, vigilance, and rules. Nothing can ever happen here. And then once again the ball is pitched—sent on its quick, planned errand. The bat flashes, there is a new, louder sound, and suddenly we see the ball streaking wild through the air and then bounding along distant and untouched in the sweet green grass. We leap up, thousands of us, and shout for its joyful flight—free, set free, free at last.

Several Stories with Sudden Endings

Even before Reggie Jackson took matters in hand, this was a rousing World Series. The Dodgers hit nine home runs, setting a National League Series record, and if they had somehow been able to carry the action into a seventh game there is good reason to think they could have won it. By far the best game, it turned out, was the first, at Yankee Stadium, and the Yankees' coup was undoubtedly the three runs they scored off the suave and redoubtable Don Sutton. The visitors, it will be recalled, bravely tied the game with a run in the ninth, but then ran smack into Sparky Lyle; deep in the unstilly night, the Yanks won it, 4–3, on a twelfth-inning double by Randolph and a single by Paul Blair. The next evening, Catfish Hunter, who had suffered through a dreary season of injuries and illness, was badly manhandled by the Dodgers, who whacked four homers and won, 6–1. Hunter, a lighthearted hero of many previous Octobers, smiled and shrugged in response to the postgame questions. "The sun don't shine on the same dog's ass all the time," he said.

Out West, within the vast pastel conch of Dodger Stadium, the Yanks now captured two fine, extremely grudging games behind some stout pitching by Torrez and Guidry, who both went the full distance. The Dodgers, apparently determined to win on pure muscle, excited their multitudes with more down-towners, but the Yankees took the first game, 5–3, on two deflected infield singles, and the second, 4–2, on some modest wrong-field hits and a solo homer by Reggie Jackson. Thurman Munson hit a homer in Game Five, and so did Jackson (a homer to be more noticed later on), but only after the

95

Dodgers had whanged out thirteen hits for Don Sutton, who coasted home in a 10–4 laugher.

With the Yankees leading the Series by three games to two, we came back to New York for the extraordinary conclusion. In this game, the Dodgers took an early 3–2 lead on Reggie Smith's home run off Mike Torrez; it was the third round-tripper for Smith, who was beginning to look like the dominant figure in the Series. The other Reggie came up to bat in the fourth inning (he had walked in the second) and instantly pulled Burt Hooton's first delivery into the right-field stands on a low, long parabola, scoring Munson ahead of him and putting the Yankees ahead for the rest of the game and the rest of the year. Jackson stepped up to the plate again in the next inning (Elias Sosa was now pitching for the Dodgers), with two out and Willie Randolph on first, and this time I called the shot. "He's going to hit it out of here on the first pitch," I announced to my neighbors in the press rows, and so he did. It was a lower drive than the first and carried only four or five rows into the same right-field sector, but it was much more resoundingly hit; at first it looked like a double, or even a loud single, but it stayed up there—a swift white message flying out on an invisible wire—and vanished into the turbulent darkness of the crowd.

My call was not pure divination. With the strange insect gaze of his shining eyeglasses, with his ominous Boche-like helmet pulled low, with his massive shoulders, his gauntleted wrists, his high-held bat, and his enormously muscled legs spread wide, Reggie Jackson makes a frightening figure at bat. But he is not a great hitter. Perhaps he is not even a good one. A chronic overstrider and overswinger, he swings through a lot of pitches, and the unchecked flailing power of his immense cut causes his whole body to drop down a foot or more. He often concludes a trip to the plate (and a Yankee inning) with his legs grotesquely twisted and his batting helmet falling over his eyes—and with the ball, flipped underhand by the departing catcher, rolling gently out to the mound. It is this image, taken in conjunction with his salary and his unending publicity in the sports pages, that seems to enrage so many fans. "Munson!" they cry, like classicists citing Aeschylus. "Now, you take Munson—*there's* a hitter!" And they are right. But Reggie Jackson is streaky and excitable. I have an inexpungeable memory of the two violent doubles he struck for the Oakland A's against Tom Seaver in the sixth game of the 1973 World Series, and of the homer he hit the next day against Jon Matlack to destroy the Mets. I remember his gargantuan, into-the-lights home run in the All-Star Game of 1971 in Detroit. And so on. Reggie Jackson is the most emotional slugger I have ever seen. Late in a close big game—and with the deep, baying cries from the stands rolling across the field: "Reg-gie! Reg-gie! Reg-gie!"—he strides to the plate and taps it with his bat and settles his batting helmet and gets his feet right and turns his glittery regard toward the pitcher, and we suddenly know that it is a different hitter we are watching now, and a different man. Get *ready*, everybody—it's show time. And, besides, Reggie had been crushing the ball in batting practice and he had hit a homer in each of the last two games against the Dodgers. Hence (to sound very much like Howard Cosell) my call.

I did not call the third homer. One does not predict miracles. This one also came on the first ball pitched—a low and much more difficult pitch, I thought, from knuckleballer Charlie Hough. The ball flew out on a higher and slower trajectory—inviting wonder and incredulity—this time toward the unoccupied sector in faraway center field that forms the black background for the hitters at the plate, and even before it struck and caromed once out there and before the showers of paper and the explosions of shouting came out of the crowd, one could almost begin to realize how many things Reggie Jackson had altered on this night. The game was won, of course (it was 8–4 in the end), and the Yankees were world champions once again. It was their first full title since 1962, and their twenty-first in all. Jackson's five homers for the Series was a new record, and so were his ten runs and twenty-five total bases. The three home runs in a single Series game had been done before— by Babe Ruth, in 1926 and again in 1928, but neither of Ruth's splurges had come on consecutive at-bats, and neither had been conclusive. Reggie Jackson's homer in the previous game had been hit on his last trip to the plate, and his base on balls in the second inning had been on four straight pitches. This meant that he had hit four home runs on four consecutive swings of the bat—a deed apparently unique in the annals of the game. But Jackson's achievement, to be sure, cannot properly be measured against any of the famous *sustained* one-man performances in World Series history—by Brooks Robinson in 1970, for instance, or by Roberto Clemente in 1971. Reggie's night—a thunderclap—was both less and more. It was out of the park. Jackson, in any case, had won this game and this World Series, and he had also, in some extraordinary confirming fashion, won this entire season, reminding us all of its multiple themes and moods and pleasures, which were now culminated in one resounding and unimaginable final chord.

O

This World Series was famous at the very end, but it was notorious all the time. Even while they were winning, the Yankees continued their off-the-field bickerings and grudges and complaints. During the Series, clubhouse reporters wrote that Thurman Munson hoped to play for Cleveland next year, that Mickey Rivers and Graig Nettles were also eager to be traded, that Ed Figueroa had almost jumped the team, and that Reggie Jackson was bitterly critical of Billy Martin's use of Catfish Hunter in the second game. A news-magazine story claimed that in the middle of the season two Yankee players had asked

George Steinbrenner to fire Martin; Thurman Munson said that the story was a lie. A press conference was convened by the Yankees at which it was announced that the club was giving Billy Martin a new car and a bonus. Reggie Jackson, who is never at a loss for words, continued to grant startling interviews to great masses of media people. "I couldn't quit this summer, because of all the kids and the blacks and the little people who are pulling for me," he said at one point. "I represent both the underdog and the overdog in our society."

In the Dodger camp, the tone of the news, at least, was different. Manager Tom Lasorda, who did a remarkable job on the field this summer and this fall, attracted hundreds of reporters to pregame interviews, during which he told a lot of Vegas-style standup-comic jokes, and also declared his love for his country and his family and the Dodger organization. "During the national anthem," he said at one point, "a tear came to my eye—I'm not ashamed to admit that. It's the kind of guy I *am*." He made frequent mention of the Big Dodger in the Sky. One day, he confirmed to reporters that he and his wife had had dinner the night before with his good friend Frank Sinatra and *his* wife. Lasorda said that his friend Don Rickles had come to the clubhouse before the fourth game to invigorate his players with insults. "Our team is a big family," he said. "I *love* my players. They've got manners, they've got morals. They're outstanding human beings." The Dodger players, who are clean-shaven and neatly dressed and youthful in appearance, were friendly and cheerful with the press. (The Dodgers are instructed in public relations during spring training, and many of them who live in and around Los Angeles appear at community dinners and other Dodger-boosting functions during the off-season.) Steve Garvey, asked by a reporter what he thought about the Yankee Stadium fans, paused for a moment and then said, "Well, throwing things on the field is not my idea of a well-rounded human being."

I think I prefer the sour Yankee style to the Dodgers' sweetness, since it may bear a closer resemblance to the true state of morale on a professional ball team during the interminable season. It probably doesn't matter much either way. The outcome of this World Series suggests that neither of these contrasting public images had anything to do with what happened on the field. What we can be certain of is that none of this will go away. We live in an unprivate time, and the roar of personality and celebrity has almost drowned out the cheering in the stands. The ironic and most remarkable aspect of Reggie Jackson's feat is that for a moment there, on that littered, brilliant field, he—he, of all people—almost made us forget this. Suddenly he confirmed all our old, secret hopes. He reminded us why we had come there in the first place—for the game and not the news of the game, for the feat and not the feature. What he had done was so difficult and yet was done so well that it was inexplicable. He had become a hero.

Wilver's Way

The New Wave

Quite a year, all in all. Surprising things kept taking place in the National League, where the Montreal Expos and the Houston Astros, both relentless losers in the past, stubbornly clung to the top of their divisions for most of the summer; both fell in the very last week, but their new hordes of fans must have recovered from their disappointment by now and can think back upon their heroes' ardent efforts with pleasure and gratitude. Most of the Astro players are exceptionally tall and thin; when seen at play, in their astounding orange-and-red-and-yellow-swatched uniforms (on which numerals appear at groin level), they sometimes suggest a troupe of gazelles depicted by a Balkan corps de ballet. Often there was a Sylphide-like quality to their games as well, which can be understood after a glance at their team statistics. Although they finished only a game and a half out of first place, and a full ten games ahead of the third-place Dodgers, the Astros scored fewer runs than anyone else in the National League—five hundred and eighty-three, which is only one run more than their pitchers gave up, over all, to their opponents. The Astros hit forty-nine homers for the year— one more than Dave Kingman's personal total—and whacked more triples (fifty-two) than homers. Jeff Leonard, who batted cleanup for the Astros most of the time, did not hit one homer. None of this, it should be understood, is easy to do. Speed and pitching made up for a lot. Five of the Astro regulars stole more than twenty bases apiece, and three Houston pitchers—James Rodney Richard, Joe Niekro, and Ken Forsch—finished in the top ten in the league, and threw forty complete games among them. *Close* games, we may assume.

Montreal, whose pitching was even better than the Astros'—the best in the league, in fact—moved out to a six-game lead in its division early in July, after winning twenty-six of its first thirty-two home games. Rapturous crowds at the Stade Olympique delivered a standing ovation for every Expo maneuver, including sacrifice bunts and discerning bases on balls. Winning at home is the traditional sign of a young team, and most of the screaming of *les Exponents* (as the Montreal rooters call themselves) centered upon the vivid play of the three dashing outfielders, Warren Cromartie, Andre Dawson, and Ellis Valentine; the estimable catcher, Gary Carter; the immense, bearded third baseman, Larry Parrish; and an infielder named Rodney Scott, who were all twenty-five years old this summer. I visited the Stade at the very end of July—almost too late for the party, I realized, for on the day of my arrival the sports section of Montreal's *La Presse* bore sombre headlines: "PIED DE NEZ DES PIRATES—*Double Défaite des Expos Devant une Foule Record*." The onrushing Pirates (the team had been aroused by the recent acquisition of Bill Madlock, a two-time National League batting champion, who came over from the Giants in a stunning trade) had swept a doubleheader the previous night, before 59,260 *Exponents effrayés*, to cut the Expos' lead to a bare half game. This margin vanished, too, after three or four minutes of the next game, when Dave Parker swatted a two-run homer toward the "BUVEZ 7UP" sign in right field in the top of the first inning, to put the visitors ahead for the night. There were brave ovations even after the Expos had dropped behind by 5–0, but the audience was plainly miserable about the loss of first place, which its team had occupied since the middle of June. (Bill Lee had told me that the pressures of the pennant race had begun to show during the previous week, when the first fistfights of the year broke out in the stands.) During the game, a glowering *amateur* just in front of me (I was sitting in the lower-deck *corbeille*, behind third base) kept up a hoarse nine-inning stream of muttered and sometimes shouted criticism and commentary, which I listened to yearningly, as if at a performance by the Comédie-Française; the burden of the message was clear enough, but I missed all the nuances.

Happiness and first place were restored on the following afternoon, a Sunday, when Andre Dawson hit a providential checked-swing, wrong-field triple to drive in three runs, in a game that Montreal won by 5–3. The hero of the day, however, was Rusty Staub, the Expo first baseman. Staub, who as *le grand Orange* was the most popular member of the team a decade ago, during its tottering first seasons as an expansion club, had been purchased from the Detroit Tigers a few days earlier, and his return to the lineup was acclaimed in the papers in terms ("*un merveilleux talent allié au charisme*") previously reserved for Maurice Richard, the hockey immortal. Staub, a serious chef off the field, had evidently not been getting much exercise as a designated hitter for the Tigers, and his movements afield caused one press-box observer to murmur, "It's like having Julia Child playing first." Mrs.

Child, however, can't hit. Rusty rapped out two singles during the after-noon—each accompanied by another standing O. and a curious, rolling volley of sound that I could not quite identify. Then I noticed that the bottoms of the plastic seats in the grandstand of the Stade Olympique—an immense and truly ugly concrete egg, built for the Olympic Games of 1976—were hinged and spring-operated, like theatre seats; when forty thousand Expo fans jump to their feet in ecstasy, one instantly hears Montcalm and Nelson Eddy and the Northwest Mounted Police galloping out of the forests to save the day.

The Pirates won back first place early in August, and began to win important games in the sudden-accident style that often characterizes pen-nant-bound clubs—a pinch-hit grand-slam homer by John Milner, a tenth-inning three-run homer by Phil Garner, and so on. The Expos slipped slowly backward, exactly as I had expected they would, and trailed by three games at the end of the month. Then, without my expecting it at all, Montreal won ten straight games, and then seventeen out of eighteen games, and squeezed back into first by a sliver of a percentage point on September 11th. In the ensuing ten days, the two clubs exchanged the lead four times. The history of this year's Pirates is now secure in the records and in our memories, but attention should still be given to the courage and tenacity of the young Montrealers and the skill of their manager, Dick Williams, which together very nearly unmade the whole story before it began. The club slipped out of first place for good in the last week, by which time they looked worn and jumpy (the Expos were not, in truth, a very good defensive team), but they were still in the race on the final Sunday, the very last day of the season, when they were shut out in Montreal by Steve Carlton and the Phillies, before fifty thousand cheering, standing, heartbroken *Exponents*.

Family Matters

"O!" (*hands in a circle over the head*)—"R!" (*left arm forms semicircle, with fingers at rib level; left leg extends*)—"I!" (*feet together; hands together over head*)—"O!" (*as above*)—"L!" (*right arm is raised, left arm extends*)—"E!" (*left leg extends; right and left arms extend to left, parallel to each other*)—"S!" (*body turns left; left arm is pointed away from forehead in Egyptian-frieze style, and right arm points astern*), followed by banner-wav-ings and tumultuous cries.

Hundreds of thousands of Baltimore and other Maryland citizens know this ceremonial by heart, and they roared out the message on every imagin-able occasion this summer at Memorial Stadium. Their shaman was Wild Bill Hagy, a large, bearded, gap-toothed cabdriver from the Dundalk area of Baltimore, who instituted the letter-cheer two years ago in Section 34 of the upper deck; this year, it swept the park and the city, and Hagy, in his well-stuffed orange T-shirt and straw cowboy hat, became a Baltimore institution, like white stone stoops. (Near the end of the last home game of the regular season, manager Earl Weaver and the rest of the Orioles came out on the grass in front of the dugout and went through the spelling dance together, in honor of the fans.) The Orioles succeeded this year not only in their league but at the gate, which has been a much more difficult challenge for them over the years. They drew 1,680,561 fans—almost three-quarters of a million above their average attendance in the past two decades, during which time they were winning more games than any other team in baseball. The youthful, hopeful, extremely informal Baltimore multitudes who screeched and sang during the local playoff games and then through the World Series were a delightful addition to the autumn scene, for they perfectly matched the young, informal, optimistic Orioles. The new fans came just in time. The Orioles were sold this summer to the Washington attorney Edward Bennett Williams, and there was talk that the team would be moved to the capital within a couple of seasons. Not now, though. Who wants to body-spell "W-A-S-H-I-N-G-T-O-N"?

The American League playoffs started briskly in Baltimore, with the Angels' Dan Ford smashing a first-inning home run off Jim Palmer, and with Nolan Ryan fanning seven Orioles in the first three innings. The home side achieved a pair of unearned runs in the third, however, and held on, at 3–3, until Ryan departed the premises in the eighth, suffering from a tightened calf muscle. This was a pure gift for the Hagy hordes, because Ryan, whose fastball is a liquid streak of white, habitually throws harder in the later innings than in the early ones—often going from timed speeds of about ninety-two or ninety-three miles per hour up to the nearly invisible environs of ninety-six and ninety-eight. His successor, John Montague, sustained the tension until the bottom of the tenth inning, when, with two Orioles on base, he threw two admirable forkballs to a left-handed pinch-hitter, John Lowenstein, and unwisely followed them with a third, which Lowenstein banked into the left-field stands, for the game.

The next evening, the Orioles pitched their ace, Mike Flanagan (who later received the Cy Young Award as the best pitcher in his league this year), and handed him a helpful 9–1 lead after three innings—a laugher, in short. But the Angels, who averaged more than five runs per game this season, scored another in the sixth, another in the seventh, three more in the eighth, and two more in the ninth, and now suddenly had the bases loaded. Like everyone else in the park, I kept running down my scorecard and counting the dots in the crowded Angel boxes. Could it be? Six, seven . . . yes, *eight* runs. The donor of the last two California counters was Don Stanhouse, the best reliever on the deep Oriole staff, and Earl Weaver, the veteran Baltimore logical positivist, now elected to stay with him a bit longer. Stanhouse thrives on crises, and often seems to invent them in order to inspire himself: a firebug fireman. Deluged with disbelieving screams, he cranked and threw only a fairish pitch, a slider, to the extremely dangerous Brian Downing, the California catcher, who slapped the ball directly at Doug DeCinces, the Baltimore third baseman. DeCinces seized it on the base path and stood there like a traffic cop to tag the oncoming Dan Ford for the last out. "It wasn't pretty by no means," Stanhouse said of his performance after the game. Still, I admired Earl Weaver for his patience, if only because he would have been unmercifully criticized if the Angels had gone on to tie or win the game against Stanhouse. Weaver doesn't give a damn what anybody will think later, which makes him a pearl among managers and men.

No team has ever come back from a two-game initial deficit in the playoffs, and the Angels came to the brink of expiring in three when they trailed by 3–2 in the ninth inning of the next game, which was played on their own rock-hard turf, in Anaheim. I was watching on television, and I was startled but pleased when the Angels suddenly rallied and won it in the ninth on two hits and a walk (Rod Carew cracked a double to start it all) and a frightful error by Oriole fielder Al Bumbry, who dropped an easy, series-ending fly ball in short center. Even before this gift, it was a thrilling game for the local rooters, with some sprinting, sliding catches in the outfield, an enemy base runner cut down at the plate, and a home run by their slugger and favorite, Don Baylor. More than two and a half million Angels fans turned out this summer, benumbing the local freeways, and friends who were at the Anaheim playoff games told me that the Californians' decibel level outdid even the Baltimore roarers'. Game Three was the reward that every Angels fan deserved. The summer ended for them the next afternoon, when Scott McGregor shut them out, 8–0, in a game illuminated by a diving, airborne catch over third base by Doug DeCinces that expunged the only California rally of the day.

The Cincinnati Reds showed grit in the first two games of their playoffs against the Pirates, forcing each of them into extra innings before succumbing by 5–2 in eleven and 3–2 in ten. (The Reds, by the way, won their division this year with a new manager, John McNamara, and a new third baseman, Ray Knight; their immediate predecessors were Sparky Anderson and Pete Rose. Unawed by his burdens, Knight batted .318. The club also got some useful work from Tom Seaver, who won eleven straight games in midsummer.) The opener was an austere, tautly played game, with thoughtful, excellent pitching by Seaver and John Candelaria, and two behemoth home runs, by George Foster and Willie Stargell; the latter's, a three-run shot against Tom Hume, won the game. Game Two was much less rewarding, thanks to some ghastly base-running on both sides. I was watching these encounters on television, and neither game aroused me as much as it should have, given the close scores. Perhaps the trouble had to do with the prim, doubt-stricken Cincinnati fans, who maintained a disapproving silence whenever their team fell behind. At one moment, while the NBC cameras panned across the silent, staring thousands, Joe Garagiola murmured, "This is not a painting."

The third game, an afternoon affair at Pittsburgh, which I attended, was delayed by a heavy rainstorm (a gruesome meteorological omen, had I only known it) but then began in lively fashion, when the Pirates got a run in the first inning on pure zeal. The lead-off man, Omar Moreno, walked, and stole second on the very next delivery by the Cincinnati pitcher, Mike LaCoss. Tim Foli then hit a high bounder to Dave Concepcion, on which Moreno unexpectedly proceeded to third, slithering under the startled shortstop's peg. Then he scored on a fly. In the third, Phil Garner, the dandy Pittsburgh second baseman, saved a run by diving on his belly to knock down Concepcion's single behind the bag, and in the bottom of that inning Stargell and Bill Madlock each hit home runs. The Reds, by contrast, looked corpselike at the end, as Bert Blyleven went the distance for the Pirates, who won by 7–1, to take the pennant. All year at Three Rivers Stadium, the field loudspeakers blasted out the Pirates' theme song during the seventh-inning stretch—a thumping, catchy disco-rock number, "We Are Family," by the Sister Sledge group. This time, with the late-summer shadows deepening and the championship at last in hand, the wives of the Pirate players suddenly moved forward from their seats, just behind the screen, and clambered up onto a low, curving shelf that rims the field behind home plate. At first, there were only a few of them, but more and more of the young women ran down the aisles and were pulled up onto the sudden stage, and then they were all dancing together there arm in arm, jiving and boogieing and high-kicking in rhythm, in their slacks and black-and-gold scarves and long, ballplayer-wife's fur coats, all waving and laughing and hugging and shaking their banners in time to the loud music. It was terrific. Since then, I have heard cynical comments about this party, and wry suggestions from writers and fans that the much repeated and much reported Pittsburgh theme song and the players' evident closeness and joy in one another were nothing more than a publicity device, and reminders that *all* winning teams are families, for as long as they win. I don't agree. It is true that the smallest flutter of a spontaneous incident—in sports, or anywhere else in public life in this country—is now seized upon and transformed at once into a mass-produced imitation or a slogan or an advertising gimmick. Bill Hagy was appearing on a television commercial in Baltimore during the playoffs and showed up repeatedly on local TV interviews and game shows. I have no doubt that by next summer two or three major-league teams will come up with organized fans' cheering sections and letter-cheers, in imitation of the Orioles, or even a wives' cheering-and-dancing group, in imitation of the Pirates. It is dispiriting, but we can't let ourselves miss the moment of humor and exultation when it does come along, or deny its pleasure. I thought about the Pirates' family when I visited the Cincinnati clubhouse after the last playoff game and saw the Reds preparing to depart for the winter. Joe Morgan was taking off his Reds uniform for the last time. He will venture into the free-agent market this year, but he is thirty-six now, and he had had a disappointing season, batting .250 and looking much slower afield; he had gone hitless in the playoffs. Just three years ago, Morgan and his teammates destroyed the Yankees in the World Series for their second World Championship in a row, and Joe Morgan was named the Most Valuable Player in the National League for the second straight year. That team was a family, too—the Big Red Machine—and now there was almost nothing left of it. But surely nobody understands all this better than the ballplayers themselves—the players and their wives—for that is the nature of their business. Injured, traded, slumping, benched, or simply playing for the wrong team, they are forever, or nearly forever, falling short of their best expectations, while their youth and their skills inexorably fade. Most big-league players never get to play in a World Series at all. When it does happen, then—the unexpected great year, when a whole team comes together, against all the odds, and wins—it should be celebrated, for the good times almost surely will not last. Why not dance?

Class

Whatever its drawbacks in weather and fielding, this World Series restored some credibility to the wall sampler which proclaims that sports build character. I have no idea how much of this came through on television, but those of us who were on the scene and in the clubhouses remarked again and again on the poise and generosity and intelligence of the players on both teams. This was a refreshing and surprising change from the demeanor of several more famous clubs and better-paid athletes in recent Octobers. The tone of the occasion—the absence of moneyed cool or aggrieved silence—was struck by Phil Garner, who said one day, "Yes, of course there's pressure. I feel anxiety about these games—why deny it? If you don't feel anything, a thump of the heart, about playing in the World Series, then I don't want you on my team. I'm excited. I get to the ballpark very early every day. I can hardly wait for the games to begin."

Both teams seemed to have this eagerness of spirit, and both of them, I believe, had absorbed it in great part from their managers. Earl Weaver and Chuck Tanner, the Pirates' skipper, are exceptionally good company, because at every moment of the season they appear to be caught up in the intellectual and emotional challenges and pleasures of their calling. Ask either one of them a question, and you get back instant strategy and history, example and perception, psychology and comedy and (in Tanner's case) homily, all in a rush. It is a treat and an education. Both of the pennant-winning teams were known in their leagues for the looseness and high spirits of their clubhouses. The Orioles' den often suggested a high-school or college locker room, full of euphoria and flying towels. The Pirates' quarters, by contrast, were an overcrowded city block in some ethnically confused but exuberant neighborhood—people eating, people drinking, people playing cards, people playing backgammon, people urging the game-players to come and do something else, knots of people shouting at one another in apparent rage and then collapsing in laughter, somebody sleeping and somebody else preparing to wake up the sleeper in a singularly frightful or comical fashion, several people deep in mysterious conversation with visiting strangers, people playing quietly with their young children or with their neighbors' children, people getting dressed and talking at length about one another's clothes and jewelry and hats, people bursting into song, and, over and through it all, the pounding, ear-wrenching noise of music—rock and disco and salsa—blasting out from enormous stereos and tape decks, and filling every corner of the room and the mind. All this was delightful, but in the end I was more impressed and convinced by the way the players and the coaches on both teams talked about themselves and each other, showing a pervasive tone of modesty and common sense that is often notably missing on clubs where money or public relations or consuming ambition tinges the entire operation.

Ray Miller, the Orioles' pitching coach, discussing the teams' apparently endless supply of extraordinary young pitchers: "We try to simplify a simple game. You listen to some coaches and managers and they make baseball sound like chess or something. The idea of pitching is to keep ahead of the batter, to make him hit your pitch. Never give him the chance to look for a good pitch. Don't walk him. Don't fall behind. We emphasize teaching the change-up to every pitcher, starting at the rookie level. Get in the habit of using your defense to get outs. Most of all, we try to take care of our young arms. We watch for the right spots for them, and we watch their mistakes. We never just throw them in the fire. If you look back two or three years, you'd see that pitchers like Dennis Martinez and Mike Flanagan were kept back and brought out of the bullpen only in long-relief situations or for spot starts. That's how you get to learn the league. Now they're regulars, and Mike may be the best in the business. You have to be patient."

Frank Robinson, the great Reds and Orioles slugger, who later managed the Indians and is now an Orioles coach: "When we're filling out the roster at the end of spring training, we spend a lot of time on the last four or five names that come up. We weigh this against that—left-hand and right-hand, can he throw, can he run, and all the rest—but in the end you pick because of character. You take a Terry Crowley because he's a pinch-hitter and he knows it, and he can sit week after week and then jump off the bench and do the job. You pick a Dave Skaggs because he's got a good personality. He doesn't play every day, but he'll sit there for months with no complaints and be *ready*. We're all in this, all twenty-five. That and Earl. Earl has always believed in himself, and he's always prepared. He's almost never caught short. That's why the players believe in him. He wins."

Earl Weaver (he always seems to enter a conversation at a full sprint, and his voice is hoarse with cigarettes and intensity): "I don't care about all that looseness and laughing in our clubhouse. That don't mean a thing. The only thing that matters is what happens on that little hump out in the middle of the field. Or if the pitcher isn't doing it, it's what the hitters are doing. Nothing else matters. We want to make a man believe in what he's doing. We tell the pitchers if you can get a batter out with your fastball, then stick to the fastball. Don't get beat fooling around out there with four or five different pitches. And the man at the plate is the one you want to get out. If you've got men on base, still concentrate on the man up there at bat. If you get him out, then you can work on the *next* man up there. It's all basic, but"—his voice drops to a whisper—"it ain't so damned easy to do it."

Chuck Tanner (his face is pleasant and lightly lined, with a bulge of Red Man in one corner): "I don't think a manager should be judged by whether he wins a pennant but by whether he gets the most out of the twenty-five men he's been given. There are third- or fourth-place managers who have done as well or better than the fellow who finishes up on top. It's easy to manage a team with no problems: everybody drinks milkshakes and hits .325. Nowadays, a lot of young ballplayers come up who have been hitting way over .300 in the minors, but when they get here they look around and suddenly baseball becomes a job for them, because they're trying so hard. The manager's real work, as I see it, is to reach the kid who's sitting over in the corner of the dugout and get him to play with the same attitude he had back in American Legion ball."

Phil Garner, on the racial composition of the Pirates—a club that included fifteen black or Hispanic players on its twenty-five-man roster this fall: "There really is no distinction between black and white on this club. If I didn't honestly believe that, I wouldn't say it. To keep factions from developing, you have to have someone that the blacks respect and someone that the whites respect, and the guy who puts that all together for us is Will Stargell. You know, I've heard it said that one reason we've never drawn very well here in Pittsburgh is that we have too many blacks on the club. I'm not saying that it's true, but it's sad if it *is* true, because we have such great talent. Why, you look at a Stargell, a Dave Parker, a Bill Madlock, a Manny Sanguillen, a Grant

Jackson—you can't *find* better players than that. If you play good ball, you deserve to be cheered."

Tim Foli, the Pirate shortstop (who joined the club in April, coming from the Mets in a trade; he had been known in the league as an angry ballplayer, a hard rock): "There's none of the jealousy you find with other teams—not with Stargell here. Every time somebody on the team does something in a game to help, he'll notice it and say something about it and emphasize it. You can't help being influenced. Nobody ever understood what kind of a player I was until I got here. But everything I did here was *noticed*. It gives you a different feeling."

Phil Garner, on Tim Foli, his second-base partner (the two are a little below average size and perhaps not better than average in range, but they both throw well, and they play together elegantly; they both have mustaches, and in the Pirates' boxy, old-fashioned baseball caps they suggest a pair of pugnacious bartender-infielders in a saloon league at the turn of the century): "When Timmy came, we started to turn things around on this club. We knew he was an exceptionally intelligent player, but I don't think anybody knew how good he was. He's been batting second, behind Omar Moreno, who can steal bases, and ahead of Dave Parker, who can drive in a lot of runs, and the man sure knows how to use that bat. He has changed his personality here. It just took him a little longer than it takes some others. He's grown up."

Dave Parker, on a gift he had presented to Willie Stargell during spring training last March, on Stargell's thirty-eighth birthday: "Well, it was a gold baseball. I handed it to him and I said 'Happy birthday, Pops.' He said 'What's this?' and I said it was a present to him from his favorite son. He said 'Yes, but what *is* it?' He kept looking at it and studying it. So I told him I'd taken it off the Gold Glove award I'd got for last year—the ball was part of the trophy, I mean, and I just pulled it off. Then he said, 'Aw, you shouldn't have done *that*, man,' and I said 'I never could have got the award without you.' Then we hugged each other."

Willie Stargell, at various times, on the ballplayer's life (he was born in Oklahoma, and his voice is unhurried and buttery): "We go out to have fun, but we work hard, too. It's supposed to be fun. The man says 'Play ball,' not 'Work ball,' you know. . . . You only have a few years to play this game, and you can't play it if you're all tied up in knots. . . . There was such a closeness this year. We were all so proud of ourselves. I said we worked hard, and I also mean the wives, who had to stay up so late so many nights because of us, or go to meet a late plane, and who had to look after the children when we were away so much, and try to be a father to them as well as a mother. It wasn't easy for anyone. I feel so grateful when I look back on this year. Oh, my, there was a day in San Diego, when Dave Roberts came in to pitch in a game we was losing. The bases were loaded for them, and a three-and-oh count on the batter, and Dave came in and made these three *outstanding* pitches and struck the man out, and we came back, caught up, and won. That was a moment when we knew what this team was like. Or, you know about the time the Hammer come up to pinch-hit, and . . ."

The Winter Games

The weather was appalling. The opening game of the Series was postponed for a day, and the next morning it snowed considerably in Baltimore and then rained all afternoon. At game time, the temperature stood at forty-one, and it went down from there. The next night was a bit warmer at first, but a late-inning drizzle turned the field to slime—the worst conditions, several players said, they had ever encountered. Game Three, in Pittsburgh, was suspended for more than an hour by a third-inning deluge, and Game Four, played in the afternoon, under scudding wintry clouds, was the coldest baseball I have ever sat through. Only in the last two games was the weather not a factor. During World Series week, there was a run on long johns and scarves and mittens in Baltimore department stores, and brave jokes were made in the press rows during the games ("If you're going inside to warm up, would you leave me your socks and shoes?" "Isn't drowsiness a symptom of freezing to death?"), but there was nothing jolly about what went on out on the field, where six errors were committed in the first game; Bruce Kison, the Pittsburgh starter, injured his arm in the cold and was finished for the year. No extended editorial comment on this weather report will be offered, since it would serve no purpose. This year's playing conditions were the worst in World Series history, but in recent years a considerable number of Series games have been played in icy winds or daunting storms, because these are perfectly normal mid-evening mid-autumn conditions in much of the country. For years, baseball has been vulnerable to this chronic disaster, because the commissioner and the owners insist on maintaining a season that runs a week or ten days too late into the fall, and because they are willing captives of network television, which wants the Series games to be played at night during the week and very early or very late in the afternoon on weekends (before or after football games, that is), since this schedule will draw the highest audience ratings. The nabobs of baseball could alter all this in a moment, if they had the wish to do so, by scheduling World Series games on afternoons in early October, but they are not so inclined, and it clearly doesn't matter to them that their famous showcase now offers a truly inferior version of the pastime, played under conditions that demean and endanger the contestants and punish the local fans. Every baseball player I have consulted on this matter is indignant about it—not so much because of the discomforts involved as because of the damage inflicted on the sport—and thousands of fans keep asking why something isn't done about it. But nothing will be done, because the ratings are right. They want it this way.

The Orioles scored five runs in the first inning of the opener, after Phil Garner threw a routine double-play ball six feet to Foli's left and into left field; later, Garner said that handling the wet ball was like trying to throw a bar of soap. Kison could not grip the ball in the cold, and gave up two walks, a wild pitch, and a two-run homer, to Doug DeCinces. The Pirates almost climbed back, but Mike Flanagan held on and won it, 5–4. Throughout the game, each player on the field was accompanied by the hovering, visible vapor clouds of his own breath, and DeCinces—who made two errors at third base and was lucky not to be charged with a third—said afterward that he had tried to blow out his breath just before each of Flanagan's pitches, so that he would have a view of the play.

The second meeting produced a tangled, tense, eventful game, stuffed with accidents and eventualities, which the Pirates won by 3–2 in the wet, with the field at the end resembling a winter salient at Verdun. Jim Palmer, the Orioles' grand master, surrendered two early runs, but then wisely shelved his fastball for the rest of the evening and did much better. The Birds caught up on two blows by their young switch-hitting slugger, Eddie Murray—a monster homer off Bert Blyleven, almost over the right-field bleachers, and then a whistling double to left, which scored Ken Singleton all the way from first. This World Series produced an amazing dossier of discussable baseball tactics and problems, and the remaining topics of the evening can be presented in a spot quiz, to which I append my own tentative answers.

Q: (a) With one out in the bottom of the sixth, was Eddie Murray (a fast man) right in trying to score from third base after Lowenstein's fly to Dave Parker in medium right field? And (b) since he did go, should he not have tried to collide with or discommode catcher Ed Ott, in the hope of jarring the ball loose?

A: (a) Sure—why not? (b) Well, Parker's throw was a laser beam, reaching the plate when Murray was still discouragingly far up the line. But yes, Eddie should have crashed.

Q: In the eighth, with the game tied, and with Murray leading off second and DeCinces off first, why didn't Earl Weaver instruct Lowenstein to bunt the runners along?

A: I still don't know. Weaver said after the game that the bunt is not his style, which is plain enough but non-responsive. As it was, Earl was cruelly punished for his flouting of classic strategy. Pirate shortstop Tim Foli was so convinced that the bunt *was* on that he broke with the pitch to cover third base as third baseman Bill Madlock charged the plate, and thus found himself perfectly positioned to field the grounder that Lowenstein bounced to the left side. Foli tried to tag Murray on the base path and missed, but threw to second for the force, and Murray was then doubled up in a rundown. (For a glimmering moment, Foli believed he even had a triple play in front of him.)

Q: Two out, top of the ninth, still a tie game. Ed Ott (a slow runner) is on second when Manny Sanguillen, pinch-hitting, singles to right against Don Stanhouse. Does hindsight offer any excuse or exoneration for Eddie Murray's impulsive decision to cut off Singleton's gentle but perhaps adequate peg home, in order to wheel and zip a faster throw to the same spot—too late, it turned out, to cut down Ott, who slid in with the winning run?

A: No.

Back home at Three Rivers Stadium and comforted by the roars of fifty thousand encircling supporters, the Pirates moved away confidently to an early lead in each of the next two games, and lost them both. They whacked the Baltimore starter, Scott McGregor, for three runs in the first two innings of Game Three, and might have dispatched him altogether if they had not damaged their own cause with some overeager baserunning. The Orioles were mysteriously succored by a third-inning cloudburst that held things up for more than an hour, because McGregor was an indomitable pitcher after the intermission, while John Candelaria, the Pittsburgh flinger, was suddenly no pitcher at all, being abruptly dispatched when the Orioles blew the game open with five runs. The key blows in their 8–4 victory were a two-run homer by Benny Ayala and a bases-clearing triple by Kiko Garcia, who wound up with four hits for the evening. These yeomen were in the lineup—Ayala in left field and Garcia at short—because both are right-handed batters, and Earl Weaver wanted an all-righty lineup swinging against Candelaria, who is a southpaw. This is a routine baseball strategy, not quite Einsteinian in its difficulty, but the tactic says a good deal about the Baltimore machine, which is made up of an unusual number of movable parts. Garcia is an uncertain fielder, to put it charitably, but he hits better than Mark Belanger, his alternate at short, who is impeccable afield but no use at all at the plate. The Orioles, it should be added, were strained for hitting all through these games, because of the different rules that govern the World Series in alternate years; this year, there was no designated hitter, which meant that the Orioles, deprived of their d.h., who is Lee May, had to make continual gingerly alterations at the plate or in the field as they tried to take up the slack. During the season, Weaver often boasted cheerfully about his club's "deep depth," but the Pirates, it turned out, were deeper.

Earl Weaver made all the right moves the next afternoon, waiting imperturbably (well, *almost* imperturbably) while the Pirates banged out fourteen hits in six innings and ran up a 6–3 lead. What he was waiting for was Kent Tekulve, the skinny, spidery, side-arming Pittsburgh relief pitcher, who now, in the eighth, came into the game during a Baltimore rally that had suddenly loaded the bases. Tekulve, a right-hander who led the élite Pittsburgh bullpen crew this summer with thirty-one saves, had been untouchable in two previous Series outings, and he had particularly embarrassed the right-handed Baltimore batters, who sometimes appeared to be wielding boathooks as they reached feebly for his dipping serves. Weaver, now beginning to play his hand, sent up the left-handed John Lowenstein to pinch-hit, and Lowenstein pulled a startling double into the right-field corner, scoring two runs. Another left-handed pinch-hitter, Billy Smith, was walked intentionally, thus reloading the bases and preparing the table for Earl Weaver's hole card, Terry Crowley, *another* left-handed pinch-hitter, who also smashed a two-run double to right, putting the Orioles ahead for keeps in the game, which they won by 9–6.

"This was the first time we've been able to keep the gun loaded right to the end," Earl said after the game. He looked like a cat with a mouthful of feathers, and who could blame him? The strategic maneuvers available to a manager are, in fact, extremely limited, and only rarely do they produce such swift and visible rewards. They are also unprovable. Tekulve, who discussed his disaster with perfect aplomb, said that, for his part, he hadn't pitched especially well, because he was releasing the ball a fraction too late, causing it to rise too much into the strike zone. Maybe he was right, at that; just after Crowley's double, Tekulve yielded a run-scoring single to Tim Stoddard, the Baltimore pitcher, who was making his very first appearance at the plate in the major leagues.

Down three games to one, the Pirates now seemed to be plucking at the coverlet. Only three teams had ever come back to win a World Series after finding themselves in such a predicament. The Pirates were whacking the ball, to be sure—the club was batting .329—but they were also playing at something less than their best, having committed eight official errors and a number of other omissions and malfeasances on the field and on the base paths. (The Orioles' six-run eighth inning had begun when Dave Parker lost track of a short fly ball by Kiko Garcia, which dropped in for a single.) Worst of all, they now faced the utter necessity of defeating Mike Flanagan, Jim Palmer, and Scott McGregor in three successive games, at a time when their own pitching was suddenly worn thin. The burden of all this kept the Pirate fans in a frenzy of apprehension during the early part of the next game—a late-Sunday-afternoon affair, and the last baseball of the year at Three Rivers Stadium no matter who won it. They shuddered and "ooh"ed at every pitch to a Baltimore batter, and then yowled and clapped and twitched their front-row bedsheet banners ("THE BIRDS WILL DIE," "FOLI'S FIENDS," "WILVER," and a heroic likeness of a rearing cobra, with Dave Parker's number, 39, under it) imploringly as each Pirate batter stepped up and dug in and stared out at the enemy pitcher under the billows of noise. Somehow, it all worked, and these vespers brought surcease and joy at the end. Chuck Tanner solved his pitching problem by giving the ball to Jim Rooker, a thirty-seven-year-old left-hander who had been twice disabled by arm miseries during the season. Holding nothing in reserve, Rooker threw fast and then faster, dismissing twelve of the first thirteen Orioles batters he faced, and departed in the middle of the fifth, after he had surrendered a lone run. He was succeeded by Bert Blyleven, in one of the extremely rare relief appearances of his career, who blew away the Birds, giving up a bare three hits the rest of the way. The final score was 7–1, Pirates, but even comfortable wins can have their hard moments and critical turns. I think the door to this game swung open in the bottom of the sixth, with two out and the score tied at 1–1, when Bill Madlock fought off several excellent Flanagan pitches with his calm, compact stroke and at last rapped a good inside fastball up the middle, to score Dave Parker from third. Madlock had four hits for the day, and afterward Earl Weaver said, "We haven't exactly learned how to pitch to him yet—or to some of the others, either. What've they got now, sixty-five hits?"

It was sixty-one hits, in fact. Sixty-one hits in five games.

Pictures in the Fire

As we know, the Pirates won the last two games as well, by scores of 4–0 and 4–1, and their sustained aplomb and courage in winning the championship against such unlikely odds made the World Series the most satisfying event of this eventful baseball year, which is as it should be. At the same time, it must be said that the sixth and seventh games, like the fifth, were unsatisfying entertainments. In all these games, the Orioles gave up the eventual winning run in the sixth or seventh inning, and the Pirates then went on and increased their lead in the late going. It should take nothing away from the Pirates' triumphant, unrelenting style of play to recall that the Orioles died at the plate in these three games, scoring two runs in the twenty-seven innings and never really mounting anything that could be called a threat along the way. Their cleanup hitter, Eddie Murray, went hitless in his last twenty-one times at bat. Baltimore was no better afield, making five errors in the three games and, more significantly, repeatedly failing to come up with the big play. True baseball fans are insatiably, and properly, critical in their demands, and most of them, I think (I exempt the Pittsburgh fans, of course), will look back on this Series with a sense of disappointment because of these unexpected Orioles failures. This was a flat spell but certainly not a collapse. The Orioles are a young and wonderfully talented team—Eddie Murray is twenty-three years old and has already hit seventy-nine major-league home runs—and I think we will be watching them again in October in the years just ahead.

What we remember about baseball after the game or the season is over is its marvellous moments—the sudden situation that offers a flashing succession of difficulties and chances and possibilities, all in the space of a second or two, and is then abruptly and sometimes shockingly resolved. That and the players' own moments—the images of the best of them that we carry with us into the coming winter. All of us, of course, will keep hold of our picture of Willie Stargell's home run against Scott McGregor, which won the last game. The Orioles were leading, 1–0, in the sixth, and McGregor had been pitching so well, spotting the ball and throwing a lot of sinkers, that a lot of the now terribly doubtful Baltimore fans must have begun to allow themselves to think that the one run just might be enough. (Tekulve, still waiting in the bullpen and all the more formidable, somehow, because of his brief recent loss of form, meant that there probably wouldn't be more than one run.) Bill Robinson's sixth-inning single was only the fourth Pirate hit of the evening. He led off first base as McGregor delivered the next pitch to Stargell—a low curve (a little *too* low, McGregor said later, for Stargell is a murderous low-ball hitter)—and Wilver hit it to deep right field, a high-sailing fly ball that descended just beyond the fence and just above Ken Singleton's leap and stretch and momentarily arrested empty reach. I have seen Willie Stargell hit so many home runs over the years (so many of them this fall, in fact) that I can run off the reel of this one again and again in my head, like a home movie: the preparatory forward double whirl of the bat, with his shoulders tilting and leaning forward, and with the weight of his body low and evenly placed on his feet but still somehow leaning, too—everything leaning—and then all of it abruptly rotating back in the opposite direction like an immense wheel, as weight and shoulders and arms and bat unwind together on the swing, and the circling, upswooping bat almost negligently intercepts the ball and disposes of it, and the body, finishing up, opens and rises, with the arms flying apart and the broad chest turning and facing out toward the field (as if it were watching the ball, too, along with the rest of us) while the bat, held only in the right hand now, softly finishes the circle and comes to a stop in the air behind the batter.

Willie won it all—the game and the Series, and the Most Valuable Player award for the Series, and a fistful of Series slugging records, and, best of all, something like a permanent place in our national sporting regard—and there is a special pleasure in all that, a thump of the heart, because of his way of doing things, because of the kind of man he is. Stargell's triumphs this fall were a perfect recompense for 1971, when the Pirates also beat the Orioles in a seven-game Series but one in which he played a very small part. Although he had led his league that year in home runs and had batted in one hundred and twenty-five runs, he went hitless in the playoffs and then batted only .208 in the Series, driving in one run. His sufferings at the plate were almost too painful to watch, but, as I wrote later, he endured this stretch of pop-ups and strikeouts and weakly topped grounders with unruffled calm—no bat-tossing, no puzzled head-shaking, not a word of explanation or complaint to the press. Near the end of that Series, I approached him in the clubhouse and asked how an intense, proud competitor like him could endure these disappointments and humiliations with such composure. Stargell's son, Wilver, Jr., who was then about four years old, was playing at his father's feet in the dressing cubicle, and Willie nodded toward the boy and said, "There's a time in life when a man has to decide if he's going to *be* a man."

Perversely, however, I continue to prefer the complexities of baseball to its curative ultimate resolutions and simplifications, no matter how heroic they may be. For me, the best moments of this Series came in the penultimate sixth game. I will not quickly forget Jim Palmer and John Candelaria battling through the first six scoreless innings: the Candy Man again and again firing outside fastball strikes to the Oriole right-handed batters and then running his nearly sidearm slider in under their fists; and Palmer, the tall and handsome hero, in his long white uniform, standing loosely and calmly in the center of things—staring *down* at the game, one always feels—with his glove hand and pitching hand held together high on his chest, almost under his chin, and then his stiff-legged stride and downhill stagger as the ball, delivered almost over the top, descended in a sudden line and flashed dangerously through the top story of the strike zone for another swinging strike.

The situation—the deadly difficulty—began when Omar Moreno singled to right field in the top of the seventh inning (there was still no score in the game), just out of Eddie Murray's reach. Moreno was then dispatched toward second on a hit-and-run play, and Foli hit a soft, high chop over the pitcher's mound that Jim Palmer leaped for and could not quite pull in; the ball, flicking off the tip of his glove, was slightly slowed in its progress, and bounced toward second. Kiko Garcia, who had moved to cover the base when Moreno was released, was in front of the bag, and he simultaneously attempted to field the chance and step on second for the force. He mishandled the ball, which trickled past him for a hit. A more experienced shortstop—a Mark Belanger, say—probably would have made the tiny, instant mental adjustment after Palmer's deflection that would have told him to forget about Moreno and make sure of the out at first. If Palmer had fielded the ball, or if he had not touched it at all, the Orioles would have had a double play.

With first base occupied, Palmer was forced to pitch to Dave Parker, and Parker, unwinding menacingly from his unique, almost cross-footed stance (he is six feet five inches tall, with columnlike legs, and he holds his long bat at the highest possible level behind his left shoulder, like a sledgehammer in midair), smashed the first pitch toward second baseman Rich Dauer, who in one instant seemed to have the play before him, and in the next fell on his knees as the ball ricocheted oddly off the infield dirt and over his right shoulder into center field. It happened very quickly, and you could see Dave Parker still only a step or two toward first base at the moment that Dauer, on all fours in the dirt, dropped his head in despair as he understood that the ball was not in his glove, that Moreno was sprinting for the plate, and that the game was forever altered. Parker, it was agreed later, had crushed the pitch, hitting the ball exactly in its middle with the middle of his bat, so that it flew toward Dauer without any spin—a knuckleball, in short, which took a sudden and characteristic knuckleball veer at the last instant and skipped free. Tim Foli, running toward second, was the nearest witness, and he said later, "I could see the seams on the ball, so I knew what had happened. It was so strange to see a ball hit that way, and hit so hard, that I yelled 'Look out!' as it went by me. Dauer never had a chance."

So Long at the Fair

—S U M M E R   1 9 8 1

S tatistics are the food of love. Baseball is nourished by numbers, and all of us who have followed the game with intensity have found ourselves transformed into walking memory banks, humming with games won, games lost, batting averages and earned-run averages, games started and games saved, "magic numbers," final standings, lifetime marks, Series, seasons, decades, epochs. With the right data at hand (such as Joseph L. Reichler's *The Great All-Time Baseball Record Book*) one can pass a rainy summer weekend in pursuit of such esoterica as Unassisted Double Plays, Outfielder; Most Complete Games, Rookie, A.L.; Stole 2nd, 3rd, and Home in One Game, N.L. (Pete Rose did it last, against the Reds in 1980), and so forth. Just the other day, while happily meandering among Mr. Reichler's figure-thickets (Dave Kingman is the Second-Easiest Batter to Strike Out in the history of the National League; Ty Cobb batted .357 in 1927, to lead all comers in the How They Performed at Age Forty category), I was suddenly taken by surprise—knocked flat, in fact—by a statistic that fell out of the sky, so to speak: I have been a fan for fifty years.

My first reaction, of course, was guilt. A half-century of vicariousness? Fifty years (now that I think of it, it may be more like fifty-one or fifty-two) in pursuit of a *game*? For shame, sir! But age teaches us how to deal with guilt (I picked him off first base), and soon I permitted myself to smile a little about the multiple pleasures and discoveries that my foolish servitude has brought me. I have written perhaps too often (Most Years Overestimating Rookie Pitchers in Spring Training, Both Leagues) about the most immediate attractions of baseball, but now some longer, quieter rewards may be observed as well. The comforting inner glow that I feel while consulting *The Baseball Encyclopedia* or looking at Lawrence Ritter's and Donald Honig's wonderful baseball picture-album, *The Image of Their Greatness*, emanates in a strange way from the names those books contain. The many dozens or even hundreds of old ballplayers' names and faces that I can quickly recognize are accompanied in my mind—blurrily or else with a perfect, crazy clarity—by scraps of attendant statistics, mannerisms, nicknames, anecdotes, teammates, and immemorial feats and failures. All ballplayers are connected with each other through the record books, of course, but now they seem connected to me, as well, through this enveloping, delicate capillary network of memory and association. Baseball is in my blood. When I stop to think about the sport this way—to think about how much almost every fan comes to know, almost without effort—I am reminded of my earliest feelings about baseball, when I had just begun to follow the fortunes of my first real heroes, Joe DiMaggio and Carl Hubbell, through the long summers of my teens. Even then, I must have sensed that more was involved in baseball than the accomplishments of a few athletes and teams, and that I was now attached in a rather mysterious way to a larger structure, to something deep and rooted, with its own history, customs, records, honored and dishonored warriors, founders, superstitions, and clouded lore. I belonged and I cared, and because I have been lucky enough to go on caring, I have belonged to baseball now for almost half of its history.

For me, going through the baseball record books and picture books is like opening a family album stuffed with old letters, wedding invitations, tattered newspaper clippings, graduation programs, and curled up, darkening snapshots. Here are people from my own branches of the family—the Giants, the Red Sox, the first Mets—and, in among them, page after page, the names and looks of other departed, almost forgotten in-laws and cousins and visitors. Everyone is here. The White Elephants and Gashouse Gang and the Big Red Machine. Hank Aaron and Hank Greenberg. Clemente and Brooksie. Gabby and Pie and Sunny Jim. Doc Cramer. (Why do I always think of Doc Cramer the instant I think of Sunny Jim Bottomley? Because, each in his own league, they were the same kind of players—invaluable, indestructible, and somehow never quite famous. Because each of them got six hits in a single game—with Sunny Jim batting in *twelve* runs in his.) Harvey Kuenn. Willie and Duke and the Mick. Jackie Robinson. *Frank* Robinson. Country Slaughter. Catfish Hunter. Columbia Lou (Old Biscuit-Pants) and the Fordham Flash ("Oh, those bases on balls!"). Stan the Man. The Meal Ticket. Schoolboy Rowe. The Yankee Clipper. Ron Swoboda, sliding on his face. Bill Klem. (An umpire, yes. He spent five thousand afternoons on the field, far more than anyone else in baseball history, and invented the umpire's essential creed: "In my heart, I never called one wrong.") The Babe. The Dutchman. Christy Mathewson. Frank Chance, the Peerless Leader. The Big Train. Cap Anson . . . An Iliad of names.

Many of these players, of course, were before my time, but I have noticed that this makes very little difference to me now. I have read so much about the old-timers and heard older players and writers and fans (including my father) talk about them so often that they are almost as visible to me as the stars I have watched on the field. I did see Babe Ruth play ball—once or (I think) twice, I saw him and Lou Gehrig hit homers back to back—so he is in my mind's eye, all right, but the sight of him is less to me than some of the things I have read about him: things I know because I am a fan. Almost everyone remembers something large and unlikely about this unlikely man, but the deed I come back to most often—I can't get over it—is his final one. On the last Sunday of his career, only a week before his retirement—when he was fat and worn-out at forty-one and had gone off to play for the Boston Braves because no other team would have him—he came up to bat four times against the Pirates, in Forbes Field at Pittsburgh, and hit a single and three homers. The last home run—the last one of his career, No. 714—flew over the roof of the double-decked grandstands in right field. It was the first ball anyone had ever hit out of Forbes Field. Goodbye, baseball.

Baseball history has made some different prodigies visible to me as well—men who illuminated the game not with their play but with their imagination, their will, their passionate selves. Two such men leap to mind.

The first one was short and dumpy, only five feet seven, and the weight he carried in later years made him look even smaller. He played the game for sixteen years (his lifetime batting average was .334), but he was made to be a manager. He managed the same club for thirty years. In time he bought a piece of the team, but in another sense he had always owned it. For every day and every game of those thirty years he was unquestionably the most vivid figure on any field where his team was playing. He was a master tactician in a time when runs were scratched out singly, out of luck and speed and connivance. He was too impatient to qualify as a great developer of talent, but he was a marvelous coach and a cold and deadly trader. He kept a distance between himself and his players, and the only two for whom he permitted himself to hold a deep affection both died young and before he did. He had great success, but terrible things happened to his teams on the field—immortal bonehead plays, crucial bases left uncovered, pennant-los-ing collisions on the base paths, malevolent bounces off invisible pebbles in the dirt. The bitter, enraged expression that settled on his thick face in his last years was the look of a man who had fought a lifelong, bareknuckled fight against bad baseball luck. They called him Little Napoleon. His name was John McGraw. "The main idea," he said, "is to win."

The other man was a lawyer, a churchman, a teetotaler—a straight arrow who made an early promise to his mother never to play ball or watch it on Sundays, and who kept his promise. He had flowing hair and bushy eyebrows and bow ties that he wore like a flag. He was a rhetorician, a nineteenth-century orator, a front-office man who enlivened trade talks with torrents of polysyllables and quotations from Shakespeare and Pope. Ideas and cigar smoke streamed from him. He thought up baseball tryouts. He put numbers on uniforms. He invented Ladies Day. He had the most discerning eye for young baseball talent that the game has ever known, and it was appropriate that he should have been the man who thought up and perfected the farm system. By the time World War II came along, his club, the Cardinals, had a chain of thirty-two minor league teams that employed more than six hundred ballplayers. Each year, the best of his young phenoms came up to the parent club, crowding its famous roster and forcing so many trades that in time half the dugouts of the National League seemed to be populated with muscular, mountain-bred throwers and long-ball hitters whom he had first spotted in some cinderstrewn Appalachian ballyard.

Then he, too, moved along to other clubs, still spouting phrases and ideas. "Judas Priest!" he cried. There was something about him of the travelling medicine-show man, something of W. C. Fields. But his ultimate alteration of the game, the destruction of baseball's color bar, was an act of national significance—an essential remedy that had awaited a man of subtlety and stubborn moral courage to bring it about. He refused to accept awards or plaudits for the deed, since it had only reversed an ancient and odious injustice. It would shame a man, he said, to take credit for that. He was the Mahatma: Branch Rickey. "Baseball," he said, "has given me a life of joy."

Quite a pair of forefathers. Judas Priest! And here comes another one, walking east on 93rd Street, in New York, at eight-thirty on a spring morning in 1932—a square-shouldered, medium-sized gent with a double-breasted suit, a small bow tie, a small white mustache, pink cheeks, and twinkly, shoe-button eyes: Colonel Jacob Ruppert, the owner of the Yankees, on his way to work at his brewery, over on Third Avenue. Coming toward him is a boy in knickerbockers, carrying books and a baseball mitt—myself, at eleven, on the way to school. Just before we pass, I tuck the books under one arm and whack my fist two or three times into the pocket of the mitt. Colonel Jake stops me, there on the street, while he extracts a calling-card from the pocket of his vest and scribbles something on it with his fountain pen. "Young man," he says, handing me the card, "take this up to the Stadium tomorrow morning for a tryout. And good luck to you." Does he actually say this to me? Did this really happen? Well, maybe not on that particular morning, nor on several dozen others when our paths crossed, there on 93rd Street. But it almost happened, surely, and one of these days, in my dreams, the Colonel will relent.

Now travel north with me about sixty blocks and about two decades and try to pick up a bespectacled, prematurely bald editor-writer at the wheel of his beat-up Ford tudor, westbound on the McCombs Dam Bridge on an early-summer Saturday. Beneath him is the Harlem River; ahead of him, uphill and off to the right, lies the Polo Grounds. Seated beside him in the front seat is his first child—a daughter, age four. He leans forward to adjust the dial on the car radio, which is bringing in the sounds of a ballgame in progress, as described by Russ Hodges. Struck by something odd, I point to the ballpark up ahead and say, "Callie, the game we're listening to is being played right over there, right now. That's the game we're listening to, and this is the Polo Grounds, where the two teams are playing it, see? It's hard to explain, but—"

The girl nods, not much interested. Then she hears something in the broadcast and sits up suddenly and stares out at the great green barn beside her. When she turns, her eyes are wide. "*Giants* are playing in there?" she asks.

○

Among relatives, jokes mean more than triumphs or ancestors. In the press box, a cloud of gossip and one-liners and irritable, over-familiar bonhomie hovers over the absorbed, half-bored regulars, as it does at a family breakfast table. Baseball writers work hard, but there is always a sense of playful companionship around them, because they must spend so much time together over the endless season and because they share the knowledge that they have all escaped doing something drearier and more serious in their lives. Even the white-haired scribes have this gleam, this boyhood joy of their occupation about them. Baseball writing has some drawbacks, but it has its moments, too. Before the opening game of the 1970 World Series, an eminent baseball writer for one of the New York dailies was on the field at Riverfront Stadium during batting practice when he noticed that the flag-draped, front-row Commissioner's box, next to the home-team dugout, contained a telephone—an instrument installed for the occasion in order to keep Mr. Kuhn in touch with God knows what advisers in case of unforeseen emergencies: with God Himself, perhaps. The reporter idly jotted down the number of the phone, and after the game had started he informed his neighbors up in the press rows about his odd discovery. Then, between innings, he dialed the number.

Watched intently by the flower of the American sporting press, Mr. Kuhn heard the ring and reached down under his seat for the receiver. "Hello?" he said cautiously.

"Hello, Chicken Delight?" said the writer-genius briskly. "I got a big order here—it's a picnic. We want eight of the Jumbo Baskets of Southern-fried, nine barbecue specials, six—"

"No, no," said Mr. Kuhn. "I'm afraid you have the wrong number. This is the Commissioner of Baseball. I'm sorry."

". . . Eleven orders of french-fries, eight cole slaw—no, make that *twelve* fries," the reporter went on, fully audible to us all. Weeping with pleasure, several dozen writers tried to keep their game binoculars steady on the Commish.

"No, you've made a mistake," Mr. Kuhn said, a trifle impatiently now. "I don't know how this could happen. This is the Commissioner of Baseball— I'm here at the *game*."

"Hold the barbecue sauce on one of the specials," the writer said. "Lots of ketchup. Lots of pickles. Last time, you forgot the pickles."

"Goodbye," said Mr. Kuhn politely, his cheeks scarlet. He hung up.

The call was placed again in the fourth inning, of course—more urgently, because the big order hadn't turned up—and again in the sixth, to diminishing returns. By this time, Mr. Kuhn had figured it out—he was in on a joke—and, to his credit, he was laughing, too. Once, he replaced the receiver and directed a sudden long stare at the press box—where everyone was deeply absorbed in his scorecard and stat sheets or busily banging out his running story. Nobody here but us scribes, Bowie. . . .

Somewhere in my files, I still have my scorecard for the Series game, with "Chick. Del." scribbled on the margin, because I have no symbol for bliss. I keep all my scorecards, of course—hundreds and hundreds of them—but I don't consult them much, to tell the truth, once the season is over. Except one. This game-scheme, now matted and prettily preserved in a grass-green frame, hangs on my office wall, and every few days or weeks I take it down and play its innings over again, out by out, in my imagination. The card is filled out far more neatly than any other scorecard I have ever seen, the names and symbols and numbers executed with an almost Oriental calligraphic care. It is not a scorecard of my own making but one that came to me by mail, two or three years ago, with a modest covering letter from its creator, a Seattle artist named Alan Douglas Bradley. I do not know Mr. Bradley, but he seems to know me. He knows, for instance, that I am a Red Sox fan, of long and painful good standing. The game he has sent me is an invention—a fabulous all-star exhibition contest in which the greatest lineup in the history of baseball is pitted against a pathetic assemblage of nondescript Red Sox footsoldiers and benchwarmers, most of whom I did not recognize or know much about until I had consulted *The Baseball Encyclopedia*. They include Hobe Ferris, who compiled a batting average of .239 while playing third base for the Bosox between 1901 and 1907; right fielder Skinny Graham, who batted .246 in twenty-one games for the Sox in 1934 and '35; Mike Herrera, at second, with .275 in eighty-six games in the mid-twenties; and so forth. The pitcher for this hopeless nine is not to be found even in the all-encompassing agate of *The Baseball Encyclopedia*, for he is me. The opening lineup for the Immortals, by contrast, requires no elucidation: Cobb,

Lajoie, Wagner, Ruth, Gehrig, J. DiMaggio, Traynor, and Berra. Cy Young is on the mound. They bat first (we are playing at Fenway Park), and in the top of the opening inning they load the bases, with one out—hits by Cobb and Wagner, a sensible intentional pass to Babe Ruth—but fail to score, because Gehrig unexpectedly raps into a 6–4–3 double play. This establishes a pattern; the All-Timers keep putting men on base—two walks in the third, a single and a double and a walk in the fifth, and so on—but somehow can't push across any runs. Babe Ruth strikes out with the bases loaded to end one threat—so weak with laughter at my curveball that he can't see straight, no doubt—and pinchhitters Willie Mays and Hank Aaron fan, in the third and sixth, probably because the proximity of the Green Wall in left field has them overswinging at my 50-m.p.h. heater. With one away in the top of the eighth, Mickey Mantle triples, and an ugly little scene is barely averted when I am warned by the homeplate ump—it must be Bill Klem—for intentionally plunking the next batter, pinch-hitter Pete Rose. (I may be overmatched but I am all heart out there—a Don Drysdale glaring in at my enemies.) Then Johnny Bench flies out to center, and Mantle is doubled up at the plate, on a close play, to end the inning.

Meantime, my Sad Sox have been able to do almost nothing against the offerings of Cy Young and his mound successors: Dizzy Dean, Sandy Koufax, and Walter Johnson. In the home fourth, we do get a man as far as third base, with two out, but Old Diz fans me in the clutch. By the top of the ninth, the game is still somehow scoreless and the stands are going *crazy*. Tris Speaker leads off with a single, and another pinch-hitter, Stan Musial, also singles. I retire Eddie Collins on strikes but walk Honus Wagner, to load the bases. (I am bushed by now, almost done, but gamely refuse to quit the mound.) The next batter, Ruth again, hits a screamer up the middle off the first pitch. I throw up my hands in self-defense (this part is not in the scorecard, to be sure, but a trained scorecard-reader learns how to sense such things) and the ball miraculously sticks in my glove; a flip over to third doubles off Speaker to end the inning, and the Gray Eagle, a step or two away from home, shakes his head in disbelief. In the bottom half, with one out, Pumpsie Green triples against Early Wynn (Pumpsie Green *triples*?), and then trots home with the game-ending counter, the only run of the game, which has been driven in on a sacrifice fly lofted to center by old Guess Who. What a game!

Alan Bradley's scorecard, it seems to me, is much more than a joke. It is also beyond art, for he has contrived to keep score during a game that only could have been played in my head. He can do this, of course, because we are both fans, he and I, and he knows that true fans still schedule these fanciful, unpardonably boyish entertainments to light up the miserable pre-dawn darkness or the endless late-afternoon of middle age. He is thoughtful enough to remember, from some writings of mine, that I would want to pitch and that the scene of my triumph is always the Fens. He and I have never met, but we are friends now—friends in baseball. This way of connecting, this family feeling, means almost more to me, I find, than the boisterous excitements of the World Series or the aesthetic tingle of a neatly executed hit-and-run play. The game has kept my interest, over many years, for reasons I have tried to set down, but its most surprising attribute may be its effortless, disarming capacity to bring its adherents closer together. A great many strangers write me baseball letters throughout the year—men and women, teen-agers, junior-college players, retired minor-leaguers, a female concert violinist, a corporation lawyer, housewives, law students, a minimalist painter from Virginia, a college president, a soldier in Germany, an eighty-four-year-old widow in Maine, many others—to express their feelings about our pastime. Often they start by thanking me (or correcting me) for something I have written, but then there is a shift (and another page or two or three of the letter) as they begin to put down their own baseball recollections and attachments, and, very often, to express their anger and sadness over its recent alterations, and by the end of the letter I sense that I have been offered not just a view of the game but a view of life. I can never respond adequately to such a compliment—I am always weeks and weeks behind in my baseball correspondence—but now and then these disarming, funny, intensely private letters have led to a longer correspondence (with a Tiger-smitten oral surgeon in Detroit, say) and to the beginning of a lifelong friendship. The same thing—the same suddenly offered glimpse of self—happens sometimes when I am on the field or in some clubhouse or in the stands, in pursuit of a story. An old pitcher, now a scout, tells me about his farm-boy beginnings in North Carolina that were first altered one morning when a shiny black Cadillac rolled up the red-dirt road to his house and yielded a dapper, citified Cardinals' scout who had come to watch him throw. A great present-day pitcher unexpectedly begins to describe his work as art, as ballet, and, on another afternoon, a famous catcher points out the trifling, everyday patterns of the game—the arrangement of infielders in response to a foul ball—that he finds so moving and satisfying. A Hall-of-Fame fireballer and a never-was, one-season Class A southpaw talk about their craft with equal seriousness and passion, and a suddenly and tragically failed Pirate hurler goes through an imaginary inning for me, pitch by pitch, against a great team—just as I do alone sometimes, in the dark, with Alan Bradley keeping score. We are all moved, or want to be, and the game invites us to that end. As E. M. Forster said (I can still see him, with one spiked foot up on the top step of the dugout and his keen, Ozark-blue eyes, under the peak of the pulled-down cap, fixed on some young batter just now stepping up to the plate), Only connect.

Distance

On the afternoon of October 2nd, 1968—a warm, sunshiny day in St. Louis—Mickey Stanley, the Detroit Tiger shortstop, singled to center field to lead off the top of the ninth inning of the opening game of the 1968 World Series. It was only the fifth hit of the game for the Tigers, who by this time were trailing the National League Champion St. Louis Cardinals by a score of 4–0, so there were only minimal sounds of anxiety among the 54,692 spectators—home-town rooters, for the most part—in the stands at Busch Stadium. The next batter, the dangerous Al Kaline, worked the count to two and two and then fanned, swinging away at a fastball, to an accompanying roar from the crowd. A moment later, there was a second enormous cheer, louder and more sustained than the first. The Cardinal catcher, Tim McCarver, who had straightened up to throw the ball back to his pitcher, now hesitated. The pitcher, Bob Gibson, a notoriously swift worker on the mound, motioned to his battery mate to return the ball. Instead, McCarver pointed with his gloved hand at something behind Gibson's head. Gibson, staring uncomprehendingly at his catcher, yelled, "Throw the goddam ball back, will you! C'mon, c'mon, let's *go!*" Still holding the ball, McCarver pointed again, and Gibson, turning around, read the illuminated message on the center-field scoreboard, which perhaps only he in the ballpark had not seen until that moment: "Gibson's fifteenth strikeout in one game ties the all-time World Series record held by Sandy Koufax." Gibson, at the center of a great tureen of noise, dug at the dirt of the mound with his spikes and then uneasily doffed his cap. ("I *hate* that sort of thing," he said later.) With the ball retrieved at last, he went to work on the next Tiger, Norm Cash, a left-handed batter, who ran the count to two and two, fouled off several pitches, and then struck out, swinging at a slider. Gibson, a long-legged, powerfully built right-hander, whose habitual aura of glower-

125

ing intensity on the mound seemed to deepen toward rancor whenever his club was ahead in the late stages of a game, now swiftly attacked the next Detroit hitter, Willie Horton. Again the count went to two and two and stuck there while Horton fouled off two or three pitches. Gibson stretched and threw again, and Horton, a righty batter, flinched away from the pitch, which seemed headed for his rib cage, but the ball, another slider, broke abruptly away under his fists and caught the inside corner of the plate. Tom Gorman, the home-plate umpire, threw up his right hand, and the game was over. McCarver, talking about this moment not long ago (he is now a radio and television broadcaster with the Phillies), said, "I can still see that last pitch, and I'll bet Willie Horton thinks to this day that the ball hit him—that's how much it broke. Talk about a batter *shuddering!*"

Bob Gibson's one-game World Series record of seventeen strike-outs stands intact, and so do my memories of that famous afternoon. In recent weeks, I have firmed up my recollections by consulting the box score and the inning-by-inning recapitulations of the game, by watching filmed high-lights of the play, and by talking to a number of participants, including Gibson himself. (He had had no idea, he told me, that he was close to a record that afternoon. "You're concentrating so hard out there that you don't think of those things," he said.) Gibson seemed to take absolute charge of that game in the second inning, when he struck out the side on eleven pitches. By the end of four innings, he had run off eight strikeouts. Not until I reëxamined the box score, however, did I realize that there had been only two ground-ball outs by the Tigers in the course of nine innings. This, too, must be a record (baseball statistics, for once, don't tell us), but the phenomenally low figure, when taken along with the seventeen strikeouts, suggests what kind of pitching the Tiger batters were up against that afternoon. Most National League batters in the nineteen-sixties believed that Gibson's fastball com-pared only with the blazers thrown by the Dodgers' Sandy Koufax (who retired in 1966 with an arthritic elbow) and by the Reds' Jim Maloney. Gibson's pitch flashed through the strike zone with a unique, upward-moving, right-to-left sail that snatched it away from a right-handed batter or caused it to jump up and in at a left-handed swinger—a natural break of six to eight inches—and hitters who didn't miss the ball altogether usually fouled it off or nudged it harmlessly into the air. The pitch, which was delivered with a driving, downward flick of Gibson's long forefinger and middle finger (what pitchers call "cutting the ball"), very much resembled an inhumanly fast slider, and was often taken for such by batters who were unfamiliar with his stuff. Joe Pepitone, of the Yankees, concluded the All-Star Game of 1965 by fanning on three successive Gibson fastballs and then shook his head and called out to the pitcher, "Throw me that slider one more time!" Gibson, to be sure, did have a slider—a superior breaking pitch that arrived, disconcertingly, at about three-quarters of the speed of the fastball and, most of the time, with exquisite control. Tim McCarver, who caught Gibson longer than anyone else, says that Gibson became a great pitcher during the summer of 1966 (his sixth full season in the majors), when he achieved absolute mastery of the outside corner of the plate while pitching to right-handed batters and—it was the same pitch, of course—the inside corner to left-handed batters. He could hit this sliver of air with his fastball or his slider with equal consistency, and he worked the opposite edge of the plate as well. "He *lived* on the corners," McCarver said. A third Gibson delivery was a fastball that broke downward instead of up and away; for this pitch, he held the ball with his fingers parallel to the seams (instead of across the seams, as was the case with the sailer), and he twisted his wrist counterclockwise as he threw— "turning it over," in mound parlance. He also had a curveball, adequate but unextraordinary, that he threw mostly to left-handers and mostly for balls, to set up an ensuing fastball. But it was the combination of the devastating slider and the famous fastball (plus some other, less tangible assets that we shall get to in time) that made Gibson almost untouchable at his best, just as Sandy Koufax's down-diving curveball worked in such terrible (to hitters) concert with his illustrious upriding fastball.

"Hitting is rhythm," McCarver said to me, "and if you allow major-league hitters to see only one pitch—to swing repeatedly through a certain area of the plate—eventually they'll get to you and begin to hit it, even if it's a great fastball. But anybody who can control and switch off between two first-class pitches will make the hitters start reaching, either in or out, and then the game belongs to the pitcher. Besides all that, Bob had such great stuff and was so intimidating out there that he'd make the batter open up his front shoulder just a fraction too fast, no matter what the count was. The other key to good hitting, of course, is keeping that shoulder—the left shoulder for a right-handed batter, I mean, and vice versa—in place, and the most common flaw is pulling it back. Gibson had guys pulling back that shoulder who normally wouldn't be caught dead doing it. Their ass was in the dugout, as we say."

Mike Shannon, who played third base behind Gibson in the 1968 Series opening game (he didn't handle the ball once), remembers feeling pity for the Detroit batters that afternoon. "Most of them had never seen Gibby before," he said, "and they had no *idea* what they were up against." Shannon, who is now a television game announcer with the Cards, told me that he encounters some of the 1968 Tigers from time to time in the course of his baseball travels, and that they almost compulsively want to talk about the game. "It's as if they can't believe it to this day," he said. "But neither can

I. I've never seen major-league hitters overmatched that way. It was like watching a big-league pitcher against Little League batters. It was frightening."

Gibson, of course, was already a celebrated winning pitcher by 1968. Like many other fans, I had first become aware of his fastball and his unique pitching mannerisms and his burning intensity on the mound when he won two out of the three games he pitched against the Yankees in the 1964 World Series, including a tense, exhausting victory in the clinching seventh game. Then, in 1967, I had watched him capture three of the Cardinals' four October victories over the Red Sox, again including the seventh game—a feat that won him the Most Valuable Player award for that Series. I had also seen him work eight or ten regular-season games over the previous five years or more. Although he was of only moderate size for a pitcher—six feet one and about a hundred and eighty-five pounds—Gibson always appeared to take up a lot of space on the mound, and the sense of intimidation that McCarver mentioned had something to do with his sombre, almost funereal demeanor as he stared in at his catcher, with his cap pulled low over his black face and strong jaw, and with the ball held behind his right hip (he always wore a sweatshirt under his uniform, with the long, Cardinals-red sleeves extending all the way down to his wrists), and with his glove cocked on his left hip, parallel to the ground. Everything about him looked mean and loose—arms, elbows, shoulders, even his legs—as, with a quick little shrug, he launched into his delivery. When there was no one on base, he had an old-fashioned full crank-up, with the right foot turning in midmotion to slip into its slot in front of the mound and his long arms coming together over his head before his backward lean, which was deep enough to require him to peer over his left shoulder at his catcher while his upraised left leg crooked and kicked. The ensuing sustained forward drive was made up of a medium-sized stride of that leg and a blurrily fast, slinglike motion of the right arm, which came over at about three-quarters height and then snapped down and (with the fastball and the slider) across his left knee. It was not a long drop-down delivery like Tom Seaver's (for contrast), or a tight, brisk, body-opening motion like Whitey Ford's.

The pitch, as I have said, shot across the plate with a notable amount of right-to-left (from Gibson's vantage point) action, and his catchers sometimes gave the curious impression that they were cutting off a ball that was headed on a much longer journey—a one-hundred-foot fastball. But with Gibson pitching you were always a little distracted from the plate and the batter, because his delivery continued so extravagantly after the ball was released that you almost felt that the pitch was incidental to the whole affair. The follow-through sometimes suggested a far-out basketball move—a fast downcourt feint. His right leg, which was up and twisted to the right in the air as the ball was let go (all normal enough for a right-handed pitcher), now continued forward in a sudden sidewise rush, crossing his planted left leg, actually stepping over it, and he finished with a full running step toward the right-field foul line, which wrenched his body in the same direction, so that he now had to follow the flight of the ball by peering over his *right* shoulder. Both his arms whirled in the air to help him keep his balance during this acrobatic maneuver, but the key to his overpowering speed and stuff was not the strength of his pitching arm—it was the powerful, driving thrust of his legs, culminating in that final extra step, which brought his right foot clomping down on the sloping left-hand side of the mound, with the full weight of his body slamming and twisting behind it. (Gibson's arm never gave him undue trouble, but he had serious difficulties with his knees in the latter stages of his career, and eventually had to have a torn cartilage removed from the right knee, which had pushed off to start all the tens of thousands of his pitches over the years and had then had to withstand the punishing force of the last stage of his unique delivery.) All in all, the pitch and its extended amplifications made it look as if Gibson were leaping at the batter, with hostile intent. He always looked much closer to the plate at the end than any other pitcher; he made pitching seem unfair.

The players in the Detroit clubhouse after Gibson's seventeen-strikeout game had none of the aggrieved, blustery manner of batters on a losing team who wish to suggest that only bad luck or their own bad play kept them from putting away a pitcher who has just beaten them. Denny McLain, the starting Tiger pitcher, who had won thirty-one games that summer but had lasted only five innings in the Series opener, said, "I was awed. I was *awed*," and Dick McAuliffe, the Detroit second baseman, said that he could think of no one he had ever faced with whom Gibson could be compared. "He doesn't remind me of anybody," he said. "He's all by himself."

I was awed, too, of course, but nothing I had seen on the field at Busch Stadium that afternoon startled me as much as Gibson's postgame comportment in the clubhouse. In October of 1964 and again in 1967, I had noticed that Bob Gibson often appeared to be less elated than his teammates in the noisy, jam-packed, overexuberant World Series locker rooms—a man at a little distance from the crowd. But somehow I must have expected that his astounding performance here in the 1968 opener would change him—that his record-breaking turn on the mound would make him more lighthearted and accommodating; he would be smiling and modest and self-deprecating, but also joyful about his feat, and this would diminish that almost immeasurable distance he had just established, out on the field, between himself and the rest of us. He would seem boyish, in short, and we, the grown-up watchers of the game, would then be able to call him by his first name (even if we didn't know him), and forgive him for what he had done, and thus to love him, as is the ancient custom in these high sporting dramas. But Gibson was unchanged. Talking to the sportswriters gathered in a thick, uncomfortable crowd around his locker, he looked at each reporter who asked him a question (Gibson is an exceptionally handsome man, with small ears, very dark skin, and a strikingly direct gaze) and then answered it gravely and briefly. When one writer asked him if he had always been as competitive as he had seemed on this day, he said yes, and he added that he had played several hundred games of ticktacktoe against one of his young daughters and that she had yet to win a game from him. He said this with a little smile, but it seemed to me that he meant it: he couldn't let himself lose to anyone. Then someone asked him if he had been surprised by what he had just done on the field, and Gibson said, "I'm never surprised by anything I do."

The shock of this went out across the ten-deep bank of writer faces like a seismic wave, and the returning, murmurous counterwaves of reaction were made up of uneasy laughter and whispers of "*What* did he say?" and some ripples of disbelieving silence and (it seemed to me) a considerable, almost visible wave of dislike, or perhaps hatred. This occasion, it should be remembered, was before the time when players' enormous salaries and their accompanying television-bred notoriety had given birth to a kind of athlete who could choose to become famous for his sullenness and foul temper, just as another might be identified by his gentle smile and unvarying sweetness of disposition. In 1968, ballplayers, particularly black ballplayers in near-Southern cities like St. Louis, did not talk outrageously to the press. Bob Gibson, however, was not projecting an image but telling us a fact about himself. He was beyond us, it seemed, but the truth of the matter is that no one at Busch Stadium should have been much surprised by his achievement that afternoon, for it was only a continuation of the kind of pitching he had sustained all through that summer of 1968—a season in which he won twenty-two games for the Cardinals while losing nine, and also compiled an earned-run average of 1.12 runs per game: the best pitching performance, by that measurement, in the history of modern baseball.

O

When Bob Gibson retired, at the age of thirty-nine, at the end of the 1975 season, after seventeen summers with the Cardinals, he had won two hundred and fifty-one games, and his record of 3,117 strikeouts was second only to Walter Johnson's 3,508. Last year, however, Gaylord Perry, who is still going strong at the age of forty-two, passed Gibson on the lifetime-strikeout list (Perry is now with the Yankees and has 3,267 whiffs to his credit at this writing), while three other active pitchers—Nolan Ryan, Tom Seaver, and

Steve Carlton—may surpass Gibson's mark next summer.* This kind of erosion of the game's most famous fixed numbers—the landmarks of the pastime—by swirling tides of newcomers is always happening, of course; it is the process that makes baseball statistics seem alive and urgent to the true fan. But Gibson's displacement unsettled me, and when I read in the sports pages last spring that he was among the players who would become eligible for election to baseball's Hall of Fame at the end of this season, after the obligatory five-year post-retirement waiting period (the qualifications for official immortality are established by the Baseball Writers Association of America, whose three hundred-odd members conduct a Hall of Fame balloting in the off-season each year), I sensed that Gibson might be about to slip away into the quiet corridors of baseball history. It is always a discomfiting moment for a long-term follower of the game when a favorite player, whose every feat and gesture on the field still retain clarity and color, is declared safe for embronzement, but the possibility of Bob Gibson's imminent apotheosis at Cooperstown came as a shock to me. He seemed too impatient, too large, and too restless a figure to be stilled and put away in this particular fashion; somehow, he would shrug off the speeches and honorifics when they came, just as he had busied himself unhappily on the mound when the crowd stopped the rush of the game to cheer him at Busch Stadium that afternoon in 1968. For me, at least, Bob Gibson was still burning to pitch to the next batter. But in another, oddly opposite sense it seemed wrong to think of Gibson as a participant in the soft, sweet rituals with which newly elected baseball immortals are inducted into the Hall of Fame at the ceremonial in Cooperstown each August—the reading of the players' records and their official citations; their speeches of acceptance and gratitude; the obligatory picture-taking, with the still-young heroes, in civilian clothes, holding up their plaques and standing among the smaller, white-haired, earlier great figures who have come back for the occasion: old gents at a reunion, blinking in the hot upstate sunlight—because baseball up to now has never quite known what to make of Bob Gibson, and has slightly but persistently failed to pay him his full due as a player and as a man. With this conviction in mind, I determined early this summer to look up Gibson and try to get to know him a little better. I wanted to see how he was faring now that he could no longer stare down at the batters of the world from the height of the pitcher's mound. I knew that he was still living in Omaha, his home town, and when I reached him there by telephone he told me to come on out if I wanted to. Not a warm

*By the end of the 1981 season, Gaylord Perry had accounted for 3,336 lifetime strikeouts, while Ryan stood at 3,249, Carlton at 3,148, and Seaver at 3,075. Steve Carlton's total is a new National League record, eclipsing Gibson's old mark, because, unlike Perry and Ryan, he has pitched only in that league.

invitation, but not a wary one, either. In the next week or two, I mentioned my forthcoming trip to some friends of mine—good baseball fans, all of them—and noticed that many of them seemed to have forgotten Bob Gibson's eminence and élan, if, indeed, they had even been aware of them. In the history of the game, it seemed, as in his playing days, he already stood at a little distance from the crowd, a little beyond us all. But then I talked about Gibson with some players—old teammates or opponents of his—and they responded more warmly.

Pete Rose, who talks in the same runaway-taxi style in which he runs bases, said, "I'm always afraid I'll forget some pitcher when I start rating them, because I've faced so many of them. I started out against people like Warren Spahn, you know. But the best pitcher I ever batted against was Juan Marichal, because he threw so many goddam different kinds of good pitches against you. The hardest thrower of them all was Sandy Koufax, and the greatest competitor was Bob Gibson. He worked so fast out there, and he always had the hood up. He always wanted to close his own deal. He wasn't no badman, but he never talked to you, because he was battling you so hard. I sure as hell don't miss batting against him, but I miss him in the game."

Billy Williams, now a coach for the Cubs, who hit four hundred and twenty-six home runs during his sixteen years with that team and two years with the Oakland A's, told me, "Bob Gibson always got *on* with it. He didn't stand around out there and look around the park, you know. You always got the same message from him: 'Look, I'm goin' to throw this pitch and either you hit it or I get your ass out.' You like a guy like that. The infielders were never on their heels out there behind him. Everyone's on their toes, and it's a better game for everybody. I used to love the afternoon games at Wrigley Field when Gibby pitched against our Fergie Jenkins, because you could always plan something early for that evening. They *hurried*. Gibby was as serious as anybody you ever saw, and you had to be ready at all times. There was hitters that tried to step out on him, to break his pace, but if you did that too often he'd knock you down. He let you know who was out there on the mound. Made himself felt. He never let up, even on the hottest days there in St. Louis, which is the hottest place in the world. Just walked out there in the heat and threw the ball past people."

Tim McCarver said, "He was an intimidating, arrogant-looking athlete. The arrogance he projected toward batters was fearsome. There was no guile to his pitching, just him glaring down at that batter. He wanted the game played on his own terms. He worked very fast, and that pace was part of his personality on the mound, part of the way he dominated the game. One of the things he couldn't stand was a catcher coming out there to talk to him. In my first full year with the Cardinals, when I was only twenty-one years old, our manager was Johnny Keane, who was a fanatic about having a catcher establish communications with his pitcher. So I'd get a signal from Keane that meant 'Go on out there and settle him down,' but then I'd look out and see Hoot glaring in at me." McCarver laughed, and shook his head. "Well, sometimes I'd walk out halfway, to try to appease both parties!"

McCarver is an intimate friend of Bob Gibson's, and he told me that Gibson was much the same off the field as on the mound. "Bob is relatively shy," he said. "He's a nice man, but he's quiet. He doesn't enjoy small talk. He doesn't like to waste his time with anything that's weak or offhand. He wants to deal from strength all the time. That's why he projects this uppity-black-man figure that so many people in baseball seem to hate. He's very proud, you know, and he had a ghetto upbringing, so you could understand why he was so sensitive to bigotry—up to a point. But we have a great relationship—me, a kid from Memphis, Tennessee, and him, an elegant black man from Omaha. Any relationship you get into with Bob is going to be intense. He's a strong man, with strong feelings."

Joe Torre, the manager of the New York Mets, who played with Gibson from 1969 to 1974, is also a close friend. When I called on him late in June, in the clubhouse at Shea Stadium, and told him I was about to go west to visit Gibson, he beckoned me over to a framed photograph on one wall of his office. The picture shows the three friends posing beside a batting cage in their Cardinals uniforms. Torre, a heavy-faced man with dark eyebrows and a falsely menacing appearance, and McCarver, who has a cheerful, snub-nosed Irish look to him, are both grinning at the photographer, with their arms around the shoulders of Bob Gibson, who is between them; it's impossible to tell if Gibson is smiling, though, because his back is turned to the camera. "That says it all," Torre said. "He alienated a lot of people—most of all the press, who didn't always know what to make of him. He has this great confidence in himself: 'Hey, I'm me. Take me or leave me.' There was never any selling of Bob Gibson. He's an admirable man. On the mound, he had very tangible intangibles. He had that hunger, that killer instinct. He threw at a lot of batters but not nearly as many as you've heard. But he'd never deny it if you asked him. I think this is great. There's no other sport except boxing that has such a hard one-on-one confrontation as you get when a pitcher and a hitter go up against each other. Any edge you can get on the hitter, any doubt you can put in his mind, you use. And Bob Gibson would never give up that edge. He was your enemy out there. I try to teach this to our pitchers. The more coldness, the more mystery about you, the more chance you have of getting them out.

"I played against him before I played with him, and either way he never talked to you. Never. I was on some All-Star teams with him, and even then he didn't talk to you. There was the one in Minnesota, when I was catching him and we were ahead 6–5, I think, in the ninth. I'm catching, and Tony Oliva, a great hitter, is leading off, and Gibby goes strike one, strike two. Now I want a fastball up and in, I think to myself, and maybe I should go out there and tell him this—tell him, whatever he does, not to throw it down and in to Oliva. So I go out and tell him, and Gibby just gives me that look of his. Doesn't say a word. I go back and squat down and give him the signal— fastball up and in—and he throws it *down* and in, and Oliva hits it for a double to left center. To this day, I think Gibby did it on purpose. He didn't want to be told *anything*. So then there's an infield out, and then he strikes out the last two batters, of course, and we win. In the shower, I say, 'Nice pitching,' and he still doesn't say anything to me. Ask him about it."

Torre lit a long cigar, and said, "Quite a man. He can seem distant and uncaring to some people, but he's not the cold person he's been described as. There are no areas between us where he's withdrawn. Things go deep with him. I miss talking to him during the season, and it's my fault, because I'm always so damn busy. He doesn't call me, because he never wants to make himself a pain in the ass to a friend. But he is my friend. The other day, I got a photograph of himself he'd sent me, and he'd signed it 'Love, Bob.' How many other ballplayers are going to do that? How many other friends?"

Most ballplayers who are discussing a past rival or a teammate go directly to the man's craft—what pitches he could hit, his arm, his range afield, or (with pitchers) his stuff and what he threw when the count was against him. But I had begun to notice that the baseball people talking about Bob Gibson all seemed anxious to get at something deeper; Gibson the man was even more vivid and interesting to them than Gibson the great pitcher. Bill White, the well-known TV and radio announcer with the Yankees, played first base behind Gibson with the Cards for seven years, and was then traded to the Phillies and had to play against him. "He was tough and uncompromising," White told me. "Koufax and Don Drysdale were just the same, with variations for their personalities—they had that same hard state of mind. But I think a great black athlete is sometimes tougher in a game, because every black has had it tough on the way up. Any black player who has a sense of himself, who wants to make something of himself, has something of Bob Gibson's attitude. Gibson had a chip on his shoulder out there—which was good. He was mean enough. He had no remorse. I remember when he hit Jim Ray Hart on the shoulder—he was bending away from a pitch—and broke his collarbone. Bob didn't say anything to him. I'd been his roomie for a while on the Cards, but the first time I batted against him, when I went over to the Phillies, he hit me in the arm. It didn't surprise me at all."

And, once again, Mike Shannon: "I think every superior athlete has some special motivation. With Bob Gibson, it wasn't that he wanted to win so much as that he didn't want to lose. He *hated* to lose. He just wouldn't accept it."

○

It was ninety-seven degrees at the Omaha airport when I landed there early one evening in July, and when I called Bob Gibson from my motel he invited me to come on out and cool off with a dip in his pool. He picked me up in his car—a black 1972 Mercedes SEL, lovingly kept up, with CB equipment (his call signal is Redbird) and terse "BG" license plates. Gibson looked well kept up himself, in tailored jeans, a white polo shirt, thin gold spectacles, a gold bracelet on his left wrist, a World Series ring, and a necklace with a pendant "45" in gold—his old uniform number. He is forty-four years old, but only his glasses spoiled the impression that he was perfectly capable of working nine tough innings the next afternoon. I asked him what he did for exercise these days, and he said, "Nothing." I expressed surprise, and he said, "I played sports hard for thirty years, which is enough. Now I'm tired of all that." No apology, no accompanying smile or joke: no small talk. He spoke pleasantly enough, though, in a light, almost boyish voice, and when he did laugh—a little later, after we were more used to each other—the sound of it made me realize that only in the world of sports would he be considered anything but a young man. There were some quiet spells in the car during our longish drive out to his house, in Bellevue, a comfortable suburban district on the south side of town, but by the time we got there I had lost any sense of foreboding that I might have had about imposing myself on such a famously private man.

Bob Gibson has done well for himself in Omaha. He was born and grew up there in the black North Side ghetto; his mother was a laundress, and his father died before he was born. He was the youngest of seven children—his three sisters and three brothers are all still living—and at the time of his birth the family lived in a four-room shack. When he was an infant there, he was bitten on the ear by a rat. By the end of his playing days, Gibson was earning more than a hundred and fifty thousand dollars a year, which made him one of the two or three best-paid players of his time, and he invested his money with care. Today, he is the chairman of the board—an interracial board—of the Community Bank of Nebraska, which he helped get started seven years ago, and which does most of its business in the black community of Omaha. He is also the co-owner and the active, day-to-day manager of a new and successful medium-sized bar-restaurant called Gibby's, a couple of blocks away from Creighton University, which Gibson entered as a freshman on a basketball scholarship in 1954. Much of Gibson's life these days seems new. Gibby's opened in late 1978, and last November he was married to Wendy

Nelson, whom I met at their home, to the accompaniment of frenzied barking from their four-month-old miniature schnauzer, Mia. ("Kill, Mia!" Gibson said delightedly. "Kill, girl!") Wendy Gibson, a composed, striking-looking blond woman in her late twenties, is in the financial division of the local telephone company, where she works, by preference, on the very early shift, driving to work each day shortly after dawn in the family's *other* Mercedes. (Gibson's previous marriage, to Charline Johnson, ended in divorce some years ago; their children, Renee and Annette, are grown up and have moved away from Omaha. A captivating oil portrait of the two girls and their father—all of them much younger then—hangs in Gibson's study in his new house; the artist is an old friend and teammate, Curt Flood.) Wendy and Bob Gibson moved into their house last May. It is a spacious, comfortably furnished and carpeted three-story contemporary wooden structure, with a sundeck that looks over a steep hillside and a thick green growth of oaks and cottonwoods. A flight of steps leads down from the deck to a big swimming pool, which had had its inaugural only a week before my arrival. Bob Gibson is handy. He helped design the new house, and he put in the deck stairs and built a raised wooden patio beside the pool, and also did most of the landscape work on the grounds, laying in some old railroad ties to form a rose garden and planting shrubs and young trees everywhere. The pool was built to Gibson's design; its sides and bottom are painted black—a da Vinci-like idea of his, meant to help the water hold the heat of the sun in the spring and fall. Somehow, though, he had not remembered the warmish midsummer Nebraska sunshine, and when he and I slipped into the inky waves, the water temperature stood at ninety-two degrees—only a fraction cooler than the steamy, locust-loud night air. "Another mistake," Gibson said mildly. Swimming was a bit like sloshing through black-bean soup, but after a couple of turns up and down the pool he and I settled ourselves comfortably enough on the top steps at the shallow end, with our legs dangling in the water, and while Mia sniffed and circled me warily we talked a little baseball.

I asked Gibson if he recalled the low-and-inside pitch he had thrown to Tony Oliva in that All-Star game, against Joe Torre's signals.

"Well, I never really liked being on the All-Star team," he said. "I liked the honor of it, being voted one of the best, but I couldn't get used to the idea of playing with people from other teams in the league—guys who I'd have to go out and try to beat just a couple of days later. I didn't even like having Joe catch me—he was with the Braves then—because I figured he'd learn how to hit me. In that same game, he came out and told me not to throw the high fastball to Harmon Killebrew, because the word was that he ate up that pitch." Gibson's voice was almost incredulous as he said this. "Well, hell. I struck him out with three high fastballs. But in any of the All-Star games

136

where I got to pitch early"—Gibson was voted onto the National League All-Star squad eight times—"I'd always dress right away and get out of there in a hurry, before the other players got done and came into the clubhouse. I didn't want to hang around and make friends. I don't think there's any place in the game for a pitcher smiling and joking with the hitters. I was all business on the mound—it *is* a business, isn't it?—and I think some of the writers used to call me cold or arrogant because of that. I didn't want to be friends with anybody on the other side, except perhaps with Willie Stargell—how could you not talk to that guy? None of this was meant to scare guys, or anything. It was just the way I felt. When Orlando Cepeda was with us, I used to watch him and Marichal laughing and fooling around before a game. They'd been on the Giants together, you know. But then Cepeda would go out and *kill* Marichal at the plate—one of the best pitchers I ever saw—and when it was over they'd go to dinner together and laugh some more. It just made me shake my head. I didn't understand it."

I had been wondering how to bring up the business of his knocking down his old roommate Bill White, but now Gibson offered the story of his own accord. "Even before Bill was traded, I used to tell him that if he ever dived across the plate to swing at an outside pitch, the way he liked to, I'd have to hit him," he said. "And then, the very first time, he went for a pitch that was *this* far outside and swung at it, and so I hit him on the elbow with the next pitch. [Some years earlier, Gibson hit Duke Snider after similar provocation, and broke his elbow.] Bill saw it coming, and he yelled 'Yaah!' even before it got him. And I yelled over to him, 'You son of a bitch, you went for that outside ball! That pitch, that part of the plate, belongs to *me*! If I make a mistake inside, all right, but the outside is mine and don't you forget it.' He said, 'You're crazy,' but he understood me."

I mentioned a famous moment when Gibson had hit Tommie Agee, of the Mets, on the batting helmet with the very first pitch of the first inning of the first Cardinals spring-training game in 1968. Agee had come over from the Chicago White Sox and the American League in the previous winter, and when Gibson's first swallow of the spring conked him, several Gibson students among the Mets and Cardinals baseball writers in the press box at Al Lang Field called out, "Welcome to the National League, Tommie!" (Agee went to the hospital for observation, but was found not to have suffered serious injury.)

Gibson was silent for a moment, and then he said, "It's very easy to hit a batter in the body with a pitch. There's nothing to it. It's a lot harder to hit him in the head. Any time you hit him in the head, it's really his own fault. Anyway, that was just spring training."

Joe Torre had told me that the Agee-plunking was an accident, but I noted now that Gibson had not quite denied intention in the affair. He had put doubt in my mind, just as Torre had told me he would. He still wanted that edge.

"I did throw at John Milner in spring training once," Gibson went on, paddling his legs in the water. "Because of that swing of his—that dive at the ball." Milner, an outfielder then with the Mets and now with the Pirates, invariably takes a full-scale, left-handed downtown swing at the ball, as if he meant to pull every pitch into the right-field stands. "I don't like batters taking that big cut, with their hats falling off and their buttons popping and every goddam thing like that. It doesn't show any respect for the pitcher. That batter's not doing any thinking up there, so I'm going to *make* him think. The next time, he won't look so fancy out there. He'll be a better-looking hitter. So I got Milner that once, and then, months later, at Shea Stadium, Tom Seaver began to pitch me up and inside, knocking me down, and it took me a minute to realize that it must have been to pay me back for something *in spring training*. I couldn't believe that."

There was a little silence at poolside while I digested this. Gibson sounded almost like a veteran samurai warrior recalling an ancient code of pain and honor. I suggested that there must be days when he still badly missed being out there on the mound, back in the thick of things.

"No, I have no desire to get out and throw the fastball again," he said quietly. "Even if I wanted to, I couldn't."

I had noticed that Gibson limped slightly as he walked around the pool, and the accounts of some of his baseball injuries and how he had reacted to them at the time came back to me. In July of 1967, while pitching against the Pirates in St. Louis, he was struck just above his right ankle by a line drive off the bat of Roberto Clemente. He went down in a heap, but after the Cardinals trainer had treated the injury with a pain-deadening spray, Gibson insisted on staying in the game. He walked Willie Stargell, retired Bill Maze-roski on a pop-up, and then, firing a three-two pitch to Donn Clendenon, came down hard on the right leg with his characteristic spinning follow-through and snapped the already cracked bone. Dal Maxvill, then a Cardinals shortstop and now a Cardinals coach, said to me recently, "That was the most extraordinary thing I ever saw in baseball—Gibby pitching to those batters with a broken leg. Everyone who was there that day remembered it afterward, for always, and every young pitcher who came onto our club while Gibson was still with us was told about it. We didn't have too many pitchers turning up with upset stomachs or hangnails on our team after that."

Gibson came back to win three games against the Red Sox in the World Series that fall, but his next serious injury, in midseason of 1973, took a heavier toll. Leading off first base in a game against the Mets at Shea Stadium, he made a sudden dive back toward the base after an infield line drive was caught, but collapsed when his right knee buckled. The trainer and the team doctor came out to succor him, but Gibson cried "Don't touch it! Don't touch it!" and again refused to be taken out of the game. When the inning ended, he walked to the mound and began his warmup tosses and fell heavily to the ground. The surgeon—Dr. Stan London—who performed the cartilage operation the next day said afterward that Gibson had the knees of an eighty-year-old man. Gibson recovered in time to pitch and win a game that September, and he continued for two more full seasons on the mound, although, as he told me now, he sometimes had to sit in the clubhouse for two hours after a game before he felt able to head for the showers. "I'd had the left knee drained about seventeen times, too," he said. "I'd sit like this"—he hung his head and arms like a broken puppet—"and I'd think, *Why do I put up with this? Why, why?*" He laughed now, mocking himself. "I just couldn't give it up," he said. "Couldn't let go."

I asked if he'd become a different kind of pitcher then, using change-ups and slip pitches, the way many older hurlers do in their final seasons.

"No, I always threw hard," he said. "They didn't use me much in my final season, after I'd announced I was going to retire—I never did understand that. But once, when I hadn't pitched in three weeks, they brought me into a game against Houston in extra innings—I was the last pitcher we had—and I struck out the side on nine pitches that were nothing but fastballs. So I still had something left, even at the end. I always had pretty good control, you know, so it wasn't like I didn't know what I was doing out there. But later that season I gave up a grand-slam home run to Pete LaCock, of the Cubs, and that told me it was about time for me to get off the mound for good." Gibson spoke lightly enough, but at the time this home run was an almost insupportable blow to his pride. A pitcher who was with the Cubs that year told me that as LaCock (who is not exactly famous as a slugger) circled the bases, Gibson stalked after him around the base paths, reviling him for what he had done.

"Pitching is about ninety percent thinking," Gibson went on. "I threw hard when I was younger, but I didn't know how to get people out. I don't care how hard you throw, somebody's going to hit it if you don't think out there. It's not all that detailed—you don't think three or four pitches ahead. But one pitch might set up the next two you throw—it depends what the guy does with it. You know. If he misses a fastball by a foot, then he'll see another one. If he fouls it off or *just* misses it, he'll probably get a breaking ball next. It isn't exactly scientific, or anything."

Gibson suddenly laughed in the darkness beside me. "But not everybody understands what a pitcher *does*," he said. "About his control, I mean. I remember when Mike Shannon was moved in from the outfield and began playing third base for us—back in the middle sixties, it was. He was really nervous over there. He kept asking me where I wanted him to play—up or back, near the line or away. He wanted instructions. I always told him I didn't give a damn where he played unless there was a right-handed batter coming up with a man on first and less than two out, but then he should be ready, because he'd be getting a ground ball, right to him or around his area. And I'd throw a sinker down and in, and the batter would hit it on the ground to Mike, to start the double play, and when we came in off the field Mike would look at me with his mouth open, and he'd say, 'But how did you *know*?' He didn't have the faintest idea that when I threw that pitch to the batter he *had* to hit it to him there! He didn't know what pitching was all about."

○

To go back a little, Gibson also won his second start in the 1968 Cardinals-Tigers World Series—a 10–1 decision in the fourth game, during which he fanned ten batters and whacked a home run. It was Gibson's seventh straight World Series victory—an all-time record. The Tigers, however, captured the Series, rallying in stimulating fashion after trailing by three games to one, and beating Gibson in the memorable finale, when Detroit outfielder Jim Northrup, batting with two out and two on in the seventh inning of the scoreless game, smashed a long drive that was misjudged by Curt Flood in center field, who then slipped on the turf and allowed the ball to go over his head for a triple. The Tigers won the game by 4–1, and the Most Valuable Player award for the Series went to Mickey Lolich, a portly left-handed sinkerball specialist, who won the second, fifth, and seventh games. Gibson, however, had established a Series record of thirty-five strikeouts (still standing), and a few weeks later he was named the Most Valuable Player of the National League for 1968 and became the unanimous winner of the Cy Young Award as the league's best pitcher. The following year, 1969, Gibson compiled a 20–13 record, with an earned-run average of 2.18, and in 1970 his 23–7 won-lost mark and 3.12 E.R.A. won him the Cy Young again. Injuries began to gnaw him after that, but he declined only stubbornly, throwing a no-hitter against the Pirates in 1971 and running off eleven straight victories in the course of a 19–11 season in 1972. His lifetime earned-run average of 2.91 runs per game is the ninth-best in baseball history. (Walter Johnson's 2.37 leads all comers, while Tom Seaver, at 2.62, and Jim Palmer, at 2.73, stand third and fourth on the all-time list at this writing.)

Many observers (including this one) believe that Gibson's 1.12 earned-run average in 1968 is one of the Everests of the game, ranking with Joe DiMaggio's fifty-six-consecutive-game hitting streak in 1941 and Hack Wilson's hundred and ninety runs batted in in 1930. Gibson's record, however, was not much noted or celebrated in its time, partly because it was achieved in a summer during which the pitchers in both leagues established a mesmerizing dominance over the batters. The leagues' combined batting average fell to an all-time low of .237, and twenty-one percent of all games played were shutouts. Many pitchers came up with startling performances that summer. Gaylord Perry, of the Giants, and Ray Washburn, of the Cardinals, threw no-hit games on successive days at Candlestick Park; Jerry Koosman, a rookie, won nineteen games for the Mets; Denny McLain, as I have noted, won thirty-one games for the Tigers; and Don Drysdale, of the Dodgers, ran off fifty-eight and two-thirds consecutive shutout innings—a record that still stands. At the end of the year, the baseball fathers studied these figures and determined to rebalance the game by shaving five inches off the height of the mound (reducing it to ten inches), and by closing up the upper and lower limits of the strike zone. Gibson's golden season may always appear a mite tarnished by these circumstances, but even a brief rundown of his 1968 summer outings suggests that in that single season he came as close to some ideal of pitching as most of us are ever likely to witness or wish for. Younger fans may argue for Ron Guidry's marvellous 25–3 season for the Yankees in 1978, when he threw nine shutouts and wound up with a 1.74 earned-run average. Others will cite Steve Carlton's one-man-band performance in 1972, when he finished with an earned-run average of 1.97 and a record of 27–10— all this for a frightful last-place Phillies team that won only fifty-nine games in all—while geezers may bring up Carl Hubbell's 23–12 and 1.66 earned-run mark for the Giants in 1933. But no matter: these great case studies of the game are forever moot.

On May 28, 1968, Bob Gibson lost to the Giants, 3–1, and saw his record for the year decline to three victories and five defeats. Surprisingly, however, his earned-run average of 1.52 for the young season was fifth in the National League at this point—an oddity explicable by the fact that his teammates had supplied him with a total of four runs in the five games he lost: starvation fare. On June 2nd, Gibson pitched the Cardinals into first place (this was before the leagues had been subdivided into East and West sectors) with a 6–3 victory over the Mets; the final Mets run—a homer by Ed Charles—came in the seventh inning. It was also the final run that Gibson surrendered in the month of June, for he threw shutout games in his next five outings. Only the last of these brought him much attention from the national press, and that came because reporters had noticed that his next appearance, on July 1st, would be against the Dodgers in Los Angeles, and that his mound opponent there would be Don Drysdale, whose record shutout skein of fifty-eight and two-thirds innings had been set over a span of six games in late May and early June. A matchup between the two seemed exciting indeed, for Drysdale, who was six feet five and threw almost sidearm, had a hostile scowl, a devastating fastball, and a reputation for knocking down batters he didn't care for: another intimidator. Gibson by now had forty-eight scoreless innings to his credit, but the tension of the famous confrontation vanished in the very first inning, when two Dodgers singled and Gibson, while pitching to Ron Fairly, let go a wild pitch that allowed Len Gabrielson to score from third base. Gibson had lost the duel with Drysdale and a shot at his record, but he won the game, by 5–1. He then pitched a shutout against the Giants, beat Houston by 8–1, and afterward shut out the Mets and the Phillies in succession. On July 30th, once again facing the Mets, Gibson surrendered a run with two out in the fourth inning, when Ed Charles scored on a double by Eddie Kranepool—the same Ed Charles who had homered against him on June 2nd. In that span—from June 2nd to July 30th—Gibson had given up two earned runs (and two runs in toto) in ninety-six and two-thirds innings.

Gibson won that Mets game, and he did not lose a game, in fact, until August 24th, when he fanned fifteen Pirates but lost, 6–4, after giving up a three-run homer to Willie Stargell. Between May 28th and August 24th, Gibson had won fifteen straight games, ten of them shutouts. He threw two more shutouts in his next two outings, and somebody figured out that in the course of three straight games in August, Gibson's infielders had to make only eight assists. (His shortstop, Dal Maxvill, told a reporter, "It's like having a night off out there when he's pitching.") Possibly tired by now—or perhaps a bit understimulated, since his club had run away with the league by this point, having established a fourteen-and-a-half-game lead over the second-place Reds by August 1st—Gibson lost three games in September, one of them to the no-hitter by Gaylord Perry. His final victory, on September 27th, was a 1–0 decision over the Astros—his thirteenth shutout. His season was over; the World Series and the Tigers were just ahead.

A further thin cement of statistics will finish the monument. Gibson completed twenty-eight of the thirty-four games he started in 1968, and was never removed in the middle of an inning—never knocked out of the box. His 1.12 earned-run average is second only to the all-time low of 1.01, established by the Red Sox' Hub Leonard in 1914, and it eclipsed the old National League mark of 1.22, set by Grover Cleveland Alexander in 1915. Gibson's thirteen shutouts are second only to the sixteen that Alexander achieved the following summer. But those very low early figures, it should be understood, must be slightly discounted, for they were established in the sludgy, Pleistocene era of the game, when aces like Leonard and Alexander and Walter Johnson and the White Sox' Red Faber regularly ran off season-long earned-run averages of two runs or less per game, thanks to the dead ball then in use. The lively ball, which came into the game in 1921, when the owners began to notice how much the fans seemed to enjoy watching a young outfielder (and former pitcher) named George Herman Ruth hit towering drives into the bleachers, put an end to the pitchers' hold over the game, and none of the four worthies I have cited ever pitched consistently in the

less-than-three-runs-per-game level after 1922. Bob Gibson, we may conclude, was the man most responsible for the *next* major change in the
dimensions of the sport—the lowering of the mound and the shrinkage of
the strike zone that came along in 1969. Gibson, like all pitchers, complained
bitterly when these new rules were announced, but Bob Broeg, the sports
editor of the St. Louis *Post-Dispatch* and the dean of Cardinals sportswriters,
told him he had only himself to blame. "I said, 'Goddam it, Gib, you're
changing the game!' " Broeg told me not long ago. " 'It isn't fun anymore.
You're making it like hockey.' "

○

On another day, Omaha slowly came to a broil under a glazy white sun
while Gibson and I ran some early-morning errands in his car—a visit to
his bank, a stop at the drive-in window of another bank, where he picked
up the payroll checks for Gibby's—and wound up at the restaurant, where
the daytime help greeted the boss cheerfully. Gibson seemed in an easy
frame of mind, and he looked younger than ever. I recalled that many of
his teammates had told me what good company he was in the dugout and
on road trips—on days when he wasn't pitching. He was a comical, shrill-
voiced bench jockey, and a grouchy but lighthearted clubhouse agitator,
who was sometimes known to bang a bat repeatedly and horribly on the
metal locker of a teammate who was seen to be suffering the aftereffects of
too many ice-cream sodas the previous evening. While he drove, Gibson,
with a little urging, recalled how he had pitched to some of the prime hitters of his day—inside fastballs to Willie Mays (who feasted on breaking
pitches), belt-high inside deliveries to Eddie Mathews, low and away to
Roberto Clemente, and so on. He said that Frank Robinson used to deceive
pitchers with his plate-crowding (Robinson was a right-handed slugger of
fearsome power, whose customary stance at the plate was that of an impatient subway traveller leaning over the edge of the platform and peering
down the tracks for the D train), because they took it to mean that he was
eager for an inside pitch. "Besides," he said, "they'd be afraid of hitting him
and putting him on base. So they'd work him outside, and he'd hit the shit
out of the ball. I always tried him inside, and I got him out there—sometimes. He was like Willie Mays—if you got the ball outside to Willie at all,
he'd just *kill* you. The same with Clemente. I could throw him a fastball
knee-high on the outside corner seventeen times in a row, but if I ever got
it two inches up, he'd hit it out of sight. That's the mark of a good hitter—
the tiniest mistake and he'll punish you. Other batters—well, somebody
like Joe Adcock was just a guess hitter. You'd pitch him up and in, and he'd
swing and miss every time. He just didn't give a damn. I don't know what's

the matter with so many hitters—it's like their brains small up." He shook his head and laughed softly. "Me, too. I got beat by Tommy Davis twice the same way. In one game, I'd struck him out three times on sliders away. But I saw that he'd been inching up and inching up toward that part of the plate, so I decided to fool him and come inside, and he hit a homer and beat me, one–oh. And then, in another game, I did exactly the same thing. I tried to outthink him, and he hit the inside pitch for a homer, and it was one–oh all over again. So I could get dumb, too."

I said that he didn't seem to have made too many mistakes in the summer of '68. Gibson thought for a moment or two and said, "You can't say it was a fluke, although some people *have* said that. Just say it was totally unusual. Everything I threw that year seemed to go where I wanted it. Everything was down, all year. I was never that good again, because they went and changed the rules on me. The next year was a terrific struggle. I had a good season, but I never worked so hard in my life, because so many of my breaking pitches were up. I'll never know, but I doubt very seriously I'd have had another one-point-one-two E.R.A., even if they'd left the mound where it was. I'd like to think I'd really perfected my pitching to that point, but I'll never know."

The talk shifted to pitchers, and Gibson (echoing Pete Rose) said he thought that Juan Marichal had been the best hurler of their time, because of his absolute control. "I had a better fastball and a better slider, but he was a better pitcher than me or Koufax," he said. Among contemporary pitchers, he had warm things to say about the Phillies' Steve Carlton, once a young teammate of his on the Cards. "He's always had a great arm," he said. "And if you have a good arm and you're in the game long enough, you're going to learn how to pitch. He sure knows how now. What makes a player great to me is longevity."

I named some other mound stars of the sixties and seventies, and Gibson shrugged and shook his head. "I guess I was never much in awe of anybody," he said. "I think you have to have that attitude if you're going to go far in this game. People have always said that I was too confident, but I think you'll find that most guys who can play are pretty cocky." The locution "He can play"—as in "Carl Yastrzemski can play a little"—is a throwaway line, the professionals' designation for star-quality athletes. "They're not sitting around worrying about who they're going to pitch against or bat against the next day. You hear a lot of talk about the pressure of the game, but I think most of that comes from the media. Most guys don't let things worry them. Pressure comes when you're not doing well. I've always thought that you only really enjoy baseball when you're good at it. For someone who isn't at the top of the game—who's just hanging on somewhere on down the totem pole—it's a real tough job, every day. But when I was playing I never wished

I was doing anything else. I think being a professional athlete is the finest thing a man can do."

I asked about the source of his great confidence in himself, and he said, "I've always been that way. After all, I was playing basketball with grown men when I was thirteen years old. I always thought I was good enough to play with anyone. I don't know where that came from."

When Gibson was playing baseball, he was considered one of the two or three very best athletes in the game. His early basketball experience had come when he was a water boy with an itinerant black basketball team, the Y Travellers (named for Omaha's North Branch Y.M.C.A.), which was coached by his grown-up oldest brother, Josh; whenever the Travellers ran up a comfortable lead over some local Nebraska or Iowa all-star club, Josh would send his kid brother into the game, just to rub things in a little. Bob Gibson won city and statewide basketball honors at Technical High School, in Omaha, and a few in baseball, too (he was a catcher in the beginning), and he broke every basketball record at Creighton, where he was the first black student to be given a basketball scholarship—and, for that matter, to play on the team. After leaving Creighton, he played for the Harlem Globetrotters during the 1957–58 season, after he had signed on as a pitcher with the Cardinals organization. "It was all right being with the Trotters," Gibson told me, "but I hated that clowning around. I wanted to play all the time—I mean, I wanted to play to win."

In spite of Gibson's spinning, staggering pitching motion, which certainly did not leave him in the squared-away, weight-on-both-feet attitude that coaches recommend as the proper post-delivery fielding stance for the position, he was agile enough out there to win the Gold Glove award as the best defensive pitcher in his league every season from 1965 through 1973. Fans and writers and players still talk about some of his fielding plays in the same awestruck tones they use for the seventeen-strikeout Series game. In one play (I can still see it) in the 1964 World Series, he scampered over and plucked up a hard-hit ball struck by Joe Pepitone that had nailed him on the hip and caromed halfway to third base; Gibson leaped and turned one hundred and eighty degrees in midair and made an overhead throw to first—a basketball one-handed fall-away jumper—that nipped Pepitone at the bag. There was also a nationally televised game in which he ran down a ball that a Giants batter had bounced over his head out on the mound; Gibson caught up with it while running full tilt away from the plate and toward second base, and he flipped it, underhand and right-handed and away from his body (try it), to first for the out. Tim McCarver, who weighs a solid hundred and ninety pounds, told me that one day when he and Gibson were horsing around on the field, Bob had suddenly seized him and lifted him above his head at arm's length, holding him aloft like some Olympic weight lifter at the end of a clean and jerk. "The man is somewhat startling," McCarver said.

○

Gibby's is a welcoming sort of place—a squared-off, three-sided bar down-stairs, with strips of stained-glass decoration on the far wall and a short flight of steps up to the sun-filled upper level, where there are some comfortable wooden-backed dining booths and hanging plants everywhere. On a busy night—on Saturdays, for instance, when a jazz group comes in to play—Gibby's has room for about a hundred and thirty diners and twenty more customers at the bar. I was not surprised to learn that Gibson had had a hand in the restaurant's design and construction. He is there every day, starting at eight in the morning, when he turns up to check the books for the previous night's business, to inspect the incoming meat and produce (the menu is modest, and is built around steaks and shrimp and delicious hamburgers), and generally to keep an eye on things. "I want to make sure nobody is throwing out the forks with the garbage," he said lightly. He went to bartend-ers' school for three months before Gibby's opened—not so much to learn how to mix cocktails, although he can now whip up eighty different drinks, as to learn how veteran waiters and bartenders can fleece a rookie owner. "What I *should* have done was to become an accountant," he said. "About ninety per cent of the job is damned paperwork." Gibby's clientele is an interesting mixture of races and ages and sexes—a "neat crowd," according to the owner ("neat" is a favorite word), and perhaps the only such cosmo-politan mixture in Omaha. The waiters are mostly young black men, and the bartenders mostly young black women. Gibson is a calm and approachable boss; the staff seems to care about him, and vice versa. When a small, very young waitress began putting coins into a cigarette machine near us, Bob said reprovingly, "Those aren't for *you*, are they?" (They weren't.) Later on, he let slip that the previous week he had taken the four-year-old daughter of one of his female bartenders out to his new pool for the afternoon when her mother couldn't find a babysitter. At the last moment, he also asked the daughter of one of his regular customers to come along, too. "I used to have little girls myself," he said to me. A lot of the arriving diners and drinkers at Gibby's say hello to him in an easy, friendly way, but there isn't much hearty bar chatter with the host. Not many people would feel impelled to buddy up to Bob Gibson. I suggested that he must be exposed to a good deal of barside baseball expertise at his place of work, and he said, "Who wants to talk to fans? They always know so much, to hear them tell it, and they always think baseball is so easy. You hear them say, 'Oh, I was a pretty good ballplayer myself back when I was in school, but then I got this injury. . . .' Some cabdriver gave me that one day, and I said, 'Oh, really? That's funny, because when *I* was young I really wanted to be a cabdriver, only I had this little problem with my eyes, so I never made it.' He thought I was serious. It went right over his head."

Gibson's impatience with trifling or intrusive strangers accounted for considerable coolness between him and the media during his playing days—a mistrust that may even keep him out of the Hall of Fame for a year or two, since some members of the Baseball Writers Association have been known to allow personal pique to influence their judgment. (Each writer selects up to ten names of eligible former players he thinks worthy of the Hall of Fame, and a player must be named on seventy-five per cent of the ballots in order to be immortalized.) A couple of years ago, when Willie Mays first came up for election, twenty-three members of the B.W.A. resolutely omitted him from their ballots.* A good many St. Louis reporters still recall the time in 1967 when Gibson had the cast removed from his broken leg and then, annoyed by their clubhouse importunings and questions, taped a sheet of paper to his shirtfront on which he had written "1. Yes, it's off; 2. No, it doesn't hurt; 3. I don't know how much longer"; and so on. The club was in a pennant race, of course, and Gibson's condition was a matter of daily concern to Cardinals fans everywhere, so his broadside was not taken in good part.

"I don't like all this personal contact with the press," Gibson told me. "The press expects everyone to be congenial. Everyone's *not* congenial! They want to put every athlete in the same category as every other athlete. It's as if they thought they owned you." I had been told of a St. Louis television reporter who had once done something to offend one of Gibson's teammates and had then tried to reassure Gibson about their relationship. "You know I'll never do anything to hurt *you*, Bob," he said. Gibson looked at him incredulously and said, "Why, hell, the only way you could ever hurt me is if you happened to be a pretty good fastball hitter!" One longtime Cardinals writer said to me, "Bob was a thorny, obdurate personality, and there weren't too many people who were crazy about him. If he'd had a little more give to him, he could have owned this city. If he'd had Lou Brock's personality, he'd still be working for the Cardinals somewhere."

There is a standoff here. The price of Bob Gibson's owning St. Louis seems to be his agreeing—in his mind, at least—to let the press own him. I have considerable sympathy for any writer who had to ask Bob Gibson some sharp, news-producing questions two or three times a week over the span of a decade or more, but wanting Gibson with a sunny, less obdurate temperament would be to want him a less difficult, less dangerous man on the mound—not quite a Bob Gibson, not quite a great pitcher. The man is indivisible, and it is the wonder of him. It is my own suspicion that both

*Not to worry. Gibson sailed into the Hall in 1981, his first year of eligibility.

sportswriters and fans are increasingly resentful of the fame and adulation and immense wealth that are now bestowed so swiftly upon so many young professional athletes, and are envious of their privileged and apparently carefree style of living. The resentment is a half-conscious appreciation of the fact that they themselves—the fans and the media people, that is—have to a great degree created these golden youths, and because of that there is indeed a wish to own them; to demand ceaseless, inhumanly repeated daz-zling performances from them on the field, and to require absolute access to their private lives as well. Most athletes, who are very young when they first come to prominence and, for the most part, have a very limited experi-ence of the world, respond to these demands either with a convulsive, wholly artificial public "image" of affability, or (more often, of late) with surliness or angry silence. Bob Gibson did neither. Somehow, he has always kept his distance and his strangeness, and there is something upright and old-fash-ioned about such stubborn propriety. He is there if anyone really wants to close that space—the whole man, and not a piece of him or an image of him—but many of us may prefer not to do so, because at a distance (from sixty feet six inches away, perhaps) he stands whole and undiminished, and beyond our envy: the athlete incarnate, the player.

Gibson had allowed me to close this space a little by his willingness to talk about himself, and I had begun to sense the intensity of relationships with him that Tim McCarver had told me about, and the absence of any withdrawn places in him that Joe Torre had mentioned. There is reason to believe that he has allowed himself to become more approachable since he left the game. Bob Broeg, who covered Gibson from his first day in spring training as a rookie, in 1958, to his retirement at the end of the 1975 season, said to me, "Bob didn't know how his personality worked against him. I don't think I wrote many things about him over the years that weren't appreciative of his great skills—he and Dizzy Dean were the two best pitchers I ever saw here—but he was always indifferent to me. One day, late in his career, I was in the clubhouse with him, and he was as closed off as ever, and I finally said, 'You've never said a kind or personal word to me in the years I've known you.' I walked away, and he chased me all the way across the room to ask what I meant. I'd pinked him, and he was extremely upset. He just didn't realize how cold he could be in everyday relationships."

But other intimates of Gibson's from his Cardinals days have a very different view of him. Gene Gieselmann, the team's trainer—he is thirty-three years old but looks much younger—counts Gibson among his closest and warmest friends. "My memories of baseball are all shiny where he's con-cerned," he said. "I cherish him. I think his problems with people go back to his never having had a father. He never knew him, you know. He dearly loved his mother, but I don't think he was very close to anyone else in his family. So when somebody, especially a white person"—Gieselmann is white—"showed him over a long period of time that he could be more than just a trainer or more than just another ballplayer, and that there could be something deeper in their relationship—well, that meant a lot to him, and then he showed how sensitive and generous he really was."

Gibson is a compulsive truthteller, and he appears to have a wry understanding of the burdens of that self-imposed role. At one point, he was talking with me about the difference between himself and Joe Torre when it came to dealing with writers and other strangers, and he said, "Joe knows everybody, and he recognizes them right away. I don't. I always had a hard time remembering people's names and recognizing their faces." There was a moment of silence, and then he added, "That's only half of it. I didn't *care*. And if I think somebody's wrong I'm going to say it."

I suddenly recalled an incident some years ago involving Gibson and another player, a well-known American League infielder, who were members of a small troupe of ballplayers making a postseason tour of military bases in the Pacific. Gibson's roommate on the trip was a public-relations man with one of the major-league teams, who was acting as an escort and travel agent for the group. Early in the trip, the infielder let drop some plainly anti-Semitic remarks about the P.R. man, who was Jewish, and Gibson stopped him in midsentence and advised him to keep his distance and not to talk to him for the remainder of the trip. "And if I ever pitch against you," Gibson said levelly, "I'm going to hit you on the coconut with my first pitch." Fortunately (or perhaps *un*fortunately), the two never did play against each other.

Gibson told me that racism had been easy to find when he came into baseball. When he first reported to the Cards' spring-training camp, in St. Petersburg, in 1958, he presented himself at the Bainbridge Hotel, where the club was quartered, and asked for his room, but he was guided out a side door, where a taxi picked him up and drove him to the house of a black family on the other side of town; the same arrangement had been made for all the team's black players. (Three years later, the entire club moved to a different, unsegregated hotel in St. Pete.) Earlier, when he was an eighteen-year-old sophomore at Creighton, Gibson and the rest of the college's basketball team had gone to Oklahoma by train for a game against the University of Tulsa, and on the way Gibson was told that he wouldn't be able to eat or sleep with his teammates there. "I cried when I was told that," Gibson said to me. "I wouldn't have gone if I'd known. I wasn't ready for that."

At one point, I said to Gibson that when I had seen him play I had always been very much aware of the fact that he was a black athlete; somehow, his race had always appeared to be a considerable part of what he brought to the mound when he went to work out there.

He didn't respond—he simply said nothing at all—and I understood that my remark was not a question that anyone could easily respond to; it was not a question at all. But a little later he mentioned the many times he had been harassed by semi-official white people—hotel clerks and traffic cops and the like—who later began fawning on him when they learned that he was *the* Bob Gibson, the famous pitcher. "It's nice to get attention and favors," he said, "but I can never forget the fact that if I were an ordinary black person I'd be in the shithouse, like millions of others." He paused a moment, and then added, "I'm happy I'm *not* ordinary, though."

All this was said without surface bitterness or cynicism but with an intensity that went beyond his words. Some days later, Bill White, who is also black, commented on this tone of Gibson's. "He was always so proud," he said to me. "You could see it in his face and in the way he met people and talked to them. He never dropped it. I used to tell him, 'You can't be as tough on people as you are—it hurts you.' And he would say, 'You can do that, take all that, but I can't.' We didn't agree. But, of course, you never know what it's been like for another person. Some people have the ability to forget these things, but Bob Gibson always had the ability to make everybody remember what he had been through."

○

Gibson and I spent the afternoon at the restaurant, and he and Wendy had me to dinner at their house that night: steaks and mustard greens, prepared by the Gibsons together, and a Cabernet Sauvignon. (He is a demanding, accomplished cook; when he was playing, he invariably got his own meals at home when he returned from road trips and road cooking.) It was our last evening. Bob showed me some of the nineteenth-century American antiques he collects—a delicate bevelled-glass-front walnut secretary, an immense Barbary Coast-style sideboard, and so on—and took me into a basement room where he keeps his HO-gauge model-railroad set: an entire railhead in miniature, with yards and sidings and a downtown terminal, complete with surrounding streets and buildings. He said he didn't use the trains much anymore. The three of us took another swim in the pool, and Bob and I played a little noisy one-o'-cat with Mia in the living room with an old tennis ball. Gibson was relaxed and playful, but, as always, there was a silence about him: an air not of something held back but of a space within him that is not quite filled. At one point, I asked him if he liked Omaha, and he said, "Not all that much. It's all right. It's what I know." Then I asked if he liked the restaurant business, and in the same brusque way he said, "It isn't much, but it sure is better than doing nothing."

I knew that Gibson had had a brief career in sports television with the American Broadcasting Company, shortly after his retirement as a player. He was a "color man" with ABC's "Monday Night Baseball," and on one occasion he conducted an impromptu, nationally televised interview with the Pittsburgh Pirates' John Candelaria, just after Candelaria had pitched a no-hit game. Gibson's questions centered on the future financial rewards of Candelaria's gem, but this insidey banter between co-professionals was evidently not a line of sports talk that the network brass approved of, and Gibson's media career declined after that, although he has since done some baseball broadcasts with the HBO cable network. It was a disappointment to him.

When Gibson was out of the room for a moment, I said to Wendy that I sensed something missing or incomplete in Bob, and she said, "Yes, he's still looking for something, and I don't know if the right thing for him will ever come along. It's sad."

Last winter, Gibson made inquiries with the Cardinals and the Royals and the Mets and the Giants in the hope of landing a job as a pitching coach; interest was expressed, but nothing quite worked out. One difficulty may be the very modest salaries of big-league coaches, but when I talked to Bob about his joining some team in this capacity I got the feeling that he might be willing to make a considerable financial sacrifice in order to get back into the game. Several of Gibson's old friends and teammates told me later that they had heard of his wish to get back into baseball, and without exception they hoped he would. They said that the game would be better off with a man of Gibson's character back in uniform. But some of them went on to express their doubt that he would be satisfied with a job of such limited rewards as that of a pitching coach. "It won't be enough for him," one man said. "Nothing will ever be enough for him now."

"I don't miss pitching," Gibson said to me on that last evening, "but I can't say that I don't miss the game. I miss it a *little*. There's a lot I don't want to get back to. I don't want the fame or the money or all that attention. I always hated all the waiting around a pitcher has to do. I used to wish I could press a button the minute I'd finished a game and make the next four days just disappear. I sure as hell don't miss the travelling. I think it's the life I miss—all the activity that's around baseball. I don't miss playing baseball but I miss . . . baseball. *Baseball*. Does that sound like a crazy man?"

For the first time in our long talks, he seemed a bit uncertain. He did not sound crazy but only like a man who could no longer find work or a challenge that was nearly difficult enough to nurture his extraordinarily demanding inner requirements. Maybe there was no such work, outside of pitching. Baseball is the most individual and the most difficult of all team sports, and the handful of young men who can play it superbly must sense, however glimmeringly, that there will be some long-lasting future payment exacted for the privileges and satisfactions they have won for themselves. Like other team sports, baseball cannot be played in middle age; there is no cheerful, companionable afternoon to the game, as there is for old golfers and tennis

151

players and the like. A lot of ex-ballplayers become sentimental, self-pitying, garrulous bores when they are cut off from the game. Some of them, including some great stars, go to pieces.

Thinking of what Wendy had said, I told Bob Gibson that I was sometimes aware of a sadness in him.

"Sad?" he said uncomprehendingly. "No, I'm not sad. I just think I've been spoiled. When you've been an athlete, there's no place for you to go. You're much harder to please. But where I am right now is where the average person has been all along. I'm like millions of others now, and I'm finding out what that's like. I don't think the ordinary person ever gets to do anything they enjoy nearly as much as I enjoyed playing ball. I haven't found my niche now that that's over—or maybe I have found it and I don't know it. Maybe I'll still find something I like as much as I liked pitching, but I don't know if I will. I sure hope so."

Maybe he will. Athletes illuminate our imagination and raise our hopes for ourselves to such an extent that we often want the best of them to become models for us in every area of life—an unfair and childish expectation. But Bob Gibson is a tough and resolute man, and the unique blend of independence and pride and self-imposed isolation in his character—the distance again—will continue to serve him in the new and even more difficult contest he is engaged in. Those who know him best will look to him for something brilliant and special now, just as they have always done. Even those of us who have not been spoiled by any athletic triumphs of our own and the fulfillment of the wild expectations of our early youth are aware of a humdrum, twilight quality to all our doings of middle life, however successful they may prove to be. There is a loss of light and ease and early joy, and we look to other exemplars—mentors and philosophers: grown men—to sustain us in that loss. A few athletes, a rare handful, have gone on, once their day out on the field was done, to join that number, and it is possible—the expectation will not quite go away—that Bob Gibson may be among them someday. Nothing he ever does will surprise me.

The Web of the Game

—JUNE 1981

An afternoon in mid-May, and we are waiting for the game to begin. We are in shadow, and the sunlit field before us is a thick, springy green—an old diamond, beautifully kept up. The grass continues beyond the low chain-link fence that encloses the outfield, extending itself on the right-field side into a rougher, featureless sward that terminates in a low line of distant trees, still showing a pale, early-summer green. We are almost in the country. Our seats are in the seventh row of the grandstand, on the home side of the diamond, about halfway between third base and home plate. The seats themselves are more comforting to spirit than to body, being a surviving variant example of the pure late-Doric Polo Grounds mode: the backs made of a continuous running row of wood slats, divided off by pairs of narrow cast-iron arms, within which are slatted let-down seats, grown arthritic with rust and countless layers of gray paint. The rows are stacked so closely upon each other (one discovers) that a happening on the field of sufficient interest to warrant a rise or half-rise to one's feet is often made more memorable by a sharp crack to the kneecaps delivered by the backs of the seats just forward; in time, one finds that a dandruff of gray paint flakes from the same source has fallen on one's lap and scorecard. None of this matters, for this view and these stands and this park—it is Yale Field, in New Haven—are renowned for their felicity. The grandstand is a low, penumbrous steel-post shed that holds the infield in a pleasant horseshoe-curved embrace. The back wall of the grandstand, behind the uppermost row of seats, is broken by an arcade of open arches, admitting a soft back light that silhouettes the upper audience and also discloses an overhead bonework of struts and beams supporting the roof—the pigeonland of all the ballparks of our youth. The game we are waiting for—Yale vs. St. John's University—is a considerable event, for it is part of the National Collegiate Athletic Associa-

153

tion's northeast regional tournament, the winner of which will qualify for a berth at the national collegiate championships in Omaha in June, the World Series of college baseball. Another pair of teams, Maine and Central Michigan—the Black Bears and the Chippewas—have just finished their game here, the first of a doubleheader. Maine won it, 10–2, but the ultimate winner will not be picked here for three more days, when the four teams will have completed a difficult double-elimination tournament. Good, hard competition, but the stands at Yale Field are half empty today. Call them half full, because everyone on hand—some twenty-five hundred fans—must know something about the quality of the teams here, or at least enough to qualify either as a partisan or as an expert, which would explain the hum of talk and expectation that runs through the grandstand even while the Yale team, in pinstriped home whites, is still taking infield practice.

I am seated in a little sector of senior New Haven men—Townies rather than Old Elis. One of them a couple of rows in front of me says, "They used to fill this place in the old days, before there was all the baseball on TV."

His neighbor, a small man in a tweed cap, says, "The biggest crowd I ever saw in here—the biggest ever, I bet—was for a high school game. Shelton and Naugatuck, about twenty years ago."

An old gent with a cane, seated just to my left, says, "They filled it up that day the Yankees came here, with Ruth and Gehrig and the rest of them. An exhibition game."

A fan just beyond the old gentleman—a good-looking man in his sixties, with an open, friendly face, a large smile, and a thick stand of gray hair— leans toward my neighbor and says, "When *was* that game, Joe? 1930? 1932?"

"Oh, I can't remember," the old man says. "Somewhere in there. My youngest son was mascot for the Yankees that day, so I could figure it out, I suppose." He is not much interested. His eyes are on the field. "Say, look at these fellows throw!" he says. "Did you see that outfielder peg the ball?"

"That was the day Babe Ruth said this was about the best-looking ballpark he'd ever seen," the man beyond says. "You remember that."

"I can remember long before this park was built," the old man says. "It was already the Yale ballfield when I got here, but they put in these stands later—Who is this shortstop? He's a hefty-looking bird."

"How many Yale games do you think you've seen, Joe?" the smiling man asks.

"Oh, I couldn't begin to count them. But I haven't seen a Yale team play in—I don't know how long. Not for years. These fellows today, they play in the Cape Cod League in the summers. They let the freshmen play here now, too. They recruit them more, I suppose. They're athletes—you can see that."

The Yale team finishes its warmup ritual, and St. John's—light-gray uniforms with scarlet cap bills and scarlet socks—replaces it on the field.

"St. John's has always had a good club," the old man tells me. "Even back when my sons were playing ball, it was a good ball team. But not as good as this one. Oh, my! Did you see this catcher throw down to second? Did you see that! I bet you in all the years I was here I didn't have twenty fellows who could throw."

"Your sons played here?" I ask him. "For Yale?"

"My son Joe was captain in '41," he says. "He was a pitcher. He pitched against my son Steve here one day. Steve was pitching for Colgate, and my other son, Bob—my youngest—was on the same Colgate team. A good little left-handed first baseman."

I am about to ask how that game turned out, but the old man has taken out a small gold pocket watch, with a hunting case, which he snaps open. Three-fourteen. "Can't they get this *started*?" he says impatiently.

I say something admiring about the watch, and he hands it to me carefully. "I've had that watch for sixty-eight years," he says. "I always carried it in my vest pocket, back when we wore vests."

The little watch has a considerable heft to it: a weight of authority. I turn it over and find an inscription on the back. It is in script and a bit worn, but I can still make it out:

PRESENTED TO JOE WOOD
BY HIS FRIEND A. E. SMITH
IN APPRECIATION OF HIS SPLENDID
PITCHING WHICH BROUGHT THE
WORLD'S CHAMPIONSHIP
TO BOSTON IN 1912.

"Who was A. E. Smith, Mr. Wood?" I ask.

"He was a manufacturer."

I know the rest. Joe Wood, the old gentleman on my left, was the baseball coach at Yale for twenty years—from 1923 to 1942. Before that, he was a sometime outfielder for the Cleveland Indians, who batted .366 in 1921. Before *that*, he was a celebrated right-handed pitcher for the Boston Red Sox—Smokey Joe Wood, who won thirty-four games for the Bosox in 1912, when he finished up with a record of 34–5, pitching ten shutouts and sixteen consecutive victories along the way. In the World Series that fall—one of the two or three finest ever played—he won three of the four games he pitched, including the famous finale: the game of Hooper's catch and Snodgrass's muff and Tris Speaker's killing tenth-inning single. Next to Walter Johnson, Smokey Joe Wood was the most famous fastballer of his era. Still is, no doubt, in the minds of the few surviving fans who saw him at his best. He is ninety-one years old.

None of this, I should explain—neither my presence at the game nor my companions in the stands—was an accident. I had been a fervent admirer of Smokey Joe Wood ever since I read his account of his baseball beginnings and his subsequent career in Lawrence Ritter's *The Glory of Their Times*, a cherished, classic volume of oral history of the early days of the pastime. Mr. Wood was in his seventies when that book was published, in 1966, and I was startled and pleased a few weeks ago when I ran across an article by Joan Whaley, in *Baseball Digest*, which informed me that he was still hale and still talking baseball in stimulating fashion. He was living with a married daughter in New Haven, and my first impulse was to jump in my car and drive up to press a call. But something held me back; it did not seem quite right to present myself uninvited at his door, even as a pilgrim. Then Ron Darling and Frank Viola gave me my chance. Darling, who was a junior at Yale this past year, is the best pitcher ever to take the mound for the Blue. He is better than Johnny Broaca, who went on to pitch for the Yankees and the Indians for five seasons in the mid-nineteen-thirties; he is better than Frank Quinn, who compiled a 1.57 career earned-run average at Yale in 1946, '47, and '48. (He is also a better all-around ballplayer than George Bush, who played first base and captained the Elis in 1948, and then somehow drifted off into politics instead of baseball.) Darling, a right-handed fastball thrower, won eleven games and lost two as a sophomore, with an earned-run average of 1.31, and this year he was 9–3 and 2.42, with eighty-nine strikeouts in his ninety-three innings of work—the finest college pitcher in the Northeast, according to major-league scouts, with the possible exception of Frank Viola, a junior left-handed curveball ace at St. John's, who was undefeated this year, 9–0, and had a neat earned-run average of 1.00. St. John's, a Catholic university in Queens, is almost a baseball powerhouse—not quite in the same class, perhaps, as such perennial national champions or challengers as Arizona, Arizona State, Texas, and Southern California, whose teams play Sun Belt schedules of close to sixty games, but good enough to have gone as the Northeast's representative to the national tournament in Omaha in 1980, where Viola defeated the eventual winner, Arizona, in the first round. St. John's, by the way, does not recruit high-school stars from faraway states, as do most of these rival college powers; all but one player on this year's thirty-three-man Redmen squad grew up and went to school in New York City or in nearby suburbs. This 1981 St. John's team ran off an awesome 31–2 record, capturing the Eastern College Metro (Greater New York, that is) elimination, while Yale, winning its last nine games in a row, concluded its regular season with a record of 24–12–1, which was good enough to win its first Eastern Intercollegiate League championship since 1956. (That tie in Yale's record was a game against the University of Central Florida, played during the Elis' spring-training tour in March, and was called because of darkness after seven innings, with the score tied at 21–21. Darling did not pitch that day.) The two teams, along with Central Michigan (Mid-America Conference) and Maine (New England Conference), qualified for the tournament at New Haven, and the luck of the draw pitted Yale (and Darling) against St. John's (and Viola) in the second game of the opening doubleheader. Perfect. Darling, by the way, had indicated that he might be willing to turn professional this summer if he were to be picked in an early round of the annual amateur draft conducted by the major leagues in mid-June, and Viola had been talked about as a potential big-leaguer ever since his freshman year, so their matchup suddenly became an obligatory reunion for every front-rank baseball scout east of the Ohio River. (About fifty of them turned up, with their speed-guns and clipboards, and their glowing reports of the game, I learned later, altered the draft priorities of several clubs.)

Perfect, but who would get in touch with Mr. Wood and persuade him to come out to Yale Field with me for the game? Why, Dick Lee would—Dick Lee, *of course*. Richard C. Lee (he was the smiling man sitting just beyond Smokey Joe in our row) is a former Democratic mayor of New Haven, an extremely popular (eight consecutive terms, sixteen years in office), innovative officeholder who, among other things, presided over the widely admired urban renewal of his city during the nineteen-sixties and, before that, thought up and pushed through the first Operation Head Start program (for minority-group preschoolers) in the country. Dick Lee knows everybody in New Haven, including Smokey Joe Wood and several friends of mine there, one of whom provided me with his telephone number. I called Lee at his office (he is assistant to the chairman of the Union Trust Company, in New Haven) and proposed our party. "Wonderful!" he cried at once. "You have come to the right man. I'll bring Joe. Count on me!" Even over the telephone, I could see him smiling.

Dick Lee did not play baseball for Yale, but the nature of his partisanship became clear in the very early moments of the Yale–St. John's game. "Yay!" he shouted in a stentorian baritone as Ron Darling set down three St. John's batters in order in the first. "Yay, Ron *baby!*" he boomed out as Darling dismissed three more batters in the second, fanning the last two. "Now *c'mon*, Yale! Let's get something started, gang! Yay!" Lee had told me that he pitched for some lesser-known New Haven teams—the Dixwell Community House sandlot team and the Jewish Home for Children nine (the Utopians), among others—while he was growing up in the ivyless Newhallville neighborhood. Some years later, having passed up college altogether, he went to work for Yale as its public-relations officer. By the time he became mayor, in 1953, the university was his own—another precinct to be worried about and looked after. A born politician, he appears to draw on some inner deep-water reservoir of concern that enables him to preside effortlessly and affectionately over each encounter of his day; he was the host at our game, and at intervals he primed Joe Wood with questions about his baseball past, which he seemed to know almost by heart.

"Yes, that's right, I did play for the Bloomer Girls a few games," Mr. Wood said in response to one such cue. "I was about sixteen, and I was pitching for our town team in Ness City, Kansas. The Bloomer Girls were a barnstorming team, but they used to pick up a few young local fellows on the sly to play along with them if they needed to fill out their lineup. I was one of those. I never wore a wig, though—I wouldn't have done that. I guess I looked young enough to pass for a girl anyway. Bill Stern, the old radio broadcaster, must have used that story about forty times, but he always got it wrong about the wig."

There was a yell around us, and an instantly ensuing groan, as Yale's big freshman catcher, Tony Paterno, leading off the bottom of the second, lined sharply to the St. John's shortstop, who made a fine play on the ball. Joe Wood peered intently out at the field through his thickish horn-rimmed spectacles. He shook his head a little. "You know, I can't hardly follow the damned ball now," he said. "It's better for me if I'm someplace where I can get up high behind the plate. I was up to Fenway Park for two games last year, and they let me sit in the press box there at that beautiful park. I could see it all from there. The groundskeeper has got that field just like a living room."

I asked him if he still rooted for the Red Sox.

"Oh, yes," he said. "All my life. A couple of years ago, when they had that big lead in the middle of the summer, they asked me if I'd come up and throw out the first ball at one of their World Series games or playoff games. But then they dropped out of it, of course. Now it looks like it'll never happen."

He spoke in a quiet, almost measured tone, but there was no tinge of disappointment or self-pity in it. It was the voice of age. He was wearing a blue windbreaker over a buttoned-up plaid shirt, made formal with a small dark-red bow tie. There was a brown straw hat on his bald head. The years had imparted a delicate thinness to the skin on his cheeks and neck, but his face had a determined look to it, with a strong chin and a broad, unsmiling mouth. Watching him, I recalled one of the pictures in *The Glory of Their Times*—a team photograph taken in 1906, in which he is sitting cross-legged down in front of a row of men in baggy baseball pants and lace-up, collared baseball shirts with "NESS CITY" across the front in block letters. The men are standing in attitudes of cheerful assurance, with their arms folded, and their mushy little baseball gloves are hanging from their belts. Joe Wood, the smallest player in the picture, is wearing a dark warmup shirt, with the sleeves rolled halfway up his forearms, and his striped baseball cap is pushed back a little, revealing a part in the middle of his hair. There is an intent, unsmiling look on his boyish face—the same grave demeanor you can spot in a subsequent photograph, taken in 1912, in which he is standing beside his Red Sox manager, Jake Stahl, and wearing a heavy woollen three-button suit, a stiff collar, a narrow necktie with a stickpin, and a stylish black porkpie hat pulled low over his handsome, famous face: Smokey Joe Wood at twenty-two. (The moniker, by the way, was given him by Paul Shannon, a sportswriter for the Boston *Post*; before that, he was sometimes called Ozone Wood—"ozone" for the air cleaved by the hapless batters who faced him.) The young man in the photographs and the old man beside me at the ballpark had the same broad, sloping shoulders, but there was nothing burly or physically imposing about him then or now.

"What kind of a pitcher were you, Mr. Wood?" I asked him.

"I had a curve and a fastball," he said. "That's all. I didn't even have brains enough to slow up on the batters. The fastball had a hop on it. You had to be *fast* to have that happen to the ball."

I said that I vividly recalled Sandy Koufax's fastball, which sometimes seemed to jump so violently as it crossed the plate that his catcher had to shoot up his mitt to intercept it.

"Mine didn't go up that far. Just enough for them to miss it." He half turned to me as he said this, and gave me a little glance and an infinitesimal smile. A twinkle. "I don't know where my speed came from," he went on. "I wasn't any bigger or stronger-looking then than I am now. I always could throw hard, and once I saw I was able to get batters out, I figured I was crazy enough to play ball for a living. My father was a criminal lawyer in Kansas, and before that out in Ouray, Colorado, where I first played ball, and my brother went to law school and got a degree, but I didn't even graduate from high school. I ate and slept baseball all my life."

○

The flow of recollection from Joe Wood was perhaps not as smooth and rivery as I have suggested here. For one thing, he spoke slowly and with care—not unlike the way he walked to the grandstand at Yale Field from the parking lot beyond left field, making his way along the grass firmly enough but looking where he was going, too, and helping himself a bit with his cane. Nothing infirm about him, but nothing hurrying or sprightly, either. For another, the game was well in progress by now, and its principals and sudden events kept interrupting our colloquy. Ron Darling, a poised, impressive figure on the mound, alternated his popping fastballs with just enough down-breaking sliders and an occasional curveball to keep the St. John's batters unhappy. Everything was thrown with heat—his strikeout pitch is a Seaver-high fastball, but his slider, which slides at the last possible instant, is an even deadlier weapon—but without any signs of strain or anxiety. He threw over the top, smoothly driving his front (left) shoulder at the batter in picture-book style, and by the third or fourth inning he had imposed his will and his pace on the game. He was rolling. He is a dark-haired, olive-skinned young man (he lives in Millbury, Massachusetts, near Worcester, but he was born in Hawaii; his mother is Chinese-Hawaiian by birth) with long, powerful legs, but his pitcherlike proportions tend to conceal, rather than emphasize, his six feet two inches and his hundred and ninety-five pounds. He also swings the bat well enough (.331 this year) to play right field for Yale when he isn't pitching; in our game he was the designated hitter as well as the pitcher for the Elis.

"That's a nice build for a pitcher, isn't it?" Joe Wood murmured during the St. John's fifth. Almost as he spoke, Darling executed a twisting dive to his right to snaffle a hard-hit grounder up the middle by Brian Miller, the St. John's shortstop, and threw him out at first. (Hey-*hey*!" Dick Lee cried. "Yay, Ronnie!") "*And* he's an athlete out there," Wood added. "The scouts like that, you know. Oh, this fellow's a lot better than Broaca ever was."

Frank Viola, for his part, was as imperturbable as Darling on the mound, if not quite as awesome. A lanky, sharp-shouldered lefty, he threw an assortment of speeds and spins, mostly sinkers and down-darting sliders, that had the Yale batters swinging from their shoe tops and, for the most part, hammering the ball into the dirt. He had the stuff and poise of a veteran relief pitcher, and the St. John's infield—especially Brian Miller and a stubby, ebullient second baseman named Steve Scafa—performed behind him with the swift, almost haughty confidence that imparts an elegance and calm and sense of ease to baseball at its best. It was a scoreless game after five, and a beauty.

"What was the score of that game you beat Walter Johnson in, in your big year?" Dick Lee asked our guest between innings.

We all knew the answer, I think. In September of 1912, Walter Johnson came to Fenway Park (it was brand-new that year) with the Senators and pitched against young Joe Wood, who then had a string of thirteen consecutive victories to his credit. That summer, Johnson had established a league record of sixteen straight wins, so the matchup was not merely an overflow, sellout affair but perhaps the most anticipated, most discussed non-championship game in the American League up to that time.

"We won it, 1–0," Joe Wood said quietly, "but it wasn't his fault I beat him that day. If he'd had the team behind him that I did, he'd have set every kind of record in baseball. You have to remember that Walter Johnson played for a second-division team almost all through his career. All those years, and he had to work from the bottom every time he pitched."

"Were you faster than he was?" I asked.

"Oh, I don't think there was ever anybody faster than Walter," he murmured.

"But Johnson said just the opposite!" Dick Lee cried. "He said no one was faster than *you*."

"He was just that kind of fellow, to say something like that," Wood said. "That was just like the man. Walter Johnson was a great big sort of a pitcher, with hands that came clear down to his knees. Why, the way he threw the ball, the only reason anybody ever got even a foul off him was because everybody in the league knew he'd never come inside to a batter. Walter Johnson was a prince of men—a gentleman first, last, and always."

It came to me that this was the first time I had ever heard anybody use the phrase "a prince of men" in a non-satiric fashion. In any case, the Johnson-Wood argument did not really need settling, then or now. Smokey Joe went on to tie Johnson with sixteen straight victories that season—an American League record, subsequently tied by Lefty Grove and Schoolboy Rowe. (Over in the National League that year, Rube Marquard won *nineteen* straight for the Giants—a single-season mark first set by Tim Keefe of the Giants in 1888 and untouched as yet by anyone else.) Johnson and Wood pretty well divided up the A.L. mound honors that summer, when Johnson won thirty-two games and lost twelve, posting the best earned-run average (1.39) and the most strikeouts (three hundred and three), while Wood won the most games and established the best winning percentage with his 34–5 mark (not including his three World Series wins, of course).

These last figures are firmly emplaced in the baseball crannies of my mind, and in the minds of most students of the game, because, it turned out, they represent the autumn of Joe Wood's pitching career as well as its first full flowering. Early in the spring of 1913, he was injured in a fielding play, and he was never near to being the same pitcher again. One of the game's sad speculations over the years has been what Joe Wood's status in the pantheon of great pitchers would be if he had remained sound. I did not need any reminder of his accident, but I had been given one just the same when Dick Lee introduced me to him, shortly before the game. We had stopped to pick up Mr. Wood at his small, red-shuttered white house on Marvel Road, and when he came down the concrete path to join us I got out of Lee's Cadillac to shake the hand that once shook the baseball world.

"Mr. Wood," I said, "this is a great honor."

"Ow—*ow*!" he cried, cringing before me and attempting to extricate his paw.

"Oh, oh . . . I'm *terribly* sorry," I said, appalled. "Is it—is this because of your fall off the roof?" Three years ago, at the age of eighty-eight, he had fallen off a ladder while investigating a leak, and had cracked several ribs.

"Hell, no!" he said indignantly. "This is the arm I threw out in 1913!"

I felt awful. I had touched history—and almost brought it to its knees. Now, at the game, he told me how it all happened. "I can't remember now if it was on the road or at Fenway Park," he said. "Anyway, it was against Detroit. There was a swinging bunt down the line, and I went to field it and slipped on the wet grass and went down and landed on my hand. I broke it right here." He pointed to a spot just below his wrist, on the back of his freckled, slightly gnarled right hand. "It's what they call a subperiosteal fracture. They put it in a cast, and I had to sit out awhile. Well, this was in 1913, right after we'd won the championship, and every team was out to get us, of course. So as soon as the cast came off, the manager would come up to me every now and then and want to know how soon I was going to get back to pitching. Well, maybe I got back to it too soon and maybe I didn't, but the arm never felt right again. The shoulder went bad. I still went on pitching, but the fastball had lost that hop. I never threw a day after that when I wasn't in pain. Most of the time, I'd pitch and then it would hurt so bad that I wasn't able to raise my hand again for days afterward. So I was about a halftime pitcher after that. You have to understand that in those days if you didn't work you didn't get paid. Now they lay out as long as they need to and get a shot of that cortisone. But we had to play, ready or not. I was a married man, just starting a family, and in order to get my check I had to be in there. So I pitched."

He pitched less, but not much less well. In 1915, he was 15–5 for the Red Sox, with an earned-run average of 1.49, which was the best in the league. But the pain was so persistent that he sat out the entire 1916 season, on his farm, near Shohola, Pennsylvania, hoping that the rest would restore his arm. It did not. He pitched in eight more games after that—all of them for the Cleveland Indians, to whom he was sold in 1917—but he never won again.

"Did you become a different kind of pitcher after you hurt your arm?" I asked. "More off-speed stuff, I mean?"

"No, I still pitched the fastball."

"But all that pain—"

"I tried not to think about that." He gave me the same small smile and bright glance. "I just loved to be out there," he said. "It was as simple as that."

○

Our afternoon slid by in a distraction of baseball and memory, and I almost felt myself at some dreamlike doubleheader involving the then and the now—the semi-anonymous strong young men waging their close, marvellous game on the sunlit green field before us while bygone players and heroes of baseball history—long gone now, most of them—replayed their vivid, famous innings for me in the words and recollections of my companion. Yale kept putting men aboard against Viola and failing to move them along; Rich Diana, the husky center fielder (he is also an All-Ivy League half-back), whacked a long double to left but then died on second—the sixth stranded

Eli base runner in five innings. Darling appeared to be struggling a little, walking two successive batters in the sixth, but he saved himself with a whirling pickoff to second base—a timed play brilliantly completed by his shortstop, Bob Brooke—and then struck out St. John's big first baseman, Karl Komyathy, for the last out. St. John's had yet to manage a hit against him.

In the home half of the sixth, Yale put its leadoff batter aboard with a single but could not bunt him along. Joe Wood was distressed. "I could teach these fellows to bunt in one minute," he said. "Nobody can't hardly bunt anymore. You've got to get your weight more forward than he did, so you're not reaching for the ball. And he should have his right hand higher up on the bat."

The inning ended, and we reversed directions once again. "Ty Cobb was the greatest bat-handler you ever saw," Wood said. "He used to go out to the ballpark early in the morning with a pitcher and work on hitting the ball to all fields, over and over. He batted that strange way, with his fists apart, you know, but he could have hit just as well no matter how he held it. He just knew what to do with a bat in hand. And baserunning—why, I saw him get on base and steal second, steal third, and then steal home. *The* best. A lot of fellows in my time shortened up on the bat when they had to—that's what the St. John's boys should try against this good pitcher. Next to Cobb, Shoeless Joe Jackson was the best left-handed hitter I ever saw, and he was always down at the end of the bat until there were two strikes on him. Then he'd shorten up a little, to give himself a better chance."

Dick Lee said, "That's what you've been telling Charlie Polka, isn't it, Joe?"

"Yes, sir, and it's helped him," Wood said. "He's tried it, and now he knows that all you have to do is make contact and the ball will fly a long way."

Both men saw my look of bewilderment, and they laughed together.

"Charlie Polka is a Little League player," Dick Lee explained. "He's about eleven years old."

"He lives right across the street from me," Wood said. "He plays for the 500 Blake team—that's named for a restaurant here in town. I've got him shortened up on the bat, and now he's a hitter. Charlie Polka is a natural."

"Is that how you batted?" I asked.

"Not at first," he said. "But after I went over to Cleveland in 1917 to join my old roommate, Tris Speaker, I started to play the outfield, and I began to take up on the bat, because I knew I'd have to hit a little better if I was going to make the team. I never was any wonder at the plate, but I was good enough to last six more years, playing with Spoke."

Tris Speaker (Wood had called him by his old nickname, Spoke) was the Joe DiMaggio or Willie Mays of the first two decades of this century—the nonpareil center fielder of his day. "He had a beautiful left-handed arm," Joe

Wood said. "He always played very shallow in center—you could do that in those days, because of the dead ball. I saw him make a lot of plays to second base from there—pick up what looked like a clean single and fire the ball to second in time to force the base runner coming down from first. Or he could throw the ball behind a runner and pick him off that way. And just as fine a man as he was a ballplayer. He was a Southern gentleman—well, he was from Hubbard, Texas. Back in the early days, when we were living together on the beach at Winthrop during the season, out beyond Revere, Spoke would sometimes cook up a mess of fried chicken in the evening. He'd cook, and then I'd do the dishes."

Listening to this, I sensed the web of baseball about me. Tris Speaker had driven in the tying run in the tenth inning of the last game of the 1912 World Series, at Fenway Park, after Fred Merkle and Chief Meyers, of the Giants, had let his easy foul pop fall untouched between them. A moment or two later, Joe Wood had won his third game of the Series and the Red Sox were champions. My father saw that game—he was at Harvard Law School at the time, and got a ticket somehow—and he told me about it many times. He was terrifically excited to be there, but I think my mother must have relished the famous victory even more. She grew up in Boston and was a true Red Sox fan, even though young women didn't go to many games then. My father grew up in Cleveland, so he was an Indians rooter, of course. In 1915, my parents got married and went to live in Cleveland, where my father began to practice law. Tris Speaker was traded to the Indians in 1916—a terrible shock to Red Sox fans—and Joe Wood came out of his brief retirement to join him on the club a year later. My parents' first child, my older sister, was born in Cleveland late in 1916, and the next year my father went off to Europe—off to the war. My mother once told me that in the summer afternoons of 1917 she would often push a baby carriage past League Park, the Indians' home field, out on Linwood Avenue, which was a block or two away from my parents' house. Sometimes there was a game going on, and if she heard a roar of pleasure from the fans inside she would tell herself that probably Tris Speaker had just done something special. She was lonely in Cleveland, she told me, and it made her feel good to know that Tris Speaker was there in the same town with her. "Tris Speaker and I were traded to Cleveland in the same year," she said.

A yell and an explosion of cheering brought me back to Yale Field. We were in the top of the seventh, and the Yale second baseman and captain, Gerry Harrington, had just leaped high to ˜natch down a burning line drive—the force of it almost knocked him over backward in midair. Then he flipped the ball to second to double off a St. John's base runner and end the inning. "These fellows came to *play!*" Dick Lee said.

Most no-hitters produce at least one such heaven-sent gift somewhere along the line, and I began to believe that Ron Darling, who was still untouched on the mound, might be pitching the game of his young life. I turned to ask Mr. Wood how many no-hitters he recalled—he had seen Mathewson and Marquard and Babe Ruth (Ruth, the pitcher, that is) and Coveleski and the rest of them, after all—but he seemed transfixed by something on the field. "Look at *that!*" he said, in a harsh, disbelieving way. "This Yale coach has his own coaches out there on the lines, by God! They're professionals—not just players, the way I always had it when I was here. The coach has his own coaches . . . I never knew that."

"Did you have special coaches when you were coming up with the Red Sox?" I said, hoping to change his mood. "A pitching coach, I mean, or a batting coach?"

He didn't catch the question, and I repeated it.

"No, no," he said, a little impatiently. "We talked about the other players and the pitchers among ourselves in those days. We players. We didn't need anybody to help us."

He was staring straight ahead at the field. I thought he looked a bit chilly. It was well past five o'clock now, and a skim of clouds had covered the sun.

Dick Lee stole a glance at him, too. "Hey, Joe, doesn't this Darling remind you a little of Carl Hubbell on the mound?" he said in a cheerful, distracting sort of voice. "The way he picks up his front leg, I mean. You remember how Hubbell would go way up on the stretch and then drop his hands down by his ankles before he threw the ball?"

"Hubbell?" Joe Wood said. He shook his head, making an effort. "Well, to me this pitcher's a little like that fellow Eckersley," he said slowly. "The way he moves forward there."

He was right. Ron Darling had some of the same float and glide that the Red Sox' Dennis Eckersley conveys when he is pitching at his peak.

"How do today's players compare with the men you played with, Mr. Wood?" I asked.

"I'd rather not answer that question," he said. He had taken out his watch again. He studied it and then tucked it away carefully, and then he glanced over at me, perhaps wondering if he had been impolite. "That Pete Rose plays hard," he added. "Him and a few more. I don't *like* Pete Rose, exactly, but he looks like he plays the game the way we did. He'd play for the fun of it if he had to."

He resumed his study of the field, and now and then I saw him stare again at the heavyset Yale third-base coach on our side of the diamond. Scoreless games make for a long day at the ballpark, and Joe Wood's day had probably been longer than ours. More than once, I had seen him struggle to his feet to catch some exciting play or moment on the field, only to have it end before he was quite up. Then he would sit down again, leaning on his cane while he lowered himself. I had more questions for Mr. Wood, but now I tried to put them out of my mind. Earlier in the afternoon, he had remarked that several old Yale players had dropped in at his house before the game to say hello and to talk about the old days. "People come by and see me all the time," he had said. "People I don't even know, from as far away as Colorado. Why, I had a fellow come in all the way from Canada the other day, who just wanted to talk about the old days. They all want that, somehow. It's gone on too long."

It had gone on for him, I realized, for as long as most lifetimes. He had played ball for fourteen years, all told, and people had been asking him to talk about it for nearly sixty years. For him, the last juice and sweetness must have been squeezed out of these ancient games years ago, but he was still expected to respond to our amateur expertise, our insatiable vicariousness. Old men are patronized in much the same fashion as athletes; because we take pride in them, we expect their intimacy in return. I had intruded after all.

O

We were in the eighth now . . . and then in the ninth. Still no score, and each new batter, each pitch was greeted with clappings and deepening cries of encouragement and anxiety from the stands and the players alike. The close-packed rows hummed with ceaseless, nervous sounds of conversation and speculation—and impatience for the dénouement, and a fear of it, too. All around me in our section I could see the same look of resignation and boredom and pleasure that now showed on my own face, I knew—the look of longtime fans who understand that one can never leave a very long close game, no matter how much inconvenience and exasperation it imposes on us. The difficulty of baseball is imperious.

"Yay! Yay!" Dick Lee cried when Yale left fielder Joe Dufek led off the eighth with a single. "Now come *on*, you guys! I gotta get home for dinner." But the next Yale batter bunted into a force play at second, and the chance was gone. "Well, all right—for *breakfast!*" Lee said, slumping back in his seat.

The two pitchers held us—each as intent and calm and purposeful as the other. Ron Darling, never deviating from the purity of his stylish body-lean and leg-crook and his riding, down-thrusting delivery, poured fastballs through the diminishing daylight. He looked as fast as ever now, or faster, and in both the ninth and the tenth he dismissed the side in order and with four more strikeouts. Viola was dominant in his own fashion, also setting down the Yale hitters one, two, three in the ninth and tenth, with a handful of pitches. His rhythm—the constant variety of speeds and location on his pitches—had the enemy batters leaning and swaying with his motion, and, as antistrophe, was almost as exciting to watch as Darling's flair and flame.

166

With two out in the top of the eleventh, a St. John's batter nudged a soft little roller up the first-base line—such an easy, waiting, schoolboy sort of chance that the Yale first baseman, O'Connor, allowed the ball to carom off his mitt: a miserable little butchery, except that the second baseman, seeing his pitcher sprinting for the bag, now snatched up the ball and flipped it toward him almost despairingly. Darling took the toss while diving full-length at the bag and, rolling in the dirt, beat the runner by a hair.

"Oh, my!" said Joe Wood. "Oh, my, oh, my!"

Then in the bottom of the inning Yale suddenly loaded the bases—a hit, a walk, another walk (Viola was just missing the corners now)—and we all came to our feet, yelling and pleading. The tilted stands and the low roof deepened the cheers and sent them rolling across the field. There were two out, and the Yale batter, Dan Costello, swung at the first pitch and bounced it gently to short, for a force that ended the rally. Somehow, I think, we knew that we had seen Yale's last chance.

"I would have taken that pitch," I said, entering the out in my scorecard. "To keep the pressure on him."

"I don't know," Joe Wood said at once. "He's just walked two. You might get the cripple on the first pitch and then see nothing but hooks. Hit away."

He was back in the game.

Steve Scafa, leading off the twelfth, got a little piece of Darling's first pitch on the handle of his bat, and the ball looped softly over the shortstop's head and into left: a hit. The loudspeakers told us that Ron Darling's eleven innings of no-hit pitching had set a new N.C.A.A. tournament record. Everyone at Yale Field stood up—the St. John's players, too, coming off their bench and out onto the field—and applauded Darling's masterpiece. We were scarcely seated again before Scafa stole second as the Yale catcher, Paterno, bobbled the pitch. Scafa, who is blurrily quick, had stolen thirty-five bases during the season. Now he stole third as well. With one out and runners at the corners (the other St. John's man had reached first on an error), Darling ran the count to three and two and fanned the next batter—his fifteenth strikeout of the game. Two out. Darling sighed and stared in, and then stepped off the mound while the St. John's coach put in a pinch-runner at first—who took off for second on the very next pitch. Paterno fired the ball quickly this time, and Darling, staggering off the mound with his follow-through, did not cut it off. Scafa came ten feet down the third-base line and stopped there, while the pinch-runner suddenly jammed on the brakes, stranding himself between first and second: a play, clearly—an inserted crisis. The Yale second baseman glanced twice at Scafa, freezing him, and then made a little run at the hung-up base runner to his left and threw to first. With that, Scafa instantly broke for the plate. Lured by the vision of the third out just a few feet away from him on the base path, the Yale first baseman hesitated, fractionally and

167

fatally, before he spun and threw home, where Scafa slid past the tag and came up, leaping and clapping, into the arms of his teammates. That was the game. Darling struck out his last man, but a new St. John's pitcher, a right-handed fire-baller named Eric Stampfl, walked on and blew the Elis away in their half.

"Well, that's a shame," Joe Wood said, getting up for the last time. It was close to six-thirty, but he looked fine now. "If that man scores before the third out, it counts, you know," he said. "That's why it worked. I never saw a better-played game anyplace—college or big-league. That's a swell ball-game."

O

Several things happened afterward. Neither Yale nor St. John's qualified for the college World Series, it turned out; the University of Maine defeated St. John's in the final game of the playoffs at New Haven (neither Viola nor Darling was sufficiently recovered from his ordeal to pitch again) and made the trip to Omaha, where it, too, was eliminated. Arizona State won the national title. On June 9th, Ron Darling was selected by the Texas Rangers at the major-league amateur-player draft in New York. He was the ninth player in the country to be chosen. Frank Viola, the thirty-seventh pick, went to the Minnesota Twins. (The Seattle Mariners, who had the first pick this year, had been ready to take Darling, which would have made him the coveted No. 1 selection in the draft, but the club backed off at the last moment because of Darling's considerable salary demands. As it was, he signed with the Rangers for a hundred-thousand-dollar bonus.)* On June 12th, the major-league players unanimously struck the twenty-six big-league teams. The strike has brought major-league ball to a halt, and no one can predict when play will resume. Because of this sudden silence, the St. John's–Yale struggle has become the best and most vivid game of the year for me, so far. It may stay that way even after the strike ends. "I think that game will always be on my mind," Ron Darling said after it was over. I feel the same way. I think I will remember it all my life. So will Joe Wood. Somebody will probably tell Ron Darling that Smokey Joe Wood was at the game that afternoon and saw him pitch eleven scoreless no-hit innings against St. John's, and someday—perhaps years from now, when he, too, may possibly be a celebrated major-league strikeout artist—it may occur to him that his

*As baseball fans know, The New York Mets acquired Darling by means of a trade with the Rangers in 1982, and he began his distinguished Mets career the following season. Viola, meanwhile, became the winningest pitcher in the majors over the five years between 1984 and 1988, and won a Cy Young Award for his 24–7 record for the Twins in 1988. As destiny fans know, he was traded to New York the next summer, and joined Darling on the Mets' starting rotation.

heartbreaking 0–1 loss in May 1981 and Walter Johnson's 0–1 loss at Fenway Park in September 1912 are now woven together into the fabric of baseball. Pitch by pitch, inning by inning, Ron Darling had made that happen. He stitched us together.

In the Country

— AUGUST 1981

Baseball is a family for those who follow it, and members of close families like to exchange letters. Three years ago, I received a letter from a woman named Linda Kittell, who was living in Clinton, Montana.

"I was born in 1952," she wrote. "I remember listening to the Yankees—with Mel Allen, it must have been—on a little yellow transistor radio on an island in Lake Champlain, where we spent our summers. Not listening but sort of doing the everyday things of an eight- or ten-year-old—drinking chocolate milk and eating animal crackers—while my sister, two years older, flirted with her boyfriend, who *listened* to the Yankee games on the yellow radio. I only paid attention when I heard Mickey Mantle's name or Roger Maris's name. And I was in love with Whitey Ford. Maris was hitting home runs as often as we went uptown that summer—every day. . . .

"I forgot about baseball later, except in September, when I paid attention if the Yankees were close to getting into the Series. I went to college, and then to graduate school in Montana. One night in a bar in Missoula, I met a man who just about fell flat when I complained about the games on the TV set there because they didn't put on the Yankees enough. He looked at me as if he'd been struck. You're a *Yankee* fan? I told him I had a perfect right, because I was from upstate New York and because I'd been in love with Whitey Ford all my life, practically. Ron was a Mantle fan (his name is Ron Goble; he's a lanky six feet five), and I tended more toward Maris, but we both loved Whitey Ford. We talked and drank beer. He'd played Legion ball for five years in his home town of Boise, Idaho, and he'd won a baseball scholarship to Linfield College, in Oregon. He'd been scouted in school by the Yankees, the Angels, and the Pirates. He's a left-handed pitcher. His fastball was clocked at more than ninety m.p.h., and he told me he'd held

170

back on it, at that, because he was afraid of hurting his arm. He said how he'd recognized the scouts in the stands because they were all tan in May and June in southern Idaho. He talked about how he'd come to think a college education was more important than athletics, and how the student riots in the late nineteen-sixties had turned him against sports, so he'd stopped playing. He talked about Vietnam and drugs and what it was like then, and what a waste it had been for him to forget about ball.

"We started living together about three years ago. Christmases, birthdays, surprises from me—all those special days had to do with baseball. A baseball book, a baseball picture, a pack of new baseball cards—anything. Then last year Seattle got the Mariners. Our vacation from Montana was a twelve-hour train ride and three days' worth of games—*Yankee* games: the Yankees at the Kingdome. I cried when I saw them out there. Ron said I was being silly. But, God, there was Mickey Rivers. I mean, Mickey Rivers! . . .

"The third day, I found a sympathetic usher who let me stand down close to the field with about ten little kids trying to get autographs. I lied through my teeth and said one of them was my little brother. Sparky Lyle and Catfish and Chambliss were playing pepper, and then a player out beyond them called, 'Hey, you girl!' I looked up. 'Yeah, you,' and he threw me a ball. Paul Blair threw me a baseball. All the little boys waist-high around me looked disgusted. 'Why'd he throw *her* a ball?' . . . 'Mom, Dad, that one threw that *girl* a ball.' It was an Official American League ball. I read it over and rushed up to my seat, where Ron was waiting for the game to start. 'It's a real ball,' I told him. '*Look* at it.' There I was, a perfectly sensible, sensitive twenty-four-year-old woman getting goose bumps over a baseball. I asked Ron if I should go down for more autographs, but something had changed. He rubbed the ball and kept looking at it. He was years away, and sad about it. . . . I went back down, and the autograph I got in the end was Elston Howard's. Memory and imagination make you think about anything you want. I'd picked Ellie Howard—and not Mickey Rivers or Catfish Hunter or Thurman Munson— because I thought it would make him happy, and because his name reminded me of my little yellow radio back in Vermont on August afternoons. Because I'm sentimental.

"We drove back to Montana with a friend, and Ron and I sat in the back seat. 'Can I see the ball again?' he said. I handed it to him and watched Ron hold it for a fastball, a slider, a curve. He looked far-off still. . . .

"This spring, there was an article in *The Sporting News* about a Class A team being formed in Boise, called the Buckskins. Tryouts were in June, and you needed three thousand dollars from a sponsor if you made the team. Something different, all right, but it was a chance to play ball. They'd signed the Sundown Kid—Danny Thomas—and a twenty-seven-year-old catcher from southern Idaho. I wanted Ron to go down and try out. He said he wasn't in shape. He said he was happy playing on the Clinton Clowns, our town's fast-pitch softball team. It was obvious that he *wasn't* happy playing softball, and especially obvious in the fall, when he'd pitch by himself—pitch baseball by throwing rotten apples from our tree against a telephone pole, and call balls and strikes, hits and outs. . . ."

Linda persuaded Ron to try out for the Buckskins, but he didn't get around to it until a few days before their season was about to begin. A letter from the Buckskin manager, Gerry Craft, said they were looking for a left-handed pitcher, and that did the trick.

"Our truck broke down," Linda's letter went on. "Planes were on strike. Finally, Ron's brother George drove him down. Ron was signed on the first day he threw—a good rotation on his curveball, they said. I didn't even know what Ron meant by that when he told me about it by long-distance. Gerry Craft had said he could go far in baseball, but what Gerry didn't know was that Ron had thrown his arm out—just about ruined it, it turned out—with the second curve he'd thrown. So Ron waited, in ice packs. Three days later, he came home with a swollen arm and a professional baseball player's contract. Five hundred dollars a month. We started packing up his stuff and spent long hours looking for a sponsor. We ended up putting up our own money. Three thousand dollars may not sound like much to some people, but it was everything we had. I served Ron a steak dinner and kissed him goodbye.

"I don't think it really sank in until I made the trip down to Boise to see the Buckskins play in their first home stand. Ron was standing there in his tan-and-black uniform, with a satin warmup jacket and real cleats, and I was just as excited about that as I'd been when I saw Mickey Rivers on the field in Seattle. I was goofy. . . .

"Now, anyone will tell you that this Buckskins team is different. The general manager, Lanny Moss [Lanny Moss is a woman], is very religious, and so is Gerry Craft. In right field at their park there's a huge billboard with 'JESUS' written on it in twelve-foot letters. In left field there's a strange picture of Christ Himself. Craft says he had a vision that told him to look around Spokane for a cabin in the woods, and that's where he found Danny Thomas, the Sundown Kid. Danny left major-league ball [Thomas, an outfielder, had played for two seasons with the Brewers] because his religion required him to read the Bible from sundown Friday to sundown Saturday, which meant he mostly couldn't play on those days. And Craft has game strategy confirmed to him by the Bible, and stuff. Some of his ballplayers have been baptized on their road trips—I picture a clean white sink at the Salem Inn as the font, with the neat sample Ivory soap tablets resting at the side. But these ballplayers are the nicest people I've ever met.

"I'm not the typical wife/girlfriend of a baseball player—those women you see on TV with their hair done up and their Rose Bowl Parade wave to the crowds. I like to watch baseball. I love the game, and I'm one of the loudest fans in the stands. And when Ron's pitching I find myself almost praying for a win. But the Buckskins don't win many games. The newspapers around the league have put too much stress on the religious aspect of the team. The players aren't all Jesus people. Most of them drink beer and swear. Gerry Craft rhubarbs with the umps with his hands in his jacket pockets. Danny Thomas hits a grand-slammer half an hour before sunset and trots around the bases on his way to his Bible. It's all wonderful. The beer, the hot dogs with everything on them, and seeing old Ron Goble out on the mound working on his curveball and about to turn twenty-seven. What a good way to turn twenty-seven—finally doing something you've tried to ignore for eight years. I love it. It's a hit in the bottom of the ninth, with the score tied and the ball sailing over the right-field wall."

○

I answered this letter, needless to say, and in time Linda wrote back. We became baseball correspondents and baseball friends. She wrote in October that year and told me about the rest of the Buckskins' season. The team had gone bad, at one point losing eleven straight games. Money was short, and the team's religious fervor made for difficulties. After the Buckskins suffered a 25–3 loss to the Salem Senators, Gerry Craft released the losing pitcher, saying that God had made it clear to him that He didn't want that pitcher on the team. In Eugene, Oregon, Craft announced that God had told him they were going to lose a game to the Emeralds, and, sure enough, they did, blowing a 6–4 lead in the ninth. Some of the benchwarmers on the club began to wonder if they were being kept on the roster because of their three-thousand-dollar sponsor deposits—an inevitable development, perhaps. The Buckskins finished last in the Northwest League, fourteen games behind their divisional winner, Eugene, and twenty-five games worse than the eventual champions, the Gray's Harbor (Washington) Loggers. Danny Thomas led the league with a .359 batting average, but the Buckskins had the worst pitching in the league—a club earned-run average of 6.42. Ron Goble wound up with a 2–3 record and an earned-run average of 8.18—his lifetime figures in professional baseball.

There were some good moments, even in a season like that.

"I went down to Boise in August," Linda wrote in that next letter. "Ron met me at the airport, and we went straight to the field. There was talk that Charlie Finley had sent for the Sundowner, to help his Oakland A's, and talk that two new pitchers were coming from Milwaukee. It was hot—a hundred degrees, easy. I sat in the only shade in the ballpark and watched batting practice. Danny Thomas was running around with a coonskin cap on, and

Bo McConnaughy, one of my favorites on the team, came out in a bright-yellow hard hat. Bo was the Buckskins' shortstop—a ballplayers' ballplayer. He had been in the minor leagues for years, in the Orioles organization—the wrong place at the wrong time, because the Orioles had a shortstop named Mark Belanger. Then Bo had gotten too old to be of any interest to them. Bo loves baseball, and you don't notice his gray hair until he's back in street clothes.

"Raymie Odermott started the game against Bend that night, and went six and two-thirds innings, until Gerry brought in Ron with the score 4–3, Boise. Two outs, men on first and second. Ron went in, and this left-hand batter was waiting for him and got a hit that tied the score. Boise scored two runs in the seventh and one in the eighth, and Ron held Bend scoreless the rest of the game, striking out their last two batters. Just fine.

"He was off in the ozone the rest of the night. He sat over a beer with friends, quietly reviewing the game. His curveball had been right for the first time since the June tryout. We both thought—or hoped, I suppose—that the days of Tenderyl and the threat of cortisone were over. It's hard to explain how happy he was that night. It's as if he believed for a moment that he wasn't eight years too late. . . .

"Still, there were rumblings on the team. Pitchers went to Gerry and complained that they didn't get to pitch. Mark Garland was one, and he got to start. He got blown away. The next night, it was Dennis Love, who'd also complained. He looked real bad, too, and Gerry brought in Ron. Ron let up a home run—to the first batter. It was a bad time. The next day, at batting practice, Dennis Love said he'd been released, along with Mark Garland. Ron went in to talk to Gerry about *his* future, and I drove down to the Circle K to get some pop. Mark Garland was crying beside a bridge over an irrigation canal. And I hoped I wouldn't end up comforting Ron some day, squeezing his hand and talking softly to him, the way Mark's wife stood comforting him.

"The last two weeks of the season, the team played without pay, until Lanny Moss could borrow the money to pay their checks. Danny Thomas left, saying he wasn't going to play ball for free. There was no money for hotels or food. Once, the bus broke down, and the team had to sleep on the floor of a church. They left on a last road trip to Victoria and Bellingham. I went up to visit friends in Seattle and to catch some of the Bellingham games. The Kingdome didn't wow me so much this time. The Yankees were there again, but I knew more about people on the field than I used to. I got Ron Guidry's autograph, and I still loved Mickey Rivers, but it was different. People, not heroes. In Bellingham, I spent a rainy evening watching 'Monday Night Baseball' with Ron and Bo. Then I danced with all the team, at Bellingham's imitation disco.

"Season's over. Ron's been back a month. Two weeks ago, he went grouse hunting with the dogs and a friend, and came home tipsy drunk. He'd remembered his doctor's appointment the next day, and had spent his time trying to forget about it. He made a mock pitch for me, and his elbow *clicked* at the end of the motion. He said, 'At least, Gerry Craft told me I could have been in the bigs. I know that much. It's enough.'

"A shot of cortisone and rest. Ron doesn't lie to the scouts about his age, you know. He and Bo are honest about that. We have tons of fallen apples, if Ron's arm starts to come around. Bo's in Boise, studying to be a mechanic. Gerry's been released. Everybody's waiting through the winter."

o

There were more letters back and forth. It meant a lot to me to hear from someone—from two people, really—who could tell me what baseball was like far from the crowds and the noise and the fame and the big money that I had been writing about for many summers. And by this time, of course, I cared about Ron and Linda, and worried about what would happen to them. Linda wrote me that Ron and his brother George and a friend named Ray were spending a great deal of their time that winter playing an extremely complicated baseball-by-dice game called Extra Innings. From time to time, Ron would get out his mitt and persuade someone to catch him, but when he threw, in gingerly fashion, he found that his elbow was still horribly painful. He couldn't get over how foolish he had been to throw that hard curve during his Buckskins tryout. He read a book by Jim Bouton, in which Bouton said that his sore arm felt as if it had been bitten by alligators; Ron's felt exactly the same way. The Buckskins, in any case, had folded. The Phillies had expressed some interest in picking them up as a farm team, but the city of Boise would not refurbish its ancient ballpark, so the Phillies went elsewhere. Then the Northwest League adopted a rule favoring younger players and making it harder for older players to find a place on its team rosters—the last blow for Ron. That winter, he sent letters to all the major-league clubs asking for some kind of employment in their organizations, but the answers were a long time coming back. He told Linda he had really been collecting major-league letterheads. Linda described an evening of theirs on the town, and its ending: "We walked through the streets of Missoula in the 4 A.M. drizzle, Ron in his Buckskin jacket and me feeling very maudlin, remembering the walk from the field to the Buckskins' dressing room. What fun it was being a Baseball Annie, arm in arm with some semblance of a professional ballplayer, rain drizzling on my arm and on the satin warmup jacket. How romantic and far away it seems now."

At about this time, I wrote an article about the difficulties that women sports reporters had experienced in gaining access to the clubhouses of major-league ball teams on their beat, and Linda commented on that, too:

"Oh, as to women in the clubhouse, I think they're a necessity. Why, this summer when the Buckskins got locked out of their locker room, I was the only one who could fit through the window and over the top row of the lockers, to unlock the door. And for that one quiet moment between lockers and door I imagined myself in uniform, imagined the feel of oiled leather and dust, the long trip from this town to the next."

There was a long trip just ahead for Ron and Linda—from Montana to northwestern Vermont, where they moved into a farmhouse about forty miles from Burlington: "It took us six days to drive across the country in a calico Chevy truck, with the two dogs in back and a U-Haul in back of that. I think the only thing that got Ron across the plains was the radio reception. We kept tuning in game after game, from all the big-league cities along the way, including a French-Canadian station, near the end, with the Expos on it. French baseball cracked me up. We're close to Montreal here, and we went to an Expos-Cardinals doubleheader last weekend. Saw Cash's grand slam and drank Canadian beer. Ron was frustrated by the French and English announcements—a whole bunch of French with 'Ellis Valentine' in the middle of it. Whenever the Expos did anything, the French-Canadians sitting around us would slap each other on the back and pull on their pints of vodka."

Linda had come East to be closer to her family for a while. (She was born in Troy, New York, and Burlington is on Lake Champlain, where she passed those early summers listening to the Yankees.) She went to work as a feature writer and sports editor for a Vermont newspaper, the *Lamoille County Weekly*. The main object, she wrote me, was to get as many players' names as possible into her stories, so that their mothers would buy the paper. "I have a funny press pass that the publisher made up," she added. "It's an attempt to make me seem very professional, but the publisher, who's an old friend of mine, can't spell very well. 'This card,' it says, 'entitles the barer . . .' It didn't get me into the press room in Montreal."

Ron was working as a carpenter and a substitute high-school teacher, and he and Linda were excited by the discovery that Burlington had a team (more than one team, it turned out) in a local semipro league. Ron hoped to play there—hoped to pitch, in fact, if he got any help from a local orthopedist who was said to specialize in sports medicine. "We'll see," Linda concluded. "I'd rather see Ron pitching and playing than substituting Great Civilization." She urged me to come and visit them, and watch Ron pitch.

○

I put it in my mind to keep that date—it would be the coming summer, the summer of 1980—but the next letter changed my plans. Ron had cancer. They had found a lump in his abdomen, which was removed by surgery.

Subsequently, he underwent another operation and lost one testicle. It was seminoma—a highly curable form of the disease, the doctors said. Ron was going into the Burlington hospital every day for radiation treatments. "I can't stand to see him hooked up to all those tubes in the hospital, and worried about how he's going to look in the locker room," Linda wrote. "I'm not sure I understand why it is that good people and athletes can be struck this way. It's pretty weird, is all. But Ron is unflappable. He's out pitching snowballs at trees and making plans to play on the Burlington team somehow. But I have a feeling it's going to take a lot to get the boy in shape this spring. Street & Smith's are out [the early-season baseball yearbook]. Ron and his buddies are ranking the teams and giving them their finishing places this year. Winner gets a six-pack from each loser."

Ron Goble had a good summer, though—much better than he or anyone else had expected. In May and June, he coached a team of thirteen-to-fifteen-year-olds in the local Babe Ruth League, and at the same time he tried out for the Burlington A's, in the semipro Northern League, and made the club. For a time, he was so weak from the effects of his illness and the radiation that he could pitch no more than two or three innings at a stretch, but he learned how to conserve his energy by warming up only briefly and by trying to throw ground-ball outs. By the end of the brief season, he was able to pitch a full game, and he wound up with a respectable 4–1 record. He never told anyone on the club, last year or this year, that he had had cancer. Last winter, he worked as a teacher's aide at the Bellows Free Academy, in St. Albans, Vermont, and as a custodian at the local rink, but most of his energy went into an attempt to organize a new Northern League club in St. Albans. It fell through—not enough local money, not enough local commercial enthusiasm—but by springtime Ron had been signed on as a regional commission scout by the Milwaukee Brewers (Gerry Craft, his old manager, was a Brewers district scout, and had recommended Ron), and he was umpiring high-school games. He would pitch again for the A's this summer. Linda was teaching humanities courses at the local community college. Things were looking good; they wanted me to drive up and see them.

The bad news, Linda wrote, had come earlier and from far away: Danny Thomas had hanged himself in a jail cell in Alabama, where he had been facing trial on a rape charge. "It came as a real shock," Linda wrote. "What bothers me is that baseball has been a savior for Ron. Last spring, it brought back his confidence in himself and in his body. And here's someone like Danny Thomas who saw baseball as his pain. Danny had a strange look in his eyes when he talked about religion, and reporters were always after him to talk about his beliefs. Everyone knew he was slightly wacko, but the man had principles. His wife, Judy, was really afraid he'd take Charlie Finley up on that offer to come back to major-league ball. She said she couldn't stand that stuff again. Ron says Danny could hit a baseball farther than anyone he's ever seen. I saw him hit a home run out of every ballpark where I saw the Buckskins play. The last day I saw him play was in Bellingham. It was raining, and Danny's little daughter, Renee, was sitting up in the bleachers with Gerry Craft's daughter, Maizee, and singing 'Take me out to the ballgame, take me out to the ballgame,' slapping their hands on their thighs. The girls didn't know any of the other words, so they sang that over and over again."

○

On a cool, windy-bright Saturday at the end of last June, I drove straight north through Connecticut, through Massachusetts, and into Vermont, crossing and recrossing the narrowing Connecticut River along the way, and at last, over the river one more time, I found the Burlington A's at play against the Walpole (New Hampshire) Blue Jays on the Walpole home field—a neat little American Legion diamond just beneath a steep, thickly wooded hillside, hard by the Hubbard Farms fertilizer plant. At play and then *not* at play, since the A's had knocked off the Jays, 4–1, at the moment of my arrival, in the first game of a doubleheader. I met Linda Kittell at the field—a dark-haired young woman in faded bluejeans, with pale eyes, an open, alert expression, and an enormous smile. Then I shook hands with the A's manager, Paul Farrar; with Paul's wife, Sue; and, at last, with Ron Goble—a pitcher, all right: long arms, long hands, long body, very long legs, a sun-burnished nose, a surprising blondish Fu Manchu mustache, a shy smile, and one bulging cheek (not tobacco, it turned out, but sunflower seeds). Ron and Paul said what a shame it was I'd missed the opener, and then quickly ducked back out onto the field and into their little concrete dugout to get ready for the next one—Ron to chart pitches and keep score (he would pitch the next day, down in Brattleboro), and his skipper, of course, to worry. Linda and I sat down in an upper row of a tiny rack of bleachers in short right field. We had no trouble finding seats. My quick count of the house, after the nightcap had begun, came to thirty-three, including babies in strollers. Several young women— players' wives or players' girlfriends, probably—were lying on blankets spread out behind the backstop, where they took turns slathering each other's backs with suntan goop. Near the Walpole dugout, a ten- or twelve-year-old girl on an aluminum camp chair watched the game in company with a big chocolate-brown Labrador, holding him out of the action (and breaking his heart) with a yellow leash. Whenever a foul ball flew past us, someone in the audience would get up and amble after it, while we in the bleachers called out directions ("More right, more right—*now* another step!") until it had been tracked down in the thick meadow weeds around the field. There was a lot of clapping and cries of encouragement ("Good eye, batter! Good

178

eye!") from the little crowd, and between batters and innings you could hear the cool, gusty northwest wind working through the green treetop canopies of ash and oak and maple on the hillside out beyond right field.

In the first inning, the Walpole batters whacked some long drives against the visitors' starting pitcher, and some short ones, too, and pretty soon Burlington's designated hitter, Darcy Spear, came out of the dugout and began warming up with a catcher—not a good turn of events, Linda told me, because the team had been able to scrape up only four pitchers for its two-day, four-game weekend road trip here to the southern end of the league. The players had driven down in their own cars and pickups, but the team, she said, would pay for their motel accommodations in Brattleboro that night. There were no programs, and I was lucky to have Linda there to identify some of the A's whose style afield or at the plate I was beginning to pick up—a diminutive second baseman, Greg Wells, who had a nice way of looking the ball into his glove on grounders; a strong-armed shortstop named Rob DelBianco; and Tinker Jarvis, at third, who had driven in a pair of runs in the top of the first inning with a line-drive double and then singled sharply in the third. The A's wore the same combination of garish buttercup-yellow shirts, white pants, and white shoes first made famous by the Oakland A's, while the Walpole nine sported a variation of Toronto Blue Jays home whites, but there was no connection between these local teams and their big-league namesakes, Linda explained; rather, the manufacturer supplying the Northern League had offered bargain rates on these prestyled uniforms—sort of like a Seventh Avenue dress house knocking off mass copies of Diors and Balmains. A distinguishing feature of this particular summer line was the names of various home-town commercial sponsors that the players wore on their backs, and before long I realized that I had begun to identify the different A's players by these billboards rather than by the names that Linda had murmured to me. Thus Darcy Spear became Uncle Sam's Dairy Bar, and it was Coca-Cola, the left-handed first baseman, who kept up a patter of encouraging talk to Red Barn on the mound (Red Barn had settled down after that first inning), while Slayton's Roofing (Manager Farrar) paced up and down in front of his dugout and waited for a chance to send the large and menacing-looking Cake World up to pinch-hit and get something started out there. Linda said it was all right for me to think of the players this way, because they often called each other by the sponsors' names anyway, for fun—except for Ron (Community Bingo), who was called Pigeon, because of his sunflower seeds. The A's players had been expected to hunt up their own sponsors at the beginning of the season, but not all of them, I noticed, had been successful. Each sponsor had put up a hundred dollars for his walking (or running and throwing, and sometimes popping-up-in-the-clutch) advertisement, and each sponsored player had sewn on his own commercial or had prevailed upon someone else—his mother, perhaps—to sew it on for him.

The Northern League, which encompasses six teams—the Burlington A's, the Burlington Expos, the South Burlington Queen City Royals, the Walpole Blue Jays, the Brattleboro Maples, and the Saxtons River Pirates—and also plays against the Glens Falls (New York) Glensox, is a semiprofessional circuit, with the stronger emphasis, I had begun to understand, falling on the "semi." In the distant past, semipro ball teams were often composed of skilled local amateurs plus a handful of ringers—a couple of hard-hitting rookie outfielders just starting on their professional careers, perhaps, or a wily, shopworn pro pitcher at the very end of his—who played for modest salaries, or even for a flat per-game fee. This system fell into difficulties when increasing numbers of young athletes began to go off to college, where they found that they were not permitted to play varsity ball, because their semipro experience had compromised their status as amateurs. An earlier, extremely popular Northern League, with teams at Burlington, Montpelier, Rutland, St. Johnsbury, and other northwestern New England towns, came apart in 1952, partly because its Big Ten college stars were withdrawn by their schools to prevent the loss of their amateur status, and thus no longer appeared in games with professionals of the likes of Johnny Antonelli, Robin Roberts, Ray Scarborough, Snuffy Stirnweiss, Johnny Podres, and Boo Ferriss, who had all played on its diamonds at one time or another before moving on up through the minors and then to fame and success as majorleaguers. Nowadays, many semipro teams simply find summer jobs for their players—a lumber company, let's say, putting a college fastball pitcher to work in the drying sheds by day so that he may advertise the concern out on the mound at the town field by night or on weekend afternoons—but only the Burlington Expos, who are looked upon as the Yankees of the Northern League, had managed to arrange this kind of tie-in this summer, and then only for a few of their players.

The Northern League is an independent body, with its own commissioner, its own set of rules (the d.h., aluminum bats for those who want to use them), and its own ways (including a ritual handshake between the players on rival clubs at the conclusion of every game—a pleasing custom probably lifted from the National Hockey League, whose teams line up and shake hands at the conclusion of each Stanley Cup elimination series). The six clubs play an official two-month schedule, from late May to late July, with playoffs and a Championship Series thereafter—about twenty-five or twenty-seven games each, with a good number of additional, informal, outside-the-standings games thrown in whenever they can be arranged. A minimum team budget, I learned, runs about three thousand dollars, and, beyond the obvious expenditures for equipment, goes for umpires (two umps, at twenty-five dollars each, for every game), a league fee of two hundred dollars (to keep statistics, handle publicity, and stage the league's All-Star Game), a modest insurance policy covering minor player injuries, and so forth. Income, beyond sponsorships, comes from ticket sales—a dollar for adults, fifty cents for children, babies and dogs free. The Burlington A's' entire season's operation probably costs less than a major-league team's bill for adhesive tape and foul balls during a week's play, but the Northern League, now in its third year, is doing well and expects to add at least two more clubs next summer.

All semipro leagues, it should be understood, are self-sustaining, and have no farm affiliation or other connection with the twenty-six major-league clubs, or with the seventeen leagues and hundred and fifty-two teams (ranging from Rookie League at the lowest level, to Class A and Summer Class A, up to the AAA designation at the highest) that make up the National Association—the minors, that is. There is no central body of semipro teams, and semipro players are not included among the six hundred and fifty major-leaguers, the twenty-five hundred-odd minor-leaguers, plus all the managers, coaches, presidents, commissioners, front-office people, and scouts, who, taken together, constitute the great tent called organized ball. (A much diminished tent, at that; back in 1949, the minors included fifty-nine leagues, about four hundred and forty-eight teams, and perhaps ten thousand players.) Also outside the tent, but perhaps within its shade, are five college leagues, ranging across the country from Cape Cod to Alaska, where the most promising college freshman, sophomore, and junior-year ballplayers may compete against each other in the summertime without losing their amateur status; the leagues are administered by the National Collegiate Athletic Association and receive indirect support—bats, balls, uniforms, and the like—from the major leagues, whose scouts keep a careful eye on their young stars. If the college leagues are semipro, the accent there probably should fall on the second word, for a considerable number of their best batters and pitchers are snapped up in the major-league amateur draft toward the end of their college careers. Scouts cover the Northern League as well—two pitchers with the Burlington Expos were signed to professional contracts this June, and they moved along at once to join their assigned minor-league clubs—but the level of play is not up to that of the college leagues. Most of the A's players, I learned in time, are undergraduates or recent graduates of local or eastern colleges (five of them from the University of Vermont, one from the University of New Hampshire, one from Amherst, one from the University of New Haven, and so on) who play for the fun of the game and the heat of the competition, and perhaps with half an eye turned toward the stands between pitches, in search of a major-league scout sitting there one afternoon who might just possibly be writing notes about this one good-looking outfielder or batter out there, whom he had somehow passed over the first time around. Ron Goble, at twenty-nine, was the oldest regular with the Burlington A's, and one of the few players in the league with any experience in professional ball.

How well did the A's play baseball? I found the question a difficult one at first, for the over-all quality of play in any one game tends to blur one's baseball judgment, but it did seem plain that most of the young players here on the Walpole ball field were far too slow afoot to merit comparison with professionals. Some threw well, as I have said, and others attacked the ball at the plate with consistency and power, but these two gifts did not seem to coexist in any one player. Most of all, the A's seemed young. They were all extremely cheerful, and, as I now found out, they loved to win. Down a run in their last at-bats (the seventh inning, in this doubleheader), the A's put their leadoff man aboard on a walk and instantly moved him up with a dazzling bunt by second baseman Greg Wells, who also knocked the catcher's peg out of the first baseman's mitt as he crossed the bag, and was safe. A moment later, with the bases loaded, Uncle Sam's Dairy Bar (Darcy Spear) whacked a single, good for two runs, and then the commercially anonymous catcher (Bob Boucher) tripled to deep center. Walpole, whose handful of wives and parents had gone speechless with dismay, changed pitchers, but Churchill's (Tinker Jarvis) singled, too, and before it was over the visiting A's had scored six runs and won the game, 9–4, sweeping the doubleheader. Ron Goble, ambling over to join us, hugged Linda and grinned at me and asked if I couldn't take the rest of the summer off to watch the A's and thus bring them through the rest of the season undefeated.

○

Steve Gallacher pitched the opener against the Brattleboro Maples the next afternoon—a strong twenty-two-year-old right-hander with a good, live fastball. The A's took up their hitting where they had left off the previous evening and moved smartly to a three-run lead in the top of the first. Linda and I sat in the last row of the grandstand, behind the decaying foul screen; it was a high-school field, a bit seedy but with a nice view to the south of some distant farms and silos and long fields of young corn sloping down toward the Connecticut River.

Linda told me that Steve Gallacher was said to have been the last man cut at a Pirates' tryout camp a year or two ago, and later had a Dodger scout on his trail, although nothing had come of it. I asked her how many people in the league still hoped to make a career in professional ball someday.

"If you have a chance, you have to see it through," she said at once. "It doesn't mean anything if you don't do something about it—really find out. So many of these players are unrealistic to think they could ever play minor-league ball. They go out and buy these expensive A's warmup jackets, which they can't really afford. I can see them all seventy-five years from now, saying, 'Well, I used to play semipro ball.' And Ron will probably be saying, 'I pitched this one great game for the Boise Buckskins.' I'd like to see something better than that for him in the end. Ron is always looking backward, and I think I like to look ahead. When he goes out scouting for the Brewers, he watches pitchers a lot, and maybe left-handed pitchers most of all. I think he still thinks he's better than most of the young pitchers he scouts."

She had been talking in an edged, hard tone I had not heard before, but now she stopped and shook her head and then laughed at herself a little—a habit of hers, I had begun to notice. "I guess Ron is even more of a hero to me than Whitey Ford was," she said more softly. "I like heroes. I have a lot of trouble with reality, too. I hate it when he plays softball, because all the other players on his team take it so seriously. Softball is—well, it's like badminton, or something. It's nothing, compared to baseball. I've told Ron he'll have to give up baseball when he looks better in his street clothes than he does in his uniform." She laughed again—almost a giggle. "He's still a long way from *that*!" she said.

We watched the game for a while, but Linda seemed tense and distracted, and it came to me at last that she was worrying about how well Ron would pitch in the second game. Suddenly she said, "With all the people I've known in baseball, I can't think of one happy ending. Danny Thomas, Gerry Craft, Ron—none of it came out happily. You know, it isn't like Chris Chambliss coming up in the ninth inning of that playoff game and unbuttoning the top button of his shirt and then hitting that home run. You just don't see that happen. Ron hurt his arm before he got started. Gerry Craft got up as far as Lodi, in the Orioles system, and he was on his way—a good outfielder. Then he got hurt and it was all finished, overnight. Danny Thomas is dead. What's the reality? I ask myself that all the time."

The Brattleboro hitters kept after Steve Gallacher, and then caught up with him and went ahead by 5–4 in the bottom of the fifth, with three solid blows. They were looking for his fastball by this time, and I wondered what would happen if he could show them a breaking pitch now and then in a tough spot. Young pitchers love the heater, but so do good young hitters. The A's put their leadoff man aboard in the top of the seventh, but the Maples' pitcher, a young redhead named Parmenter, threw some impressive-looking sliders and shut off the rally. It was a quick, well-played game, and the local fans—a much better turnout today—gave their boys a good hand at the end.

Ron Goble started the second game, and I found that I was a bit nervous, too. I needn't have worried. He set down the side in order in the first, and even though the Maples touched him up for a pair of runs in the second, on a walk and a couple of singles, he looked unstressed and in control out there, never attempting to force a delivery or to work beyond his capacities. He ended up the inning by fanning the side—a good sign. He is a graceful-looking pitcher. My game notes about him read:

> Tall, v. long legs. Minimal rock & motion. Drops glove behind leg-crook (southpaw). Long upper-bod. and uses good upper-bod. with fastball. Fastball just fair. Good curve. Goes sidearm at times for strikeout. About ¾ otherwise. Good pitcher's build. Control fair. Long stride but doesn't drop down. Curve/slider break down. Changes speed w/o effort. Sense of flow. Pitches patterned. Intell. Knows how to pitch.

On this particular day, Ron also had the A's hitters going for him, for they came up with six runs in the third and six more in the sixth, the latter outburst including two singles, a nifty squeeze bunt, a double, a pinch-hit triple by Cake World, and a home run by Coca-Cola. The last batter of the inning was Manager Paul Farrar, who sent himself up as a pinch-hitter now that matters were in hand. He is a friendly, medium-sized man with curly hair and metal-rimmed glasses—he is also a backup catcher for the club—and his players razzed him happily when he stepped up to the plate, calling him Satch and asking if he didn't want the Maples' pitcher to throw from farther back out there. He fanned, to raucous cheers. The A's won it by 16–4—a laugher, but Ron had pitched well, surrendering only four hits. Near the end, Linda began to relax a little in her seat. At one point, she saw me watching her, and she laughed and shrugged. "Ron's mother used to tell me what to do when he was pitching," she said. "She always said, 'Watch the ball, not the pitcher. Never look at the pitcher.' I wish I could remember that."

O

Ron and Linda live in a worn brown farmhouse next to a collapsing gray shingle barn, at the very end of a twisting, climbing two-mile-long dirt road. On a map, they are in the upper northwest corner of the state. St. Albans, the nearest real town, is fifteen miles to the west, on the shore of Lake Champlain, and the Canadian border is about the same distance due north. The house, which they rent, is on the side of a hill (*everything* in Vermont is on the side of a hill) and is set about with maples, an elderly lilac bush, and a high stand of burdock. Ron's vegetable garden is up the hill, behind the house. There is a small unpainted front porch with missing steps, which makes it look a little like the front stoop of a sharecropper's place. No matter: the view from here is across many miles of hazy-green rolling farmland toward some distant blue mountains. There isn't much furniture inside—a few castoff schoolroom chairs, with iron pedestal bases, that stand around the dining table, and one overflowing easy chair. The most prominent object

184

is a modern cast-iron heating stove, right in the middle of the room, with a long outlet pipe snaking up through the ceiling. Upstairs, the bathroom has been recently panelled and fitted out with a shower. The best room in the house is a sun-filled upstairs bedroom, five windows wide. A cluster of sports pennants is pinned to one wall there, with their points all streaming to starboard, as if in a stiff breeze: the Mariners, the Yankees, Idaho U., the Clinton Clowns (Ron's old softball team), and one banner with a misshapen felt baseball and the words "I'm a Backer" (a Buckskin backer, that is) on it. On the opposite wall, there is a framed Idaho potato bag depicting (as best one can depict on burlap) a full-rigged ship and inscribed "Tradewind Brand." Linda's desk and Selectric are under one window, next to an over-flowing bookshelf: contemporary poets (she writes poetry), classics, English Lit. textbooks—everything. On one windowsill, a philodendron is growing in a small white pot in the shape of a baseball shoe; on another rests a narrow cardboard box containing the complete 1981 Topps bubble-gum baseball-card collection. At the other end of the room, another bookcase offers a considerable paperback collection of contemporary Latin-American fiction, in translation: Borges, García Márquez, Jorge Amado, Machado de Assis, and others. These, I learned, are Ron's. "When I finished my season with the Buckskins, I was told my arm might heal if I could rest it long enough," he told me, "and I began to fantasize that it *would* heal. It was an excuse not to work, so I just sat and read. I was reading García Márquez's 'Leaf Storm' just then, and when I finished that I read *One Hundred Years of Solitude* and then *The Autumn of the Patriarch*. I drank a lot of Colombian coffee while I read, and it was like I'd gone off to another country."

When Ron Goble graduated from Capital High School in Boise in the spring of 1969, he accepted a fifteen-hundred-dollar baseball scholarship at Linfield, a small (one thousand students) college in McMinnville, Oregon. He had been an outstanding player in his local American Legion baseball pro-gram for several summers (young ballplayers who start in the Little Leagues at the age of eight may graduate to the Babe Ruth League at the age of thirteen and then move along to American Legion teams at sixteen), and he had been named to the all-state team in his senior year at school, as a first baseman. His pitching arm began to mature at about the same time, and when his fastball was clocked at better than ninety miles an hour the scouts began to take notice of him. When he went to Linfield, his real hope was not just to pitch for the varsity team there but to find a more relaxed and varied social and political atmosphere. At Capital High, sports and unquestioning patriotism had seemed to go hand in hand. Capital's teams were known as the Eagles, and varsity athletes were told to keep their hair cut in the "Eagle-pride" style—so short that it couldn't be parted—and there was constant pressure on the larger and quicker boys to make their major school commitment to the football team. Ron played tight end and safety and sometimes quarterback for the Eagles, but he didn't much like football; he was also made uncomfortable by the fact that his own sport, baseball, was considered effete—"sort of a pansy game," as he put it. But things weren't much different at Linfield, he discovered. The jocks there were expected to keep their hair cut short, too, and to think more about winning seasons than about Vietnam and Cambodia and the other political and social crises that were convulsing the nation at the time. Ron was not an activist, but his parents—his father is a state fire-insurance inspector—had always encouraged their three sons to think for themselves. Ron's older brother, Dale, had been an undergraduate at Columbia during the student riots there in 1968, and had brought home tapes he had recorded of the impassioned speeches and the crowd roars during those tumultuous days, and Ron had played these over many times. He was an athlete but he was also a reader and a student, and he felt isolated at Linfield. Early in May of his freshman year, he heard the news of the appalling events at Kent State University, and he and five or six friends went to the Linfield student-union building and lowered the flags there, in honor of the demonstrating students who had been shot by National Guardsmen in Ohio. Only two or three people of the hundreds who walked by stopped to ask what the lowered flags meant, and the next day one of Ron's coaches told him that he had "the wrong orientation" about politics. The next fall, Ron transferred to the University of Idaho and gave up varsity sports.

Ron told me all this in a quiet, almost apologetic manner. His voice is modulated and unforced, and somehow suggests his pitching motion. Like some other young men and women of his generation, or quarter-generation, he takes pains never to sound assured, never to strike an attitude. "I wasn't a real political dissident, you understand," he said. "I cared—I still care—but I didn't know what I was doing. At Idaho, I went down to the R.O.T.C. Building one night and stole Richard Nixon's picture out of its frame there. Big piddly-assed deal."

He laughed, and Linda joined in the laughter. We were sitting out on their porch, drinking beer, and their two English setters, Boone and Hannah, were running and sniffing through an overgrown meadow before us, with their feathery white tails marking their progress through the long grass. Once, Boone got on the trail of something and took off downhill, but Ron turned him with a piercing, two-fingered whistle.

"Tell about the time you decided to go back and play ball," Linda said.

"Oh, geezum," Ron said, smiling. "Well, after a while there at Moscow"— Moscow, Idaho, is the university seat—"I began to reconcile sports and politics a little, and I saw that I wasn't quite the great political radical I'd thought I was. For a while, I'd even stopped collecting baseball cards, but I sure missed playing ball, especially in the spring, and so one day I went down to see the baseball coach. I was going to offer to come out, if he wanted me, but when I got there his office was closed, and I took that as a sign. I decided it wasn't my karma to play ball yet."

"It wasn't your *karma*!" Linda said, doubled over with laughter. "Can you *believe* that now!" They cracked up, thinking about it.

In his last two years at Idaho, Ron lived with two friends on a farm twenty-six miles away from the campus, where they raised chickens and helped the farmer with his planting and other chores. Ron was a pre-law student, majoring in political science, and he had looked forward to going to law school, but now something had changed for him, and he found himself more interested in the farm and in outdoor life. "I just got tired of school," he said. He had let his hair grow long, and he realized that most of his classmates probably thought of him as a hippie. After he graduated, he moved to Missoula because he loved its setting—the high country and the cold streams of the Bitterroot Range and the Garnet Mountains—and found work as a janitor at the University of Montana.

"I just wanted something to do so I could keep on fishing and backpacking," he said. "There were a lot of people with the same idea there at that time. It was what was happening. That's great country, out along the Clark Fork and the Big Blackfoot, if you like fishing. You could walk across the Milwaukee Road railroad tracks behind our house and cross the floodplain and you'd be fishing in just five minutes."

Our house: He had met Linda, and they had moved into a log cabin in Clinton, which is twenty miles southeast of Missoula. She was in graduate school at Montana, majoring in creative writing. She also tutored undergraduates in English and Greek, and after she had picked up her master's degree she worked in a Poetry in the Schools program in the state school system and then became poet-in-residence and a teacher at a private school in Missoula. She and Ron talked baseball and followed the Yankees from a distance, as she wrote me in her first letter, but softball was the only game in town.

Ron said, "Every spring, I'd think, Geezum, I've made it through the winter again—and they were long, long winters there, you know—and I'd get that little urge. I'd go off fishing, and when I got my arm working back and forth with the fishing pole [he said "pole," not "rod"] it was sort of like throwing a curveball. I was spring-strong, and I'd get to wondering what I could have done if I'd gone on in baseball. Each spring was like that. Then when I read that notice in *The Sporting News* about the Buckskins' tryout camp, I realized that it had been eight years since I'd pitched in a ballgame. I couldn't believe it."

This must have sounded self-pitying to Ron when he said it to me, there on the porch, and he corrected himself at once. "It was my own fault," he said. "There was fear, I guess, and then I began to rationalize it all and remind myself that I'd have to go to a tryout camp if I wanted to come back, and maybe I'd fail. What I'd had was a marginal talent—a pretty good high-school fastball—and if I was ever going to do something with it, I would have had to pay the price. I didn't want to have to work at it, I think, or else I just didn't want to work that hard. So I let it go by."

○

Late one afternoon that week, I watched another team of country ballplayers wearing sponsors' names on the backs of their uniform shirts—Waterville Garage, Tobin Construction, Gerald W. Tatro—in a game played on still another hillside diamond. The field was unfenced, and the woods and brush along the right-field foul line crowded in so close that there wouldn't have been room for bleachers or any other kind of seats there. It was a *field*: the shaggy grass around second base was white with clover blossoms. We were in Belvidere, Vermont—a Green Mountain village a bit to the north and east of Mt. Mansfield—and the game pitted the home team of Belvidere-Waterville against the visiting Morrisville nine. These were Babe Ruth League teams, whose players range in age from thirteen to fifteen years, but the Belvidere-Watervilles seemed to be outweighed by a couple of dozen pounds and outsized by a couple of inches at almost every position. Outmanned, too: only eight home-team players had turned up for the game, and their coach, Curt Koonz, was filling in at shortstop. The disparity was most noticeable on the mound, for the Belvidere-Waterville pitcher, Earl Domina, was so short that the white pants of his uniform were within an inch or two of swallowing his shoes. He worked hard out there, toeing the rubber in good style and hiding the ball behind his hip while he stared in at his catcher for the sign, but he wasn't big enough to get much stuff on his pitches, and it sometimes looked as if he were throwing uphill against the tall, half-grinning Morrisville boys. Earl was being hit hard—the bases were repeatedly loaded and then unloaded against him in the two or three innings I saw him play—and he also had to put up with a few throwing-uphill jokes from his own teammates, but he kept his concentration and his seriousness, jutting his jaw on the mound and staring the base runners into place before each pitch, and in time the smiles and the jokes died away. He was a battler.

I had heard a good deal about the problems and triumphs of the Belvidere-Waterville Babe Ruth League team from its previous coach, Ron Goble, who had been greeted with hand slaps and jokes and cheerful body blocks by his former troops when we turned up at the game that afternoon. (He and Linda lived in Waterville when they first came to Vermont, but their present house is some thirty miles to the northwest—too far for him to keep up with his Babe Ruth League coaching while he also continues to pitch for the A's.) Now he pointed out some of his stalwarts from the previous year's squad—Peanut Coburn, the team's best shortstop, best outfielder, best first baseman, best everything, who had graduated to assistant coach; the Eldred brothers, Keith and Mike; some others. He said that a few of his players last year had come up through a Little League program, but others had never played an inning of baseball before their season got under way. There weren't many players in either category, to tell the truth, so everybody got a chance to play, including Kim Wescom and Angie Tourangeau, who are girls. Kim, a second baseperson, always wore blue eyeshadow with her game uniform—a complicated announcement, Linda thought. All the teams that Belvidere-Waterville faced were larger and more experienced than they were, and the enemy players razzed them unmercifully for playing girls and for looking like hicks.

"Well, we *were* hicks," Ron said to me. "We were a country team, and most of our players came from poor families, so after a while we took that as our team name. We became the Hicks." The razzing never got entirely out of hand, in any case, because after a couple of innings of it, Frank Machia, the Belvidere-Waterville first baseman, would take a few steps over toward the other team bench and invite the critics there to step forward. Frank was fifteen, but he has a Boog Powell-style chest and belly, topped off by a full beard, and so things usually quieted down in a hurry. The continuing trouble—the real trouble—was that the team wasn't good enough to win. One very bad day came at Stowe, a wealthy ski-resort town at the foot of Mt. Mansfield (its Babe Ruth League team even has different uniforms for home and away games), where the game was called, by mutual consent, when Belvidere-Waterville had fallen behind by 35–3, or 36–5, or something like that.

Ron told me that one of the team's handicaps had been the lack of a decent home field to practice and play on, and after the Stowe disaster he and Linda and a few other devout team backers—Larry and Shirley Brown, Olive McClain, and Emmett Eldred—went over to the abandoned Smithville diamond, in Belvidere, which had long ago turned into a meadow, and attacked it with hand mowers. After three long, hot days' work—a horrendous job, everyone agreed—the hay was cut and raked, and a new backstop had been erected, just in time for the return game against Stowe, which turned up with a considerable entourage to watch the continuation of the slaughter.

"Well, we didn't beat them," Ron said. "It was 9–6, Stowe, in the end, but we *almost* beat them, and they sure knew they'd been in a game. We showed them we could play, and that made the whole season worthwhile."

I asked how the team had fared after that.

"The truth is, we lost all fourteen games on our schedule," he said. "No,

189

that's not right—we took one on a forfeit, when the other team didn't turn up. But it meant a lot to these kids, learning how to play ball, learning to enjoy it. By the end of the season, they were backing up plays and sometimes hitting the cutoff man on their throws, even though that was mostly because they couldn't throw the ball all the way home anyway. They're all good kids. There isn't much else to do around here in the summers, you know, and that kept them at it."

The game we had been watching ended at 11–4, Morrisville, and the young players began to drift away, some in their parents' cars and pickups, some on bikes, and some on foot. The Belvidere-Waterville bats and batting helmets were stuffed into a gunnysack and toted away. It was evening, or almost evening, by now, but the field was at once repopulated by softball players—a pickup, slow-pitch game, arranged by telephone earlier that day. Ron played and so did Earl Domina—a long pitcher and a very short one, both playing in the same outfield now—and more cars pulled up by the field as the news of the game got around, and soon there were twelve or thirteen players on a side out there in the warm, mosquitoey half-light. Linda didn't play, and I sat it out, too, keeping her company. We were at a worn, teetery old picnic table, where we gnawed on some cold roast chicken she had brought along, and in time we were joined there by Larry Brown, a shy, slightly built, soft-spoken man, who often looks at the ground when he speaks. Larry Brown is the Branch Rickey of Belvidere baseball. He is an asbestos miner—a laborer—with a modest seasonal sideline in maple syrup made from his own hillside sugar bush. Still in his forties, he has six children and two grandchildren.

He told me that he had been a catcher for the Belvidere town team when he was a younger man. "It was all town teams around here then," he said. "I'd like to see those days come back again. Maybe they will. Back when I was a boy, all I had was a bat and one old taped-up ball. It wasn't all organized, the way it is now. I don't think there's a single town team in Lamoille County, but there are eight hundred boys playing Little League and Babe Ruth ball."

His doing—in part, at least. Larry Brown got the Belvidere Little League started, about five years ago. (In fact, a Little League game had been in progress off at the other end of the same field that the Babe Ruth teams were using that afternoon, and I had been struck by the fact that all the players on both teams had full uniforms. Seeing so many players in action at the same time almost reminded me of spring ʹraining.) Larry Brown found sponsors, got the parents involved, raised the money for uniforms and bats and balls. Last year, when Ron and Linda turned up in Waterville, he sought out Ron and persuaded him to take on the town's very first Babe Ruth team. Larry didn't know that Ron was still recovering from his cancer surgery and

190

from the debilitating radiation treatments that had ensued, but Larry had been wonderfully persuasive, and the job, Ron must have realized almost at once, was a perfect one for him at that moment: cheerful and funny and full of hope. When the season ended, with most of those hopes still unrewarded, Larry Brown and his wife threw a big potluck dinner for the team. Ron gave a speech, summarizing the summer's high points—the time Mike Eldred lost both sneakers while trying to steal second base (and turned back at once to get them), Angie Tourangeau's single that didn't count because the ump said he wasn't ready, the two games against Stowe.... Everyone had such a good time at the dinner that they all decided to chip in and arrange a team trip up to Montreal for an Expos game. Later in the summer, they did it again. Baseball has caught on in Belvidere.

I asked Larry Brown if anyone from Lamoille County had ever made it to the big leagues.

"No, I don't think so," he said, still smiling and still looking at the ground. "Though there was so many that played ball and watched ball around here in the old days you'd think it'd happen, wouldn't you? Why, I can remember going over to St. Albans when they had a team in the old Northern League here—the Giants, they were—and they'd have a thousand people there at Coote Field. A thousand, easy. But we had some mighty good players around here. Don McCuin played for our team—the Belvidere team, I mean—right after the war. He was a left-handed pitcher. He was signed by the Cardinals organization, but when he got down there he found he couldn't play ball in the heat, there in the South. And there was another good left-hander, named Sonny Davis, just about that time. Funny you'd have two so good, who was both the same kind. He played for Stowe. He signed up with the Braves, back in the nineteen-forties. Sonny told me once that he'd played in a game with young Henry Aaron, who was just a beginner, too, at the time, and when Sonny saw Aaron hit some drives in batting practice he suddenly understood that he was never going to make it in major-league baseball."

All three of us laughed. It was almost dark now, and whenever somebody on the ball field made contact (with that heavy, smacking sound that a softball makes against the bat), the arching ball looked like some strange gray night bird suddenly rising out of the treetops.

"Leonard McCuin was as good as Don was, from all I hear," Larry went on. "He was Don's father. Leonard once played on a team over to Saranac Lake, where Christy Mathewson was his coach. Mathewson was there because he had tuberculosis, you know. I guess he was about dead of it by then. Funny, I always thought Don McCuin had the head for major-league baseball. It was his arm that was at fault. But I liked the way he pitched. I always compared Don to Warren Spahn—a classic left-hander with that high kick. I don't think there was ever a smarter pitcher than Spahn. But I'm not one

191

of those who goes around always saying that the old players were the best. I've been up to Montreal for some games, now that the teams are so close—I almost went *broke* the first summer the Expos was playing!—and I think there's been no better players than some we've seen in our time. You only have to go back a few years to when Aaron and Mays and Clemente were still playing, you know, and you just couldn't come up with a better outfield than that. They say Roberto Clemente was the least appreciated ballplayer of his time. Well, *I* appreciated him."

It was dark now, and the softball game had ended at last. Ron joined us at the picnic table, and some of his friends sat down with us, too, drinking beer and swatting mosquitoes. Little Earl Domina had gone home, waving shyly to us as he walked away into the shadows, and I told Larry how much I'd admired him in the Babe Ruth League game we'd seen.

"He's about half-size for his age, but he always puts out," Larry said. "There are others I wished cared as much about it as he does. Size don't have much to do with it in this game."

Roberto Clemente and Leonard McCuin, Don McCuin and Warren Spahn, Sonny Davis and Hank Aaron, Christy Mathewson and Earl Domina— they were all together in baseball for Larry Brown. For him, the game had no fences.

○

I was pleased but in fact not much surprised to find someone like Larry Brown here in a corner of Vermont, for I had already met other friends of Ron's and Linda's who seemed sustained and nourished by a similar passion for baseball. One of them was Paul Farrar, the A's manager, who normally gives six or seven hours of his day to the team during the season, beginning at four in the afternoon on weekdays, when he gets off work at the I.B.M. plant in Burlington. If there is a home game (there are also practices on some off-days) at the University of Vermont's Centennial Field, where the A's play, Farrar is usually the first man to arrive. He carries in the field rakes from his car and then unlocks the concession stand and carries out the dusty bases that have been stored there since the last game. The players begin to drift onto the field while he is raking the base paths or carefully laying down the foul lines and the batter's boxes with a lime cart, and he kids them cheerfully and asks about their bruises. Long before this, while he paused at home to put on his uniform, he has picked up the day's team telephone messages from his wife, Sue. Tinker Jarvis will have to work until past seven tonight, she told him, which means not only that he won't be there in time to play but that his girlfriend, Helen Rigby, probably won't be around to work in the hot-dog stand. Southpaw Joe Gay's arm is coming along, his father called to say, but the doctor still thinks it'll be another week before he'll be ready to pitch. One of the troubles is that Joe has this summer job as a housepainter, which makes it hard for him to give his arm the kind of rest it should have. (Why can't Joe paint *right*-handed for a while, Paul wonders for an instant.) The other team tonight will be perfectly willing to play nine innings, instead of seven, if the A's want to, but which of them will pay the seventy-five bucks that U.V.M. wants as a fee for using the lights? Then, there are the automobile arrangements to be made for the weekend doubleheader over at Saxtons River. . . . Paul thinks about some of this while he pitches batting practice, but then he tries to put it all out of his head when he makes out his lineup in the dugout and begins to concentrate on the game at hand. Who's got to play if we're going to win? Who ought to play because he hasn't got into enough games lately? . . .

Paul grew up in the Bronx and, of course, dreamed of playing in Yankee Stadium someday, as a big-leaguer. Then his family moved to South Burlington, and in time Paul went off to Rensselaer Polytechnic, in Troy, New York, where he played catcher for four years on the varsity team. Then he coached at R.P.I. for two years, as an assistant with the varsity, while he got his graduate degree. He is a senior associate engineer with I.B.M. He is twenty-six years old.

"Ron and I and Tinker Jarvis are the old men on the team," he said to me, "but I think it may be more fun for us than for the others. And managing is—well, it's *involving*. These games don't mean anything, but I play them again in my mind when they're over. The bunt signal we missed. The pitcher I maybe took out one batter too late. I lie in bed and play baseball in my head in the middle of the night."

○

Herbie Pearo lives in East Alburg, Vermont, on a peninsula jutting into Lake Champlain. He is the manager of the East Alburg Beavers, an amateur slow-pitch softball team that Ron plays for whenever the A's schedule permits it. Upstairs in his house there, one walks into a narrow room and a narrow loft above it—a baseball museum—stuffed to bursting with baseball uniforms, autographed baseball bats, autographed baseballs, caps, pairs of spikes, old baseball photographs, albums of baseball tickets, baseball programs, bubble-gum baseball cards, everything. Some of the uniform shirts are framed, showing names and numbers on their backs, and these include the shirts of many present and recently past Expos—Andre Dawson, Ellis Valentine, Steve Rogers, Rusty Staub, Warren Cromartie—for Herbie is a terrific Expos fan. He is also a former terrific Mets fan. The centerpiece of his present collection is Tom Seaver's 1967 Mets uniform (1967 was Seaver's first year in the majors), which Herbie values at one thousand dollars. "Not that I'd automatically sell it," he adds. Selling items like these is Herbie Pearo's business—a baseball-souvenir-and-tradables line known as Centerfield Eight Sales. The business is advertised in most standard baseball publications, and the turnover is brisk. Brisk but often painful, because Herbie, one senses quickly, would much rather hold on to his best stuff. He is still writhing over the recent loss of a genuine Rogers Hornsby St. Louis Browns uniform. "I *had* to do it," he says apologetically. "The man made me an offer I couldn't refuse—seven guaranteed All-Stars' uniforms, plus a lot of other things, but still . . ." His voice trails off, and in his face you can almost see the Hornsby uniform still hanging in its old place on the long wall.

Centerfield Eight is one of the hardest stores to walk out of I have ever walked into. I was there for an hour or more, and each time I edged closer to the staircase my eye would fasten on some new wonder or Herbie would draw me back to look at something else. He wasn't trying to sell me anything; he simply wanted to share it all. He was a great curator, and we were at the Louvre. . . . Here is a ball signed by Sadaharu Oh, and a bat signed by the Babe. Here is Pete Rose's very first Reds' shirt—with a rookie's number, 33, on the back. Here is a Reggie Jackson Oakland A's shirt; here is a Roberto Clemente shirt (in the old, sleeveless Pirates' style); and over here is an orange Charlie Finley baseball (Finley once lobbied to have the major leagues shift to orange baseballs); and—oh, yes—upstairs, there in the corner, is a player's battered old locker from Connie Mack Stadium, now long gone, alas. And look *here* (here in a desk drawer): a pair of genuine Phillies World Series tickets from 1964—the year the Phillies folded so horribly and didn't make the Series after all. Here is a genuine scout's contract, signed by Connie Mack himself. This is a photograph of the 1908 Portland Mohawks ("Maine's Premier Amateur Baseball Team"), and here are some 1975 White Sox World Series ducats (another blasted hope), and that's an usher's cap from Anaheim Stadium—a bargain at twenty-five bucks. But oh, *wait*! And he holds up a pair of snowy, still pressed Washington Senator home-uniform shirts on wire hangers, with a "1" on one of them and a "2" on the other—commemorative shirts made for presentation to President Nixon and Vice-President Agnew at the Senators' opening game in 1970. I stare at these particular relics in slow surprise, astounded by the possibility that I have at last come upon an object—*two* objects—in this world that may truly be said to have no meaning whatsoever.

Stunned with memorabilia, I descend the stairs at last (the balusters are bats, each with its own history), and Herbie Pearo's voice follows me down. "I wish you'd seen my Carl Furillo shirt, from the 1957 season," he says. "The real thing. I wish I hadn't sold that. I've been *kicking* myself ever since . . ."

As I have explained, my trip to visit Linda Kittell and Ron Goble was something I had looked forward to for years. It came while the midsummer major-league baseball strike was about two weeks along, but there was no connection between the two events. I was not visiting a semipro player because I would have preferred to call on a big-leaguer. I was not out to prove some connection or lack of connection between the expensive upper flowerings of the game and its humble underbrush. Everyone in Vermont talked about the strike, but not for long; we wanted it over, because we missed the games and the standings and the news of the sport, but I heard no bitter talk about money and free-agency, "spoiled" ballplayers or selfish owners. At the same time, it occurred to me again and again while I was there (it would have been impossible to ignore the comparison or not to think about its ironies) to wonder how many big-league owners and famous players and baseball businessmen (the league presidents, and so forth, and perhaps even some of the writers) had an involvement in the game—a connection that was simply part of life itself—like Ron Goble's and Larry Brown's and Linda Kittell's. Not many, I would think, and yet at the same time it seemed quite likely to me—almost a certainty, in fact—that if I had stopped and visited friends in almost any other county or state corner in the United States I would have found their counterparts there, their friends in baseball.

○

Late one afternoon, Linda and Ron and I drove into Burlington for an A's game against the Queen City Royals. We were in their wheezy, ancient red Vega, and Ron kept cocking his head and listening to the engine in a nervous sort of way; a couple of weeks earlier, the car had conked out altogether on the same trip, and he had missed the game and his turn on the mound. He was in uniform tonight, but he wasn't going to play; his next start would be the following night, against the hated Burlington Expos. We were all eating ice-cream cones.

I asked Ron if he could tell me a little more about his summer with the Boise Buckskins, when he had pitched in organized ball for the first time, and everything had gone so badly for him and his teammates.

"In some ways, it wasn't exactly what you'd call a rewarding experience," he said after a moment or two. "Our pitching was downright terrible. We won on opening day, and that was sort of the highlight. Gerry Craft said opening day was God's greatest blessing but the rest of it was our trial. We had those ugly uniforms, and the fans got on us because of the religion thing, and we were always jumping off buses and going right into some park to play. It was good we had a few things going for us, like Danny Thomas. The real battle for me was not to let any of that bother me too much. I was there to prove myself. That summer answered a lot of questions for me that I would have gone on asking myself all my life. I got that albatross off my neck at last. What I discovered was that I'd had a talent at one time for throwing the ball—

maybe not a major-league talent, at that. But I found out that although I couldn't throw by then—not really—I was at least a pitcher." He paused and then added his little disclaimer: "Although that may be too much of a complimentary term."

What was it about Danny Thomas, I asked. What had made him so special to them and to the whole team?

"Well, he was tall and he had those good long muscles," Ron said. "You know—he looked like a ballplayer."

"And that fantastic smile," Linda said from the back seat.

"Yes, there was never a better-looking ballplayer, anywhere," Ron said. "And his hitting! I remember once when we were playing against the Emeralds on a road trip, and the whole park was down on us for some reason—everyone yelling and booing and laughing. Because we'd been looking so bad, I guess. And then he hit one. I mean, he *hit* it—it went out over the lights and out of the ballpark, and even before he got to first base there was this absolute hush in the place. It was beautiful. He'd shut them up."

"Plus he wore No. 7," Linda said.

"That's right," Ron said at once. "The same number."

It was a minute before I understood. Mickey Mantle's old number had been 7.

At this moment, the Vega gave a couple of despairing wheezes and slowly glided to a halt. We came to rest at meadowside on a singularly unpopulated and unpromising stretch of macadam.

"Damn *carburetor*," Ron said. He popped the hood. "Hammer," he said, swinging his long legs out, and Linda, reaching down between her feet, found a hammer and wordlessly handed it to him, exactly like a good instrument nurse working with a surgeon. This operation entailed some thunderous banging noises from up forward—not a promising prognosis at all, I thought—but when Ron reappeared, redfaced, and restarted the engine, it spluttered and groaned but then caught. A miracle. "Remind me to park facing downhill when we get there," he muttered as we resumed our course.

And so I asked him about his pitching now—pitching for the Burlington A's.

"Well, it's still enjoyable," he said. "The thing about pitching is—it's that it requires your concentration. It requires your entire thought. There aren't many things in life that can bring that to you. And every situation, every day and every inning, is different. You have to work on so many little details. Finding the fluidity of your body. Adjusting for different mounds. Bringing the leg up higher, bringing it over more. You kind of expect standards of yourself, and when they're not there you have to find out what's going wrong, and why. Maybe you're not opening up quickly enough. Maybe you're not following through enough, or maybe you're throwing too much across your body.

Some days, you're not snapping your wrist so much. Some days, the seams on the ball aren't so nice. It's always different."

He shook his head, and laughed at himself again. "Actually," he went on, "at some level I'm always pitching in the hope that the curveball—the real old curveball—might come back someday. Geezum, wouldn't that be nice, I think to myself. It doesn't happen, though. It's gone. Now it's different, being a pitcher, and sometimes I think it's almost more fun, because you can't just throw it by them now. You've got to trick 'em, because you've got nothing much to get them out with. So you try to set them up—get them looking away and then throw them inside. Get them backing off, and go down and away. I don't play often enough to have that happen too much—just to be able to think about location like that—but that's what it's all about."

He was right: this is what pitching is all about. I have heard a good many big-league pitchers talk about their craft—hundreds of them, I suppose, including a few of the best of our time—and when they got into it, really got talking pitching, they all sounded almost exactly like Ron Goble. He probably would have denied it if I'd said it, but he was one of them, too—a pitcher.

"I know baseball is important to me," he said after another moment or two. "Playing now is like getting a present, and you don't expect presents."

○

In Burlington, Ron swung into a gravelly downhill road leading to Centennial Field, and then stopped the Vega unexpectedly and walked over to a small shed on the left-hand side of the road and took from it a large, triangular wooden sign, hinged at the top like a kitchen stepladder. He and Linda carried it up to East Avenue, which we had just left, and set it up on the sidewalk there. "BASEBALL TODAY," it read. "6:00." We parked facing downhill and went down to the park—an ancient dark-green beauty, with the outfield terminating in a grove of handsome old trees. The roofed stands were steeply tilted, and the cast-iron arm at the end of each row of seats bore a "UVM" stamped into the metal. Swallows dipped in and out of the shadows under the grandstand roof. Linda and Ron pointed out the football stadium that rose beyond the left-field fence, and then drew my attention to the back of the football press box perched on its topmost rim—a good hundred feet up there, I suppose. This was history: history made about two weeks earlier, when Darcy Spear had whacked a home run against the Expos that cleared the top of the press box—a Kingman shot, an all-timer.

Ron went off to batting practice, and Linda told me she would be selling tickets up at the main automobile gate. It was still a good hour before the game with the Queen City Royals would begin, and I went along. Linda was carrying a big roll of blue tickets and a small envelope of loose change. "Shall we abscond?" I said. She looked into the envelope. "Better wait until a few customers turn up," she said. We leaned on the chain-link fence beside the open gate, listening to the distant crack of bats from the field below, and passed a bottle of warmish beer back and forth. It was a heavy, quiet summer evening.

Linda said she had hardly ever heard Ron talk about his pitching the way he had talked in the car that night. "Basically, I realize I know absolutely nothing about baseball compared to Ron," she said. "But I get tired of the other women around players, who say 'Don't you get tired of him talking about nothing but baseball?' I *hate* that. I think I like the part of Ron that I don't understand. I feel I could get all the knowledge of baseball that he has, and still not understand, because I never played baseball. It's a mystery between us, and I like that. If you know everything about a person, it's sort of a letdown. I just have no idea what he goes through out there on the mound. I get glimpses sometimes, but that's all.

"Ron is truly modest about his talent—you've seen that. I believe all the things about him that he doesn't think or say himself. I believe he could have been a major-league pitcher. I wanted everyone to know about it when he was pitching and was still sick, but he wouldn't let me tell anyone. He didn't want to bother them with it. I think that's sort of heroic. He still doesn't have his fastball back, you know."

The first two or three cars rolled up and stopped for their tickets. "Looks like a nice evening," one man said.

"Yes, it does," Linda said. "Have a nice time, now."

She came back and leaned against the fence again. "I get scared about the day when he can't play ball anymore," she said. "I get teary thinking about it sometimes. He couldn't have planned his life any differently, but sometimes I wish he wouldn't give up on himself so much. There are a lot of other things he could have done. But if he'd planned his life differently I wouldn't be around. There's no one here he can ask, but I get the idea that he knows as much about the technical side of pitching as anyone else. He just learned it himself, I think."

I said I had exactly the same impression.

"Sometimes he asks me to watch a particular thing when he's pitching— whether he's opening his hips, say. But if he asks me about something else afterward—where his foot is coming down, or something like that—then I've totally missed it. I keep wishing his brother George was here, so he could talk baseball with him. There's so much *to* it. To me, baseball is like learning a foreign language. You never learn all the vocabulary, all the endings and idioms. It's what I love about languages."

It came back to me—it was stupid of me not to have remembered it, all this time—that Linda had gone to college right here. The main college buildings were just behind us, over the top of the hill. This was her campus. I asked her what languages she had taken, here at U.V.M.

"The Classics Department got upset with me, because I always wanted to take up more languages, all at the same time," she said, smiling. "I was studying classical Greek, modern Greek, Latin, Russian, and Japanese. I switched majors over and over. I'd do more than anyone expected of me in one thing—like creative writing—and let everything else slide. If I had to do a Milton paper, or something, I'd do it in twenty minutes and hand it in—I didn't care. But if I was studying something like rondo alliteration or chiastic alliteration, I'd get so excited I'd forget everything else." She shook her head. "Not *organized*."

I asked about her own poetry. She had declined to show me her poems.

"I'll never catch up in baseball, but I have my own world," she said. "Ron can read something I've written and he'll say 'That has a nice sound,' or something, but he doesn't see that for once I've got a good slant rhyme in there. And he'll never see things I suddenly notice when I'm reading—that 'chrysanthemum' is such a perfect iambic word, for instance—that so excite me. When we went out to some friends who were having Hayden Carruth for dinner—Ron has read maybe one poem of Carruth's, I'd say—I said to him, 'Remember, you're having dinner with Mickey Mantle.' But maybe I should have said Catfish Hunter, because Ron respects Catfish Hunter in such a special way." She giggled.

More cars were coming in now. A man in one car said, "I'm one of the umpires," and Linda waved him in. He waved back and drove in. His license plate said "UMP."

"I feel a little disappointed in my own career," Linda went on during the next pause. "But it isn't as if you're ever too old to write a good poem. But I don't know many ninety-year-old pitchers—do you? Maybe Ron and I are both wrong to make baseball so important to us. But what the hell, writing a poem isn't so important, either."

I asked what would happen to Ron in the next couple of years.

"If he isn't going to go on playing ball—and he can't for much longer—and if he can't find something that will take up as much of his attention as baseball, I don't know what's going to happen to him," she said. "Maybe he'll get into teaching, or some kind of coaching. He's supposed to teach in a kids' baseball camp later this summer, and then maybe . . ." She shrugged. "He lets things happen. He's that kind of a person. At least he found out he's a professional-level pitcher, but I think he'd feel better if it had got him to the major leagues. And he'll never feel he knows everything about baseball. Sometimes I'll watch him in the store when we're shopping together, and he'll have a cantaloupe in his hands and he'll be practicing his motion, right there in the store. It's true! And sometimes I'll see him sitting at home in the evening and shaking his head, and I'll ask him why, and he'll say, 'I can't *believe* I threw that pitch.' "

Some cars were rolling up to the gate, and Linda started over to meet them. "I know one thing," she said. "You can't rewrite a pitch."

○

The A's had another easy time of it that night. Charlie Corbally pitched and went the distance, and Darcy Spear had three hits and four runs batted in, and the team rolled to a 12–3 win over the Royals. I'd had a hard time finding out the A's place in the standings, because Ron said he couldn't always remember which games counted in the league and which were the informal ones, but he asked Paul, who said the club was now four and four in the league, and something like eight and five for the season over all. None of it mattered much. The next night was what mattered—the game against the Expos.

A lot of people turned out for that one—more than three hundred fans, including Larry Brown, who had brought his wife, Shirley, and one of his daughters, Laureen, and one of his sons, Stephen, and Earl Domina. We all sat together, behind first base. Even before the game began, I could see that the Expos—they wore the same parti-colored red-and-blue-and-white caps that the Montreal players do—were quicker and much more confident than most of the other Northern League players I had seen. They all looked like ballplayers. It was a wonderful game, it turned out, stuffed with close plays and heads-up, opportunistic baseball, and the A's won it, 3–2. Darcy Spear got the big hit once again—a two-run, two-out single in the third. Ron Goble started, but Paul Farrar had said beforehand he wouldn't let him pitch more than four innings; then he would bring in Steve Gallacher to mop up. Both pitchers were tired, and the staff was a little thin just now. Ron retired the first two Expos batters in the first and then gave up a bunt single. He walked the next man. He was falling behind on the count, and I noticed that he didn't seem to have his full, free motion out there. The next batter hit a sure third-out grounder to Greg Wells, but the ball took a bad hop at the last instant and jumped over Wells' glove for a single and an Expos run. Ron walked the next batter, and Paul came out to the mound to settle him down. Ron fell behind on the following batter, too, and eventually walked him, forcing in another run. Linda stared out at the field without expression. The next Expo rammed a hard shot toward third, but Tinker Jarvis made a good play on the ball and threw to second for the force, ending the inning.

In the next inning, Ron gave up two trifling singles through the middle. With two out, the Expos tried a fancy delayed double steal, with the base runner heading toward second intentionally getting himself hung up in the hope that his man from third could score before the out, but Greg Wells made the play perfectly, stopping and wheeling and firing to the plate in time to nail the runner there. Ron also got through the third unscathed, although he surrendered a single and hit a batter with one of his pitches. From time to time, Ron came off the mound between pitches and stared at the ground, his hands on his hips. In the top of the fourth, now defending a 3–2 lead, he walked the leadoff Expos hitter. The next Expos batter, a right-handed hitter, stood in and Ron hit him on the knee with his first pitch, and Paul Farrar came onto the field slowly and took him out of the game. It hadn't been a disastrous outing—with a couple of small breaks, Ron probably could have gone his four innings without giving up a run—but his struggles on the mound in search of his control had been painful to watch, especially for those of us who remembered his easy, elegant dominance over the batters in his previous game, down in Brattleboro. This kind of turnabout is a frightful commonplace for pitchers, as Ron had said himself, the day before in the car: It's always different.

Steve Gallacher came in and got the next Expos man to rap into an instant double play, and then retired the next man on a fly ball, ending the threat. Then Gallacher set down the remaining nine men in succession, fanning four of them—an outstanding pitching performance that nailed down the win. He got a terrific hand when he came off the field, and he deserved it.

After the game, Ron spotted Larry Brown's car just as it was about to leave the parking lot and ran over to say hello. He squatted down beside the driver's side of the car for a good five minutes, talking to Larry about the game. All around the parking lot, you could see the young Expo and A's players standing in their uniforms beside their cars, tossing their spikes and gloves into the back seats, lifting a beer here and there, and laughing with little groups of friends and with their young wives or girlfriends. I was sorry to be leaving. I was staying in Burlington that night, at a motel, so that I could make an early start back to New York the next morning.

Ron and Linda and I went to a bar-restaurant she knew, up a flight of stairs in Burlington. Linda and I ordered drinks and sandwiches. Ron asked for three large glasses of water, and drank them off, one after the other. Then he had a gin rickey and a sandwich, too. He was still in uniform.

"I learned how to drink in here, I think," Linda said, looking around. "A long time ago."

Ron said, "The last time I pitched, I started from the middle of the plate and began to work it out toward the corners. Tonight, it was the other way around. I started on the outside and I never did get it together." He shook his head. "I can't think how long it's been since I hit two batters."

"Well, at least we won," Linda said.

"Yes, at least we won," I said. "You guys ought to keep me around some more."

Ron had stopped listening. He was staring across the room, with a quiet, faraway look on his face. Linda put her hand on his crossed left leg, just above the white part of his cutouts, and watched him with an expression of immense care and affection. He was still in the game.

In the Fire

C onsider the catcher. Bulky, thought-burdened, unclean, he retrieves his cap and mask from the ground (where he has flung them, moments ago, in mid-crisis) and moves slowly again to his workplace. He whacks the cap against his leg, producing a puff of dust, and settles it in place, its bill astern, with an oddly feminine gesture* and then, reversing the movement, pulls on the mask and firms it with a soldierly downward tug. Armored, he sinks into his squat, punches his mitt, and becomes wary, balanced, and ominous; his bare right hand rests casually on his thigh while he regards, through the portcullis, the field and deployed fielders, the batter, the base runner, his pitcher, and the state of the world, which he now, for a waiting instant, holds in sway. The hand dips between his thighs, semaphoring a plan, and all of us—players and umpires and we in the stands—lean imperceptibly closer, zoom-lensing to a focus, as the pitcher begins his motion and the catcher half rises and puts up his thick little target, tensing himself to deal with whatever comes next, to end what he has begun. These motions—or most of them, anyway—are repeated a hundred and forty or a hundred and fifty times by each of the catchers in the course of a single game, and are the most familiar and the least noticed gestures in the myriad patterns of baseball. The catcher has more equipment and more attributes than players at the other positions. He must be large, brave, intelligent, alert, stolid, foresighted, resilient, fatherly, quick, efficient, intuitive, and impregnable. These scoutmaster traits are counterbalanced, however, by one additional entry—catching's bottom line. Most of all, the catcher is invisible. He

---

*The catcher's helmet, now universally in use, has made this movement nearly extinct. Rick Dempsey, of the Dodgers, still sports a cap, its brim jauntily tipped up, *under* his helmet, thus sustaining the mannerism.

does more things and (except for the batter) more difficult things than anyone else on the field, yet our eyes and our full attention rest upon him only at the moment when he must stand alone, upright and unmoving, on the third-base side of home and prepare to deal simultaneously with the urgently flung or relayed incoming peg and the onthundering base runner— to handle the one with delicate precision and then, at once, the other violently and stubbornly, at whatever risk to himself. But that big play at home is relatively rare. Sometimes three or four games go by without its ever coming up, or coming to completion: the whole thing, the street accident— the slide and the catch, the crash and the tag and the flying bodies, with the peering ump holding back his signal until he determines that the ball has been held or knocked loose there in the dust, and then the wordless exchanged glances ("That all you got?" . . . "You think that *hurt*, man?") between the slowly arising survivors. Even when the catcher has a play on a foul fly—whipping around from the plate and staring up until he locates the ball and then, with the mask flipped carefully behind him, out of harm's way, following its ampersand rise and fall and poising himself for that crazy last little swerve—our eyes inevitably go to the ball at the final instant and thus mostly miss catch and catcher.

But this slight is as nothing compared to the anonymity we have carelessly given to our receiver in the other, and far more lengthy, interludes of the game. Because he faces outward—I *think*: none of this seems certain— and because all our anticipation of the events to come (in this most anticipatory of sports) centers on the wide greensward before us and on its swift, distant defenders, our awareness of the catcher is glancing and distracted; it is as if he were another spectator, bent low in order not to spoil our view, and although at times he, too, must cover ground quickly, he is more often waiting and seemingly out of it, like the rest of us. We fear or dote upon the batter, depending on which side is up; we laugh at pitchers a little, because of their contortions, but gasp at their speed and stuff; we think of infielders as kids or terriers, and outfielders are gazelles or bombardiers or demigods; but catchers are not so easy to place in our imagination. Without quite intending it, we have probably always patronized them a little. How many of us, I wonder, have entirely forgotten "the tools of ignorance," that old sports-page epithet for the catcher's impedimenta (it was coined in the nineteen-twenties by Muddy Ruel, a catcher with the Senators, who practiced law in the off-season). And think for a moment of the way the umpire watches the catcher as he goes about his housekeeping there behind the plate. Sometimes the arbiter has actually picked up the man's helmet and mask from the ground during the play just previous, and now he hands them over with an odd, uncharacteristic touch of politeness. Both of these men wear shin guards and chest protectors and masks, and although theirs is mostly an adversary relationship, they crouch in identical postures, inches apart (some umpires actually rest one hand on the catcher's back or shoulder as the pitch is delivered), and together engage in the dusty and exhausting business down behind the batter, living and scrounging on the hard corners of the sport. For one game, that is. Tomorrow, the umpiring crew will rotate, as it does for each game, and the ump working behind home will be stationed out at third base—almost a day off for him—so that he can recover from such labors, but the same catcher most likely will still be down there bent double behind the batters. *Here y'are*, the ump's courtly little gesture seems to say. *You poor bastard.*

I thought a lot about catchers during the long winter off-season that is just now drawing to a close, and found for the first time that I was able to envision a couple of them at work at their trade, in the same way that, like most fans, I can easily bring back the mannerisms of a favorite batter— George Brett, Lou Piniella, Mike Schmidt—as he steps into the box and prepares for the pitch, or the unique pause and stare and windup motion of some pitcher—Steve Carlton, Rick Sutcliffe, Fernando Valenzuela—whose work I know by heart. Suddenly, this winter, I could envision Rick Dempsey, the dandy midsize Oriole receiver, coming up onto the balls of his feet in the crouch after delivering a sign, with his orange-daubed glove inviting an outside-corner pitch to the batter. A base runner flies away from first with the pitcher's first move, and the delivery is low and away, a very tough chance, but Dempsey is already in motion, to his right and forward—"cheating," in catchers' parlance—and he seizes the pitch with the back of the mitt nearly touching the dirt and his bare right hand almost simultaneously plucking the ball from the pocket. The catch drives the glove backward, but because Dempsey has anticipated so well, the force and direction of the pitch are simply translated into the beginnings of his rising pivot and the upcocking of his arm for the peg—a line has become an upswooping circle—and he steps eagerly but unhurriedly across the plate to start the throw to second.

Finding Dempsey in my mind's eye in January was not quite startling, since he played so well in the course of the Orioles' five-game victory over the Phillies in the World Series last fall (he won the Most Valuable Player award for the classic, in which he batted .385, with five extra-base hits, and, even more important, was the prime receiver during the Baltimore pitching staff's 1.60-E.R.A. stifling of the National League champs), but some other catchers turned up in my hot-stove reveries as well. Bob Boone, for instance. Boone, who is thirty-six, now catches for the Angels, after a decade of notable defensive work with the Phillies. He is six feet two—a large man, although there is nothing hulking or overmuscled about him—but his movements behind the plate are gliding and water-smooth. He sets up with his left foot flat and the right foot back an inch or two, with its heel up, and once the sign is delivered he tucks his right hand behind his thigh—almost standard stuff, but if you keep your eyes on him you begin to pick up the easy body movement that slips him imperceptibly into place behind each arriving pitch and the silky way the ball is taken into the glove, without haste or grabbing. If something goes wrong—a pitch bounced into the dirt off to his right, say—his motion toward the ball is quickly extended, with the whole body swinging in the same arc as the pitch: the right knee goes into the dirt, with the leg tucked along the ground, while the glove is dropped straight down to dam off the opening below the crotch. No attempt is made to catch the pitch—catchers are endlessly trained in this, since it contravenes all baseball instinct—and the ball is simply allowed to bounce off his body. Boone locates it on the ground (his mask has flown off, spun away by an upward flick of his hand) and only then looks up to check the base runner; if he's going, the play is in front of him. It's an anxious, scattery set of moves, or should be by rights, but Boone makes them seem controlled and confident, as if the mistake had been reversed and turned into something risky for the other team. Nothing in these classic maneuvers is unique to Boone, except for the thoughtful elegance of their execution; he helps you appreciate the work.

Talking to catchers is even more fun than watching them, as I discovered last season, when I began to sense how little I knew about their dusty trade and sought out a few of them for enlightenment. They were surprised to be asked, it turned out, and then they seemed eager to dispel some of the peculiar anonymity that has surrounded such a public occupation: if you want an earful, go to a man in a highly technical profession who feels he is unappreciated. My instructors—almost a dozen of them in the end—came in different sizes and ages and uniforms and degrees of experience, and they were almost a random sample. Inevitably, I missed some of the best-known practitioners (including the celebrated Johnny Bench, who retired after the 1983 season; Montreal's Gary Carter, who is paid well over a million dollars per annum for his work and is perhaps the leading candidate to succeed Bench as the No. 1 catcher; Lance Parrish, of the Tigers; Jim Sundberg, late of the Texas Rangers and now of the Brewers; and the testy Jerry Grote, who is out of baseball and living in Texas, after winding up an extended career with the Mets and three other clubs, during which he was thought of as perhaps the best handler of pitchers around), but the catchers I did talk to were so voluble and expressive in their responses that I did not come away with the feeling that any major theorems of their profession were closed to me. Indeed, their replies were so long and meaty that I realized along the way that I simply wouldn't have time to take up *every* aspect of catching with them—blocking the plate, for instance, or the nasty little problem of catching and holding the knuckleball and the spitter, or the business of learning an extraordinary physical stoicism that allows the man behind the plate to disregard or play through the daily bruises and batterings that come with the job (most regular catchers experience pain of one form or another, and in one or several places on their bodies, right through the season), or the relative importance of the pre-game strategic review of the other team's hitters, or the business of veiling your signals from enemy base runners, or the prevalence of low tricks like surreptitiously nicking or scuffing the ball in aid of your pitcher, and more. These themes would have to wait for remedial sessions. Bob Boone told me at one point that he thought it took about three hundred major-league games for a catcher to feel comfortable back there, and I realized that the best I could hope for as an outsider was a glimpse at such a body of skills.

I talked to my informants separately, beginning with extended colloquies around batting cages and in dugouts and clubhouses during the leisurely 1983 spring term in Arizona and Florida, and then coming back for some short refreshers whenever I ran into one of them during the regular season. In time, these interviews ran together in my mind and seemed to turn into one extended, almost non-stop conversation about catching, with the tanned, knotty-armed participants together in the same room, or perhaps ranged comfortably about on the airy porch of some ancient summer hotel, interrupting each other, nodding in recollection, doubling back to some previous tip or topic, laughing together, or shouting in sudden dissent. But they grew more serious as they went along. One of the surprising things about the catchers' catcher-talk, I realized after a while, was how abstract it often was. Old names and games, famous innings and one-liners and celebrated goofs seemed to drop out of their conversation as they got deeper into it, as if the burden of anecdote might distract them (and me) from a proper appraisal of their hard calling. Everything about catching, I decided somewhere along the way, is harder than it looks.

○

Terry Kennedy, the twenty-seven-year-old receiver for the San Diego Padres, is six feet four and weighs two hundred and twenty pounds—almost too big for a catcher. He is prized for his bat and his durability—in the past two seasons he played in a hundred and fifty-three and a hundred and forty-nine games (very high figures for a catcher) and batted in ninety-seven and ninety-eight runs. At one time, there was some thought of moving him out to play first base, until a year ago, when the Padres acquired a fellow named Steve Garvey in the free-agent market. Now Kennedy must stay behind the plate and work on his quickness—work to become smaller, almost.

"Throwing is where mobility matters," he told me in Phoenix one afternoon. "I'm learning to cheat a little back there, with men on base. Once I determine where the pitch is, I'm starting up. You *have* to do that, with all the fast runners we're seeing on the base paths. Coming up right is what throwing is all about. There's a two-step or a one-step release. I start with a little jab-step with my right foot and go right forward. The important thing is to be true with that throw, so you try to keep your fingers on top of the ball. If they're off to one side, the ball will banana on you"—sail or curve, that is—"as it goes out there. You can even throw a little from the side, as long as your fingers are on top."

Kennedy's home pro is Norm Sherry, the Padres' pitching coach, who put in four years as a backup catcher with the Los Angeles Dodgers and the Mets, sandwiched in the middle of sixteen seasons in the minors; he has managed at both levels (he was the Angels' skipper for a term), but, with his dark glasses, his seamed and mahogany-tanned face, and his quick, thrusting way of talking, he suggests the quintessential infantry sergeant.

"Terry's coming on and coming on," Sherry told me. "It takes a long time to learn to call a game, but Terry was much more of a catcher in the second half of the season last year. He understood situations better. You can't work on that kind of stuff in the spring, but I been pitching forty or fifty pitches to him every day—curves and fastballs and in the dirt—and he has to come up throwing. Young catchers today don't have such good mechanics, because they all rely on this one-handed glove. If you take the pitch with one hand, you don't have your throwin' hand on the ball in good position when you start back. They look up and see the guy running and make any old kind of grab at the ball, and that's where you get those errors. I try to get them to take the ball two-handed, and that also closes up the front shoulder, the way it should be to start your throw. So many of them are in a *panic* when they see somebody movin' and they lose control of everything. Sometimes you see a man even knock his mask so it sort of half slides across his face. Then he can't see anything, because he was in such a hurry. But if you just take that little half step in advance, you've done all the hurrying you need to do. You just have to stand up and take a good stride and throw it.

"So much of this started with Johnny Bench, you know, who became such a good catcher with that one-handed glove. All the young catchers started to follow him, to pick up that style. But not many guys are Johnny Bench. He had great big hands, and wherever he grabbed the ball he got seams. It was like Willie Mays and his basket catch—only a few could do it well."

Months later, Joe Garagiola showed me a trick about seams. We were standing behind the batting cage together before the first World Series game in Baltimore last fall, and when Johnny Bench's name came up—he had just closed out his distinguished seventeen-year career with the Cincinnati Reds: indisputably the greatest catcher of his era—Garagiola, after adding several accolades, suddenly echoed Norm Sherry's little demurrer. In a way, he said,

Bench had almost set back the art of catching, because of his own great skills. "You have to get that good grab on the ball," Joe said in his quick, shill-sharp way, "and you can't always do that if you're hot-doggin' with that mitt. You gotta get seams to throw straight. Here—get me a ball, somebody." A ball was sneaked from the cage, and Garagiola, blazer and all, half crouched and suddenly became a catcher again. (He had a successful nine-year career at the position, mostly with the Cardinals, before taking up his second life, behind the microphone.) "Here's what Branch Rickey made us do when we were just young catchers tryin' to come up in the Cardinal system," he said. "Take the pitch in two hands, with your bare hand closing it in there, and then *grab seams*. If you take hold of it this way"—he held the ball on one of its smooth white horseshoe-shaped sectors, with the red stitching on either side of his forefinger and middle finger—"you got no *idea* where it's going to end up. But you can learn to shift it in your hand while your arm is comin' up to start the peg. Just a little flip in the air and you can get seams. Look."

He raised his hand quickly three or four times in a row and took a fresh grip on the ball as he did so. Each time, he had seams. He laughed in his famous, engaging way, and said, "Nights in spring training, Mr. Rickey made us each take a ball with us when we went to the movies and practice that in the theatre. Three or four catchers sittin' in a row, grabbing seams!"

○

The "one-handed glove" that so many of my catching informants referred to is the contemporary lightweight mitt that everyone, including Little Leaguers, now employs behind the plate. Thanks to radical excisions of padding around the rim and thumb, it is much smaller than its lumpy, pillowlike progenitor, more resembling a quiche than a deep-dish Brown Betty. The glove comes with a prefab central pocket, but the crucial difference in feel is its amazing flexibility, attributable to a built-in central hinge, which follows the lateral line of one's palm. The glove is still stiffer and more unwieldy than a first baseman's mitt, to be sure, but if you catch a thrown ball in the pocket the glove will try to fold itself around the ball and hold it, thus simply extending the natural catching motion of a man's hand. Catching with the old mitt, by contrast, was more like trying to stop a pitch with a dictionary; it didn't hurt much, but you had to clap your right hand over the pill almost instantly in order to keep it in possession. Indeed, this technique of nab-and-grab was almost the hardest thing for a boy to learn about catching when I first tried it (and instantly gave it up), many years ago, and a mistimed clutch at the ball was often suddenly and horribly painful as well. The new glove turned up in the nineteen-sixties, and its first artisan was Randy Hundley, a smooth, lithe receiver with the Chicago Cubs. Its first and perhaps still its greatest artist, its Michelangelo, was Johnny Bench, whose extraordinary balance and quickness, coupled with the glove, allowed him to take every-thing one-handed and, moreover, to make every kind of catch back there look as effortless and natural as the gestures of a dancer. He made the lunging, manly old art look easy, which may explain why so many baseball people—including many of the catchers I talked to—seem to find it neces-sary to set Bench a little to one side when they speak of him: to mount him as a museum exhibit of catching, a paradigm locked away behind glass, and to examine it with appropriate murmurings of wonder and then walk away. "Bench was picture-perfect," Ted Simmons said. "A marvellous mechanical catcher. There's no better. In the light of all that praise, it's very hard for any other catcher to be considered in that way." Carlton Fisk said, "Bench did so many things almost perfectly that it almost seemed robotical. Everything was done so automatically that it didn't seem to have much creativity to it." Sometimes catchers can sound like authors.

○

For Bob Boone, the catcher's front shoulder is the key to strong throwing. "You have to have that closed front side, just the way you do in hitting," he told me. "When the arm goes through, the front shoulder opens up. Coming up to that position is basically a three-step movement, but some can skip all that and take just one step and throw. That takes a real strong arm. Parrish can do it. I went to it early in my career, because it was simple for me then, but I don't think it's the most effective. If your arm doesn't get all the way through—if it never quite catches up to your body and you let the throw go from out *here*—you get that three-quarters, Thurman Munson throw. Thur-man threw that way because he didn't have a strong arm, and I'm sure he weighed that quick release against velocity and accuracy. But he didn't have a choice, really. For me, that shift to get the shoulder into position is where the throw is made. Velocity is a gift—and most catchers in the majors have it—but quickness is in your feet."

Boone speaks in a deliberate, considering sort of way. He is a thoughtful man, with a saturnine look to him that contrasts strikingly with his gentle, almost sleepy smile. He is a graduate of Stanford, where he majored in psychology (not much of a help to him in baseball, he confided—not even in dealing with umpires). During the negotiations arising from the 1981 baseball strike, he represented the National League for the Players Associa-tion. Possibly because of this union activity, he was not signed to a new contract by the Phillies the next season, and crossed leagues to join the Angels, where he enjoyed immediate success, winning a Gold Glove award (his third) for his defensive prowess, and handling the theretofore listless California mound staff in a manner that helped bring the club to the cham-pionship playoffs that fall. We talked in the visiting-team clubhouse during the middle innings of an Angels-Cubs spring game at Mesa, while he slowly took off his uniform (he had played the first four innings) and showered and dressed, waiting for his teammates to be done, waiting for another team bus. I didn't think we covered much ground in our talk, but I was wrong about that; his modest, off-speed delivery fooled me. In the days and weeks that followed, I heard Boone-echoes in things that other catchers and coaches were telling me, and realized that I had already been put in the game, as it were, by what he had imparted.

One catcher's attribute that Boone always seemed to come back to in our talk was consistency—doing hard things right again and again, doing them as a matter of course. "Everyone at the major-league level has talent," he said at one point, "but the players who last are the ones who are consistent. People who can control themselves over one hundred and sixty-two games are rare, and that's why the old idea of the starting nine has sort of gone out. It seems that a lot of players get into bad spells and have to have a rest. I think you have to prepare your *mind* to play a full season, and of course you have to train for it physically. I work a lot on flexibility. You have to be able to deal with pain, to the point where it doesn't affect how you hit and catch and throw. That comes with time. You experience things and deal with them. I don't look at the catcher's job as one that's going to tire me out more than other players get tired. Getting tired is just part of the season, so you prepare for that, too."*

○

In Sarasota, Dave Duncan was talking about the great recent upsurge of base-stealing in both leagues, and what the coaching staffs were doing to combat it. (Per-team base-stealing totals have risen dramatically in the past two decades, thanks in part to the individual exploits of motorers like Lou Brock, of the Cardinals, who at the age of thirty-five set a new one-season record with a hundred and eighteen stolen bases in 1974, and Rickey Henderson, of the Oakland A's, who stole a hundred and thirty in 1982; and in part to a freethinking manager, Chuck Tanner, two of whose clubs, the A's and then the Pittsburgh Pirates, set amazing new *team* stolen-base records in

*On September 16th, 1987, Bob Boone caught his 1,919th major-league game, thereby surpassing the all-time receivers' record held by Al Lopez. By the end of the 1989 season, Boone had extended that total to 2,185 games caught, with the still-active Carlton Fisk now in close pursuit, at 1,928 games. Boone's 1988 batting average of .295 was a career best. The following year, having moved along to the Kansas City Royals as a free agent, he topped all catchers in his league by working one hundred and twenty-nine games behind the plate, and was voted his seventh Rawlings Gold Glove award (and fourth in a row) as the best defensive-catcher in the American League. He is forty-two years old, and his mind is prepared to go right on catching.

each league, in 1976 and 1977, with three hundred and forty-one and two hundred and sixty thefts, respectively. Back in the nineteen-forties and fifties, the major-league clubs averaged fewer than fifty stolen bases per year, with everyone waiting to stroll around the bases after a home run, but now National League teams average about a hundred and fifty swipes per summer, and the A.L. about forty or fifty fewer, with the difference probably attributable to the quicker, artificial-turf basepath carpets that predominate in the senior circuit.) Duncan, who is the pitching coach for the Chicago White Sox, caught for eleven years with Kansas City, Oakland, Cleveland, and Baltimore. He handled the hairy A's flingers—Catfish Hunter, Vida Blue, Rollie Fingers—during the first of Oakland's three successive world-championship seasons, in the early nineteen-seventies: yes, *that* Dave Duncan. He is a slender, soft-spoken gent with wide-spaced pale-blue eyes.

"*Everyone's* running, it seems," he said. "And everything is being timed now. I don't remember anybody putting a clock on a catcher when I was out there. Now there are three or four guys on the bench with stopwatches, and the first-base coach in the spring has a stopwatch, too. It's gotten so you can figure in advance that you've got a chance against a particular base runner if *this* guy is pitching for you and *that* guy is behind the plate. We've all learned the figures. A good time for a catcher, from the moment of his catch until the moment his peg arrives at second, is around two seconds. If you find a catcher who can get it out there in one-nine or one-eight, that's a quick release. Meanwhile, a man who takes an average lead and gets himself down to second in three-three is a good base runner. A tenth off makes him a real rabbit, and if you're going to throw him out you've got to do everything right—hold him pretty close, a quick delivery from the mound, and then a pitch that the catcher can handle easily. A catcher with a good throwing arm—a Rick Dempsey, a Lance Parrish, a Mike Heath—is almost a necessity nowadays. Bob Boone is about the best there is at calling a good game and also throwing well. He's very consistent, with good accuracy and great anticipation."

I remembered at once. "With a Rickey Henderson or a Tim Raines or a Lou Brock on base," Boone had told me, "you work at setting up the same way as always and at knowing what your own maximum speed is. If you try to go beyond that, you become erratic and you're actually slower. It's like a boxer throwing a jab. He wants to do it at his maximum all the time, but if he suddenly wants a little extra he's much less—you can see it. Actually, it's almost easier with a speedster—with a Rickey Henderson leading away out there—because you know he's going to go. The other guys, the ones you don't expect to run, are harder to keep up for, and you have to do that on every pitch, really, with a man on base. You tell yourself, 'I've got a right-handed pitcher and he's throwing a curveball here, so I have to be aware

212

of my right side, 'cause that's where it's going. O.K., *I'm prepared.*' "

In 1982, Boone was the only regular catcher in either league to throw out more than fifty percent of the opposition's would-be base stealers; he got fifty-eight percent of them, and cut down Rickey Henderson six times out of thirteen. This is still not a dazzling success ratio, to be sure, and since it is demonstrable that athletes today are much quicker afoot than their predecessors, it seems certain that not even time-motion studies and smart catchers are going to keep base runners from sprinting off for second in ever-increasing numbers in the seasons just ahead. It has occurred to me that this phenomenon may represent the first breakdown of baseball's old and beautiful distances: if ninety feet from base to base is no longer enough to keep a single or a base on balls from becoming an almost automatic double, then someone may have to go back to the drawing board at last in order to restore caution to the austere sport—and to cheer up catchers a little, too.

"I admire Bob Boone and this kid Tony Peña, with the Pirates," Tim McCarver said from across the room, so to speak; we were in St. Petersburg, where McCarver, now a Mets broadcaster, was preparing to do a Mets–Red Sox game. He played in four different decades, from the late fifties to the early eighties, mostly for the Cardinals (he was Bob Gibson's favorite receiver), and he is humorous, snub-nosed, and cheerfully opinionated. "Peña does so many things right already that he makes me *salivate*," he said. "The Phillies let Bob Boone go because they said he couldn't throw anymore—a terrible rap. So he goes over to the Angels and leads the league in throwing out runners and takes the Angels right to the doorstep of the World Series. He's conscientious and he's always in great shape, and his throwing is only a little part of it. I never could throw well, so I always thought calling a game was the biggest thing. That will never become a noted part of the game, because there are no stats for it, and the fans don't care about it, and most of the scouts don't know a whole lot about it, either. Even today, scouts and some managers will say, 'He can really catch,' when they mean 'He can really throw.' This is real bullshit, because throwing just isn't a very important part of it, when you think about it. Gene Mauch is one of the few managers who really understood and appreciated catching. I always felt some resentment about not being appreciated, but that was balanced out by pitchers who knew what I was doing back there. Some of them didn't appreciate me until the time came when they had to pitch to somebody else." He laughed.

○

All right, forget about throwing. Think about catching the ball instead—seizing that imminent, inbound, sinking or riding, up-and-in or down-and-away, eighty-to-ninety-five-m.p.h. hardball, and doing it, moreover, in a way that might just turn the umpire's call to your advantage. Terry Kennedy told me that sometimes you can take a pitch close to the inside edge of the plate (inside to a right-handed batter, that is) and slightly rotate your glove to the left at the last instant—he shifted his mitt so that the thumb moved from two o'clock to noon—and thus win a strike call from the ump. "But you can't hold it there, to make the point," he said. "They *hate* it if you keep the glove up there, and it's almost an automatic ball."

Milt May said that just catching the ball cleanly was a big help to the umpires, and led to better calls, while Tom Haller (we will meet these deponents in a minute) told me that Del Crandall, the celebrated Milwaukee Braves receiver of a quarter of a century ago, had taught him how to catch an away pitch, on the outside corner, with his glove parallel to the ground, and to take the ball in the webbing instead of in the pocket. "The ball could be an inch or two off the strike zone and he still might call it a strike, because the glove itself is still over the plate," Haller said. "And a high pitch you can take with a little downward move sometimes. You teach a young catcher to take most pitches as close to the plate as possible, because the farther back you are, the more it can bend out of the strike zone. If your glove is back to where that pitch looks like a ball now, the crowd may even react to it, and then the ump thinks, Hell, I'm going to call that a ball after all."

Bob Boone again: "There are a few little tricks of framing and catching the ball that might convince an umpire—shifting your body instead of your glove, or maybe the way you collapse your glove as you make the catch. But you don't want to work on that umpire too much. More often, a catcher will take a strike away from the pitcher by catching it improperly—knocking it out of the strike zone, or moving the glove with the pitch so that it carries the ball out of the strike zone after the catch, and even if you roll your glove you might help the umpire to make up his mind the wrong way."

He left the umpires for a moment and segued into the problems of setting up for the pitcher—presenting the best sort of target for each pitch. "Some pitchers want to throw to your whole body, and not just the glove," he said. "Then if you want the pitch outside, on that far corner, you have to get yourself on out there in a way that the batter won't notice. There's an art in that—it takes time to learn it. You slide over at the last second—and it's much harder to do that against a batter with an open stance, of course: somebody like Rod Carew, on our club—and you also try to get a little closer, which makes it that much tougher for him to spot you. There are some guys who can always seem to sense where you are, no matter what you do. And of course there are a few peekers, too."

I said that he sounded disapproving.

"Well, you tell them to cut it out," Boone said. "But if it goes on you can just say a word to your pitcher. Then you set up outside and he throws inside.

That usually stops it right away, and if the batter says anything about it you just say, 'Hey, you were *looking*.' "

But let's finish the introductions. I remember Milt May when he was a blond, promising rookie receiver with the Pittsburgh Pirates, almost fifteen years ago. Now much of his hair has gone, and he is on the down side of a respectable, journeyman sort of career that has taken him by turns to the Astros, Tigers, White Sox, Giants, and—early last season—back to the Pirates again, where he is now a backup to the effulgent Peña. I talked to him in Arizona last spring, while he was still a Giant. Milt May, incidentally, is the son of Pinky May, an infielder with the Phillies around the Second World War. Oddly enough, Terry Kennedy is the son of Bob Kennedy, who was a major-league infielder-outfielder and later on served in various capacities, as coach, manager, and front-office executive, with, among other clubs, the Cubs, Cardinals, and Astros; and Bob Boone's pop, Ray Boone, was a well-known American League shortstop and third baseman in his day. Maybe *not* so oddly: perhaps years of serious baseball talk at the family breakfast table adds a secret something—a dab of sagacity, say—to the Wheaties and thus turns out good catchers down the line.

Tom Haller put in a dozen years at catcher for the Giants and Dodgers and Tigers. Now he runs the baseball side of things for the Giants, as V.P. for Baseball Operations. The other catchers in our group, who are leaning forward in the chairs a little restlessly over there as they wait to be heard from, are probably more familiar. The long lanky one is Carlton Fisk, and the intense fellow, smoking a cigarette, is Ted Simmons. In a *minute*, you guys— all right?

Surprisingly, there was more agreement about umpires among the panelists than about anything else. Grudging respect was what I heard for the most part, and then, after the conversation had run in that direction for a few minutes, even the grudgingness seemed to drop away. Ted Simmons, the Milwaukee Brewers veteran, described the catcher-umpire relationship in social terms. "It's like meeting people at a cocktail party," he said. "Some you like and some you can't stand, but you know you have to be at least polite with everybody in order to keep things going."

"You can beef about pitches, but you always do it when you're walking back toward the plate from the mound—after a play maybe," Haller put in. "You don't turn around and do it, you know. Young catchers are always being tested by the umps, and they have to learn to take some bad calls and not say anything. Catchers who are moaning and bitching all the time really can hurt their team, but there's such a thing as being too quiet, too. You hear an umpire say, 'Oh, he's a good catcher—you never hear a word of complaint out of him,' but to me that's a catcher who isn't sticking up for his team out there."

"I don't mess with umpires," young Terry Kennedy said. "Let 'em sleep. They say, 'The ball missed the corner,' and I say unwaveringly, 'No, it *hit* the corner,' but I'm quiet about it." He laughed, almost helplessly.

Carlton Fisk: "Any game where there's a lot of situational friction—all that yelling and screaming—it can suddenly be very hard on your team. Young umps and young catchers are both new kids on the block, trying to establish themselves, but in time the respect appears, and it can grow. After a while, a good umpire knows you're not going to give him a hard time, and you start to feel he won't squeeze you too much back there. I got along real well with Bill Haller"—he's Tom Haller's older brother—"who just retired. The same for Richie Garcia and Dave Phillips and Steve Palermo. I get along with Ken Kaiser, who can't get along with a lot of players. He umpired with me in the minor leagues, so we go back a long way together. With most of them, it's strictly professional—a 'How's it going?' And then you get on with the game."

Tom Haller: "Al Barlick was the best ball-and-strike umpire I ever worked with. He took a lot of pride in that. Others—well, Dusty Boggess was on the way out, I think, when I was coming up, and one day I'd been getting on him back there and I said something he didn't like. The next pitch was right down the middle and I'd hardly caught it when he yelled 'Baw-ell!' In time, I learned. As I got older, I began to appreciate how good most of them were."

Bob Boone: "The umpire has to be himself, so I try to be as honest with him as I can. You're not going to fool a major-league umpire for long. If one of them asks me about a borderline pitch that went for us—a called strike, I mean—he may do it a couple of pitches later: 'What did you think about that pitch?' and I'll tell him, even if I'm saying 'Well, I thought it was a little outside' or 'I thought it was a little high.' That way, he knows if I make a gripe on a pitch later on I'm not trying to steal anything from him."

Milt May: "They respect your opinion because they know you respect them. Some days, *I'm* not seein' the ball too well, and after the hitter's gone I might ask, 'Say, where was that second pitch? Did you think it was high enough?'—or whatever. I think the instant replays have made the umps look good, because it's turned out they're right so much of the time. Only a catcher who's down there with them can know how hard it is. They don't know what pitch is coming'—whether it's meant to be a slider or a sinker, or what. That ball is *travelling* and doin' different things, and maybe one half inch of it is going to catch the black. If there's a hundred and forty pitches in a game, fifty of them are balls and fifty are strikes, and the other forty are so close—well, dad-*gone*, somebody's going to be mad."

Carlton Fisk: "If I know an umpire's preferences, that gives me some borders to aim at. Some are notorious high-ball umps, and others have a very low strike zone. If you have a high-strike umpire and your pitcher is a sinkerball specialist, you might remind the umpire early in the game: 'Hey, this guy's keepin' the ball down real good the last few games—he's pitching real well.' That puts him on notice. And if your pitcher is the kind that's around the strike zone all the time he'll always get more calls from the umpire."

Tom Haller: "Umpires tend to be good at what a pitcher is good at because they anticipate that pitch."

Bob Boone: "When you change leagues, the way I did, you have to learn the new umpires' strike zones, and when you can argue and when you can't. Paul Runge has a low strike zone—he's going to make you swing that bat when you're up there. He's got a little bigger plate than some, but he's very consistent. You certainly can't change him. Lee Weyer has an extremely wide strike zone. Everyone knows it, and the catchers sort of count on it. Others have a smaller strike zone, and they're known as hitters' umpires." (Both Runge and Weyer are National League umps, and later on, after this part of our conversation, I realize that Boone, a diplomat, has not discussed his umpire preferences in the American League, where he now goes to work.)

Milt May: "You come to appreciate a pitcher who's always around the plate, because he's helping himself with that ump so much. He might miss the black by an inch sometimes, but the umpire will ring it up right away, because he's come to expect strikes from him. It's only natural."

Bob Boone: "The real negotiation isn't between the catcher and the umpire—it's between the *pitcher* and the umpire. The pitcher has to show that he can put the ball where he wants it and move it around. If he establishes that he knows where the ball is going, and that he's not just lucking out on the corners, the umpires will be a lot more forgiving with him than they will with the man who's all over the place and suddenly comes in with something close. A good pitcher—a Tommy John, who *lives* on the corners—sets up a rhythm with the umpire, and anything he throws will get a good long look. That's what control is all about."

Milt May: "The only thing that gets me upset is having two or three pitches in the same spot that are called strikes, and then you come back to that spot and the umpire misses it, just when you most needed that strike. But—well, I'd hate to call about twenty of those pitches myself."

Bob Boone: "When I'm back there, I want my umpire to call his very best game ever. That's the ideal."

○

Every catcher exudes stability and competence—there's something about putting on the chest protector and strapping on those shin guards that suggests a neighborhood grocer rolling up the steel storefront shutters and then setting out the merchandise to start the day—but Milt May seemed a little different from the other professionals I consulted. For some reason, I kept thinking that he and I could have played on the same team. I am much older than he is, and I never even lettered in baseball, so this was a dream of some sort. May and I talked during a Giants morning practice in Scottsdale, and he apologized to me each time he had to break off and go take his hacks in the batting cage. He was thirty-two, but he looked a bit older—or perhaps only wearier. Established catchers take on a thickness in their thighs and a careworn slope around the shoulders. Or possibly we only imagine that, from thinking about all those bent-over innings and hours—many thousands of them in the end. But May sounded young and even chirpy when he talked baseball, and up close his face was almost boyish. He hadn't shaved yet that day, and the stubble along his chin was red-gold in the morning sunshine. At one point, he said, "I think I'm like some other catchers—if I hadn't been able to catch I probably wouldn't have been able to make it to the big leagues at all. Maybe you can't run, but if you've got good hands and don't mind the work you can play. Not too many people want to do it." A bit later in the day, I noticed that when May flipped off his mask behind the plate his on-backward cap pushed his ears out a little on either side of his head. Then I understood my dream. Milt May is the kind of kid who always got to catch back when I played on pickup teams as a boy. He was big and slow, and he looked sort of funny out there, but he didn't mind the bumps and the work and the dirt, because that way he got to play. None of the rest of us wanted the job, and most of us couldn't have done it anyway.

○

That afternoon, Tom Haller and I sat on folding chairs in a front-row box in the little wooden stadium in Scottsdale and took in an early-March game between his Giants and the Seattle Mariners. Haller is a large, pleasant man, with an Irish-touched face, and a perfect companion at a game—silent for good long stretches but then quick to point out a telling little detail on the field or to bring up some play or player from the past, for comparison. He was watching his own rookies and stars out there, of course, but he had generous things to say about the young Mariner receiver, Orlando Mercado, who somehow folded himself down to about the height of a croquet wicket while taking a pitch.

"These kids we're seeing today—this one, and that Peña that the Pirates have—are lower than anybody I used to play with," he said in his light, faintly hoarse voice. "Maybe they're better athletes than they used to be—more agile, and all. I still wish they'd move the top half of their bodies more when they're after the ball. That glove has made everybody lazy. You just stick out your hand."

There was an infield bouncer to deep short, and Mercado trailed the play, sprinting down behind first base to back up the peg from short. Haller nodded in satisfaction. "It's hard on you physically behind the plate," he said. "All that bending and kneeling. One way to help yourself is to get on down to first base on that play and do it every single time. You let yourself out a little, so you're not cramped up all day."

A bit later, he said, "Mainly, you have to be a student of the game. There are so many little things to the job. You have to look the same when you're setting up for the fastball and the breaking ball, so you don't tip the pitch. A batter steps up, and he may have moved his feet in the box since the last time you saw him play, and that might completely change the way you and your pitcher've decided to pitch to him. You can't stop everything and call a conference to discuss what to do. You have to decide."

Then: "What you do can get sort of subtle sometimes. If you're ahead by a few runs or way behind in a game, you might decide to give a real good hitter the pitch that he's waiting for—his favorite pitch. Say he's a great, great breaking-ball hitter. Normally, you'd absolutely stay away from that pitch with anything over the plate, but in that special situation you might think, Let's let him have it, this once—let him hit it. That way, you put it in his head that he might get it again from you, later on in the game or the next time he faces that same pitcher. He'll be looking for it and waiting for it, and he'll never see it again. You've got a little edge on him."

In the game, the Giants had base runners on second and third, with one out, and the Mariners chose to pitch to the next batter, outfielder Chili Davis, who instantly whacked a double to right, for two runs. "If you've got an open base, you should try to remember to use it," Haller observed. "So often, you have the intention of putting a good hitter on, rather than letting him hurt you. You go to work on his weakness—let's say, something outside and away—and you get lucky and get two strikes on him, and then the pitcher decides, Hey, I can strike this bozo out. So you come in with the fastball and, bam, he kills you. You got greedy and forgot.

"Sometimes the little breaks of the game begin to go against your pitcher, and you can see him start to come apart out there. You have to watch for that and try to say something to him right off, because you can't do much to settle down a pitcher once he really gets upset. If he's sore, it means he's lost his concentration and so he's already in big trouble. You go out and try to get him to think about the next pitch, but you know he's probably not going to be around much longer."

The game flowed along quietly—nothing much, but not without its startlers. Orlando Mercado, batting against a Giants right-hander named Segelke, in the fifth, spun away from a sailing fastball, but too late—the pitch caught him on the back of his batting helmet and he sagged to the ground. It looked bad for a minute—we'd all heard the ugly sound of the ball as it struck and ricocheted away—but in time Mercado got up, albeit a little groggily, and walked with a Mariner trainer back to his dugout, holding a towel to his ear, which had been cut by the edge of the helmet.

In another part of the game, the Seattle second baseman, Danny Tartabull, cued a high, twisting foul up over the Giants dugout. Milt May came back for it, but it was in the stands, close to the front rows somewhere, and as I peered up, squinting in the sun, I realized at last that it was *very* close to the good seats. I cringed away, holding my notebook over my dome, and Tom Haller stood up beside me and easily made the bare-handed catch. Sensation. The Giants dugout emptied as the San Francisco minions gave their boss a standing O and Haller's friends in the stands—hundreds of them, by the sound of it—cheered noisily, and then a couple of former Giant managers, Wes Westrum and Charlie Fox (they are both scouts now), waved and called over to him from their seats nearby to express raucous awe. Haller flipped the ball to Bob Lurie, the Giants' owner, who was in an adjoining box. "I think I just saved you three bucks," he said. He was blushing with pleasure.

It had been a good five years since anything hit into the stands had come anywhere near that close to me—and, of course, it was the most *immediate* lesson in catching I was to get all year. Then I realized I'd missed the play again. "How did you take that ball, Tom?" I said. "I—"

He made a basket of his hands. "I was taught this way," he said. "Then if you bobble it you can still bring it in to your chest."

Haller's paws are thick and gnarled, and there seems to be an extra angle in the little finger of his right hand. He saw me looking at it now, and held out the hand. "Richie Allen hit a foul and tore up that part," he said. "I had a few dislocations and broken fingers along the line, and this split here needed seven stitches. Usually, you looked for blood, and if there wasn't any that meant you were all right. You could pop a dislocation back in and stay in the game. We were trained to tuck your right thumb inside your fingers and curve the fingers around, so if there was a foul tip the ball would bend them back in the right direction. Nowadays, catchers can just hide that hand behind their leg, because of the new glove. So it has its advantages."

Late in the game, the third Mariner catcher of the afternoon—a rookie named Bud Bulling—was struck by a foul that caromed into the dirt and up into his crotch. He remained on his knees in the dirt for a minute or two, waiting for that part of the day to be over, while the Giants players called to him in falsetto voices. "I got hit like that in the spring of my very first year up with the Giants," Haller said. "I tried not to say anything, and when I got back to the clubhouse I took the cup out of my jock all in pieces. Each spring, you wait for that first shot between the legs and you think, *All* right, now I'm ready to start the season."

The game ended (the Giants won it, and Chili Davis had racked up a homer, two doubles, and a single for the day), and as we stood up for the last time Haller called to a Mariner coach out on the grass. "I see some of us get old and gray!" Tom said.

"Yeah, I saw you," the coach said. "Your hands still look pretty good!" He waved cheerfully.

"That's Frank Funk," Haller said to me. "Frank was my first roommate in organized ball. We were in spring training together in the Giants' minor-league complex in Sanford, Florida, in 1958. He was a pitcher and I was a catcher, and they put us together to see if we could learn something."

He'd had a great afternoon—you could see that. He was tickled.

○

No catcher of our time looks more imperious than Carlton Fisk, and none, I think, has so impressed his style and mannerisms on our sporting consciousness: his cutoff, bib-sized chest protector above those elegant Doric legs; his ritual pause in the batter's box to inspect the label on his upright bat before he steps in for good; the tipped-back mask balanced on top of his head as he stalks to the mound to consult his pitcher; the glove held akimbo on his left hip during a pause in the game. He is six-three, with a long back, and when he comes straight up out of the chute to make a throw to second base, you sometimes have the notion that you're watching an aluminum extension ladder stretching for the house eaves; Bill Dickey, another straightback—he was the eminent receiver for the imperious Yankee teams of the thirties and forties—had that same household-contraption look to him when getting ready to throw. Fisk's longitudinal New England face is eroded by reflection. He is a Vermonter, and although it has been three years now since he went over to the White Sox, he still looks out of uniform to me without his Fenway habiliments. Pride is what he wears most visibly, though, and it's also what you hear from him.

"I really resent that old phrase about 'the tools of ignorance,' " he said to me in the White Sox dugout in Sarasota. "No catcher is ignorant. I've caught for pitchers who thought that if they won it's because they did such a great job, and if they lost it's because you called the wrong pitch. A lot of pitchers need to be led—taken to the point where they're told what pitch to throw, where to throw it, when to throw it, and what to do after they've thrown it. The good pitcher knows that if you put down the fastball"—the catcher's flashed signal: traditionally one finger for the fastball, two for a breaking ball, three for a changeup, and four for variants and specials—"it's also meant to be down and in or down and away, and if you put down a breaking ball then it's up to him to get that into some low-percentage area of the strike zone. The other kind just glance at the sign and fire the ball over the plate. That's where you get that proverbial high hanger—and it's your fault for calling it. But you know who the best pitchers are, and they know you. I worked with Luis Tiant as well as with anybody, and if he threw a fastball waist-high down the middle—well, it was nobody's fault but his own, and he was the first to say so. Not many fans know the stats about catchers, but smart pitchers notice after a while that they'll have a certain earned-run average with one catcher, and that it'll be a point and a half higher with another catcher on the same club. Then they've begun to see that it isn't just their talent that's carrying them out there."

There are some figures that even fans can understand, however: in 1980, Fisk's last year in Boston, the Red Sox won sixty-eight games and lost forty-four when he was behind the plate but were fifteen and thirty-three when he was not. His bat helped, then and always (he is a lifetime .281 hitter, with two hundred and nine career homers, and of course he is the man whose twelfth-inning home run won the sixth game of the 1975 World Series—still a high-water mark of the October classic), but Fisk, in conversation, showed a splendid ambivalence about the two sides of his profession. Hitting mattered, but perhaps not as much as the quieter parts of the job.

"Catchers are involved every day," he said, "and that's one of the reasons why, over the years, they've been inconsistent in their productiveness. You can go a month and make a great offensive contribution, and then maybe a month and a half where there's little or none. But because of the ongoing mental involvement in the pitcher-batter struggle you don't have the luxury of being able to worry about your offensive problems. You just haven't got time. I think catchers are better athletes than they used to be. They run better and they throw better, and more of them hit better than catchers once did. I'm not taking anything away from the Yogi Berras and the Elston Howards and the rest, but there never were too many of them. With the turn of the seventies, you began to get catchers like myself and Bench and Munson, and then Parrish and Sundberg and Carter, and then Peña—you go down the rosters and they're all fine athletes. Bench started hitting home runs and Munson started hitting .300, and that old model of the slow, dumb catcher with low production numbers started to go out of date."

Then there was the shift: "It always bothered me that catchers seemed defined by their offensive statistics—as if a catcher had no other value. Famous guys who hit twenty-five or thirty home runs or bat in a hundred runs may not have as much value as somebody hitting .250 or less—a Jerry Grote, say—but his pitchers and his teammates sure know. Look at Bill Freehan, with that good Detroit team back in the sixties and early seventies. He was a very average sort of runner, with an average, quick-release sort of arm, and nothing very startling offensively. But you just can't *measure* what he did for that Tiger pitching staff—people like McLain and Lolich and Joe Coleman."

He had brought up a side issue that has sometimes troubled me. There have been a hundred and seven Most Valuable Player awards since the annual honor was instituted by the Baseball Writers Association of America, in 1931, and thirteen of them have gone to catchers—very close to a one-in-nine proportion, which looks equitable. Catchers who are named M.V.P.s tend to get named again—Roy Campanella and Yogi Berra won the award three times apiece, and Johnny Bench twice—but it is hard not to notice that almost every M.V.P. catcher posted startling offensive figures in his award-winning summers: Gabby Hartnett batted .344 in 1935, Ernie Lombardi batted .342 in 1938, Bench had a hundred and forty-eight runs batted in in 1970. And so forth. Only one M.V.P. catcher—Elston Howard, in 1963—had offensive statistics (.287 and eighty-five R.B.I.s) that suggest that his work behind the plate had also been given full value by the voting scribes. The B.B.W.A.A. is engaged in an interesting ongoing debate about whether pitchers should be eligible for the M.V.P. award (as they are now), given the very special nature of their work. I think we should look at the other end of the battery and consider the possibility that, year in and year out, each of the well-established veteran catchers is almost surely the most valuable player on his club, for the reasons we have been looking at here.

Fisk cheered up a little after his musings. He tucked a nip of Skoal under his lower lip, and told me that catching left-handed pitchers had been the biggest adjustment he'd had to make when he went over to the White Sox. "Except for Bill Lee, we didn't have that many left-handers my twelve years in Boston," he said. "Because of the Wall. But there are good left-handers on this club, and that's taken me a little time. When you're calling a game with a left-handed pitcher against a lot of right-handed batters, you have to do it a little differently. A left-hander's breaking ball always goes to my glove side, and his fastball and sinkerball run the other way. That fastball up over here, from a lefty pitcher, is a little harder for me to handle, for some reason. I'm still conscious of it, but I'm beginning to have a better time of it now."

I thought about Fisk often and with great pleasure last summer, while his White Sox streaked away with the American League West divisional title. He batted .289, with twenty-six homers, for the year, and the Chicago pitchers (including LaMarr Hoyt, whose 24–10 and 3.66 record won him the Cy Young Award) outdid themselves. Fisk's season ended in the White Sox' excruciating 3–0 loss to the Orioles in the fourth game of the American League championship series, at Comiskey Park, in a game in which Britt Burns, the young left-handed Chicago starter, threw nine innings of shutout ball before succumbing in the tenth. Fisk had but one single in five at-bats in that game, but I think he found some rewards just the same. There in Sarasota, he'd said, "When things are working well and the pitcher stays with you the whole way and you're getting guys out and keeping in the game—well, there's just no more satisfying feeling. You want to win it and you want to get some hits, but if your pitcher is doing his best, inning after inning, then you know you've done your job. It doesn't matter if I don't get any hits, but if I was an outfielder in that same game and all I'd done was catch a couple of routine fly balls— why, then I wouldn't have anything to hang my hat on that day."

Tim McCarver also spoke of this sense of deeper involvement. Like many useful long-termers, he was moved to easier positions when the demands of the job began to wear him down, but he didn't like it much not catching. "Joe Torre had been through that same shift," he said to me, "and he told me that when I changed position I'd be amazed how much my mind would begin to wander. When I moved out to first base—I played more than seventy games there in 1973—I couldn't believe it. I had to keep kicking myself to pay attention."

○

Calling a game, of course, is the heart of it, and what that requires of a catcher, I came to understand at last, is not just a perfect memory for the batting strengths and weaknesses of every hitter on every other club—some hundred and sixty-five to a hundred and ninety-five batters, that is—but a sure knowledge of the capabilities of each pitcher on his staff. The latter is probably more important. Milt May said, "If I had a chance to play against a team I'd never seen before but with a pitcher I'd caught fifty times, I'd much rather have that than play against a team I'd played fifty times but with a pitcher I didn't know at all."

The other desideratum is a pitcher with good control—far rarer, even at the major-league level, than one might suppose. "There are very few guys who can really pitch to a hitter's weakness," May said. "Most of 'em just want to pitch their own strength. Young pitchers usually have good stuff—a good moving fastball—and they pitch to hitters in the same pattern. Most of their breaking balls are out of the strike zone, so they go back to the fastball when they're behind, and of course if you're up at bat you notice something like that."

Here is Bob Boone again: "It's much more fun catching a guy with excellent control, because then you feel you're part of the whole jockeying experience. Here's a ball that's just inside—fine. Now go back outside and put the ball on the corner this time. You're *orchestrating* that. Catching somebody like Tommy John is more work mentally, but it's much more pleasurable, and after it's over you'll both think, Hey, we had a great game. There's no doubt that a catcher can help a pitcher, but he can't be a dictator out there. When you've established that rapport with a pitcher you know, what you put down in a situation is almost always just about what he's thinking. When that happens, it gives the pitcher the confidence to throw a good pitch. You adjust as you go along—to the hitter and to your pitcher's abilities on that given day. If you can do it, you want to save something to use late in the game, because there are always a few batters you can't get out the same way more than once. If you've got through the order the first time without using your pitcher's whole repertoire, you're a little ahead. But pitchers change as a game goes along, of course, and then you have to adjust to *that*. Say your pitcher's best pitch is his slider, but then by the way he warms up for the next inning you think *Uh-oh*, because suddenly it isn't anymore—not at that moment. But then four pitches later it may be back again. It's a feel you have, and that's what you really can't teach to young catchers.

"Sometimes you get a sudden notion for an exotic call—something that's really strange in a certain situation that you somehow know is the right thing. You're jamming the man—throwing the ball right by him—and suddenly you call for a changeup. Ordinarily, you don't do that, but even if I'm watching a game from the bench I can sometimes feel when the moment comes: *Now throw him the changeup*. It's strange and it's strictly feel, but when it happens and you have that closeness with the pitcher he'll come in after the inning and say, 'You know, I had exactly the same idea back there!' But in the end, of course, it's how he throws those pitches that matters."

Pitchers can always shake off a catcher's sign, to be sure—some shake-offs are only meant to set up doubt in the batter's mind—and catcher-pitcher negotiations go on between innings or during a mound conference. These last are not always diplomatic murmurings. "There almost has to be a lot of screaming and yelling between pitchers and catchers if they're going to get along," Tim McCarver told me. "With Gibby"—Bob Gibson, that is—"it sometimes happened right out on the mound. I remember a game against the Pirates when Clemente hit one of his patented shots to right field, and when Gibby came past me to back up the throw in he yelled, 'Goddam it, you've got to put down something more than one finger back there!' "

Ted Simmons said, "Sometimes you have to persuade your pitcher out of a certain pitch in the middle of the game. It's hard for him to remain objective in the heat of battle. If he's had some success, I might go out there and ask what he's thinking, and if he says, 'Over the years, I've gotten this guy out with this pitch in this situation, even though it's dangerous'—let's say there are two on and he's getting ready to throw a changeup—then I say, 'Fine. Let's go.' But if I go out there and he says, 'Well, I just got a *feel*, man,' and he's lookin' at me with cloudy eyes, I say, 'Look, we'll do that next time—O.K.?' It's a matter of being convincing."

Ted Simmons, I should add, is one of the most convincing men in baseball. He is a sixteen-year man in the majors—the last three with the Brewers, the rest with the Cardinals—and is one of the prime switch hitters in the game: in 1975 he batted .332 for the Cards and drove in a hundred runs. He is known for his intelligence and knowledge of the game—splendid assets, but what I most enjoy about Simba is his passionate way of talking baseball. He talks the way Catfish Hunter used to pitch—feeling for the corners early on and then with a widening flow of ideas and confidence and variation in the late going: Cooperstown stuff. When we sat down together at Sun City last spring, I asked him about the difference between National League and American League pitching—almost an idle question, I thought, since I was pretty sure I knew the answer: a lower strike zone in the National League, and more breaking balls in the A.L.

"I don't know how it began, but it's there, all right," Simmons said. "It's a difference of *approach*. The National League, in my mind, throws the slow stuff early in the count and then throws the fastball late, with two strikes on the batter. To me, that makes more sense, because you're forcing the batter to hit the ball—that's the objective—and the odds are always against a base hit, even with the best hitters. The American League approach, from what I've seen of it in two years, is to throw hard early—to get two strikes and no balls, or 2–1 or 2–2—and *then* go to the slow stuff. So if you're 2–1 in the A.L., you're apt to go to 3–2 every time, because they'll throw a curveball and you'll foul it. Then a curve or a slider, and you'll take it, for 3–2. Then another slider or curve, and you'll foul it, then *another* curveball, and you'll swing and miss it for a strikeout or hit a fly ball for the out. So there are three or four extra pitches on almost every batter, and that's one reason why the American League has such long games. The A.L. philosophy is to get two strikes and then don't let him hit, and the N.L. thinks, Get two strikes and *make* him hit it."

I asked him which league had the better pitchers, and he thought about it for a while. "I think the American League pitchers are *probably* better, on balance," he said at last, "because they have to be refined when the count is against them—to throw that breaking ball and get it over the plate, throw it in a way to get the man out. The very best of them may be more subtle and refined and tough than the N.L. pitchers. I'm talking about guys like Dave Stieb, of the Toronto Blue Jays, and Pete Vuckovich here. Vukey was with me on the Cardinals, you know, but he made the adjustment very fast when he came over to this league. But there are always exceptions. Somebody like Steve Rogers"—of the National League Montreal Expos—"could pitch very well in this league."

Bob Boone and Milt May have also had experience in both leagues, but they both gave a slight edge to National League pitching. May said that the

N.L.'s preference for the slider—the faster breaking ball—as against the American League's prejudice for the curve, might make the crucial difference. Boone said, "I think the real difference between the leagues is about six National League pitchers. Soto, Seaver, Carlton, Rogers, maybe Reuss, and any one of three or four others. Put 'em over in the American League, and they're even." (Tom Seaver, who came to the Chicago White Sox over this winter, has already made the switch.) "I would guess there are deeper counts in the A.L., but I wouldn't know for sure. I know there's more confidence in control in the A.L. In either league, it's hard as hell to get a base hit, most days."

Simmons wanted to be sure that I understood the extent of the catcher's involvement with other aspects of the game—with his manager, for instance, and with the deployment of the defense on the field. "With some managers," he said, "you can come to them in the dugout in the middle of the game and say, 'This pitcher has *had* it. I assume you know that. But I want you to know I'm having to struggle with every pitch in every inning. I can't set up a program with this man, because he's faltering. Now I want some notion about your objectives. Do you intend to pitch him one more inning, or three more?' Then if the manager says, 'Wow, let's get somebody up out there,' I can say, 'Well, O.K., I can get him through one more inning,' and you work that inning like it's the ninth, with nothing held back. But there are some managers who can't respond to that assertive approach, because of their personalities—I can think of a half dozen of them that I've been involved with—and with those, well, you have to find some other way to get the message across."

We moved along to defensive alignments, and I noticed that sometimes the intensity of his message made Simmons lift his hands to either side of his face as he talked, as if he were peering out of his mask at the game.

"You have to move your people around," he said. "It's part of your job, and part knowing how your manager wants things done. You've got a left-handed pull hitter up there, and you decide you're going to do one of two things. You're going to throw him low fastballs away and hope he tries to pull it, or slow stuff inside and *make* him pull it. So you set up your defense accordingly. Your second baseman plays in the hole, your shortstop is back of second base, and everyone in the outfield moves over two steps toward right. But if your second baseman is still playing at double-play depth, then you've got to stop and move him over. You can do that with a little gesture, just before you put down the sign—and I never put down anything until I know I have the second baseman and the shortstop's attention anyway. I just look them right in the eye and go—" He waggled his glove hand imperceptibly. "If he still has a question, when you get back to the bench you can say, 'Hey, don't you see how we're pitchin' that guy?' This happens a lot, but people don't always appreciate it. Sometimes you'll see catchers with large reputations who'll stop and turn to the umpire and call time out and turn to the world and walk out a few steps and gesture to the man they want to move over, and everyone in the stands will say, 'Ah, yes, there's a man who knows what he's doing.' But it just isn't essential. It isn't done."

The ultimate responsibility—for the game itself, Simmons suggested—is more difficult. "The catcher is the man who has to be able to think, and he has to make the decisions—and to face the consequences when he's wrong," he went on. "Whether it's fun for you or a burden, that's where it's *at*, and the real satisfaction in catching is making that decision for everyone—for your pitcher, your team, your manager, and the home crowd. It's all in your lap. Think of a situation. Think of something that happens all the time. The count is two balls and one strike, they have a man on first base, and you're ahead by one run. There's a pretty good hitter up—he doesn't strike out much. Now, you're the catcher and you've got to decide if they're going to hit-and-run. And with that you've got to decide if you're going to pitch out and negate all that, and what the consequences will be if you're wrong.

"*Now* we've got to where the fun is—where you know your allies, the capabilities of your pitcher and your team, and you also know the opposition, to the point where you're playin' with their heads. Because you know their manager and their way of playing, you know already what they're going to do. You have a gut feeling about it: *God, he's going to run*. You *know*. But instead—it's so easy to do this—you think, Well, I'd better play it safe, because I'm not sure, and we don't want 3–1 on this good hitter. So you call a fastball away to that right-handed batter, and he does hit the ball to right on the hit-and-run—the runner's gone—and now you've got first and third, which is much, much worse. And you say to yourself, God *almighty*, I *knew* they were going to run! Why didn't I pitch out? Well, what you learn later on, when you've grown up as a catcher, is not to fight that urge, because you understand that if you were in their dugout and you were that manager you'd run. So you learn to stop being just a catcher, and to be them as well as yourself. Until you can get to that point, accept that burden, you're not in control. Once you do, you're a successful catcher—the man everyone relies on and looks to for leadership, whether they know it or not."

○

Ted Simmons had a good season last year, in spite of the sudden late-summer collapse of the defending-champion Brewers, who wound up in fifth place in their division, eleven games behind the Orioles. He kept his stroke when all about him were losing theirs, and wound up with a .308 average and a hundred and eight runs batted in. For all that, it was probably Simmons' last year of regular work behind the plate. During the off-season, Milwaukee traded for Jim Sundberg, and it is expected that he will now take over the day-to-day catching chores for the Brewers. Simmons, who has suffered from a chronic problem in his right shoulder, looked slow and work-worn behind the plate in most of the games in which I watched him last year, and he is at an age when many full-service catchers begin to wear down physically. I think he will find surcease in his new role as a designated hitter—if his pride allows him to accept this limited service. But I still felt bad when I heard the news of the trade, since it seemed to mean that Simmons' passionate involvement in the flow of things would now become distanced and muted. The game is no longer in his lap. His change of fortune made me recall a remark of Dave Duncan's last spring: "By the time you've learned it all, by the time you're really proficient, you're almost too old to go on catching."

I cheered up pretty quickly, however, when I recalled one more little talk I'd had with Ted Simmons, which had made me realize that his special feeling for the subtleties and rewards of catching will never be entirely lost to his teammates. On another day in Arizona last spring, I watched a few innings of a morning B-squad game between the Padres and the Brewers. Simmons wasn't playing, but then I spotted him in the Milwaukee dugout, where he was seated between two younger Brewer catchers, Ned Yost and Bill Schroeder; Simmons kept moving and gesturing, and when I changed my seat, moving a little closer to the diamond, I saw, without much surprise, that he was talking excitedly. When the game ended, I sought him out and asked him about it.

"We were just talkin' catching," he said. "I feel that every ballplayer, including myself, has the responsibility of training his replacement. People who are afraid to do that aren't very secure. What we saw was what you saw in that game—do you remember it? There was a time in the fifth when they're up at bat, with a man on first, and the count on the batter went to 2-2. I said to the guys with me, 'You've got two alternatives on the next pitch—what are they?' They both had the answer: fastball in or slider away. I said fine, but how do you decide which to call, and they didn't know. I said, 'Based on your pitcher'—and never mind right now which pitcher we were talkin' about. 'Based on your knowledge of this pitcher, can he throw the 3-2 slider for a strike?' They both said no, and I said, 'Well, then, you have to call for the slider on the 2-2, so that if the pitcher misses with it, then he'll be able to come back with the fastball on 3-2. But if he's a pitcher who *can* throw the slider on 3-2, then you can put down the fastball on 2-2—the fastball inside, to lock him out. If you miss, then you go to the slider on 3-2, and he's dead.'

"Our other catcher, Steve Lake, was in the game, so I didn't talk to him. He was in the fire, and we were lookin' into it. But that's all there is to it, you know. Does the man back there know what's going on? If he does, he can throw bad and he can run bad and block bad, but he's still the single most important player on the field."

Life in the Pen

— J U L Y 1 9 8 5

On a summer Saturday in Kansas City, I kept an appointment with Dan Quisenberry, the Royals' prime short reliever. Quis is a slim, angular right-hander, with sharp shoulders and a peaceable, almost apologetic mien. He has pinkish-red hair, a brushy ochre mustache, and round pale-blue eyes. Nothing about his looks is as surprising as his pitching delivery, however. He is a true submariner—a man "from down under," in baseball parlance—and every pitch of his is performed with a lurching downward thrust of his arm and body, which he must follow with a little bobbing hop off toward third base in order to recover his balance. At perigee, ball and hand descend to within five or six inches of the mound dirt, but then they rise abruptly; the hand—its fingers now spread apart—finishes up by his left shoulder, while the ball, plateward-bound at a sensible, safe-driving-award clip, reverses its earlier pattern, rising for about three-quarters of its brief trip and then drooping downward and (much of the time) sidewise as it passes the batter at knee level or below. One way or another, the pitch almost always finds part of the strike zone, but most people in the stands—even the home-town regulars in Royals Stadium—are so caught up in the pitcher's eccentricities that they don't always notice this. The oversight is forgivable, since Quisenberry is not a strikeout pitcher. But he doesn't walk batters, either; in his six hundred and thirty-five major-league innings (going into this season), he had surrendered a total of eighty-four bases on balls—one for each seven and a half innings' work, which for him comes out at about one walk every fourth game—and had plunked only two batters with pitched balls. Yet Quisenberry when pitching invites more similes than stats. His ball in flight suggests the kiddie-ride concession at a county fairgrounds—all swoops and swerves but nothing there to make a mother nervous; if you're standing close to it, your first response is a smile. At other

230

times, the trajectory of the pitch looks like an expert trout fisherman's side-arm cast that is meant to slip the fly just under an overhanging clump of alders. The man himself—Quis in mid-delivery—brings visions of a Sunday-picnic hurler who has somehow stepped on his own shoelace while coming out of his windup, or perhaps an eager news photographer who has suddenly dropped to one knee to snap a celebrity debarking from a limousine. If some of these images are shared by batters in the American League, they probably play a part in Quisenberry's extraordinary record of success as a short reliever. The night before our meeting, I had watched him close down the Yankees in his typically unspectacular fashion, to record his third save in four days and his twentieth of the year, which put him ahead of all American League relief pitchers in that department. Last year, Quisenberry had forty-four saves in all, the most in his league, and figured in sixty percent of the Royals' winning games; the year before that, he established a new major-league record with forty-five saves.

None of the pride and bulldog resolution that makes for numbers like these was apparent in Quisenberry's demeanor when we met in the spacious Royals clubhouse on Saturday afternoon. The coming game, a night affair, was still hours away, but Quis, who habitually arrives very early at the park, was already in uniform and ready for the next thing. Like other veteran ballplayers I have encountered, he seemed exceptionally contented in his clubhouse; he looked almost dug in, and, watching him there, with his friends and his mail and his keepsakes (there was a child's red fireman's hat, with a red headlight on it, perched on top of his cubicle), I thought of the Badger at home in his slippers, in "The Wind in the Willows." Quisenberry is a genial and respected figure in the clubhouse (he is the Royals' player representa-tive: their elected union delegate in the Players Association), and so many overlapping conversations were swirling around his corner of the den that I was glad when he suggested that we walk out to visit his other place of business—the bullpen. There were a couple of other players in view outside as we strolled across the warm ungrass—the home bullpen is in right field at Royals Stadium—but the sunstruck table of the field and the rising tiers of gleaming empty seats encircled us in a silent bowl of light.

"There's Charlie Leibrandt over there, throwing up on the sidelines," Quis said, nodding his head toward one of the Royals playing catch. He watched for my reaction—this is a first-year–Little League baseball joke—and I laughed in spite of myself. "This year's bullpen is starting to develop," he went on. "It's a good group. Each year, the makeup of the pen is a little different, and the feeling changes. Our new man out here is Mike LaCoss"—LaCoss, an experienced National League right-handed pitcher, had been signed as a free agent over the winter—"and we're getting to know him a little. We call him Buffy and Izod, or Izod, and Buffenstein. I never know

231

where all the nicknames come from. He likes to mix it up—get on guys and have them get on him. He's an expert bridge player, or thinks he is. Then there's Mike Jones, Joe Beckwith, and John Wathan, the catcher—he always sits a little bit apart—and the rest. Joe watches All-Star wrestling, and he likes to show us all the new holds. Renie Martin used to bring pencil and paper, and he'd draw little cartoons of things that happened in each game. Mike Armstrong and I used to do some games in Spanish—I just remembered. Broadcasts, I mean. Of course, neither of us could *speak* Spanish, but that didn't stop us. The trouble with bullpens is that they keep changing. The people in them come and go, so you can't always keep things going. Last year was a good crossword bullpen, but we're not so big on that this year for some reason. But we still do the crossword in the paper first thing every day, and then Izod looks at the bridge hand and tells us how Omar Sharif would have played it. The early part of the game is given to the starting pitcher and the other guys on the field, and Muggsy—Jimmie Schaffer (he's our bullpen coach)—sets the tone. We're critical, I mean. If a pitcher in the game gets behind in the count, he says, 'How can you not throw strikes with *that* garbage?' and you know he's saying it about you when you're in the game. There's a total freedom in the bullpen—freedom of speech, freedom of action. One of the great things about baseball is that everything gets out in the open."

I asked if he'd heard from the others in the pen when he was having troubles this year, and he said, "Oh, sure. I was called Firecan and Arson and—well, much better stuff than that, if I could remember it. Silence would be terrible under those circumstances. We get on everybody, except there's sort of a compact about the rookies—you go easier with them. And then of course you don't say much to the next man who's going to come into the game—he's off in his little world, getting ready."

Quisenberry, I'd been told, starts to get ready after the sixth inning or so. He becomes withdrawn and abstracted, preparing for what is to come. Players call this "putting on your game face."

There were local legends, Quis explained—the bullpen pitchers who have put on groundskeepers' uniforms and joined the crew sweeping down the infield in the middle of a game, and so forth. Jim Colborn was the first Kansas City pitcher to think of that one, years ago. Quisenberry joined the Royals too late to see Colborn throw his no-hitter against the Rangers, back in 1977, but he knew the story. Colborn, a free spirit, was so entranced with his work that day that he became convinced that he would pitch *another* no-hitter on his next outing, and insisted that he wouldn't need anybody in the bullpen that day to back him up. All the relief men obliged him and stayed in the dugout when the game began—except for one cynic, Steve Mingori, who trudged on out as usual. Mingori watched Colborn pitch to three or four batters and then got to his feet and began to wave frantically for more help out there. He was right, it turned out: Colborn got bombed.

We had reached outer right field by now, and Quis pointed to a spot on the AstroTurf about twenty feet short of the right-field foul pole. "This is where the ball landed when Robin Yount hit a shot against me here once. Clint Hurdle dove for it and missed, and it turned into an inside-the-park home run. Sometimes when you're sitting over here in the pen, you can see a line drive disappear into the right-field corner, with the right fielder chasing it. Then the ball comes flying past you on the ground, going in the other direction, and then here comes the fielder again after it, like a dog after a rabbit. It's a great sight."

He stopped, and began pointing out various places in the empty right-field stands above us. "Two girls from Topeka sit up there, most games," he said. "They drive all the way here for the games, and then drive home again. Up there, there's an old gent we call Colonel Sanders—he has that look. Then there's a great fan named Joe Hess, who has a long white beard. He's Santa Claus, of course. There's a guy in Army fatigues who comes a lot—I call him Phnom Penh—and there are three or four grandmas who sit together over here: old sweethearts. You get to know the real fans. Some Sunday games, on days when it's real hot, I get out the ground crew's hose and spray the fans, who line up to hang over that incline over the pen. I only do it in the middle of the sixth inning, and the fans who want to cool off come over and crowd around for it. It's a custom by now, I guess."

We reached the bullpen—a row of orange grandstand seats under an oblong fibre-glass roof and behind a high chain-link fence, with one larger, round, overstuffed black chair in the corner: Muggsy Schaffer's throne. The phone to the dugout was on an adjacent wall. There were a dozen or more little marks scratched on the telephone receiver box, and when I pointed them out Quisenberry said they were left over from the previous season, when the bullpen people had begun keeping track of the outstanding fielding plays made by the new Royals first baseman, Steve Balboni—plays that, in their judgment, his predecessor at the position, Willie Aikens, would proba-bly *not* have made. Behind the bullpen chairs were two pitcher's mounds and two home plates set out along a stretch of lush, beautiful grass—the only natural lawn in the park. It is a small irony of contemporary baseball that the Royals' George Toma is considered the best groundskeeper in the business and now has no grass to cultivate except in the bullpens and down some tilted strips of turf that surround the celebrated Royals Stadium fountains, beyond the fences. Quisenberry pointed out Toma's office, which is under the stands, to one side of the bullpen, and then took me into a vast concrete equipment shed stuffed with mowers and rakes and rollers, a couple of John Deere tractors, coils of thick hose, and so forth. Just beyond this was a long, upcurving concrete tunnel, which held more equipment; several cars were parked in the tunnel.

"This is all wonderful," Quis said, "because what you want most in a bullpen is distraction. During a long game, you can walk over here and visit with George. His office is air-conditioned, and sometimes he'll give you a cup of coffee or some of that iced tea he's made by leaving a pitcher of water and tea bags out in the sun all day. You can watch TV there or read the horticultural news on his bulletin board. You can sit in one of the cars and turn on the radio, and sometimes even bring in another game that's being played somewhere. There are odometers and things. There are the ground-crew guys to talk to. Sometimes you can even sneak a ride on George's Suzuki tricycle."

I asked Quisenberry about the requisites for a good bullpen, and he mentioned distance from the fans ("You don't want to hear *everything* they're saying to you"), some kind of roof for rain protection, a good bathroom, and a screen to keep balls from getting loose on the field when you're warming up. He much prefers enclosed bullpens to the ones that border the outer stretches of the playing field in foul ground. California's bullpen is beyond the fence, and so are the pens in Chicago, Yankee Stadium, and Baltimore; Oakland and Minnesota and Toronto have sideline pens. And so on. Seattle has a sideline pen and no bathroom; the visiting pen there was moved from right field to left field last year, and a player who needs to use the bathroom has to come in between innings, passing both dugouts along the way. (Quis had begun to sound like a *Guide Michelin*, and I began to envision glyphs illustrating the amenities and points of interest for a young pitcher making his first grand tour of the American League.)

The Royals Stadium bullpen's bathroom is outstanding, Quis said: air-conditioning, heating for cold nights, a door that locks, a sink, and a mirror. The Fenway Park can, by contrast, has no light and no sink, and the door doesn't lock.

I asked about the odd bullpens in Tiger Stadium, which are sunk below ground level in foul territory, with a little screen above them to protect the occupants' heads from foul balls.

"We used to make out that's a submarine," Quis said eagerly. "We'd make those pinging sounds, and if a ball came near us it was a depth charge, and we'd fire our torpedoes. If the ball bounced off the little screen, that was a direct hit, and we'd panic and then ask for damage reports. Then there's always Cleveland, which is interesting in a different way. They've gone and reversed their home-team and visiting-team pens this year, too. The pens there are down the line, but they do have shelter and plenty of grounds equipment and all. That and the biggest spiders in the league. Now that they've put us on the other side of the field, I don't know if the spiders will be as good this year. I don't know their names yet. It's always wet and damp in Cleveland, and there are lots of mosquitoes, but you can catch the mosquitoes and feed them to the spiders—just toss them into the web. There's almost always a rain delay there, so there's plenty of time for all that." He was laughing.

Not So, Boston

—F A L L   1 9 8 6

Y es, it was. Yes, we did. Yes, that was the way it was, really and truly . . . The baseball events of this October—the Mets' vivid comeback victory over the Boston Red Sox in seven games, and the previous elimination of the Houston Astros and the California Angels in the hazardous six-game and seven-game (respectively) league championship playoffs—will not be quickly forgotten, but disbelief is a present danger. Sporting memory is selective and unreliable, with a house tilt toward hyperbole. In inner replay, the running catch, the timely home run become incomparable, and our view of them grows larger and clearer as they recede in time, putting us all into a front-row box seat in the end, while the rest of that game and that day—the fly-ball outs, the four-hop grounders, the fouls into the stands, the botched double play, the sleepy innings, the failed rally, the crush at the concession stand, the jam in the parking lot—are miraculously leached away. This happens so often and so easily that we may not be prepared for its opposite: a set of games and innings and plays and turnabouts that, for once, not only matched but exceeded our baseball expectations, to the point where we may be asking ourselves now if all this really did come to pass at the end of the 1986 season and if it was all right for us to get so excited about it, so hopeful and then so heartbroken or struck with pleasure. To which let it be said again: Yes, it did. Yes, it was. Yes, absolutely. What matters now, perhaps, is for each of us to make an effort to hold on to these games, for almost certainly we won't see their like again soon—or care quite as much if we do.

Purists are saying that the postseason baseball this year was not of a particularly high quality. In the World Series, the first five games were played out without a vestige of a rally, or even of a retied score; that is, the first team to bring home a run won the game. Each of the first four games, moreover, was lost by the home team: not much fun for the fans. One of the games turned on an egregious muff of a routine ground ball, and another produced the decisive event (it turned out) on the third pitch of the evening—a home run by the Mets' Lenny Dykstra. Neither of the pennant winners' famous and dominant young starters, Dwight Gooden and Roger Clemens, won a game in the Series. In the playoffs, the Angels committed three errors in one inning in the abysmal second game, and gave up two and then seven unearned runs in their last two games. In that same series, a plunked batsman figured significantly in the outcome of the critical fourth game—and again in the fifth. The Astros, over in the other league, contributed to their own downfall with an errant pick-off throw in the twelfth inning of their penultimate game, and with a butchered fly ball, a throwing error, and two wild pitches in the sixteenth inning of the finale.

No matter. These games, although slipshod and human in their details, were of a different order from the sport we thought we knew—"too fairy-tale-ish," in the words of one Mets pitcher. As the long eliminations ran down, the events on the field sometimes seemed out of control—not the plays or the players but the game itself, the baseball. The World Series became the focus of mass hopes and private wells of emotion, not just because of the rival kinships and constituencies of the Red Sox and the Mets, of Boston and New York (Athens and Sparta, in the words of Peter Gammons in *Sports Illustrated*), but because of a cumulative fan sense of intensity and gratitude that grew around them near their amazing end, by which time the strongest feeling seemed to be a wish that there should not be a loser. But probably that was a second wish, after we knew how it did end, and maybe not one that is felt much to this day in New England. In mid-October, however, caring had become an affliction. More and more, we fans wanted each game to go our way, to come out right, to end the right way—our way—but again and again, it seemed, that wish was thwarted or knocked aside, and we would find ourselves tangled in a different set of baseball difficulties and possibilities, and pulling for *that* to end right somehow. We wanted to be released, and until the very end the games refused to do that; the baseball wouldn't let us up. And if we were sometimes sorry for ourselves, because of these wearying repeated pains and disappointments and upsets, I think we felt worse about the players and the managers (sometimes the managers most of all), because they, too, were so clearly entwined in something they couldn't handle, couldn't control or defeat, in spite of all their efforts and experience and skill.

"Come on," we fans said again and again, addressing the team or the score or the situation. "Come *on!*" In the end, that cry didn't seem to be directed at anything except the sport itself, which twisted and wrung us, day after day, to the point where we wanted the games over with and this strange trial ended, even while we laughed and smiled at each other and wanted it to go on forever. "Wasn't that wonderful!" we cried. "My God, wasn't that terrific?" And "Did you *see* that? I couldn't bear it! Wasn't it awful!" And then "I just can't *take* it anymore. It's too much."

No poll or instrument can determine whether such paroxysms of fan feeling were felt in more distant parts, away from the big-city narcissism of Mets-mania or from the peat fires of devotion and doubt of the Red Sox faithful, but it is my guess that every fan was affected by these games to some degree. It's hard to be sure—and here a bias must be confessed. As readers of these reports may know by now, I am a baseball fan as well as a baseball writer (most scribes, however grizzled and game-worn, are fans at heart, although they love to deny it), and although I am capable of an infatuated interest in almost any accomplished or klutzy nine that I happen to watch over a span of four or five games, the true objects of my affection down the years have been the Mets and the Red Sox. I have written almost as many words about these two clubs as I have put down about the twenty-four other major-league teams combined. I have publicly exulted in their triumphs (the World Series captured by the boyish Mets in 1969; the wholly unexpected pennant in 1973, after the Mets went into first place in the National League East and reached the .500 level on the same evening in mid-September; the autumn weeks in 1967 when the Red Sox' Carl Yastrzemski seemed to have taken a pennant and a Series into his own hands; the sudden, scintillant glory of Game Six of the 1975 World Series), and I have put forth nostrums and philosophies to explain their much more frequent disasters and stretches of ineptitude. It did not occur to me that an October might arrive when my two true teams would come face to face in a World Series, and that I would have to discover and then declare an ultimate loyalty. The odds against two particular teams' meeting in a World Series in any given year are so extreme (a hundred and sixty-seven to one against, in fact) that I felt safe in moonily wishing for this dream date: when it came closer, during this year's pennant races and then again late in the playoffs, I became hopeful and irritable, exalted and apprehensive, for I didn't know—had no idea at all—which outcome would delight me if they did play, and which would break my heart. In dreams begin responsibilities, damn it.

Twenty postseason ballgames (the same total was rung up last year, when the league championships were first expanded from a three-out-of-five-game playoff to the full four-out-of-seven format that governs the World Series) are too many to keep in mind, even with the help of line scores and summations, and at this late date it may be possible to recapture some trace of these vivid and engrossing baseball doings and to glimpse the men on the field in their moments of duress and extremity only by concentrating on a handful of particular games, with perhaps more of our attention going to the league championships than to the World Series itself, for there is little doubt in my mind that the earlier events surpassed the classic. This was the possibility foreseen and deplored by so many baseball people (including this one) when the expansion of the playoffs was first proposed, but after it happened it didn't seem to make any difference. An exceptional set of games, wherever it may come, enhances our appreciation of the richness and surprises of the pastime, and there is a carryover of involvements and good feeling that burnishes the next game we see, and the one after that. Baseball is cumulative, and rewards the stayer.

What will not be set forth here is much news of the regular league seasons—two thousand one hundred and two games (three late-season dates were cancelled by natural causes, and there was one tie that was never untied) that will now vanish by magical elision, since they did not produce a vestige of a pennant race in any division. Lost in this process is a proper full appreciation of some players who enjoyed remarkable seasons while toiling for clubs that did not make the finals. Mike Schmidt, for instance, at the age of thirty-seven, led his league in homers (he had thirty-seven) for the eighth time and in runs batted in (a hundred and nineteen) for the fifth, and later was voted his third Most Valuable Player award. Don Mattingly, who failed for the second year in a row to beat out Wade Boggs as the American League batting champion (.352 to Boggs' .357), nonetheless put together an altogether brilliant year at the plate, becoming the first American League player to surpass thirty homers, a hundred runs batted in, and two hundred and thirty hits in a single season; his two hundred and thirty-eight hits were the most ever by a Yankee batter. His teammate, the relief wizard Dave Righetti, accounted for an all-time-record forty-six saves; and their skipper, Lou Piniella, beat perhaps even longer odds when he was rehired to manage the Yankees for another year. Fernando Valenzuela, of the Dodgers, won twenty games for the first time (he was 21–11 at the end), and so did his fellow-countryman Teddy Higuera (20–11), for the Brewers; the two Mexicans were the talk of the All-Star Game, when they went head to head in three blazing middle innings. The Indians, of all people, came up with a genuine star in their third-year outfielder-slugger Joe Carter (.302, twenty-nine home runs, two hundred hits, and a hundred and twenty-one runs batted in); his nearest rival in the last category was Oakland's rookie bombardier Jose Canseco, who had thirty-three homers and was perhaps the best of a notable freshman class in the American League that also included the Rangers' Pete Incaviglia, the Mariners' Danny Tartabull, and the Angels' Wally Joyner.

The real news around the leagues, however, was the manner in which the four divisional winners entirely suppressed the opposition throughout the summer. The calendar is conclusive. The Mets took over the top of their division for good on April 23rd, the Red Sox on May 15th, the Angels on July 7th, and the laggard Astros on July 21st. The Mets' four starting pitchers—

Dwight Gooden, Ron Darling, Bob Ojeda, and Sid Fernandez—had a combined record of forty-one wins and ten losses at the midseason All-Star-Game break, by which time the club led its nearest pursuer, the Expos, by thirteen games. Its ultimate 108–54 won-lost record for the season tied the modern National League level set by the 1975 Reds (the 1954 Indians went 111–43, to establish the modern American League and major-league mark, but it should perhaps be noted that the Mets' .667 winning *percentage* is less remarkable. Twenty-six previous clubs, most of which date back to the one-hundred-fifty-four-game schedules in effect prior to the league expansions in the early sixties, surpassed that win-two-lose-one ratio, including Frank Chance's stone-age 1906 Cubs, who finished up at 116–36, or .763; the thunderous 1927 Yankees, with 110–44, or .714; and even the 1942 Dodgers, whose 104–50, .675, season only won them second place, two full games behind the Cardinals). The Mets' home attendance total of 2,762,417 was the best ever for any New York team in any sport. In retrospect, the Red Sox' one important (or perhaps only symbolically important) game of the summer seems to have been a series opener at Yankee Stadium on June 16th, when Roger Clemens bested Ron Guidry in a 10–1 blowout and ran his record to 12–0 for the season to that date; it was Guidry's sixth loss in a row. The injury-depleted Sox sagged a bit during a swing west in late July, but stood firm against all comers thereafter (to the amazement of their careworn, wary fans and many of their writers), running their lead from three and a half games to ten in the first twelve days of September.

Nobody finished like the Astros, however. Pitching and defense was their game—or let's just say pitching. On September 23rd, in Houston, rookie left-hander Jim Deshaies struck out the first eight Dodgers of the evening and shut out the visitors, 4–0, on two hits. The following night, Nolan Ryan gave up no hits to the Giants in the first six innings, and wound up with a 6–0 two-hitter, and the night after *that* Mike Scott beat the same team with a 2–0, no-hit game that clinched the Astros' divisional pennant in the National League West. The absence of a race or of any sort of rival to these top four teams did not deter fans from coming out to the games this summer; 47,500,347 turned up in all, which was a new record, and, for the first time ever, no club drew fewer than a million in its own park. The pennant races were a success in another way as well, for they produced divisional winners that, for once, really were the best four teams in baseball. The championships promised well, and that promise was kept.

Game Three,
National League Championship Series

It came on a chilly gray afternoon at Shea Stadium, and by the end of the second inning the Mets were in heavy weather of their own making, down by 4–0 to the Astro left-handed starter Bob Knepper. These N.L. playoffs, it will be recalled, had opened at the Astrodome with a dominant, almost suffocating 1–0 shutout performance by the Astros' big, sleepy-faced right-hander Mike Scott, who had struck out fourteen Mets batters with his darting split-fingered fastball and high heater, thus nullifying a strong effort by Dwight Gooden. The visitors had evened matters the next day, when the Mets, blown away by Nolan Ryan in his first trip down their batting order, jumped on him for five quick runs on their second look, to win 5–1, behind their left-handed off-speed precisionist Bob Ojeda. But here at Shea the sudden four-run Houston lead looked serious, for Knepper, a ten-year veteran with exquisite control, had defeated the Mets three times during the regular season, and we knew that Scott, the best pitcher in the National League this year, would be back for the Astros the very next day. Watching these glum proceedings from my press seat in deep left field (the foul pole actually blocked my view of the mound), I was afflicted by grumpiness and self-pity. The night before, at home by my television set, I had watched the Red Sox drop a 5–3 game to the Angels out in Anaheim, to slip behind in *their* playoffs by two games to one. My dream was already coming apart, and here at my sixth game in five days (two up at Fenway Park and three via television) I felt baseballed out. Ron Darling, the Mets' starter, had composed himself after two egregious innings (five hits, a base on balls to the No. 8 batter, two stolen bases, a wild pitch, and a two-run homer by second baseman Bill Doran), but the Mets in their dugout—as viewed unsteadily through my binoculars—looked glum and wintry, with their arms crossed and their paws buried in the pockets or the armpits of their shiny blue warmup jackets. In among them I could pick out Wally Backman and Lenny Dykstra, the Mets' dandy two-cylinder self-starting machine that had figured in so many uprisings this summer; Dykstra bats from the left side and Backman is a switch hitter who does much better against right-handers, and so both were sitting out Knepper. ("I don't care how fiery you are," Mets manager Davey Johnson said about Dykstra before the game. "It's on-base average that counts.") The Shea multitudes made imploring noises from time to time, but they, too, looked muffled and apprehensive. Nothing doing.

Kevin Mitchell led off the Mets' sixth with a single over third, and Keith Hernandez followed with a modest fly ball that dropped into short center field for another hit—nothing *much*, except that Craig Reynolds, the Astro shortstop, now booted a grounder by Gary Carter (a double-play ball, in fact), sending Mitchell home, and Darryl Strawberry lofted Knepper's next pitch into the first deck in right field, to tie the game. I revived instantly, but also briefly, for the Mets now handed back the gift run—a walk (Rick Aguilera was pitching for the home side by now), a throwing error by Ray Knight, and an infield out—and very soon thereafter had to deal with Charlie Kerfeld, the Astros' lumpy, menacing right-handed rookie flamethrower, who blew out the candle in the eighth on a handful of pitches. Kerfeld is a hotdog—all shades, chaw, belly, and heat out there—and when he somehow reached behind his back to spear Carter's hard one-hop grounder to the mound, he pointed at Gary as he ran up the line, relishing the moment before he threw him out.

I had improved my seat by a section or two during the afternoon, scrounging the places of no-show reporters closer to the action, but at the end of the eighth I decamped for the interview room, just beyond the Mets clubhouse in the nether corridors of the park—a way to beat the crowds, and a pretty good vantage point from which to watch the last few outs of a game, by means of a giant television monitor. Panting, but certain of my long wisdom in these matters, I attained my goal, to find the room virtually deserted: somebody had forgotten to set up the monitor. And so it happened that I got to see not the longest game-winning home run of my life but certainly the smallest—the sudden two-run, bottom-of-the-ninth smash to right by Lenny Dykstra that I watched, huddling with similarly misplaced media friends, via a palm-size Sony Watchman TV set that one foresighted reporter had brought along to the game. Peering like microbiologists, we watched the mini-replays and filled in the missing details. Backman, pinch-hitting, had dropped a leadoff bunt down the first-base line and made a skidding slide into the bag around an attempted tag by first baseman Glenn Davis; then he had motored along to second on a passed ball. The Houston pitcher was the Astros' short-relief specialist Dave Smith, who had been wheeled in by manager Hal Lanier to wrap things up, thus expunging Kerfeld. Now a postage-stamp-size Backman, seen in black-and-white slow-motion replay, flung up his arms as he watched Dykstra's homer sail into the Mets' bullpen and then began his jumping, backward-running dance toward third, while the rest of the Mets streamed onto the field to celebrate the 6–5 victory and their sudden lead in the playoffs. Dykstra, it should be explained, had come into the game in the seventh, when he fanned against Knepper. Davey Johnson was proud of this maneuver (he likes to have his pair of deuces in there late in a game), and explained that he had guessed—guessed right, it turned out— that Knepper would shortly be done for the day, leaving Dykstra still in there to swing against a right-hander his next licks.

Dykstra is a pistol. In this, his first full season, he not only had won the job in center field (moving Mookie Wilson to left, on most days, and permitting the club to drop the increasingly ineffective George Foster) but had quickly emplaced his engaging and brattish mannerisms in our mass Shea consciousness—his odd preliminary forward lean in the batter's box, with bat held upright, as if to conk a burglar; the facial twitches, winces, and squinchings as he prepares for the pitch, and, before that, the peculiar, delicate twiddling of a gloved fingertip along his brow; the joyful little double jump and hand pop as he comes to a dusty stop beyond first with another base hit; and, contrariwise, his disbelieving, Rumpelstiltskin stamp of rage when a pitcher has caught a corner against him for strike three. Here in the interview room, Lenny was all cool and charisma—a guest on some late-night talk show. He said that the only other time he had hit a winning home run in the bottom of the ninth was in Strat-O-Matic (a board game), against his kid brother, Kevin.

In the clubhouses, I heard more talk about Strawberry's home run than about Dykstra's. Strawberry had suffered through a ghastly midsummer batting slump (he was booed horrendously by the upper-deck critics at Shea, where he went 0 for August), and had looked particularly helpless against left-handed pitching. The three-run homer struck off Knepper meant something, then—something beyond this game. Keith Hernandez said, "Baseball is a constant learning experience. Nothing happens very quickly for most hitters, and you have to remind yourself that Darryl is still only twenty-four years old. He's played four years in the majors, but he's still a baby. It isn't often that a Gehrig or a Mattingly comes along, who can do it all at the plate right away. When I first came up, the Matlacks and Koosmans and Carltons of this league—all those left-handers—gave me fits. Jim Rooker just killed me at the plate. You have to be patient and try to learn to adjust, and Darryl is still learning."

What happened on this afternoon (and again in the fifth game of the playoff, when Straw whacked another telling homer against the Astros) did not quite turn Strawberry's year around, for he batted only .208 in the World Series, with six strikeouts and a lone, superfluous home run and run batted in on his very last at-bat. He is an enigma and a challenge, perhaps to himself as much as to us and to his club, and his style (those thick, long young arms; the looping, easeful swing; the long-loping catch in right-center field that ends with a casual heavenward reach to suck in the ball, with the gesture of somebody taking down a hat from a top shelf) is always so effortless that it looks magical when it succeeds and indolent when it fails. Each year, we wait for the performance that will lift his numbers (.259 this year, with twenty-seven homers and ninety-three runs batted in) to the next level, which is superstardom; each year, that once-certain goal seems a little farther away.

Here in the clubhouse, Strawberry said that Knepper had been throwing him breaking balls all afternoon (he'd nubbed one down the third-base line in the fifth, for a thirty-foot single), and he had guessed fastball the next time up—guessed right, that is. The batting and first-base coach Bill Robinson said, "When Darryl got on base after that little hit, I said 'That's the way to beat on that ball!' and he told me maybe that at-bat would make him stay in the next time up. And that's what he did do—he kept his right side in on that swing and didn't pull off the ball. I tell them all, '*Guess fastball.*' You can adjust to a curveball, a knuckleball, a slider, or a change off the fastball, but it's tough to guess a curveball, a knuckleball, a slider, or a change and then hit the fastball. I believe most pitchers will throw the fastball six out of ten times. So six out of ten times I'm sitting on dead red and knowing I still have a chance on the others. If Knepper throws me a good slider or something outside that's nasty, I'm not going to hit it anyway. You can count the good breaking-ball hitters in this league on the fingers of one hand—well, the fingers of *two* hands. We're all fastball hitters in the end."

Game Five,
American League Championship Series

Home in fine fettle after the Mets' sudden resurrection that Saturday, I had a drink and some dinner, and took my ease in front of the set, where my Red Sox, out in the late sunshine at Anaheim Stadium, played resolute, patient ball in their almost boring Game Four, eventually dispatching the ancient and wily Don Sutton in the seventh inning. (I should explain that the two sets of playoffs never exactly overlapped in their progression, thanks to the vagaries of the network schedulers.) The Sox' 3–0 lead midway through the ninth looked safe as houses, for their pitcher was Roger Clemens, their soon-to-be winner of both the Cy Young and the Most Valuable Player awards in his league; he had gone 24–4 for the season, after winning his first fourteen decisions in a row, and had also established a new all-time record by striking out twenty batters in an April game against the Seattle Mariners. So far in this game, Clemens had simply brushed aside the Angels, allowing no one to reach third base; three more outs would bring the teams even in their playoff, at two games apiece. But in fact Clemens was running out of gas, and after a leadoff home run by Doug DeCinces in the ninth and one-out singles by Dick Schofield and Bob Boone he was abruptly gone. His successor, the young fastballer Calvin Schiraldi, suffered a nasty shock when a well-hit but catchable fly by Gary Pettis became a run-scoring double because Jim Rice lost the ball in the lights. With the score now 3–2, and with the bases loaded after an intentional pass, Schiraldi fanned Bobby Grich and went to two strikes and one ball on Brian Downing, but then hit him on the thigh with his overreaching next pitch ("Oh, *no!*" I cried, badly startling the snoozing terrier at my feet as I sailed up out of my chair, to the invisible balletic accompaniment of three or four million Sox fans to the north and east of me—along with *their* dogs, I suppose), to force in the tying run. The Angels won it in the eleventh (oh, yes), bringing exquisite joy to their rooters but ruin to my overcrowded baseball day.

Game Five, played out lengthily at Anaheim the next afternoon, has already taken its place on the little list of Absolute All-Timers, and I must assume that its immoderate events are known by heart by even the most casual followers of the pastime. The Angels pitched their main man, Mike Witt, a spidery right-hander with an exceptional curveball, which he throws in two variant modes; he had eaten up the Red Sox batters in the playoff opener, retiring the first seventeen in a row. Now he survived a two-run homer by Rich Gedman in the early going and was still in command as the ninth began, with his club ahead by 5–2, three outs away from a pennant. The last two California runs had come in when Dave Henderson, the second Boston center fielder of the day (he had entered the game after Tony Armas twisted an ankle), made a fine running catch of Grich's deep drive, only to have the momentum of his effort carry the ball up over the top of the center-field wall and, appallingly, out of his glove for a home run. In the ninth, Witt gave up a single to Bill Buckner, fanned Rice, and then threw a pretty good breaking ball, down and away, to Don Baylor, who reached out and drove it over the left-field fence: a sobering moment there in Southern California.* Dwight Evans popped up for the second out, though, and manager Gene Mauch called in a left-hander, Gary Lucas, to pitch to the left-side batter Gedman, in search of one more out and a championship. The tactic, arguably logical (and arguably the only appropriate occasion for "arguably" ever to see print), since Gedman had ripped Witt for a homer, a double, and a single for the day, didn't work, because Lucas plunked Gedman on the hand with his first pitch, thereby setting up the next confrontation, between Dave Henderson and the Angels' less than imperious right-handed relief stopper Donnie Moore, who had thrown well in his most recent appearance. With the crowd putting up an insupportable din, with the ushers arrayed along the baselines and police stuffing the dugouts and bullpens, with the Angels up on their topmost dugout step for the pennant sprint and the huggings and the champagne, Henderson worked the count to two and two, fouled off two fastballs, and then hit the next delivery—a forkball, perhaps—into the left-field seats.

Silence and disbelief out there. Exultation on the opposite coast. The

*Baylor's home run, which I watched again and again in taped replay during the winter, ranks as Feat of the Month in this feat-filled October. Witt's pitch broke sharply away over the farthermost part of the strike zone, and Baylor not only got his bat on it but somehow muscled the ball in the opposite direction and out of the park.

Angels, it will be recalled, quickly made up the new one-run deficit in their half of the ninth, and even had the next winning run—the pennant-winner once again—poised at third base when DeCinces popped to short right field and Grich lined out softly to the pitcher. These extended melodramatics had settled nothing so far (Al Michaels, the exemplary ABC television play-by-play man, summed things up along about here by saying, "If you're just tuning in, too bad"), but now it suddenly seemed clear that the Red Sox *would* win, although that took a couple of innings: a hit batsman (it was Baylor), a single, an unplayable bunt by Gedman, and the winning sacrifice fly to center—by Henderson, of course. Schiraldi came in at the end and got the save. The Angels repacked their gear and de-iced the champagne (I guess) and returned to Boston, where they lost their last two games of the year, 10–4 and 8–1. "I don't think we ever should have had to come back here," Donnie Moore said when it was all over.

My eagle-eye view of Game Five was not nearly as clear as I have depicted it, since duty forced me to leave my TV set in the middle of the ninth that evening and head back to Shea for the fourth Mets-Astros affray, and I picked up most of the amazing and extended events in Anaheim over my car radio while tooling along on the Grand Central Parkway. Taking pity on his old man, my son taped the action on our VCR, and when I got home very late that night (the Mets had lost again to Mike Scott, just as I had feared) I played the last three innings over for myself, and, sure enough, the Red Sox won, 7–6, in eleven innings. It was the first time all month I didn't have to keep score.

I thought back on this game many times after the Red Sox had won their championship and the Angels had packed up and gone home for the winter, but with a good deal less than pure pleasure. These last-moment reprieves and reversals are so anguishing for the losing players and coaches (and the fans, too, to be sure) that one's thoughts return to them unbidden, long after the winners' celebrations have been forgotten. Players in the winning clubhouse always look like boys (and not just because they are behaving like infants), while the ones in the other clubhouse resemble veteran combat soldiers who have barely survived some dreadful firefight. They look worse after a playoff defeat than after the World Series, because the losing team in a championship elimination has won nothing at all; it has become a trivia question. Even the Red Sox players, I noticed later on, talked about their narrow escape in Game Five with dire, near-funereal images. "We were on our deathbed," Roger Clemens said. "The heartbeat meter was on a straight line." John McNamara, who has a whispery, monsignorlike habit of speech, said to me, "We were dead and buried. When Henderson went to two strikes and the police were all set to go, I looked over and saw Reggie taking off his glasses in their dugout, getting ready for the celebration. That's how close we were."

I feel bad about the Angels, who were a team made up of some distinguished, or very well-known, older players—Don Sutton, Reggie Jackson, Doug DeCinces, Bob Boone, Brian Downing, George Hendrick, Rick Burleson, and Bobby Grich (Sutton and Jackson are in their forties, and the others in their upper thirties)—who fitted well with younger stars like Dick Schofield, Gary Pettis, Mike Witt, Kirk McCaskill, and the splendid rookie first baseman Wally Joyner. (He missed all but the first game of the playoffs with a leg infection.) I see that I have just referred to the Angels in the past tense, which is understandable, for this particular Angels team has ceased to exist. Grich has already retired, Jackson is a free agent—with no assurance that anyone will pick him up for next season—and so are Downing, Boone, and DeCinces, and management has been extremely quiet about which of the other expensive old-timers we will see in Anaheim next summer. I feel sorry for Gene Autry, the seventy-nine-year-old president and chairman of the board, who is revered in the game (he is known as the Cowboy) and has owned the still pennantless team ever since its inception, as an expansion club, in 1961.

I even feel bad about the Angels fans. There is a popular dumb theory here in the East that there is no such thing as a California Angels fan, and that those two-and-a-half-million-attendance totals at Anaheim Stadium, year after year, are made up of moonlighting sunbathers and foot-weary families resting up from Disneyland. This is parochial nonsense, of course, and it's about time we old-franchise inheritors admitted the Angelvolk to the ranks of the true sufferers—the flagellants, the hay-in-the-hair believers, the sungazers, the Indians-worshippers, the Cubs coo-coos, the Twins-keepers, the Red Sox Calvinists: the *fans*. I have heard from a few of them by mail. One pen pal, a professor of Byzantine history from Canoga Park, California, sent me a five-page single-spaced typed letter delineating his pains and his heroes down the years, starting in 1961, when the Angels played at the Pacific Coast League Wrigley Field, in Los Angeles, and won seventy games in their very first season. "Now we know that rooting for the Angels is just like rooting for the Red Sox," he wrote. "One does it guardedly, always looking over one's shoulder." Another Angels correspondent, a medical-journal editor who lives in San Francisco, sent along his scorecards for the A.L. playoff games this fall—beautifully detailed, meticulously executed, pitch-by-pitch delineations of the seven games, which concluded with a gigantic, smudgy execration of Gene Mauch scrawled across the bottom of the seventh-game scorecard: the last Angels loss of the year. My correspondent apologized for this in a covering note: "I'm sorry—I was very upset. I still am."

I feel bad about Gene Mauch, too—*everybody* feels bad about Mauch by now—who has managed in the majors for twenty-five years without ever setting foot in the World Series, although he had come excruciatingly close before this. In 1964, his Phillies led the National League (this was before divisional play) by six and a half games with two weeks to go, and then lost ten of their last twelve games and, on the last day, the pennant. Four years ago, his Angels led the Milwaukee Brewers in the five-game American League playoffs by two games to one but lost—an outcome so painful that Mauch moved up to the front office for a couple of seasons, and took up the managerial burdens again only last year. He is a dour, unapologetic baseball chancellor (a former colleague of his told me that he'd never heard Mauch ask an opinion or invite a discussion about any move he had made, on or off the field), who has acquired a sharply divided body of passionate loyalists and dedicated doubters in the press boxes and front offices of the game. He has also been second-guessed as much as anyone in his hard profession, but this, I have come to believe, is due not so much to his hard-shell exterior or to his reputation for over-managing as to a deep wish, however unconscious, among other managers and players and watchers of the game to prove that baseball really is more tractable, more manageable in its results, more ame-nable to tactics and patience and clear thinking, than it seems to have been for him. All of us—even us fans—want the game to be kinder to us than it has been to Gene Mauch, and we are terribly anxious to find how that could be made to happen. No group of games in recent memory had produced anything like the second-guessing of managers that one heard at these two championships, but this is explained, to my way of thinking, by the fact that five of the thirteen games were settled in the ninth inning or later—in the ninth, tenth, eleventh, twelfth, and sixteenth, to be precise—and that pro-longing reties were also produced, twice in a ninth inning and once in a fourteenth.

Mauch's moves during Boston's ninth inning of that fifth game, when the three-run Angels lead was converted to a one-run deficit, will be a Gettysburg for tactical thinkers for years to come. An old friend of mine who has managed extensively in both leagues was in Anaheim that afternoon, and later on I asked him what it was like when it all began to come apart for the Angels out there, and what he would have done in the same circumstances.

"When Baylor hit his home run, the game still didn't have that feeling of doom," he said. "You thought, All right, you don't win 5–2, you win 5–4. There were so many different directions Gene could have gone—he just chose the one that didn't work. Gedman looked like the problem, because he'd gone three for three against Witt. But for me, the one to worry about, the key batter, is the *next* guy, the right-handed hitter Henderson, and I'm not too worried about him, because my very best right-handed pitcher—my best pitcher of all—is still in the game. Mike Witt, I mean. He's just struck out

Rice and popped up Evans, so he can't be all that tired. If he loses Gedman somehow, he just needs to get Henderson out, and if he can't do *that*, then we don't deserve the pennant. And Henderson would have a whole lot more trouble against him than against a Donnie Moore.

"We know that Gene went to Lucas, and Lucas came in and hit Gedman. Gene's move could have worked, but I think *the wrong man hit Gedman*. If Witt hits him, it's a very different story. With Witt on the mound and Gedman coming up to bat and all eager for that next rip at my pitcher, I would have walked out to Witt and said, 'Look, the *next* batter is the one you want. Don't worry about Mr. Gedman. Hit him on the hip with your first pitch, and if you miss go back and hit him with the next one. Then go after Henderson and we're out of this and into the World Series.'

"You know, when Donnie Moore came in after Lucas, I had the same little feeling I'd had back in Milwaukee when Gene's Angels got so close in '82: Now, *wait* a minute: this is ours, but it isn't quite ours yet—let's not gather the bats. And then it all happened again. The fans took it hard, but I think they felt, Well, O.K., we still just need one of the two games back in Boston. But you only had to look at the players' faces to know that it had gotten away from them and it might never come back. Once that phoenix gets out of the ashes, he wants to fly."

My friend the manager told me that he felt terrible about Gene Mauch. "He's been in this place for so long, and he won't give in to it and he won't walk away from it. This one's going to be very tough for him. He gets within one pitch and one run of the Series, but all those 'ones' are still there for him. I know Gene, and I know all the cigarettes that have been smoked and the drinks that have been drunk and the miles that have been paced over this kind of thing, down the years. He'll pay that price to get there, but now I don't know if it will ever happen for him. How do you go on?"

Game Six,
National League Championship Series

I wasn't there, and had to pick up most of its extended, convoluted, and startling events in bits and pieces—by television and cab radio and word of mouth and television again—and then put them together in my head at last with the help of another tape made for me by the Mets screamers at my house. I was in Boston for the American League finale, and the Mets and Astros, as we know, had moved back to the Astrodome. The day before, I had seen the Mets go one up in their playoffs, in a makeup afternoon game at Shea (the thing had been rained out the night before), in which Nolan Ryan and Dwight Gooden pitched each other to a 1–1 standstill over the regulation distance. Ryan, who is thirty-nine years old, fanned twelve Mets and threw a two-hitter, but one of the two was a home run by Strawberry. Ryan left after nine innings and Gooden after ten, and the Mets won in the twelfth, when Gary Carter rapped a run-scoring single past Kerfeld's rump, which Charlie this time did *not* grab behind his back, although he tried. The Astros were sore about an umpire's out call at first base, which had cost them a run back in the second inning, but nothing could be done about it, of course.

I took in most of Game Six the next afternoon by television in my Boston hotel room—not much sport, to tell the truth, for the Mets instantly fell behind by three runs in the first inning, and could do nothing at all against Bob Knepper over their initial eight. It's embarrassing to curse and groan and shout "*C'mon!*" twenty or thirty times in an empty hotel room, but yelling and jumping up and down on the bed—which is what I did during Dykstra's pinch-hit triple, Mookie's single, Keith's double, and Ray Knight's game-tying sac, all in the Mets ninth—is perfectly all right, of course. And here, perhaps, we should pause for statistical confirmation of the kind of baseball week that it had turned out to be. Somebody along about here had noticed or discovered that in the six hundred and forty-two postseason games played prior to 1986 no team had ever made up a deficit of more than two runs in its final chance at bat. Now it had happened three times in five days.*

Darkness had fallen on the Public Garden by the time the Mets got all even, and I was overdue at Fenway Park. Four or five times, I turned off the set, grabbed my game gear, and headed for the door, only to come back and click on again for another out or two. (I didn't know it at the time, but millions of Mets fans in New York were in the same pickle; baseball had burst its seams and was wild in the streets.) The Mets scratched out a run at last in the fourteenth, against Aurelio Lopez (possibly a leftover character actor from a Cisco Kid movie), and that was good enough for me: the Mets had it in hand for sure. I doused the game and headed out to keep my other date, and so missed Billy Hatcher's gargantuan solo home run into the left-field foul-pole screen, which retied things in the bottom half. The sixteenth did wrap it up at very long last, but my patchwork impressions of its events (snatches over somebody's radio just ahead of me on the outside staircase at Fenway Park, and then glimpses on a TV monitor at the back of the overstuffed rooftop pressroom while several scribe friends tried to catch me up, viva voce, at the same time) have required subsequent firming up by tape. The Mets' three runs in the top half of the sixteenth and the Astros' gallant but insufficient answering pair in the bottom are still thrilling, of

*Bobby Thomson's miracle ninth-inning, three-run homer in 1951, which put down the Dodgers and won the pennant for the Giants, has not been overlooked here. The two clubs had finished their seasons in a tie, and the homer came in the final game of a two-out-of-three playoff. This was an extension of the season, in short, and batting and pitching records in the games were included in the 1951 league statistics.

course, but the fatigue and bad nerves of the principals make you jittery, even in replay. Strawberry's mighty-swing semi-bloop fly became a double when the Houston center fielder, Hatcher, got a very late start in for the ball, and a throwing error by right fielder Kevin Bass and two wild pitches helped the Mets almost as much as Knight's single and then Dykstra's. Jesse Orosco (who won three games in the playoffs) was so arm-weary by the uttermost end that fastballs became an impossibility for him; one last, expiring sinker fanned Bass, with the tying run at second, and that was the pennant. A moment or two earlier, Davey Johnson (he told some of us about this back in New York), with the enormous, domed-in roarings of the Houston multitudes cascading and reverberating around him, noticed that his nearest companion in the Mets' dugout, pitching coach Mel Stottlemyre, looked a tad nervous. Davey leaned closer and said, "Come on, Mel, you knew this had to come down to one run in the end. It's that kind of game."

What I missed by not being in Houston that day may have been less than what I missed by not being in New York. The pennant-clinching celebrations in Boston were happy indeed (about a four on the Roger Scale), but the excruciating prolongation and eventual exultation of the Mets' Game Six were something altogether different—a great public event, on the order of a blackout or an armistice. The game began at 3:06, New York time, and ended at 7:48, and in that stretch millions of Mets fans in and around New York, caught between their daywatch of the game and some other place they had to be, found themselves suspended in baseball's clockless limbo, in a vast, mobile party of anxious watching and listening and sudden release. Sports can bring no greater reward than this, I think. In time, I—like many others, I imagine—began to collect Game Six stories: where folks had been that night, and what they had seen and heard and done during the long game's journey into night. There was no rush hour in New York that evening, I kept hearing: so many office workers stayed in their offices to follow the game that the buses and avenues in midtown looked half empty. Subway riders on the I.R.T. platform at Grand Central heard the score and the inning over the train announcer's loudspeaker. A man I know who was in bed with the flu or something said that he rose to a sitting position during the Mets' rally in the ninth, and then left his bed and paced the floor; when it was all over, he got up and got dressed and was cured. Another man, a film editor— not at all a fan—was running around the Central Park Reservoir when a strange, all-surrounding noise stopped him in his tracks. It came from everywhere around the Park, he said, and it wasn't a shout or a roar but something closer to a sudden great murmuring of the city: the Mets had won.

Men and women on commuter trains followed the news by Panasonic or Sony, clustering around each radio set for the count and the pitch, and calling the outs and the base runners to the others in their car. At the

Hartsdale platform, in Westchester, a woman with a Walkman, having said goodbye to other alighting commuters as they hurried off to their car radios, started up a stairway and then stopped and cried "Oh!" Her companions from the train stared up at her, stricken, and she said, "Gary got thrown out, stealing." There were portables and radios at Lincoln Center, too, where the ticket holders at the Metropolitan Opera's performance of "The Marriage of Figaro" reluctantly gave the game up at seven-thirty and went in and took their seats for the overture. After a moment or two, a man in the orchestra section sprang up and disappeared through a side exit; he slipped back in a few minutes later (he'd found someone in the cloakroom with a radio, he subsequently explained) and, resuming his seat at the beginning of Figaro and Susanna's opening duet, turned and signalled, "Seven-four in the sixteenth!" on his fingers to the rows around him, and then did a thumbs-up to show he meant the Mets. A newspaperman heading back home to New York stopped off in an airport bar at Boston's Logan Airport, where the game was on, and fell into Mets conversation there with a woman who turned out to be a Merrill Lynch investment broker; they missed the three-o'clock, the four-o'clock, and the five-o'clock Eastern shuttles, somehow tore themselves away for the six-o'clock—and discovered that the game was still on when they deplaned at La Guardia. A colleague of mine who lives in New Jersey said that while going home he'd followed the game by stages over a spontaneous electronic relay network that had sprung up along the way—a TV set in the fire station on Forty-third Street, a wino's radio in Grace Plaza, a big TV in the window of a video store on Sixth Avenue, some kids with a boom box in the doorway of a Spanish deli, and then a crowd-encircled gray stretch limo parked in Herald Square, with its doors open and the windows rolled down and, within, a flickering tiny television set turned to the game. Radios on his PATH train went blank during the journey under the Hudson but they came back to life in the Hoboken station, where he changed to a New Jersey Transit train, and where the Astros retied the game in the fourteenth. A frightful communications disaster—the long tunnel just before the Meadowlands—was averted when his train, a rolling grandstand, unexpectedly ground to a halt ("Signal difficulties," a conductor announced), and stood there right through the top of the sixteenth, when the Mets scored three and service resumed.

Writer friends wrote me about the game, too. A woman's letter began, "My friend Sandy came over to my place for the game with a quart of beer and some snacks—he doesn't have a color TV set. Sandy and I had been to a couple of games at Shea together, and I assumed it would be just about the same, but this was more like the time we'd been to see the movie 'Dawn of the Dead'—he kept turning his face away from the screen in dread. I kept up a casual, chatty, reassuring act, saying comforting things like 'It's all right now. Ojeda is totally in command,' but then there was this one terrifying closeup of Knepper out on the mound—eyes burning and steam coming out of his ears. A real image from a horror movie. As the game went on, I realized that I was living it through the Mets pitchers, maybe because the pitcher's motions can give you that trancelike feeling of security. Just about all I was aware of late in the game was McDowell's right leg coming down and that little bow-legged hop he takes after every pitch, over and over. As long as I kept seeing that, I knew we'd be all right."

An art critic who lives in the East Village wrote, "At our apartment during the late innings of Game Six were my wife Brooke, our daughter Ada, myself, two dinner guests, and two people who had dropped in on short notice and then stayed around. One of the guests was Nell, a film director we like a lot, even though she's one of those people who can't believe that anyone of your intelligence actually cares about baseball. One of the drop-ins, an Australian poet named John, knew nothing—nothing!—about baseball but took a benign attitude, asking polite, wonderfully dumb questions about the game. The other drop-in was Aldo, our neighborhood cop on the beat, a Mets fan and a friend. Aldo was in full cop gear, and voices crackled from his walkie-talkie: cops out there talking about the game.

"Nell is one of those people who don't know any policemen and who can't believe that you do. She looked at Aldo for a while and then said, 'Excuse me, but what are you doing here?' I had to explain that it was all right, he was here for the game.

"I don't remember it all, but of course I do remember the growing delirium—like trying to explain to John what a foul ball was and how to throw a slider, and Nell becoming more and more agitated, and Brooke assuming her old rally posture in a particular doorway we have, and then, at the very end, all the whooping and hollering and inaccurate high-fiving, and some wild hugging. Nell was leaning out the window shrieking with joy."

Game Five, World Series

This was less than a classic, perhaps, but there was spirit and pleasure in it. The home-team Red Sox ravished their Fenway supporters with a 4–2 win, behind their mettlesome left-hander Bruce Hurst, and defeated Dwight Gooden for the second time in the process. This was the Sox' high-water mark (it turned out later), putting them ahead by three games to two, but it also felt like the first game in which the Series competition was fully joined. The Bostons, it will be recalled, had won the Series opener down at Shea, with a splendid 1–0 effort by Hurst against Ron Darling, in which the only run had come in on an error by Mets second baseman Tim Teufel. A promised Gooden–Clemens thriller the next day came to nothing when the Sox won by 9–3, doing away with Dwight almost without effort; Clemens, for his part, was wild, and was gone in the fifth inning. This was Dwight Evans' great game: a mighty two-run homer that caromed off a tent marquee out beyond left-center field, and then a lovely sliding, twisting catch against Dykstra in right. Up in Boston, the Mets, now in a jam, rebounded strongly, with four first-inning runs against Oil Can Boyd in Game Three; Dykstra's leadoff home run set the tone, all right, but the central figure of the evening may have been the Mets' lithe left-hander Bobby Ojeda, a member of the Red Sox pitching corps last year, who nibbled the corners authoritatively ("You don't live in one place in this ballpark," he said later) in the course of his 7–1 outing, and became the first left-hander to win a postseason game at Fenway Park since Hippo Vaughn turned the trick for the Cubs in 1918. Those two quick losses to the Red Sox in the early games meant that Davey Johnson would be overdrawn at the pitching bank in the ensuing games, but he got even at last in Game Four, when Ron Darling shut down the Sox for seven innings (he gave up no earned runs at all in his first two outings), and the Mets roughed up Al Nipper et al. with twelve hits, including two homers by Gary Carter. (A missing figure in the Red Sox pitching rotation was Tom Seaver, who suffered a knee-cartilage tear in September and was forced to sit out all the postseason games: hard news for Sox fans—and for Mets fans, too, I believe.)

Hurst's work here in Game Five was the kind of pitcher's outing that I have most come to admire over the years—a masterful ten-hitter, if that is possible. This was his fourth start in postseason play, and although he was not nearly as strong as he had looked during his gemlike shutout at Shea, he used what he had and kept matters in check, scattering small hits through the innings and down the lineup, and racking up ground-ball outs in discouraging (to the Mets) clusters with his forkball. ("IT HURSTS SO GOOD," one Fenway fan banner said.) The pitch, which disconcertingly breaks down and away from right-handed batters, sets up the rest of his repertoire—a curve and a sneaky-quick fastball—and although Hurst resolutely refers to it as a forkball, it is in fact the ever-popular new split-fingered fastball (*sort* of a forkball), which Hurst learned in 1984. He didn't actually have enough confidence to use the pitch in a game until late June last year, at a time when he had been exiled to the Red Sox bullpen, but it revived his career wonderfully, transforming him from a journeyman 33–40 lifetime pitcher (in five and a half seasons) to a 22–14 winner in the subsequent going. Hurst missed seven weeks this summer with a groin injury, but he deconvalesced rapidly, wrapping up his season's work by going 5–0 and 1.07 in his last five starts, which won him a league accolade as Pitcher of the Month in September. Despite all this, I think we should be wary about making too much of one particular delivery, for pitching is harder than that. Hurst, it should be noticed, belongs to the exclusive Fenway Lefties Finishing School, which numbers two other

polished and extremely successful southpaw practitioners among its graduates: Bob Ojeda and John Tudor, who pitched the Cardinals to a pennant last
year with a tremendous 21–8, 1.93 summer and then won three games in
postseason play. Ojeda, for his part, had an 18–5 record with the Mets this
year, which was the best won-lost percentage compiled by any of the Mets'
celebrated starters; it was the best in the league, in fact. Previously, Ojeda
had toiled for six summers in Fenway Park, and Tudor for five. The uniting
characteristics of the three Wallmasters are control, extreme confidence, and
a willingness to come inside. At Fenway Park, the inside pitch to a right-
handed hitter is what it's all about, for it discourages him from leaning out
over the plate in the hope of something he can rap onto or over the Green
Monster, and requires him, in fact, to compete with the man on the mound
for his—the pitcher's—part of the plate and for his sector of the ballpark,
which is to say outside, and to right or right-center: a mismatch. The inside
pitch, it should be added, is mostly thrown in the early innings, to plant the
idea of it in the batter's head, but is then eschewed in the late going, when
weariness is more likely to result in a tiny, fatal mistake. Actually, it doesn't
have to be thrown for a strike in order to have its effect, and unless you are
a Clemens or someone of that order, it's probably a much better pitch, all
in all, if it's a ball. "What Ojeda does, over and over, is one of the beauties
of the game," Keith Hernandez said at one point in the Series. "When you
miss, you've got to miss where it doesn't hurt you. That's what pitching is all
about." For his part, Hurst, who throws over the top and finishes his delivery
with a stylish little uptailed kick of his back leg, works with great cheerfulness
and energy, and here in Game Five he finished his evening's work with a
flourish, fanning Dykstra for the last out of the game, with Mets runners on
first and third. "BRUCE!" the fans yowled. "BRUUUUCE!"

It was a great night at the Fens. A gusty wind blew across the old
premises (left to right, for the most part), and a couple of advertising bal-
loons out beyond the wall bucked and dived in the breeze, tearing at their
tethers. The long cries from the outermost fan sectors (the oddly slanting
aisles out there looked like ski trails dividing the bleacher escarpments)
came in wind-blown gusts, suddenly louder or fainter. The wind got into the
game, too, knocking down one long drive by Henderson in the second (it was
poorly played by Strawberry) and another by Jim Rice in the fifth, which
sailed away from Dykstra and caromed off the top railing of the Sox' bullpen—triples, both of them, and runs thereafter. It was the kind of game in
which each player on the home team (in that beautiful whiter-than-white
home uniform, with navy sweatshirt sleeves, red stirrups, the curved, classical block-letter "RED SOX" across the chest, and a narrow piping of red around
the neck and down the shirtfront) seems to impress his own special mode
or mannerism on your memory: Rich Gedman's lariatlike swirl of the bat

over his head as he swings through a pitch; Rice's double cut with the bat when he misses—swish-*swish*—with the backward retrieving swing suggesting a man trying to kill a snake; Boggs' way of dropping his head almost onto the bat as he stays down in midswing; Buckner (with that faro-dealer's mustache and piratical daubings of anti-glare black on his cheeks) holding the bat in his extended right hand and, it seems, aiming it at the pitcher's eyes as he stands into the box for an at-bat. And so on. Almost everyone out there, it seemed—every one of the good guys, that is—had his moment in the game to celebrate and be put aside in recollection by the fans: Hendu's triple and double, Marty Barrett's walk and single and double (he batted .433 for the Series), a beautiful play by Boggs on Kevin Mitchell's tough grounder in the second, and, best of all, Billy Buck's painful and comical hobbling gallop around third and in to the plate in the third inning to bring home the second run of the game on a single by Evans. Buckner can barely run (can barely play) at all, because of his sore back and his injury-raddled ankles; it takes him two hours to ice and wrap his legs before he can take the field. He had torn an Achilles tendon in the September 29th game and was playing in this one only on courage and painkillers and with the help of protective high-top boots. No one wanted to laugh at his journey home after Evans bounced the ball up the middle, but you couldn't help yourself. He looked like Walter Brennan coming home—all elbows and splayed-out, achy feet, with his mouth gaping open with the effort, and his head thrown back in pain and hope and ridiculous deceleration. When he got there, beating the throw after all, he flumped belly-first onto the plate and lay there for a second, panting in triumph, and, piece by piece, got up a hero.

This was the last home game of the year for the Red Sox, and when it was over the fans stayed in the stands for a time (John Kiley gave them "McNamara's Band" on the organ again and again), clustering thickly around the home dugout and calling out for Hurst and Billy Buckner and the others, and shouting "We're Number One!" and waving their white Red Sox painters' caps in exuberance. There had been great anxiety about this game, because of the Mets' sudden revival in Games Three and Four, but now the Sox were moving down to New York for one more win, with a rested Clemens going on Saturday and with Hurst ready again, if needed, on Sunday, and I don't think anyone there at the end that night really thought it might not happen. There is great sadness in this, in retrospect, since the team's eventual loss (and the horrendous way of it, on each of the last two days) has brought back the old miasmal Boston baseball doubt and despair—the Bermuda low that has hung over this park and this team perhaps since the day in 1920 when owner Harry Frazee sold a good young outfielder named Babe Ruth to the Yankees, two seasons after Ruth, then a pitcher, had helped bring the Sox their last (to this day) World Championship. Once again, New England's fans have been sent into the winter with the dour nourishment of second-best to sustain them: Indian pudding. If they wish, they may once again ponder the wisdom of George Bernard Shaw's opinion that there are two tragedies in this world: one is never getting what you want, and the other is getting it—a dictum they would love to put to the test someday.

But enough of this. Glooming in print about the dire fate of the Sox and their oppressed devotees has become such a popular art form that it verges on a new Hellenistic age of mannered excess. Everyone east of the Hudson with a Selectric or a word processor has had his or her say, it seems (the *Globe* actually published a special twenty-four-page section entitled "Literati on the Red Sox" before the Series, with essays by George Will, John Updike, Bart Giamatti—the new National League president, but for all that a Boston fan through and through—Stephen King, Doris Kearns Goodwin, and other worthies), and one begins to see at last that the true function of the Red Sox may be not to win but to provide New England authors with a theme, now that guilt and whaling have gone out of style. I would put forward a different theory about this year's loss and how it may be taken by the fans. As one may surmise from the *Globe*'s special section, the Red Sox have become chic: Pulitzer Prize winners and readers of the *New York Review of Books* hold season tickets behind first base, and the dropped "Geddy" and "Dewey" and "Roger" and "the Can" clang along with the sounds of cutlery and grants chat at the Harvard Faculty Club. The other, and perhaps older, fan constituency at Fenway Park has not always been as happy and philosophical about the Sox. The failures of the seventies and early eighties were taken hard by the Boston sports crowd (the men and women who care as much about the Celtics and the Patriots and the Bruins as they do about the Sox), and the departure of Carlton Fisk, Rick Burleson, Freddy Lynn, and Luis Tiant, and the retirement (at long last) of Yastrzemski, left a very bitter taste, and so did the team's persistent, almost stubborn unsuccess in this decade. (It finished fifth, fourth, and sixth in the American League East in the three years before this one, an average nineteen games behind the leader.) The ugly "Choke Sox" label was much heard, and the team's ancient, stubbornly held style of play, characterized by insufficient pitching, insufficient or nonexistent speed, a million ground-ball double plays (by the Sox, I mean), and an almost religious belief in the long ball, had become a byword in the game, a "pahk your cah" joke around the league. Nothing could change this, it seemed. But this year it changed: a baseball miracle. This year, the Red Sox not only won their division and the American League playoffs and, very nearly, the World Series but became a different sort of team, to themselves above all. Nineteen-eighty-six turned around for the Red Sox because of Roger Clemens (and perhaps because of Schiraldi's sudden midseason arrival as a bullpen stopper), but a more significant alteration was one of attitude—a turnabout that began when Don Baylor came over from the Yankees and almost immediately became the team leader, something the Sox had been lacking for as long as anyone could remember. He told the young pitchers that they had to pitch inside if the team was to win; he persuaded the batters to take the extra base, to look for ways to get on base in the late innings (like getting hit with pitches, for instance: a Baylor specialty), to find that little edge—the one play or moment or lucky hop—that turns games around. Tom Seaver came aboard in June, and deepened this same aura with his maturity, his ease, and his sense of humor and proportion. The Sox grew up this summer: you could see it on the field—in Jim Rice choking up on the bat by an inch or so when he got to two strikes (this for the first time ever) and stroking the ball to right-center now and then, so that though his homers went down by seven (to twenty), his batting average improved by thirty-three points and his hits by forty-one—and in the results. The players spoke of it themselves. "We have more character," they said, and "We're going to win"—words unheard by this writer from any Boston club of the past.

What fans think about their team is subtle and hard to pin down, but I am convinced that everything was changed this year by one game—by that stubborn and lucky and altogether astounding Red Sox return from near-defeat in the fifth game out at Anaheim, when they came back from extinction and a three-run deficit in the ninth inning and won by 7–6. It almost carried the month, and it is startling to notice, in retrospect, that the Red Sox actually won five games in a row right in the middle of the postseason—the last three of their championship playoffs and the first two of the World Series. There is no prize for this, of course, but no other team in October played quite so well for quite so long. In its killing last-minute details, their loss to the Mets in Game Six (they fell after holding a two-run lead in the tenth inning, with no one on base for the Mets) was so close to what the Angels had experienced that their fans—even the most deep-dark and uncompromising among the bleacherites, I think—must have seen the connection, and at last sensed the difficulties of this game and how much luck and character and resolve it takes to be a winner in the end. History and the ghost of Sox teams past had nothing to do with it. The Choke Sox died in Anaheim, and this losing Red Sox team will be regarded in quite a different way in New England this winter. It will be loved.

Game Six, World Series

The Mets are not loved—not away from New York, that is. When the teams moved up to the Hub, with the Mets behind by two games to none, there was a happy little rush of historical revisionism as sportswriters and baseball thinkers hurried forward to kick the New York nine. Tim Horgan, a columnist with the Boston *Herald*, wrote, "Personally, I don't think anything west of Dedham can be as marvelous as the Mets are supposed to be. I wouldn't even be surprised if the Mets are what's known as a media myth, if only because New York City is the world capital of media myths." Bryant Gumbel, on NBC's "Today" show, called the Mets arrogant, and ran a tape of Keith Hernandez' bad throw on a bunt play in Game Two, calling it "a hotdog play." Sparky Anderson, the Tigers manager, declared over the radio that the Indians, the traditional doormats of his American League division, put a better nine on the field than the Mets, and a newspaper clip from the heartland (if San Diego is in the heart of America) that subsequently came my way contained references to "this swaggering band of mercenaries" and "a swaying forest of high fives and taunting braggadocio." Much of this subsided when the Mets quickly drew even in the games, and much of it has nothing to do with baseball, of course; what one tends to forget is that there is nothing that unites America more swiftly or happily than bad news in Gotham or a losing New York team. Some of these reflections warmed me, inwardly and arrogantly, as Game Six began, for I was perched in a splendid upper-deck-grandstand seat directly above home plate, where, in company with my small family and the Mets' mighty fan family, I gazed about at the dazzlement of the ballpark floodlights, the electric-green field below, and the encircling golden twinkle of beautiful (by night) Queens, and heard and felt, deep in my belly, the pistol-shot sounds of clapping, the cresting waves of "LETSGO-METS! LETSGOMETS! LETSGOMETS!," and long, taunting calls—"Dew-eee! DEW-EEEE!" and "Rog-errr! ROG-ERRRR!"—directed at some of the Bosox below: payback for what the Fenway fans had given Darryl Strawberry in the last game in Boston. And then a parachutist came sailing down out of the outer darkness and into the bowl of light and noise—a descending roar, of all things—of Shea. "GO METS," his banner said as he lightly came to rest a few steps away from Bob Ojeda in mid-infield and, encumbered with minions, went cheerfully off to jail and notoriety. We laughed and forgot him. I was home.

Game Six must be given here in extreme précis—not a bad idea, since its non-stop events and reversals and mistakes and stunners blur into unlikelihood even when examined on a scorecard. I sometimes make postgame additions to my own scorecard in red ink, circling key plays and instants to refresh my recollection, and adding comments on matters I may have overlooked or misjudged at the time. My card of Game Six looks like a third grader's valentine, with scarlet exclamation points, arrows, stars, question marks, and "Wow!"s scrawled thickly across the double page. A double arrow connects Boggs, up on top, to Spike Owen, down below, in the Boston second—a dazzling little hit (by Wade)-and-run (by Spike) that set up Boston's second score of the game. Two red circles are squeezed into Jim Rice's box in the Boston seventh—one around the "E5" denoting Ray Knight's wild peg that put Rice on first and sent Marty Barrett around to third, and the other around the "7–2" that ended the inning, two outs and one run later, when Mookie Wilson threw out Jim at the plate. A descendant arrow and low-flying exclamation points mark Clemens' departure from the game after the seventh (the Red Sox were ahead by 3–2, but Roger, after a hundred and thirty-one pitches, had worked up a blister on his pitching hand), and an up-bound red dart and "MAZZ PH" pointing at the same part of the column denote Lee Mazzilli's instant single against Schiraldi, while the black dot in the middle of the box is the Mazzilli run that tied the score. But nothing can make this sprawling, clamorous game become orderly, I see now, and, of course, no shorthand can convey the vast, encircling, supplicating sounds of that night, or the sense of encroaching danger on the field, or the anxiety that gnawed at the Mets hordes in the stands as their season ran down, it seemed certain, to the wrong ending.

The Red Sox scored twice in the top of the tenth inning, on a home run by Dave Henderson ("Hendu!" is my crimson comment) and a double and a single by the top of the order—Boggs and then Barrett—all struck against Rick Aguilera, the fourth Mets pitcher of the night. Call it the morning, for it was past midnight when the Sox took the field in the bottom half, leading by 5–3. Three outs were needed for Boston's championship, and two of them were tucked away at once. Keith Hernandez, having flied out to center for the second out, left the dugout and walked into Davey Johnson's office in the clubhouse to watch the end; he said later that this was the first instant when he felt that the Mets might not win. I had moved down to the main press box, ready for a dash to the clubhouses, and now I noticed that a few Mets fans had given up and were sadly coming along the main aisles down below me, headed for home. My companion just to my right in the press box, the *News'* Red Foley, is a man of few words, but now he removed his cigar from his mouth and pointed at the departing fans below. "O ye of little faith," he said.

It happened slowly but all at once, it seemed later. Gary Carter singled. Kevin Mitchell, who was batting for Aguilera, singled to center. Ray Knight fouled off two sinkers, putting the Red Sox one strike away. (Much later, somebody counted up and discovered that there were *thirteen* pitches in this inning that could have been turned into the last Mets out of all.) "Ah, New England," I jotted in my notebook, just before Knight bopped a little single to right-center, scoring Carter and sending Mitchell to third—and my notebook note suddenly took on quite a different meaning. It was along about here, I suspect, that my friend Allan, who is a genius palindromist, may have taken his eyes away from his set (he was watching at home) for an instant to write down a message that had been forming within him: "Not so, Boston"—the awful truth, no matter how you look at it.

Schiraldi departed, and Bob Stanley came on to pitch. (This was the Steamer's moment to save what had been an unhappy 6–6 and 4.37 season for him, in which his work as the Sox' prime right-handed stopper had received increasingly unfavorable reviews from the Fenway bleacher critics; part of me was pulling for him here, but the game was out of my hands—and evidently out of his as well.) Mookie Wilson, batting left-handed, ran the count to two-and-two, fouled off two more pitches, and then jumped away, jackknifing in midair, to avoid a thigh-high wild pitch that brought Mitchell flying in from third, to tie it. Wilson fouled off two more pitches in this at-bat of a lifetime and then tapped a little bouncer down toward first, close to the baseline, that hopped once, hopped twice, and then slipped under Buckner's glove and on into short right field (he turned and stared after it in disbelief), and Knight thundered in from around third base. He jumped on home plate with both feet—jumped so hard that he twisted his back, he said later—and then disappeared under an avalanche of Mets.

The post mortems were nearly unbearable. "This is the worst," Bob Stanley said.

"I'm exhausted," Ray Knight said. "My legs are trembling."

"As close as we came . . . " whispered John McNamara. "As close as we came, I can only associate it with California."

"It's baseball," said Dave Henderson. "It's baseball, and we've got to live with it."

Questions were asked—they always are after major accidents—and some of them must be asked again, for this game will be replayed, in retrospect, for years to come.

Q: Why didn't Davey Johnson double-switch when he brought in Jesse Orosco to get the last out of the eighth inning? Without an accompanying substitute at some other slot in the order, Jesse was forced to depart for a pinch-hitter an instant later, in the Mets' half, thus requiring Johnson to wheel in Aguilera, who was a much less certain quantity on the mound, and who quickly gave up the two runs that so nearly finished off the Mets. A: I still don't know, for Davey is a master at the double switch—a textbook maneuver in National League tactics, since there is no designated hitter—and a bit later on he made a much more questionable switch, which removed Darryl Strawberry from the game. It came out all right in the end, but I think Davey just forgot.

Q: Why didn't McNamara pinch-hit for the creaking Buckner in the tenth, when another run could have nailed down the Mets for sure? And, having decided against this, why didn't he at least put the much more mobile Stapleton in to play first base in the bottom half—perhaps to gobble up Wilson's grounder and make the flip to the pitcher? More specifically, why didn't he pinch-hit Baylor, his designated hitter, who batted in the No. 5 slot throughout the regular season and in the playoffs but rode the bench (no D.H.) almost to the end during the games played at Shea? A: Johnny Mack has defended himself strongly against both of these second-guesses, citing Buckner's excellent bat (a .267 year, with eighteen home runs and a hundred and two runs batted in) and Buckner's glove ("He has good hands," he said), in that order. His answer to the Baylor puzzle is to say that Baylor never pinch-hits when the Red Sox are ahead—sound strategy, one can see, until a game arrives when they might suddenly fall behind at the end. McNamara also claims that Stapleton normally substitutes for Buckner at first base only if there has been an earlier occasion to insert him as a pinch-*runner* for Buckner; this is mostly true (it wasn't the case in Game Five), but the fact remains that Stapleton was playing first base in the final inning of all three games that the Sox did win. My strong guess is that McNamara is not beyond sentiment. He knew the torments that Buckner had gone through to stay in the lineup throughout the season, and the contributions he had made to bring the club to this shining doorstep (he had mounted a seventeen-game hitting streak in mid-September, and at one stretch drove in twenty runs in a span of eight games) and he wanted him out there with the rest of the varsity when the Sox seemed certain to step over it at last.

O

We need not linger long on Game Seven, in which the Mets came back from a 3–0 second-inning deficit and won going away (as turf writers say), 8–5. It was another great game, I suppose, but even noble vintages can become a surfeit after enough bottles have been sampled. A one-day rainout allowed us to come down a little from the sixth game and its astounding ending, but then we came to the last day of all, and the sense of that—a whole season rushing to a decision now—seized us and wrung us with almost every pitch once play resumed. Ron Darling, who had given up no earned runs in the Series so far, surrendered three in the second inning (Evans and Gedman whacked home runs on successive pitches) and was gone in the fourth. Hurst, for his part, permitted only a lone single in five full innings, but ran dry in the sixth, when the Mets evened the game. They had specialized in this sleeping-dragon style of play all through the championship season, and this last time around they showed us once again how dangerous they really were: nine hits and eight runs in their last three innings of the year. Somehow, the anguish of the Red Sox mattered more than the Mets' caperings at the very end, because it was plain by now that it could have just as easily gone the other way. In the Boston clubhouse, Al Nipper, who was badly battered during his very brief appearance in the New York eighth, sat at his locker with his back turned and his head buried in his hands. Dennis Boyd, who had not been called on in the Sox' extremity, rocked forward and back on his chair, shaking his head in disbelief. Friends of mine said later that they had been riveted by a postgame television closeup of Wade Boggs sitting alone in the dugout with tears streaming down his face, and a couple of them who are not fans asked me how it was possible for grown men to weep about something as trivial as a game. I tried to tell them about the extraordinary heights of concentration and intensity that are required to play baseball at this level, even for a single trifling game in midseason, but I don't think they believed me. Then I remembered a different moment on television—something I saw a couple of years ago on a trip abroad, when the captain of the Australian cricket team was interviewed over the BBC just after his eleven (I *think*) had lost a protracted test match to the West Indies. I listened to the young man's sad recapitulations with predictable American amusement—until I suddenly noticed that there were tears in his eyes. He was crying over *cricket!* I suppose we should all try to find something better or worse to shed tears for than a game, no matter how hard it has been played, but perhaps it is not such a bad thing to see that men can cry at all.

The acute moment in Game Seven was produced in the Mets' sixth, when Keith Hernandez came up to bat against Hurst with the bases loaded and one out and the Red Sox still ahead by 3–0. Anyone who does know baseball understood that this was the arrangement—this particular batter and this precise set of circumstances—that the Mets wanted most and the Red Sox least at the end of their long adventures. It was the moment that only baseball—with its slow, serial, one-thing-and-then-another siftings and sortings—can produce from time to time, and its outcome is often critical even when reexamined weeks later. I think the Red Sox would have won this game if they had got Hernandez out. As it was, he took a strike from Hurst (a beautiful, dipping off-speed breaking ball) and then rocketed the next pitch (a fastball, a bit up) to deep left-center for a single and the Mets' first two runs and the beginning of their championship comeback. I'm not sure that anyone remembered at the time, but we should remember now that Hernandez, then a member of the Cardinals, hit a crucial two-run single up the middle in the sixth inning of the seventh game of the 1982 World Series, to start that team on its way to a comeback 6–3 victory over the Milwaukee Brewers.

Many fans think of Gary Carter as the quintessential Mets player, while some may see Lenny Dykstra or Wally Backman or Dwight Gooden, or even Ray Knight (who won the Series M.V.P. award), or perhaps Mookie Wilson in that role (Mets-haters despise them all, for their exuberance, their high-fives, their cap-waving encores, their vast publicity, their money, and their winning so often: winning is the worst mannerism of all), but for me the Mets are Keith Hernandez. His game-long, season-long intensity; his classic at-bats, during which the contest between batter and pitcher seems to be written out on some invisible blackboard, with the theorems and formulas being erased and rewritten as the count progresses; his style at the plate, with the bat held high (he is mostly bare-armed), and his pure, mannerism-free cuts at the ball; and, above all, his demeanor afield—I would rather watch these, I think, than the actions of any other player in the game today. Watching him at work around first base—he is sure to earn his ninth consecutive Gold Glove for his performance at the position—you begin to pick up the little moves and glances and touches that show what he is concerned about at that instant, what dangers and possibilities are on his mind. Holding a base runner close, with a right-handed pull hitter up at bat, he crouches with his left foot planted on the baseline and toeing to right—a sprinter's start, no less—and he moves off so quickly with the pitch that he and the runner appear to be tied together, one mass zipping along the base path. When there's a left-handed batter in the box under the same circumstances, Keith leaves his post just as quickly once the pitcher lets fly, but this time with a crablike backward scuttle, quicker than a skater. He makes the tough 3–6 peg down to second look easy and elegant, and he attacks bunts with such assurance that he sometimes scoops up the ball on the third-base side of the invisible pitcher-to-home line (I have seen only two or three other first basemen pull this off even once; Ferris Fain, of the late-nineteen-forties Athletics, was one of them) and then gets off his throw with the same motion. If you make yourself notice where Hernandez has stationed himself on the field, you will sometimes get a sudden sense of what is really going on down there. Wade Boggs, the best hitter in baseball, usually raps the ball up the middle or to left, even though he is a left-handed swinger, but his failure to pull even one pitch up the line to right in the course of the World Series allowed Hernandez to play him more and more into the hole as the Series went on, and contributed to Boggs' problems at the plate in these games. Even one pulled foul would have altered his positioning, Keith said after the Series ended; he was amazed that Boggs hadn't attacked him in this way.

Hernandez is probably not an exceptionally gifted athlete, but his baseball intelligence is remarkable. Other Mets players say that he always seems to be two or three pitches ahead of the enemy pitcher and catcher, and that he almost seems to know the other team's coaches' signals without looking, because he understands where they are in their heads and what they hope to do next. He shares all this with his teammates (keep count in a game of the number of different players he says something to in the course of a few innings), and the younger players on the club, including Darryl Strawberry, will tell you that Keith's counsel and patience and knowledge of the game and its ways have made them better ballplayers, and winners. All this comes at a price, which one may guess at when watching Hernandez chain-smoke and put away beers (there is a postgame ice bucket at his feet by his locker) in the clubhouse as he talks and comes down after the game. The talk is a season-long seminar that Mets writers attend, day after day, taking notes and exchanging glances as they write. The man is in the game.

Davey Johnson also has some baseball smarts, and in this last game he showed us, if we needed showing, how far ahead he had been all along. Sid Fernandez, the Mets' dumpling left-handed strikeout pitcher—their fourth starter this year, and during some stretches their best—came into the game in the fourth inning, with the Mets down by 3–0, and stopped the Sox dead in their tracks: a base on balls and then seven outs in succession, with four strikeouts. "That did it," Keith said afterward. "When Sid was in there, we began to feel that we might win this game after all. He was the necessary hero." Johnson had passed over Fernandez as a starter in the Series (he is streaky and emotional), but he had brought him along, all right. Fernandez had pitched a shaky one-third of an inning in Game Two, surrendering three hits and a run late in a losing cause; in Game Five, which the Mets also lost, he had pitched four shutout innings, with five strikeouts. He was Series-tested by the end, and he became Johnson's last and best move.

The Sox, for their part, mounted a courageous rally in their eighth inning, when three successive solid blows accounted for two runs and closed the score to 6–5 before Orosco came in and shot them down for good. By this time, the Mets hitters had done away with Schiraldi and were loose in the Boston bullpen—John McNamara's worst dream come true. Strawberry's homer and the cascade of Mets runs at the end released the fans at last, and their celebrations during the final outs of the year—the packed thousands together chanting, roaring out the Freddie Mercury rock chorus "We will, we will . . . ROCK YOU!" while pointing together at the Boston bench—were terrific fun. There was a great city party there at Shea, and then all over town, which went on into the parade and the ticker tape (it's computer paper now) the following afternoon, but when it was all over I think that most of us, perhaps all of us, realized that the victory celebration didn't come up to the wonderful, endless sixteen innings of Game Six, back during the playoffs. As one friend of mine said later, "For me, that night was the whole thing. Whatever there was to win had been won."

There was a surprise for me, there at the end. I am a Mets fan. I had no idea how this private Series would come out, but when the Mets almost lost the next-to-last game of the Series I suddenly realized that my pain and foreboding were even deeper than what I had felt when the Red Sox came to the very brink out in Anaheim. I suppose most of my old Red Sox friends will attack me for perfidy, and perhaps accuse me of front-running and other failures of character, but there is no help for it. I don't think much has been lost, to tell the truth. I will root and suffer for the Sox and the Mets next summer and the summers after that, and if they ever come up against each other again in the World Series—well, who knows? Ask me again in a hundred and sixty-seven years.

FROM

La Vida

—SUMMER 1987

O ne spring in Mesa, Arizona, I ran into Gene Autry, the owner of the California Angels, who was chatting with some of his players in the visiting-team dugout. He was wearing cowboy boots and a narrow string tie. He looked gentle and old and agreeable, the way he always does. When the Angels lost the American League playoff in 1982 by dropping three games in a row to the Brewers (after winning the first two games), and then threw away another championship series last year under even more unlikely and scarifying circumstances, everybody in baseball felt bad, because they so wanted a Gene Autry team in a World Series. We chatted a little, and he told me about his baseball beginnings. "I was always a Cardinals fan then," he said, "because I came from Oklahoma, and they had the Dean brothers and Pepper Martin and all those other Okies playing for them. Then I followed the Cubs, because I'd started in singing over Station WLS, in Chicago. The Gabby Hartnett–Charlie Grimm Cubs, I mean. Oh, I had a lot of baseball friends. I have a photo at home of me and Casey Stengel and Mantle and Whitey Ford. I wouldn't take anything in the world for that photo. You know, I was thinking just the other day about the old days down home, when we'd listen to Bob Kelley, who did those game re-creations from the Coast over the radio, from a telegraph ticker. You don't remember that, I imagine. There'd be nothing, and then you'd hear the ticker begin to go and you'd know something was happening in the game, and then he'd describe it. He could bring it all alive for you."

But I did remember. I still do—me, at ten or eleven, with my ear next to the illuminated, innerly-warmed gold celluloid dial of the chunky, polished-wood family radio, from which there emerges, after an anxious silence, the clickety, train-depot sounds of a telegraph instrument suddenly bursting with news. Then a quick, closer *tock!*—the announcer or some studio hand rapping on the mike with a pencil, I suppose—and the re-creator, perched in his imaginary press box, says, "Uh-oh. . . . Hafey really got hold of that delivery from Fat Freddie. The ball is rolling all the way to the wall in left, and here come two more Cardinal runs across the plate . . . " The front door slams—my father home from work, with the New York *Sun* under his arm (and the early-inning zeros of that same Giants road game on the front page, with the little white boxes for the rest of the line score still blank), and I get up to meet him with the bad news.

O

Spring training is the life. One March day in Phoenix Municipal Stadium, I strolled slowly away from the batting cage in the dazzling desert sunlight and climbed the shallow grandstand steps behind the Oakland home dugout, on my way to grab a pre-game hamburger and a cold Coors at the little freeload picnic grounds for the media out by left field. The fans were coming in—old folks carrying seat cushions and scorecards, college kids in T-shirts and cutoff jeans, young women in sandals with serious tans and white "A's"-emblazoned painter's caps, kids balancing mammoth cups of popcorn—and unhurriedly scouting around for good seats in the unreserved rows. A last fly ball rose and dropped untouched behind second, where an Oakland coach and a batboy were picking up the batting-practice balls and dropping them into a green plastic laundry basket. The first visiting ballplayers, fresh off their bus, were playing catch over in front of their dugout; it was the Giants this time, and I was looking forward to seeing Al Oliver again and to watching this kid pitcher Garrelts (if he did work on this day, as promised) and a couple of others, but there was no hurry about the game's starting, of course, and nothing to worry about even if I did miss a few pitches and plays while I lingered over my lunch. A friend of mine, a beat man with the San Francisco *Chronicle*, came along and fell into step beside me. Smiling a little behind his shades, he nodded toward the field and the players and the filling-up stands and murmured, "You know, it's a shame to have to mess all this up with the regular season."

Teams in Arizona and Florida play with identical rules and before the same sort of audiences, but the two spring flavors are quite different. I don't understand it. Florida ball seems more citified, hurried, and temporary; no matter how rustic the setting, I always have the sense that the regular season impends, and that these humid, sunny afternoons are just postcards, to be glanced at later on and then thrown away. Arizona baseball is slower, sweeter, and somehow better fixed in memory. For one thing, there seem to be more young children in attendance at the western parks; the stands are stuffed with babies and toddlers—or else I just notice them more. In Phoenix one afternoon, a small barefoot creature came slowly and gravely up the aisle behind the home dugout wearing nothing but a Pamper. Six- or seven-year-old home-team batboys are already veterans of two or three Arizona seasons. In one game at Scottsdale, matters were suspended briefly when a very young rookie batperson in pigtails went out on the field after a base on balls, picked up the bat (they were both the same length: the thirty-three-inch model), and paused, staring slowly back and forth, until she remembered which dugout she had come from, and then returned there, smiling in triumph. The home-plate umpire, I noticed, made a good call, holding up one hand and watching over his shoulder until we were ready for baseball once again. It wouldn't have happened in Florida.

For me, Arizona baseball is personified by a young woman vender at Phoenix Stadium I came to recognize, after several springs, by her call. She would slowly make her way down an aisle carrying her basket and then sing out a gentle, musical "*Hot* dog! . . . *Hot* dog!"—a half note and then down four steps to a whole note. She'd go away, and later you heard the same pausing, repeated cry at a different distance, like the cry of a single bird working the edge of a meadow on a warm summer afternoon. "*Hot* dog!"

Old fans and senior scribes want the spring camps to remain exactly the same; they should be like our vacation cottages at the lake or the shore—a fusty and familiar vicinity in which we discover, every year, the sparkle and renewing freshness of another summer. The wish is doomed, of course. Each succeeding March, the small ballparks are visibly more crowded and the audiences younger and more upscale, with affluent, Hertz-borne suburban families on the kids' spring break lately beginning to outnumber the cushion-carrying retirees in the stands. Authors and television crews cram the sidelines at the morning workouts, and by game time the venders at the souvenir stands look like Bloomingdale's salesgirls during Christmas week. Spring training is "in," worse luck, and even the most remote baseball bivouacs are incipient Nantuckets. Out in Mesa, descending hordes of Cubs fans absolutely swamp little HoHoKam Park every game day, lining up at breakfast time to buy up the twenty-three hundred unreserved seats that go on sale at ten o'clock; the park put in new bleacher seats in 1985, enlarging its capacity to eight thousand, but this was insufficient to handle the numbers of the new faithful. A friend of mine—a retired Chicago baseball writer who lives in Arizona now—told me that he drove over to the Cubs training complex on the very first day of spring training that same year, when only the pitchers and catchers had reported, and counted license plates from twenty-six states in the parking lot. "There were maybe a thousand fans at the workout," he said. "A thousand, easy, just watching the pitchers doing sit-ups."

Chain O'Lakes Park, the Red Sox training site in Winter Haven, Florida, is less frantic, but it has changed, too. It was an inning or two into my first game there in 1985 when I saw the difference: the old, fragrant orange grove out beyond the right-field and center-field fences was gone, replaced by a cluster of low, not quite finished white buildings, with a drooping banner out front that said "LAKEFRONT CONDOMINIUMS." I gestured miserably at this phenomenon, and my seatmate, a Boston writer, said, "Yes, I know. Remember when we used to write 'and Yaz hit it into the orchard'? Now what do we say?"

Trying to perk me up, he pointed out that the two nesting ospreys I had seen here on prior spring trips were still in residence in their big, slovenly nest on top of the light pole in short right-field foul ground; just the day before, he said, a batter with the visiting Reds had skied a foul ball that had landed in the nest—landed and stayed there, that is—but the birds did not seem discomposed. I kept an eye out, and over the next few innings I saw one or perhaps both of them depart and return to their perch, coming in with a last flutter of their great wings and then settling down on whatever they were keeping there above the field. Someday soon, I decided, we would hear about the first confirmed sighting of a young red-stitched osprey (*Pandion ueberrothiensis*) here, hard by the banks of Lake Lulu. I cheered up. A little later in that game, we had a brief shower—the first rain in weeks, I was told—and some of the older fans got up from their unprotected seats along the left- and right-field lines and came and stood in the aisles of the roofed grandstand, out of the wet. The game went on, with the sitting and standing fans quietly taking it in, and I had a sudden, oddly familiar impression (this has hit me before, in this park at this time of year) that I had found my way into a large henhouse somewhere and was surrounded by elderly farmyard fowls. We perched there together, smelling the aroma of mixed dust and rain, and waited for the sun to come out again.

○

On another afternoon that March, I found comfort at Terry Park, in Fort Myers, where the Royals get their spring work done. Fort Myers is seventy-five miles down U.S. 41 from the next-nearest Gulf Coast diamond (at Sarasota), and this distance seems to have preserved the sweetness that I had lately missed in some other spring parks. Dowager nineteen-twenties palms line the narrow downtown avenues of Fort Myers, and some of the old folks coming into the stadium at game time tote little plastic bags of seashells that they have plucked from the beach that morning.* In the park, there is Astro Turf within the bases and green grass beyond—possibly a metaphor representing the 1985 Royals, who have very young pitching and a comfort-

---

*These happy grounds are now lost to big-league baseball. The Royals gave up their Fort Myers camp in 1987 and moved to Orlando, where their spring workouts form part of a "Boardwalk and Baseball" theme park.

ably mature defense. One afternoon in the press box (an upright, boxy shack that perches on top of the grandstand roof like a diner on a siding), I was startled by a stentorian squawking—*"Whooh!"* . . . *"Whooh!"* . . . *"Whoo-ooh!"*—that progressed by slow degrees around the stands below me, from right field to left. I made inquiry, and was told that this was the Screecher, an ancient local species of fan, who had not missed a Terry Park game for many years. He was Mr. Bruce McAllister, who brought his unique avian rooting here more than twenty years earlier, back when the Pirates were the spring incumbents; before that, I learned, he had screeched at old Forbes Field, in Pittsburgh.

Earlier that day, I had a rewarding conversation with Joe Cunniff, a Chicago teacher who takes the winter semester off every year in order to be near baseball. He is a spring assistant to the Royals' P.R. people, watching over things in the press box, keeping statistics, and the like. The rest of the year, he teaches music and art at De Paul University and the City Colleges of Chicago—adult-education courses, for the most part. He told me that his baseball vacation at Fort Myers was a cultural counterpart of his fellow pedagogues' summer trips to Greece and Italy. Cunniff is in his upper thirties—an engaging, thick-set baseball zealot with a black mustache and a shy, polite way of talking.

"I love that sound of bats cracking in the morning air," he said at one point. (We were sitting in the cool, shady Royals dugout during batting practice.) "Every year, you see a new player in the games here who sticks out in your mind. Last year, Jack Morris came down here with the Tigers and struck out six of our batters in three or four innings, and I called my brother in Chicago that night and told him that Morris would be unbeatable during the season. Sure enough, Morris came to Comiskey Park in the first week of the season and threw a no-hitter against the White Sox. My brother was *impressed*."

Cunniff said that he'd started out as a White Sox fan as a boy in Chicago, but that in recent years he had become entranced by the pleasures of the bleachers at Wrigley Field and had just about made the great moral switch-over to the Cubs. "I suspect that if most people in Chicago really told the truth they'd admit that they're perfectly happy when either team does well, and that they secretly shift over and begin to root for that team and claim it as their own," he said. "Baseball's really about fun, you know, and I don't think we have to have these deep antagonisms. But now the suburbs have discovered the Cubs, and I think it's going to be different from here on. I almost preferred it when they were in last place, and we regulars would be out there in center field, cheering them on. It's the best life you can imagine. Down here, I care about the Royals—they're a great team and a great organization. I go see them and root for them when they come to Chicago, and that way

I get to see the writers I know and my other friends in the press box."

One of those friends, Tracy Ringolsby, of the Kansas City *Star-Times*, told me about his favorite moment of spring training at Terry Park. An hour or more after the final game of the 1984 spring season, he and a *Star-Times* colleague, Mike Fish, were alone in the press box, clicking out their final pre-season wrapups, when they noticed a lone figure out on the diamond. The stands were empty, the players and the groundskeepers had long since left the field, the bases were up, and an angling sun illuminated the field below. The man out there was not in uniform, and he had no glove, but he had stationed himself at shortstop and was taking infield practice—the last workout of the year. It was Joe Cunniff. Unnoticed in their perch, Ringolsby and Fish watched, mesmerized ("It was beautiful," Ringolsby told me. "It took your breath away"), as Cunniff charged an invisible slow hopper and flipped sidearm over to second. Then he grabbed a bullet line drive down by his heels and whipped the ball over to first quickly, trying to double off a runner. Then he flew into the hole, far to his right, pulled down the hard grounder, planted his foot, and made the long peg over to first, waiting an instant for the ump's call over there, and then slapping his fist into his phantom glove in triumph: *out!* He had made the hardest play at the hardest position in the game.

○

The life—baseball as a side order, so to speak—is not necessarily slow or reflective. What I remember about an October now seven years gone isn't an unmemorable World Series between the Dodgers and the Yankees (the Dodgers won it) but the crowds at the Stade Olympique, up in Montreal, during the stirring Dodgers–Expos playoff games there. All that is still clear: the middle innings of Game Three, say (the clubs had come back from Los Angeles with the series tied), with the Dodgers' Jerry Reuss and the Expos' Steve Rogers locked in hard combat, and the Dodgers up a run—the only run of the game so far—and the encircling, in-leaning rows upon rows of avid, baseball-mad Canadians, seeming to sway and shudder and groan and cry in the chilly northern night air with every pitch and movement of the fray. And to sing. When I wrote about this, several days later, I still half heard in the dusty back chambers of my head the vapid, endlessly repeated chorus of that damnable Expo marching song—*"Val-de-ri! Val-de-rah!"*—that the locals bellowed together, in enormous and echoing cacophony, at every imaginable stitch and wrinkle of the games' fabric. The song is not some famous indigenous voyageurs' chantey, as one might suppose, but only the old, implacably jolly "Happy Wanderer" hiking ditty that generations of sub-adolescents across the continent have had to warble through ("Val-de-ra-ha-ha-ha-ha-ha!") during mosquitoey marshmallow roasts at Camp Pine-away. But the Montrealers sang it with a will—sang it because they *wanted* to, of all things—and they won my heart. I didn't even mind the weather, which was unsuitable, if never quite unbearable, or the appalling ballpark. The round, thick-lipped, inward-tilted concrete upper wall of the Stade Olympique appears to hang over the stands and the glum, Astro-Turfed field in a glowering, almost threatening way, shutting out the sky, and fastballs and hard-hit grounders are so hard to see from above, for some reason, that the accompanying noise from the crowd is always an instant or two out of sync. This time I didn't care, because the teams and the players and the quality of play were all so good that every part of the games mattered and made you glad you were there and no place else in the world just then.

In the sixth inning of that third game, the Expos tied things up with a single and a walk and a little roller by Larry Parrish, *just* through between Cey and Russell at third and short. Reuss, perhaps ever so slightly distracted by the blizzards of torn-up *journeaux*, and the layered explosions of noise, and the illuminated "PLUS FORT!" up on the scoreboard, and the back-and-forth billowings of an enormous white Québecois flag, and the hundredth or perhaps thousandth bellowed cascade of "*Val-de-ri!*"s and "*Val-de-rah!*"s—now got a fastball a millimeter or two higher than he wanted to against the next batter, outfielder Jerry White, who socked the ball up and out into the left-field stands for a homer and three more runs and, it turned out, the game.

I imagine everyone who thinks of himself or herself as an Expo fan still clings to that moment, for the team lost the next two games—lost them late, under grindingly painful circumstances—to miss out on the World Series, and sank into a long baseball torpor. Sometimes it's wiser to remember the byplay of big games—the songs and the rest of it—instead of their outcome, because losing hurts so much. Players understand this all too well. A day or two before the end, Steve Rogers, talking about all the singing and happiness in the Montreal stands, shook his head a little and said, "Yes, it's beautiful, but—well, euphoria is not always the name of the game."

○

People who don't follow baseball very closely assume that fans care only about their own club. I don't agree. Whenever I happen upon a Little League game or a high-school game or a Sunday game in Central Park between a couple of East Harlem amateur nines, it only takes me an inning or so before I find myself privately rooting for one of the teams out there. I have no idea how this choice is arrived at, but the process is more fun if the two sides offer a visible, almost moral, clash of styles and purpose, and—even better—if each seems to be personified by one of its players. At that 1982 Cardinals-Brewers World Series, York and Lancaster were brilliantly depicted by the rival center fielders; the frail, popeyed, apologetic-looking Cardinal rookie,

Willie McGee; and the hulking, raggedy-ass veteran Brewer slugger, Gorman Thomas. McGee had a great series, it turned out, both at the plate and in the field; in the third game, which the Cardinals won, 6–2, he smacked home runs in two successive at-bats, and in the ninth he pulled down a mighty poke by Gorman Thomas (of *course*) after running at full tilt from mid-center field into deep left center and then to the top of the wall there all in one flowing, waterlike motion—a cat up a tree—with no pause or acceleration near the end to adjust for the catch; at the top of his leap, with his back to the field, he put his glove up and a bit to his left, and the ball, in the same instant, arrived. The play almost broke my heart, for I had already somehow chosen the Brewers and Gorman Thomas as my own. Thomas, as it happened, did nothing much in the Series—three little singles, and this after a summer in which he had hit a league-leading thirty-nine home runs—so I certainly wasn't front-running. The frowsy Thomas was a walking strip mine; he had worn the same pair of uniform stockings, now as threadbare as the Shroud of Turin, since opening day of 1978. I recall a moment in the Brewer clubhouse during the Series when a group of us were chatting with Thomas's father—he was the retired postmaster of Charleston, South Carolina—and some genius reporter asked what Gorman's room had looked like back when he was a teen-ager. "Turrible!" Thomas *père* said, wincing at the thought. "Why, I could hahdly make myself look in theah!"

O

Events on the field qualify in the life, as well; they only have to be a little special. In September 1986, during an unmomentous Giants–Braves game out at Candlestick Park, Bob Brenly, playing third base for the San Franciscos, made an error on a routine ground ball in the top of the fourth inning. Four batters later, he kicked away another chance and then, scrambling after the ball, threw wildly past home in an attempt to nail a runner there: two errors on the same play. A few moments after *that*, he managed another boot, thus becoming only the fourth player since the turn of the century to rack up four errors in one inning. In the bottom of the fifth, Brenly hit a solo home run. In the seventh, he rapped out a bases-loaded single, driving in two runs and tying the game at 6–6. The score stayed that way until the bottom of the ninth, when our man came up to bat again, with two out, ran the count to 3–2, and then sailed a massive home run deep into the left-field stands. Brenly's account book for the day came to three hits in five at-bats, two home runs, four errors, four Atlanta runs allowed, and four Giant runs driven in, including the game-winner. A neater summary was delivered by his manager, Roger Craig, who said, "This man deserves the Comeback Player of the Year Award for this game alone." I wasn't at Candlestick that day, but I don't care; I have this one by heart.

Or consider an earlier concatenation that began when Phil Garner, a stalwart Pirate outfielder, struck a grand slam home run against the Cardinals at Three Rivers Stadium one evening in 1978. Every professional player can recall each grand slam in his career, but this one was a blue-plate special, because Garner, who is not overmuscled, had never hit a bases-loaded home run before—not in Little League play; not in Legion or high-school ball; not in four years with the University of Tennessee nine; not in five years in the minors; not in six hundred and fifty-one prior major-league games, over two leagues and five summers. Never.

We must now try to envisage—perhaps in playlet form—the events at the Garner place when Phil came home that evening:

P.G. (*enters left, with a certain swing in his step*): Hi, honey.

Mrs. P.G.—or C.G. (her name is Carol): Hi. How'd it go?

P.G.: O.K. (*pause*) Well?

C.G.: Well, what?

P.G.: What! You mean . . .

C.G. (*alarmed*): *What* what? What's going on?

P.G.: I can't believe it. You missed it . . .

Yes, she had missed it, although Carol was and is a baseball fan and a fan of Phil's, as well as his wife, and was in the custom of attending most of the Pirates' home games and following the others by radio or television. When he told her the news, she was delighted but appalled.

C.G.: I can't get over not seeing it. You can't imagine how bad I feel.

P.G. (*grandly*): Oh, that's O.K., honey. I'll hit another one for you tomorrow.

And so he did. He hit his second grand slam.

○

Attention must be paid. In March, 1984, I watched a talented left-handed Blue Jay rookie pitcher named John Cerutti work three middle innings against the Red Sox at Winter Haven; at one point he struck out Jim Rice with a dandy little slider in under his fists. I talked to Cerutti after the game and learned that he was four credits away from his B.A. degree in economics at Amherst (he has since graduated) and that his senior thesis had to do with the role of agents in major-league player salaries. I also discovered that he had a baseball hero: Ron Guidry.

"I don't have many fond memories of baseball until I was about eighteen and pitching for the Christian Brothers Academy, in Albany," he said. "Then I got the notion that I might make it in the game someday. I had a real good year that year—it was 1978—and, of course, that was the same time that Guidry had *his* great year. I was a Yankee fan—always had been—so naturally I followed him and pulled for him, and that spring I began to notice that something weird was happening to us. I mean, I won seven games in a row, and he won his first seven. Then I was 9–0 when he was exactly the same— we were winning together, me and *Ron Guidry*! School ended and I graduated, but I went on pitching in American Legion ball. I was 13–0 when I lost my first game, and I thought, Uh-oh, that's the end of it, but that very same night Guidry lost, too, for the first time—I was watching on TV—so we were still the same. Well, I guess you know he finished up the year with a 25–3 record, and was the Cy Young winner and all, and I ended at 25–2. So you could say we both had pretty good years. That affinity began."

Cerutti said all this a little offhandedly—with a trace of college-cool irony, perhaps—but his face was alight with humor and good cheer.

"So do you want to know my dream now?" he went on. "My dream is that first I make this club some day, and then I end up pitching a game against Ron Guidry. It's a big, big game—a Saturday afternoon at the Stadium, one of those big crowds, with a lot riding on it—and I beat him, 1–0. It could just happen."

"I know," I said.

"Keep watching," he said.

"I'll be there," I said.

Making the Blue Jays took a little longer than Cerutti had expected, but when he was called up from Syracuse in the spring of 1986, it was noticed that he had his stuff together at last; he went 9–4 for the season, with a shutout along the way, and took up his place in the Toronto starting rotation. I was happy about the promotion (I had renewed acquaintance with him briefly a couple of times in the interim, mostly in Florida), and in June this summer I watched him work a game against the Yankees in New York one evening—watched him over the tube, I mean. It was a significant game for both clubs, since the Blue Jays were a half game up on the Yankees at the top of the American League East. There I was, with my dinner and a drink before me and with John Cerutti, big as life, up there on the screen, when several rusty synapses clicked on at last. "My God!" I cried. "It's Guidry, too. It's happened."

I had blown our date, but Cerutti kept his, all right, beating the Yankees by 7–2, it turned out, to solidify his team's hold on first place. Not Cerutti's plan *exactly*, but close enough. I considered rushing up to the Stadium to catch the later innings, but I didn't. I got there early the next evening, however, and at batting practice a couple of writer friends said, "You see John Cerutti? He was looking for you last night."

He came in from the field at last—he had been doing his sprints out there—and found me in the dugout. "Hey," he said cheerfully. "Where were you?"

"I blew it," I said. "I'm sorry, John—I stood you up. I feel bad about it. Only you said it would be a *Saturday*."

"Well, I looked for you," he said. "Everyone else was here. I heard a couple of days ago that it might be me and the Gator, so I called my mom and she came down for it. In the end, I had to leave sixteen tickets for people from home. They knew how long I'd been waiting. It was all just the way I'd dreamed about it. In the first couple of innings, I kept thinking, Here I am, with my spikes on the same pitching rubber where Ron Guidry's spikes were a minute ago. It was a thrill."

"I know—I saw it at home," I said miserably. "There's no excuse, only well, you know . . . I didn't believe it. Life isn't *like* this."

"I know," he said. "But this is different."

"This is baseball, you mean."

"That's right," he said. "In baseball—well, stuff can happen."

The Arms Talks

T he lesser wonders of baseball—the sacrifice fly, the three-six-three double play, the wrong-side hit-and-run bouncer through a vacated infield sector, the right-field-to-third-base peg that cuts down a lead runner, the extended turn at bat against an obdurate pitcher that ends with a crucial single squiggled through the middle—are most appreciated by the experienced fan, who may in time also come to understand that expertise is the best defense against partisanship. This game can break your heart. No other sport elucidates failure so plainly (no other sport comes close), or presents it in such painful and unexpected variety. My favorite team, the Mets, won a World Championship last fall, but the pleasure of that drained away much more quickly than I thought it would, and now, in company with their millions of other fans, I am stuck with the increased anxieties and diminished pleasures of a possible repeat performance. The 1986 league championships and World Series produced so many excruciations and twists of the knife that these, I suspect, are now remembered more vividly than anything else. Hundreds of thousands of TV spectators must have fallen in love with baseball in the course of watching these soap operas, but during the winter I sometimes wondered how many of those newborn fans would stay with the game once they perceived its slower and less melodramatic midsummer flow, and whether (if they were Mets rooters) they were giving thought to the lingering, inexorably recalled off-season sufferings of the worthy (and, together, much more numerous) fans of the Astros and the Angels and the Red Sox, some of whom or all of whom may have to wait for many seasons—decades, perhaps—before they find better luck and a shot at redress. There are easy days and lesser rewards for every fan, of course, but losing, rather than winning, is what baseball is about, and why, in the end, it is a game for adults.

Trying to learn the game, as I have suggested, protects us from its overattachments and repeated buffetings, and for me, as the years go by, this has become almost the best part of baseball. This spring and last spring, I passed many hours in the company of coaches and managers and players— older players, for the most part—as I tried to learn a bit more about pitching. I wasn't so much concerned with strategy—where the ball is pitched, and with what intention, to different batters in different game situations (the heart of the game, in fact)—for that art is better pursued during the regular season, when each pitch matters. Rather, I wanted to learn for certain how the different pitches are thrown and why; how the ball is held and what happens to it in flight and which styles in pitching and pitchers' thinking are undergoing alteration. (In the course of these talks, I often found myself moving a ball this way and that in my right hand—I pitch and write righty—while some pitcher or coach tried to arrange my fingers around it in different ways, and I would suggest to readers who wish to accompany me closely over the ensuing paragraphs that they might do well to hunt around the house for an old baseball and keep it close by as a teaching aid.)

Early on, I found out about—or was confirmed in my guesses about—an amazing revolution in pitching style and theory that has been in progress for more than a dozen years now. Pete Rose put it well (Pete puts *everything* well) in Tampa a year ago. "The two biggest changes I've noticed in baseball in my twenty-three-year career are, first and obviously, the much bigger salaries and, second, the maturity of big-league pitchers today," he said. "There's a reason for this, which is that in every class and level of baseball today there is a pitching coach. It didn't use to be that way when I was coming up. I don't think the pitchers are faster than they used to be, but I think they're better. By the time a pitcher is twenty or twenty-one years old now, he's very comfortable throwing 2–0 changeups and 3–1 curveballs. We've gotten used to that, but it's something real different. When I first came up, most of the relievers were freak-ball pitchers, who threw screwballs or knuckleballs or forkballs or palmballs. Now the hardest throwers—I'm only talking National League, because that's where I've been—the hardest throwers are in the bullpen. Gooden is an exception. Most of the other burners—Gossage, Lee Smith, Jeff Reardon, Ted Power, Niedenfuer—are coming out of the pen." Ted Power, it should be noted, was moved into the Reds' starting rotation last summer—a move made by the Reds' manager, Pete Rose. "I mean, the top relievers are smokers, and most of the starters are the other way," he went on. "More and more, the starters in this league pitch backward—2–0 breaking balls and changeups, and 0–2 fastballs. They don't give in to you. It's a good way to pitch, if you can do it, because you can win that way."

Steve Garvey, the first-base perennial—he is thirty-eight years old and is now in his nineteenth season in the majors—agreed with Pete Rose right down the line, and said as well that the advent of the new split-finger fastball (which we will examine in more detail shortly) has brought a fresh dimension of difficulty for the batter. He thinks that the batter who tends to go with a pitch and rap it up the middle of the diamond—a hitter like his Padre teammate Tony Gwynn, for example—will have more success against the new pitch than someone who likes to pull the ball. Garvey told me that the swift arrival of very talented relievers in a game also adds to the batter's burdens. "The second guy to pitch now is as good as a fifth starter," he said, "and that's pretty decent." The man up at bat gets to see three and maybe four pitchers pitch in the same game, he noted, each with a different style and size and delivery point, and batting averages in both leagues are drooping as a result. Garvey feels that the old respectable, upper-level .280-to-.295 hitter is being forced down into mediocrity merely by much better pitchers and tougher pitches.

"Basically, we're all fastball hitters," Garvey said. "If we couldn't hit the fastball, we wouldn't be here. But if you have to look at breaking balls all the time you're only as good as your ability to adjust. It's a whole different game. When I came up, there was more of that pure challenge from the starting pitchers. Seaver threw hard, Jerry Koosman threw hard. Bob Gibson threw, I mean, *hard*. Fergie Jenkins threw hard and had that good slider away. Jerry Reuss and Steve Carlton threw hard when they were together on the Cardinals in the seventies. So did Candelaria, when he came along, and that same Pirates team had Terry Forster and Goose Gossage coming out of the bullpen. Hard throwers. The 2–0 breaking ball used to be a special trait of the American League, because they had smaller ballparks and it's harder to hit the breaking ball out. But now, because of free agency, the National League has a lot of American League pitchers in it, and even with our bigger ballparks the whole pitching staff is saying, 'Why don't we do it that way, too, instead of being the hardball league?' It's tougher on hitters every day."

Joe Rudi told me that when he first came up the slider was a relatively new pitch and he had to deal with the new masters of the genre, like Jim Lonborg. "Now it's this split-finger fastball," he said. "It seems like the pitchers are always getting ahead. The real change, to me, is that middle-innings relief specialist—the long man. You hear pitching coaches talking about your rookies, and they'll say, 'This guy is going to be a real good middle-innings pitcher.' That's something new. What it really means is you never get that fourth at-bat against a great pitcher. I used to have to face Jim Palmer in maybe three or four games a year, and the first two or three at-bats against him were tough, believe me. But the fourth time up I thought maybe I had a chance. Nowadays, that pitcher is out of the game by then and you're looking at a sinker-baller like Quisenberry or a Jay Howell throwing gas. That good last at-bat is gone."

Doug DeCinces, the California third baseman, said he almost missed the old challenge of waiting for a guaranteed fastball ("sitting dead fastball," in baseballese) on a 3–1 count, but not if the pitcher was Goose Gossage. He said, "You didn't want *that* every day, but Goose sure liked it. It was 'Here it is, what are you going to do about it?' You knew that before you stepped in there. But I wouldn't say that the hard throwers are all the same. I mean, they're not dumb. I remember when I was younger I was with the Orioles, and Nolan Ryan threw a no-hitter against us at Anaheim Stadium one day. He struck out Bobby Grich on a 3–2 changeup for the last out of the game. He made Bobby look so bad it was pathetic. I mean, everybody in the park knew that with a 3–2 count it had to be a fastball coming. Only it wasn't."

There were echoes and variations on these themes everywhere. In Mesa, Herm Starrette, the Cubs' pitching coach (he has held the same post with the Braves, the Giants, the Phillies, and the Brewers), said, "There's no doubt in my mind that pitchers are better than they used to be. They know more things." Starrette is kindly and gently pedagogic in manner; he wears outsized spectacles and reminds you a little of a small-town insurance man. "I think a starting pitcher in the big leagues has to have three pitches he can get over the plate in any situation, and now the man who comes in and relieves him is just about as good," he went on. "You don't follow a starter with a reliever who has the same kind of delivery. It's like dancing with somebody—if you shift to a partner with a different sense of rhythm, it takes a time around the floor to get used to it. It's not easy for the batter to pick up the change—from left-hander to right-hander, or a new release point of the pitcher's hand, or whatever—and by the time he does the game is about over. Then here comes Lee Smith, who's throwing ninety-per or better, and now he's got a slider to go with it, and that hard sinker, too. It's unfair. I think pitchers are the smartest people on the field. They've got to know every batter and understand every situation in the game. If a guy wins twenty games, he's real smart. If he doesn't—well, he's proved it: he's not so smart." He laughed.

○

HOTDOG: Nothing is easy in baseball, of course, even for the pitchers. In Phoenix Stadium last spring, Bill Rigney and my teen-age son, John Henry, and I watched from behind home plate while Oakland's Joaquin Andujar worked in a little B-game against the Indians one day. It was about ten-thirty in the morning—a time of day when a ballgame feels like a special treat, like a children's birthday party—and the desert sunlight was putting a fresh-paint sheen on the empty rows of reserved-seat stands around us. Four or five scouts sat together on little metal chairs in a box-seat section down behind the screen, and now and then one of them would pick up a coffee container from between his feet and sip at it and put it down again. There were about thirty fans in the rest of the park, and the only unhappy folks in view may have been Andujar, out on the mound, and Rig, just to my right, who were equally unimpressed with the pitching just then. Andujar, a combustible 21–12 pitcher with the Cardinals the year before, had been acquired in a trade over the winter and was expected to add some zing to the lackluster Oakland pitching corps. Rigney, a former manager of the Giants and the Twins and the Angels, is the chief baseball adviser to the Athletics, and now he exchanged a couple of sharp glances with me as Andujar kicked unhappily at the rubber and stared around at a couple of Cleveland base runners he had put aboard on a walk and then a single that was hit off an unimpressive 3–1 pitch. A white-haired, mahogany-tan gent with a cigar came along the aisle and sat down behind us and put his arms up on the back of our row of seats. "You see it, don't you, Rig?" he said instantly in a deep, mahogany-colored voice. "The whole key to Joaquin is that front knee. If he don't pick it up in his motion and bring it right up 'long-side the back leg, it opens him up too soon. There—he just did it again. He throws three-quarters that way, and when he's three-quarters the goddam ball gets up, and his slider just goes *shh-shh-shh*. When he gets tired, he does that all the time, and his sidearm is horseshit. He's got to tuck in that front knee—just that much more gives him time to get up on top of the ball. . . . Like *that*—he did it that time."

Our new companion was Hub Kittle, a legendary erstwhile pitching coach with the Cardinals. Now seventy, he has become a traveling instructor in the Cards' farm system and a part-time scout. He was dressed in several eye-shattering shades of Cardinals red, with a thong tie and a turquoise tie clasp. Rig introduced us, and Kittle buried my hand in his, but his eyes stayed on the field.

"Oops—there's that little forker I taught him," he said. "But that forearm has got to come down, *down* onto his goddam knee. He's so quick you don't see where he's going wrong." He curled his right hand into a spyglass and peered through it with one eye. "Close out the batter, close out the hitter and the ump, and then you can see him," he muttered. "I had him at Houston and down in the Dominican for five years, and I know you got to stay on his goddam ass. 'O.K., now,' you say to him. 'O.K. *¡Bien! ¡Arriba! ¡Bueno!*' You keep on his case so the *brujo* don't get him—the witch doctor. He gets in those spells out there."

Andujar gave up a little single, which scored a run, and then the home-plate ump—the woman umpire Pam Postema—called a balk when he tried to pick off the runner at first.

"Oh-oh," Kittle said. "Now he's pissed. See him stompin' around out there. He's talking to himself again." Kittle half rose and shouted something in Spanish to Andujar. "Go full circle!" he roared. "Keep the ball down, *hombre!*"

Joaquin, struck dumb, stared around the stadium in confusion—I think for a moment he looked straight up at the sky. Then he spotted Kittle and waved his glove. The next two pitches were good breaking balls, and then he struck out the batter with a fastball to end the half inning.

"There," said Kittle. "That's the *pistola*. He's still got it."

"I think you should have been part of the deal," Rig said. "This man"—he grabbed Kittle by the knee—"this man and I played together on the Spokane Hawks in 1938," he went on, to John Henry and me. "He was a pitcher, and I was a kid shortstop. That was a B League, and it was my first professional team. Wes Schulmerich was finishing up his career there." He shook his head. "Nineteen thirty-eight . . . "

○

The split-finger fastball is baseball's Rubik's Cube of the eighties—a gimmick, a supertoy, a conversation piece, and a source of sudden fame and success for its inventor. It is thrown at various speeds and with a slightly varying grip on the ball, but in its classic mode it looks like a middling-good fastball that suddenly changes its mind and ducks under the batter's swing just as it crosses the plate. The pitch isn't exactly new—nothing in baseball is exactly new. A progenitor, the forkball, was grasped in much the same fashion, between the pitcher's forefinger and middle finger, but tucked more deeply into the hand, which took off spin and speed—a "slip-pitch," in the parlance. Elroy Face, a reliever with the Pirates, was its great practitioner in the nineteen-fifties and sixties, and he put together an amazing 18–1 won-and-lost record (all in relief) with it in 1959. Bruce Sutter—like Face, a right-handed relief specialist—came along with the first so-called split-finger fastball a decade ago while with the Cubs, and has employed it (and very little else by way of repertoire) to run up a lifetime National League record of two hundred and eighty-six saves, with a Cy Young Award in 1979; he later moved along to the Cardinals and is now with the Braves and in temporary eclipse, owing to a sore arm. The Sutter pitch seemed not only unhittable but patented, for no one else in the game has quite been able to match his way of combining the forkball grip with a mid-delivery upward thrust of the thumb from beneath, which imparted a deadly little diving motion to the ball in flight. Here matters rested until 1984, when Roger Craig, a pitching coach with the Tigers, imparted his own variant of the s.-f. fb. to several members of the Detroit mound staff, with instant effect. Craig went into retirement after that season (he has since unretired, of course, and manages the Giants), but he is an affable and enthusiastic gent, who loves to talk and teach pitching. He is tall and pink-cheeked, with a noble schnoz; as most fans know, he has endured every variety of fortune on the mound. Callers at his home near San Diego that first winter of retirement included a good many opportunistic pitchers and pitching coaches from both leagues who were anxious to get their hands on the dingus. Most prominent among them—now, not then— was Mike Scott, a large but as yet unimpressive pitcher with the Houston Astros (the Mets had traded him away after 1982, at a time when his lifetime record stood at 14–27); he spent a week with Craig and came home armed with Excalibur. With the new pitch, he went 18–8 in 1985 and 18–10 last year, when he won a Cy Young Award after leading the majors with three hundred and six strikeouts and a 2.22 earned-run average. He capped his regular-season work with a no-hitter against the Giants, clinching the Astros' divisional pennant, and then zipped off sixteen consecutive scoreless innings while winning his two starts in the championship series against the Mets, to whom he surrendered but one run over all. Indeed, the other great "what if" of this past winter (along with second-guessing the way the Red Sox played the tenth inning of Game Six in the World Series) is the speculation about the Mets' fate in the playoffs if they had been forced to face Scott for a third time, in a seventh and deciding game.

"The split-finger is mostly a changeup," Keith Hernandez told me in St. Petersburg. "It can be thrown in different ways, so you can say it's really a three-speed changeup, with the forkball action as the other half of it. Scott can make it run in or out, but when he throws it inside to me he throws it *hard*. It has so much velocity on it that it's a real fastball for him, plus it goes down. It just drops off the table. Sutter's was the best until this one, but Scott has perfected it. He has tremendous command over the pitch—he never makes a mistake." (Mike Scott, it should be added, might not agree with this generous appraisal, for Hernandez hits him better than anyone else in the league: .377 lifetime, according to the *Elias Baseball Analyst*.)

Roger Craig told me that both Scott and Jack Morris throw the split-finger at eighty-five miles an hour or better—faster than anyone else, although Scott Garrelts, a fireballing reliever on Craig's Giants, is now approaching that level. "Jack has his fingers up higher on the ball than Mike does," Craig said. "Mike's got the ball as far out in his hand as you can get it. He throws it about sixty or seventy percent of the time now, and there was a stretch at the end of last year when he was just unhittable. The pitch was a phantom—you'd swing and it wasn't there." (A good many batters in the National League are convinced that Mike Scott also imparts another sort of witchcraft to the baseball, by scuffing it in some secret fashion, in contravention of the rules. Steve Garvey told me that retrieved balls Scott has thrown often show a patch of lightly cut concentric circles on one of the white sectors—something that might be done with an artificially roughened part of his glove or palm. Garvey made a little sidewise gesture with his hand. "That's all it moves," he said, smiling. "It's enough.")

Craig—to get back into the sunshine here—said that the best thing about the split-finger is that it can be thrown at so many different speeds. "It depends on where you've got it in your fingers, on how you cock your wrist—on a whole lot of things," he said. "But the ultimate is when it comes out off the tips of your fingers—they just slip down along the ball on the outside of the seams—and the ball *tumbles*. That's the great one, because it's the opposite spin from the fastball. People keep telling me it isn't really a fastball, but I keep saying it is, because I want that pitcher to throw it with a fastball motion. Dan Petry, back with the Tigers, used to let up on it, because it was in the back of his mind that it was an off-speed pitch, but that's wrong. Here—gimme a ball, somebody."

We were sitting out on a bullpen bench in left field on a shining morning in Scottsdale—Craig and I and one of the Giants' beat writers. Craig has large, pale, supernally clean hands—Grandpa hands, if Grandpa is a dentist—and when he got a ball he curled his long forefinger and middle finger around it at the point where the red seams come closest together. "I start with my fingers together like this, and I say 'fastball' . . . 'fastball' . . . 'fastball' "—he waggled his wrist and fingers downward again and again—"but I have them go this way each time: just a bit wider apart. By the time you're out here"— the fingers were outside the seams now, on the white, slippery parts of the ball—"you're throwing the split-finger. There's a stage where it acts sort of like a knuckleball, but it'll come. You've started."

Craig told us that he'd discovered the pitch back in 1982, while he was coaching fifteen- and sixteen-year-old boys in California. He takes great pleasure in the fact that several older or middle-level professionals have saved their careers with the pitch (Milt Wilcox, a righty with the Tigers, was one), and that subvarsity high-school and college pitchers have made the team with it. Superior pitchers sometimes resist it, by contrast. "Jack Morris thinks he's the greatest pitcher who ever lived," Craig said. "He has that great confidence. He insisted he didn't need it, even though he was getting killed with his changeup. So I said, 'Do me a favor. Pitch one game and don't throw a change—throw the split-finger instead.' He did it, and it was a two-hitter against the Orioles."

When Craig arrived at Candlestick Park in September of 1985, as the Giants' new manager, he took all the pitchers out to the bullpen on his second day and asked for a volunteer who had never essayed the split-finger. Mark Davis, a left-hander, came forward, and Craig sent the rest of the staff down to stand behind the catcher. "Well, in about twenty, twenty-five pitches he was throwing it," Roger said, "and all my other pitchers were thinkin', Well, if he can do it, *I* can do it. That way, I didn't have to go out and try to convince them one by one." Everybody on the Giants throws the pitch now, and one of Craig's starters, Mike Krukow, went 20–9 with it last year—his best year ever. Craig hasn't counted, but he believes that thirty or forty percent of the pitchers in the National League have the pitch by now, or are working on it. Five of the Dodgers' staff—Welch, Hershiser, Niedenfuer, Young, and Leary—employ the pitch, and the American League is beginning to catch up. Gene Mauch, the Angels' pilot, told Craig this spring that all his pitchers would be working on it this year.

I suggested to Roger that he should have registered the split-finger, so that he could charge a royalty every time it's thrown in a game, and his face lit up. "*That* would be nice, wouldn't it?" he said. "Just kick back and stay home, and take on a few private pupils now and then. That would be all right! But I've stopped teaching it to other teams. About ten pitching coaches called me up last winter and asked if they could come out and pick it up, but I said no. And there was this one general manager who called me up and said he'd send me and my wife to Hawaii, all expenses paid, if I'd take on his pitching coach and teach it to him. It's too late, though—I already showed it to too many guys. Dumb old me."

Not everybody, in truth, picks up the split-finger quickly or easily, and not all split-fingers are quite the same. Ron Darling, the Mets' young right-hander, mastered the delivery last summer, after a long struggle, and when he did, it became what he had needed all along—a finishing pitch, to make him a finished pitcher. (He was 15–6, with a 2.81 E.R.A., for the year, along with a hatful of strong no-decision outings.) He has never talked to Roger Craig, and, in fact, his split-finger started out as a forkball taught to him by pitching coach Al Jackson at the Mets' Tidewater farm club in 1983. But Darling, who has small hands, could never open his fingers enough to grasp the ball in the deep forkball grip, so it became a split-finger delivery instead. (Craig told me that some pitchers he knew had even gone to bed at night with a ball strapped between their fingers, in an attempt to widen their grip.) Darling had very little luck with the pitch at first, but kept at it because of Jack Morris's example—especially after Morris pitched a no-hitter against the White Sox at the beginning of the 1984 season.

"The whole idea about pitching—one of the basics of the art—is that you've got to show the batter a strike that isn't a strike," Darling said. "More than half—much more than half—of all the split-fingers that guys throw are balls. They drop right out of the strike zone. That's a problem, because you might have a great split-finger that moves a lot, and the batter is going to lay off it if he sees any kind of funny spin. So you have to throw it for a strike now and then. Hitters adjust, you know. Most of the time, you're going to throw the pitch when you're ahead in the count. But sometimes I throw it when I'm behind, too. All you have to do is make it look like a fastball for at least half the distance. A lot of times last year, I'd try to get a strike with a fastball and *then* throw a split-finger strike. If it does get over—and this began to happen for me for the first time last year—it rocks the world, because then here comes another split-finger and the bottom drops out, but the guy still has to swing. He has no other choice. Nobody can afford not to swing at that pitch—unless he's Keith Hernandez. Umpires don't call third strikes on Keith."

○

K FOR KOUFAX: Each year, I notice, one particular old player's name pops up again and again in baseball conversations. I don't understand it. This year, it was Sandy Koufax. Roger Craig told me that he and Koufax were among the old Dodgers who had turned up at Vero Beach for a thirtieth reunion of the 1955 Brooklyn World Champions, and that Sandy immediately began asking him how to throw the new split-finger pitch. The next afternoon, he summoned Craig over to watch him working off a mound. "Well, first of all, Sandy was throwing the fastball at around eighty-five miles an hour," Craig said. "He was in great shape, as usual, and he just did it naturally—no effort at all. I couldn't get over it. He was working on the split-finger, of course, though, and already he had it down pretty good. You know how long *his* fingers are. Sandy was pretty excited, and after a while he told me he was going to unretire and get back into the game as a pitcher again. I said, 'Jesus Christ, man, you can't do *that*! You're fifty years old!' But I thought he really meant it for a while, and so did Buzzie Bavasi and some of the others who heard him. I guess somebody talked him out of it in the end, but I almost wish they hadn't. Wouldn't that've been something!"

At Winter Haven, Eddie Kasko, the Red Sox' director of scouting (and a former manager of the Bosox), was talking about Sandy, too. He had a couple of friends from Massachusetts in tow—fans down to watch the Sox in training—and at one point he told us about a day back in the early nineteen-sixties, when he was an infielder with the Reds, and he and Whitey Lockman and Ed Bailey were sitting together on the bench, watching Koufax in action for the visiting Dodgers.

"Sandy is just chewing us up out there, putting down the batters in rows with that tremendous fastball," Kasko said, "but Ed Bailey keeps saying, 'Well, he don't look like nothing special to me. That pitch isn't much. I wish they'd give me just one crack at him.' Ed loved to pinch-hit, you know—he thought there wasn't anybody he couldn't hit. Well, a little later we're way behind in the game, and Hutch sends Bailey up to bat against Sandy, and it's one, two, three strikes, you're out. Eddie swings three times and doesn't come within a foot of the ball. He walks back to the dugout and sits down, and after a while

I give Whitey a little nudge and I say, 'Well, Ed, what do you think now?' And Bailey turns around, all red in the face, and says, 'He's *too straight!*' Whitey says, 'Yes—and so is a .30–.30.' "

O

Both leagues rang up strikeout records last year—a phenomenon attributable at least in part to the split-finger—and what one makes of this depends on whether one thinks like a batter or like a pitcher. Roger Craig smiled when I asked him about it and said, "I can't call it bad." Hernandez said, "What I'm concerned with is that the sixties brought us the slider, and now here's the eighties and this pitch. What's going to happen in the nineteen-nineties? What's going to happen to us hitters? The slider was a much harder pitch to hit than the curveball, and in the end they had to change the strike zone in order to even things out a little. The only thing on our side now is that the hanging split-finger is a great pitch to hit. It's just sitting up there on a tee for you."

The change that Hernandez alluded to—a historic proceeding in baseball, which has rarely altered its essential rules and ancient dimensions—came just after the season of 1968, when the two leagues showed a combined batting average of .236. Carl Yastrzemski won the A.L. batting title with an average of .301 that year, and in the same summer a rookie pitcher—the Mets' Jerry Koosman—accounted for seven shutouts, Bob Gibson achieved an earned-run average of 1.12 (a modern record), and Gaylord Perry and Ray Washburn threw no-hitters on consecutive days in the same ballpark. The batters were dying. The remedy, put into effect the following year, was to cut down the strike zone by a couple of inches, top and bottom, and to shave the pitching mounds from fifteen inches to ten inches above field level. Offensive statistics picked up almost at once (National League hitters batted .253 last year, and those in the A.L. .262), but many contemporary hitters believe that their eventual return to form was mostly because the batters began to recognize the slider a little sooner and to attack it with more success. I have also heard them say that the same thing will happen after they've seen the split-finger pitch more often. They may be whistling in the dark. For one thing, most pitchers who have mastered Craig's Little Jiffy say that they don't know exactly where the pitch is going to end up once it has been launched; in this respect, at least, it resembles the knuckleball to some degree. We'll see.

I asked Marty Barrett (of the Red Sox) and then Wally Backman (of the Mets) how many split-finger pitches each of them sees, and what they told me suggests that the pitch is much less employed, or less trusted, in the A.L. Both Barrett and Backman are bantam-size contact hitters (well, Barrett has a bit of power: he hit thirty-nine doubles last year) who bat second in power-laden lineups, which means that pitchers tend to work them with extreme care. Barrett told me that he didn't run into many split-finger pitches, perhaps because the pitchers were afraid that they'd get behind in the count and end up walking him. "I think the pitch is for bigger guys, who aren't as selective and will probably go to swinging at pitches that end up being balls," he said. "I get more fastballs. If Jim Rice got the pitches I get, he'd hit seventy home runs."

I told Backman what Marty had said, and he was surprised. He said he saw the pitch often. To be sure, if the leadoff man got on base just ahead of him he wouldn't be served many breaking balls, but whenever the Mets were behind late in a game the whole lineup would probably see the split-finger. "A lot of times, the split-finger is a ball," he said, "but even if you know that, it's hard to lay off it sometimes. I just think there are more guys in our league who are throwing the thing."

A further ingredient in the shifting batter-vs.-pitcher wars is the indisputable evidence that in the past four or five years the umpires in both leagues have responded to the breaking-ball and sinkerball epidemic by lowering the strike zone. There was no plan to this; it just happened. The high fastball—the old Koufax or Seaver hummer that crossed the plate at the level of the batter's armpits, which is still the official ceiling of the strike zone—would probably be called a ball today, and umps today are also calling a lot of strikes on pitches that cross below the knee-level demarcation. Contemporary umpires are handing out quick warnings on brushback or knockdown pitches as well, and as a result the batters feel free to take a better toehold up at the plate and swing hard at low pitches away—"diving at the ball," in the new jargon. As I have mentioned previously, Don Drysdale, the old Los Angeles intimidator, says that modern-day batters are less wary when up at bat, and he and some other thoughtful baseball people warn that one of these days somebody is going to get beaned by an inadvertent high, inside pitch. On the other hand, it is the lower strike zone that also makes the batters so vulnerable to the split-finger's skulking little ways, because so few of them will trust the umpire to call a ball on a pitch that ends up below the strike zone.

To return to the slider, there is very little agreement about its origins but unanimity about the fact that it is easy to throw and hard to hit. Bill Rigney says that it caught on in the National League in the early fifties, after Don Newcombe's sudden flowering with the Dodgers. "Erskine and Branca had those big old wide-breaking curveballs, but then suddenly here was Newk with his hard pitch," he told me. "It only broke about *this* much, but it was a bear. It just took over the league. It was easier to control than a curveball— you could throw it for strikes—and the batters hated it. I remember riding in the team bus before the 1948 All-Star Game, and Ted Williams was asking us, 'What's this new thing over in your league—this slider?' Well, he found out about it, too. A lot of batters used to put it down, you know—they called it a nickel curve—but they still couldn't hit it."

The slider is admired but mistrusted, for the evidence seems clear that it can destroy a pitcher's arm. The Dodgers discourage its instruction in their minor-league clubs, and a great many baseball people think it can permanently damage kid pitchers who begin to fool with it at the Little League and Pony League levels. "I like the slider," Herm Starrette told me, "but I'd teach it last to a young pitcher, if at all. It's a great pitch to throw when you're behind in the count and want to throw some kind of breaking ball. But it will hurt your arm unless it's thrown properly. I teach the loose-wrist slider—the Steve Carlton pitch. It has a shorter, quicker break, and it moves downward. The stiff-wrist slider is what you call the cut fastball. It's a flat slider."

Pitchers say that the standard slider is thrown overhand, with the forefinger and the middle finger slightly off center on the ball, and that the proper wrist action gives the ball the same spiral imparted to a passed football. The fingers are off center on the cut fastball, too, but the pitch, launched with a full fastball motion, results in a brusque, twisting action of the elbow and forearm that shortens the delivery—and, in time, a career.

"Right-handed pitchers can do better with the cut fastball against a left-handed hitter than against a right-handed hitter, because for the right-handed hitter the ball comes in on the same plane as the fastball, and you have a chance to get more wood on it," Starrette went on. "But if your slider breaks across and *down* to a right-handed batter, you've got a chance he'll miss it or bump the ball on the top half for a ground-ball out. If you're a right-hander facing a left-handed batter . . . well, most left-handed batters are low-ball hitters, so if you throw the stiff-wrist slider—that cut fastball—up and in, you can get by with it, because it's on the small part of the bat, in on the fists. And that's why pitchers go back to it, even if it's dangerous for them. Anything that works will be used, you know."

The slow or sudden ruin of an arm and a livelihood is on every pitcher's mind, and examples of crippled careers are to be found on all sides, although fans and pitchers alike prefer not to notice them. Steve Garvey believes that the near-epidemic of torn rotator cuffs (it is the section of muscle that encircles the arm in the same fashion, and at approximately the same site, as the seam that attaches a shirtsleeve to a shirt) arises from pitchers' trying to throw too many different deliveries, and from overthrowing in crucial game situations. "You see a lot of guys who used to throw hard who have lost a few miles an hour on their fastball after a couple of years," he said. "Then they go to other stuff, to compensate, and they get into trouble. Stress comes into it more than it used to, because there's so much more money to be made in the game. The desire to win in important situations has gone way up."

Craig, for his part, claims that his split-finger special will be kinder to pitchers in the end, for it is thrown with a full, easy fastball motion. "Hell, you can hurt your arm throwin' a pebble or a rock, or flyin' a damn kite," he said at one point, "but there's less chance of it this way." Other coaches and managers (Sparky Anderson is among them) are dubious, and say that we'll have to wait and see about the long-range effects of the split-finger. One pitcher showed me that if you repeatedly split your throwing fingers apart you will feel a twinge in your upper forearm, and said that he does exercises to compensate. *Any* overhand pitching motion is probably unnatural, for that matter. Joe Rudi believes that the spitball (still illegal, and still in the game, of course, because it works so well) is the most dangerous delivery of all. "You're gripping the ball off the seams, which is to say your fingertips have very little resistance, nothing to pull down against," he said. "When that part of the ball is wet, the ball suddenly comes flying out of there, and there's nothing left—no resistance at all. Your arm accelerates exactly at the point when it's begun to decelerate, and that's a great way to blow it out for good. It's like when you go to pick up a bag of groceries, only there's nothing in the bag. You go *oops*—and you've thrown out your back. I don't let the outfielders on my team throw the ball any kind of a funny way, even when they're fooling around in practice. A lot of young players have no idea how vulnerable the arm really is. It's a delicate mechanism."

In 1980, by the way, a wonderful young Oakland pitching staff, featuring Mike Norris, Rick Langford, Matt Keough, Brian Kingman, and Steve McCatty, led the American League in complete games (by a mile) and earned-run average, but after three years all but McCatty were gone, with their careers in tatters. One popular theory for the debacle was that Billy Martin and his pitching coach, Art Fowler, allowed the youngsters to stay too long in too many games (the A's had almost nothing in the way of a bullpen), but another theory claimed, or whispered, that Fowler had taught the kids the spitball.

○

SCROOGIE: The first screwball pitcher I ever saw was Carl Hubbell, the great—the word fits here—Giants left-hander of the nineteen-thirties, who, along with Joe DiMaggio, became my earliest baseball hero. I recall the thrilling moment at the Polo Grounds when my father pointed out to me that Hubbell's left arm turned the wrong way around when it was at rest—with the palm facing out, that is—as a result of his throwing the screwball so often and so well. (The ball is delivered with the hand and wrist rotating in an unnatural direction—to the right for a left-hander, to the left for a right-hander—and the pitch breaks wrong, too. It's what pitchers call "turning it over.") I couldn't get over Hubbell's hand; it was like meeting a gladiator who bore scars inflicted at the Colosseum. Since then, I have talked with Hubbell a few times—he's a thin, stooped elderly gent who lives in Mesa, Arizona—and whenever I do I can't help stealing a glance at his left hand: it still faces the wrong way. The prime screwballer of our time is Fernando Valenzuela, of the Dodgers. His pitching arm looks perfectly normal so far, I'm sorry to say.

Last summer, I ran into Warren Spahn, the old Boston Hall of Famer, in the visiting-team dugout at Fenway Park. He was there for an Old Timers' Game—he's a regular at these events—and he was wearing an old Braves uniform, with that tomahawk across the chest; he played twenty years for the Braves, eight of them in Boston ("Spahn and Sain and pray for rain") and the rest in Milwaukee, and his lifetime three hundred and sixty-three victories are still the most compiled by any left-hander. Spahn, a leathery, wiry, infallibly cheerful man, was sitting with some of the Texas Rangers (they would play the Bosox that afternoon, once the exhibition innings were over), and in no time he had begun teaching his famous sinker-screwball delivery to another left-hander—the veteran Mickey Mahler, who was trying to stick with the Rangers as a middle-innings relief man.

"Look, it's easy," Spahnie said. "You just do this." His left thumb and forefinger were making a circle, with the three other fingers pointing up, exactly as if he were flashing the "O.K." sign to someone nearby. The ball was tucked comfortably up against the circle, without being held by it, and the other fingers stayed up and apart, keeping only a loose grip on the pill. Thrown that way, he said, the ball departed naturally off the inside, or little-finger side, of the middle finger, and would then sink and break to the left as it crossed the plate. "There's nothing to it," he said optimistically. "Just let her go, and remember to keep your hand up so it stays inside your elbow. Throw it like that, and you turn it over naturally—a nice, easy movement, and the arm follows through on the same track." He made the motion a few times, still sitting down, and it certainly *looked* easy—easy but impossible.

Spahn went off to join some other uniformed geezers, and I asked Mahler if he intended to work on the pitch, now that he'd had it from the Master.

"Oh, I don't think so," he said. "I'm trying to learn the screwball from our pitching coach, and this would mess me up for sure." He seemed uncomfortable, and after a couple of minutes he told me that a little earlier he and Spahn had been standing near the stands and some kids there had asked him, Mickey Mahler, for his autograph. "They asked me—not Warren Spahn," he said. "Can you *believe* that?" He was embarrassed.

O

I don't like to see young pitchers get their hearts broken in spring-training games, but it's much worse when it happens to somebody you know and remember and care about—to a veteran, I mean. In Winter Haven, the starting pitcher for the Tigers one afternoon was Frank Tanana, a thirty-three-year-old lefty with fourteen years' service in the majors. Like many fans, I remembered him as a slender, dazzling left-hander when he first came up with the Angels. He led the league then with two hundred and sixty-nine strikeouts in 1975, and went 19–10 the next year, and the year after *that* his 2.54 earned-run average was the best in the league. (A scout told me once that as a teen-ager Tanana had played in a high-school league in and around his native Detroit, where two strikes on a batter retired him and three balls meant a walk. "Nobody touched him there—it was just a mismatch," the scout said. "Everybody got home for supper early that spring.") But Tanana went down with a rotator injury in 1979 (his pitching motion was across the body—a dangerous habit for a fast-baller), and he was a different sort of pitcher after that. He lost eighteen games for the Rangers in 1982, but then he began to do better. He is smart, and he knows the corners, and he has become a master at changing speeds. Over the last four years, he won forty-six games and lost forty-seven while toiling for the Rangers and then the Tigers, but there was more arm trouble last year. Against the Red Sox, in his outing at Winter Haven, he gave up ten runs on eleven hits, and couldn't quite get the last out in the third inning. When he left, he raised his cap to the Boston fans just before he disappeared into the dugout, and got a nice little hand in return. I hated it.

The Sox' opponents the next afternoon were the Montreal Expos, a team that has systematically stripped itself of most of its expensive stars and is engaged in filling out its roster with youngsters and retreads. Len Barker threw three pretty fair middle innings for the visitors, giving up a lone run on three hits, but I felt edgy the whole time he was out there. A hulking, six-foot-four flinger with blazing speed, Barker had a brief time in the sun with the Indians at the beginning of this decade, when he led the American League in strikeouts two years running. Early in the 1981 season, in a game against the Blue Jays, he achieved the ultimate rarity, a perfect game: no hits, no walks, no runs, nobody on base. His occupational injuries began in 1983, and ultimately required extensive surgery on the elbow of his pitching arm, and he never had a successful or pain-free season after that. He moved along to Atlanta in time, and spent all of last summer with Indianapolis, a Class AAA minor-league team, but his most common address was the disabled list. He didn't make the team this year, it turned out; the Expos gave him his release just before the season started, and his career may be at an end at last. Another rotator-cuff casualty, Bruce Berenyi, gave it a last try this spring with the Expos, but the pain was too much, and he announced his retirement a few days after camp opened; he had been with the Mets and, before that, the Reds, but he never returned to form after shoulder surgery two years ago. He was a hard thrower, too. Bob McClure, a left-handed ten-year man who has worked mostly out of the bullpen, hung on and made the Expos' opening-day roster—an exception in this unhappy litany, for he has made do in the majors ever since his rotator-cuff trauma in 1981. His spring wasn't exactly carefree, however: just before the regular season began, he gave up nine runs to the Yankees in two-thirds of an inning of work, during a grisly 23–7 blowout at Fort Lauderdale.

Earlier, when I was out in Arizona, the Athletics had announced that Moose Haas, a prime starter for them last year until he was sidelined by bursitis, was suffering from a pulled muscle in the rotator cuff of his pitching shoulder and would be unable to start the season. And then, a bare day or two before the season began, Pete Vuckovich announced his retirement from baseball, thus terminating a distinguished eleven-year career that included a Cy Young Award in 1982, when he put together an 18–6 season for the Brewers, which helped take them into the playoffs and the World Series that fall. A torn rotator cuff got him the following spring. I was in the Brewers' camp at Sun City the day it was announced, and I well remember the waves of dismay that went through the clubhouse that afternoon—dismay but perhaps not surprise, for it was known that Vukey had pitched in great pain during the final stages of the pennant race the year before. In late September, two days after receiving a cortisone shot in his shoulder, he somehow went eleven full innings against the Red Sox, throwing a hundred and seventy-three pitches, and won the game. (I reported on this unhappy business at the time.) Vuckovich underwent extensive shoulder surgery early in 1984 and sat out the entire season. He was never sound again, but he just wouldn't give up. As scarcely needs saying, he is a man of enormous determination, pride, and stubbornness. The Brewers demoted him a year ago, but he refused to report to the minors; then he changed his mind and went to Vancouver after all, when he threw well enough (a 1.26 E.R.A. in six games) to be invited back to the Brewers again in September. Now it's over for him.

Vuckovich and Haas and McClure were on the same Brewer pitching staff in the early eighties, and so was Jim Slaton, who also suffered a rotator-cuff injury but eventually recovered. So was Rollie Fingers, the slim, flamboyant relief pitcher who won his Cy Young in 1981 but could not pitch for the team in the playoffs or the World Series in 1982, because of an injury to his forearm that forced his retirement three sad seasons later. And so on. I don't think we should draw any particular conclusions about the Milwaukee club of that time, beyond its famous combativeness and pride, but the point I am getting at here is that all the pitchers just mentioned, with the exception of Berenyi, came up in, and mostly pitched on, American League clubs. To go back a bit, we should also remind ourselves that the 1980 Cy Young Award winner in the American League—Steve Stone, who won twenty-five games and lost seven for the Orioles—was forced into retirement by elbow miseries after but one more summer's work. When three successive Cy Young winners in the same league—Stone, Fingers, and Vuckovich—together arrive at a point when none of them is able to throw a pitch in combat, the award suddenly begins to take on the meaning of a Purple Heart.

Tony Kubek, the NBC baseball commentator, often points out that the designated-hitter artifice, which was adopted by the league in 1973, allows a manager to stay with his starting pitcher for as long as he seems to be pitching effectively, even though his team may be behind in the game, and, furthermore, that A.L. pitchers have to make a larger number of high-level, high-strain pitches per game, because they are facing an additional dangerous bat in the lineup in the person of the designated hitter. Kubek remembers asking Catfish Hunter about the D.H. rule when it was first enacted (Hunter pitched in the A.L. exclusively), and the Cat said, "Well, it's going to make me a lot more money, and it's going to shorten my career by about two years"—a dazzling prognostication, it turned out, for Hunter's number of games won, complete games, and innings pitched suddenly rose after 1973 (he led the league in all three categories in 1975) and then almost as quickly dwindled, when arm miseries overtook him. By 1979, he was down to 2–9 with the Yankees, and by the next year he was gone, at the age of thirty-three.

Steve Garvey, another thoughtful mikado of the pastime, is also convinced that the designated-hitter rule has been a stroke of very bad fortune for the A.L. pitchers. "Because there's no pinch-hitter, the good starting pitchers stay in the game longer and run into more of those stressful late-inning situations—a men-on-base, close-game crisis, where they'll be throwing that much harder just when their arms are getting tired and are most vulnerable," he said. "There are very few easy batters in big-league lineups now, and in the American League, of course, the pitcher never gets to pitch to the other pitcher. There's no rest for him, I mean. Count up the good American League starters we've lost these past few years and see. It's not a situation you want to think about."

Perhaps we should think about David Bush instead. Last year, in the midst of spring training in Arizona, David felt some minor and then not so minor twinges of pain in his right shoulder, and finally consulted Mark Letendre, the Giants' new trainer, who had just ascended to the post. Letendre poked and pulled and then diagnosed a mild rotator-cuff injury ("My first rotator cuff!" he exclaimed to Bush), and suggested anti-inflammatory drugs and rest. Bush, who is a veteran baseball-beat writer with the San Francisco *Chronicle*, refused to baby himself, and did not miss a single deadline ("I'll play through pain," he said stoutly), and there is some hope that he may have made a complete recovery. When I inquired about the possible source of the injury, David finally confessed that it might have happened when he heaved his wife's clothesbag up on his shoulder the morning she was flying back to the Bay after a conjugal visit to Scottsdale. Lesly Bush, a stylish lady, does not travel light.

○

THE HOOK: New fans always want to know what the manager is saying to his pitcher when he goes to the mound to take him out of a game. The answer is: Nothing much. There are four or five new baseball books out every week, it seems, and soon, I don't doubt, there will be an anthology of pre-shower epigrams. In Scottsdale, I saw a thin Athletics right-hander named Stan Kyles give up a walk and a single in the fifth inning. Then he walked three batters in a row—walking himself to Tacoma, in effect. Eventually, manager Tony LaRussa showed mercy and got him out of there, and when the game was over I asked LaRussa what he'd said to Kyles. "I said it looked like he'd run into a moving target today," Tony said.

Bill Rigney told me once that one day in his first summer as a major-league manager he went out to the mound in the Polo Grounds to yank a veteran Giants relief man named Windy McCall, who had got nobody at all out during his brief stint that day. Rig said, "I walked out there and I said 'How are you?' and McCall said 'Great. How the hell are *you*?' So I never asked that question again."

○

I took a drive across the desert to visit the Indians in Tucson—in particular, to watch their two new genuine stars: Joe Carter, who rapped twenty-nine home runs last year and led both leagues with a hundred and twenty-one runs batted in; and Cory Snyder, the phenom sophomore, who, by sudden consensus, is said to have the best outfielder's arm in the majors. The Indians are trying to deal with an unaccustomed emotion—hope—and may make a real run at the leaders in the American League East. The most hopeful Indian of them all, I found—by far the most cheerful pitcher I talked to this spring—was Tom Candiotti, a youthful-looking, almost anonymous twenty-nine-year-old right-hander, who had been informed the day before by Tribe manager Pat Corrales that he would be the team's opening-day pitcher. A year ago, Candiotti was invited to Tucson for a look-see by the Indians, in spite of his most ordinary seven-year prior career, passed mostly in the bushy lower levels of the Milwaukee organization. He had a scattered 6–6 record while up with the Brewers, but had spent all of the previous, 1985 season in the minors; three years before that, he sat out an entire season after undergoing elbow reconstruction. Cleveland wanted to look at him because of some gaping vacancies on its own pitching staff and because Candiotti had experienced some recent success while throwing a knuckleball in a winter league in Puerto Rico. His early adventures with the flutterball in the American

League last summer were a bit scary—he was 3–6 by mid-June—but he finished up with an admirable 16–12 record, including seventeen complete games. Only scriptwriters fashion turnabouts like that, but Candiotti's help had come from a more reliable source—Phil Niekro, a forty-eight-year-old knuckleball grand master (only four other men in baseball history were still active players at his age), whom the Indians picked up on waivers when the Yankees released him just before the 1986 season got under way. Niekro had won his three-hundredth game at the end of the previous season, and he went 11–11 for the Tribe last year, his twenty-third in the majors; Candiotti and everyone else on the club gave him much of the credit for the younger man's wonderful record as well.

"Knucksie is my guru," Candiotti told me. (Knucksie is Niekro: sorry.) "He coached me during every game and in between. Last year—early last year—I was trying to throw the knuckleball hard all the time. It was a nasty pitch but tough to control, so I was always in trouble—3–0, 2–1. He said, 'Listen, that's not the way to do it. First of all, you *want* the batter to swing at it. You don't want to go 3–2 all day. So take a little off it, make it look tempting to the batter as it comes up to the plate.' I did that, and after a while I began to get a little more movement on my slower knuckler. I haven't come close to mastering anything yet, the way he has, but I'm better."

The knuckleball looks particularly tempting if you are a lizard or a frog. It is thrown not off the knuckles but off the fingertips—off the fingernails, to be precise—which renders the ball spinless and willful. It meanders plate-ward in a leisurely, mothlike flight pattern, often darting prettily downward or off to one side as it nears the strike zone, which results in some late and awkward-looking flailings by the batter, sudden belly flops into the dust by the catcher, and, not uncommonly, a passed ball or a wild pitch. It is the inelegance of the thing that makes it so unpopular with most managers (some of them call it "the bug"), but distinguished and wonderfully extended careers have been fashioned by wily Merlins such as Wilbur Wood, who had two twenty-four-victory seasons in the course of his seventeen-year tenure (mostly with the White Sox) in the nineteen-sixties and seventies; Charlie Hough, of the Rangers, now in his eighteenth year in the big time; and, of course, Hoyt Wilhelm, who went into the Hall of Fame after twenty-one years of knuckling, with a record—let's say "all-time" this once: with an all-time-record one thousand and seventy game appearances. The pitch, in short, is unthreatening to a pitcher's arm, and I have often wondered why it isn't practiced and admired more widely.

Candiotti, an agreeable fellow, told me that Niekro had emphasized that it was absolutely necessary for a knuckleballer to field his position well and to learn how to hold the runners close (Niekro's pickoff move is legendary), since the bug is unhurried in its flight and tends to spin weirdly when nubbed along the ground. "The pitch takes its time, you know," Tom said. I asked how much time, and he said that his knuckleball had been timed between forty-eight and seventy-one miles per hour last year. "Seventy-one is *slow*, you understand," he said. "You just can't believe how easy on your arm this pitch feels. Knucksie keeps telling me that I'll go through a lot of frustrating days with the knuckleball, and sometimes you'll get racked up. But the thing to do is stay with it."

Niekro pitched against the Giants that afternoon in beautiful little Hi Corbett Field, and tried his damnedest to stay with the pitch. It was a bright, windy afternoon (the knuckleball becomes even more flighty in a breeze, or else refuses to perform at all), and Phil gave up four runs, including a couple of walks and two doubles, in his three-inning outing. The pitch seemed to arrive at the plate in stages, at the approximate pace of a sightseeing bus.

Niekro, whom I found in the Indians' empty clubhouse after his stint, was not much cast down. "I haven't thrown a real knuckleball all this spring training," he said. "It's too dry here, and the wind keeps blowing. I can't sweat. Just can't get it right. If the knuckleball ain't there, I'm a mass of confusion. I can't defend myself with a fastball or a slider, like other pitchers. It seems like it takes me a little longer to find it each spring."

He sounded like a man who had been going through his pockets in search of a misplaced key or parking-lot stub, and it came to me that I had sometimes had this same impression when listening to Dan Quisenberry, the Kansas City sidearm sinkerballer, talk about *his* odd little money pitch. Niekro said that this feeling around for the perfect knuckleball—this sense of search—was a year-round thing with him. "You've got to sleep with it and think about it all the time. It's a twenty-four-hour pattern," he said. "The margin for error is so slight, and it can be such a little-bitty thing—your release point, the ballpark, your fingernails, the ball you've just gotten from the umpire. If anything is a fraction off, you might not have a thing out there." He crooked his fingers and waggled his wrist. "It's hunt and peck, all year long."

Niekro is lean and gray-haired, with an easy manner and a sleepy sort of smile. Watching him take off his spikes and his elastic sock supporters and the rest, and tuck his gear into his square-top travel bag (the club was going on a road trip the next day), I was reminded of an old-time travelling sales-man repacking his sample case. Niekro is unhurried and precise in every-thing he does. I have never seen a neater ballplayer. Something else about him surprises you, too, but you can't quite figure it out at first: he is a grownup.

He told me that helping Candiotti had been a treat for him, because the young man had exactly the right makeup for the job. "He knows his limita-tions," he said. "He changes pitches better than I did when I was his age. I used to go: Bang—here's a knuckleball. Bang—here's another. He's really pitching: Go at one speed, go at another. Take a little off. Throw one knuckler to set up another one. But he's sort of like me, at that. I won my first game in the big leagues at the age of twenty-six, and he won his at the age of twenty-five. So he's right on track."

Niekro's lifetime record is an herb garden of statistics—three twenty-game-or-better winning seasons, two years when he *lost* twenty games (he combined the two in 1979, when he won twenty-one games for the Braves and lost twenty), and a 17–4 record in the summer of his forty-fourth year: the best percentage in the league that season. He has thrown a no-hitter, he has struck out four batters in a single inning, and he has thrown four wild pitches in one inning and six in one game. Any day now, he and his brother Joe, who is a starting pitcher for the Yankees, will set another record when they surpass Gaylord and Jim Perry's lifetime total of five hundred and twenty-nine victories by pitcher brothers. Joe, who also throws the knuckler, is forty-two, and has won two hundred and fourteen games.

"I learned my knuckleball from my daddy," Phil said, "but Joe was a different kind of pitcher at first. He had a three-quarter mediocre curveball, a fastball, and a slider, and he was just getting by in the major leagues. I think he was on his way down when he said, 'Oh, hell—all right,' and he went into his back pocket and began throwing the knuckleball, too. It took him three or four years to make the transition, but once he got it he was as good a pitcher with the knuckleball for eight or nine years as there'd ever been in baseball."

I asked Niekro if he was ever tempted to giggle when one of his pitches danced away from a batter for strike three.

"Oh, no—you can't do that," he said. "I won't ever laugh at him, but I'll laugh with him sometimes, if I see he's laughing over it. We'll have a little fun out there." He gave me a glance, and said, "You know, there's lots of guys can throw the damn knuckler for fun. It ain't all that hard to pick up. But here's a game: You're out on the mound, here's the strike zone, and there's a man standing there with a bat in his hand. It's a 3–2 count, there's a man on third base, or maybe the bases are loaded, and now you've got to throw the knuckleball over the plate on pitch after pitch after pitch—because he's sure as hell going to foul some of them off. You just go back to it and throw it for another strike, and that's not fun. That's a little different."

Niekro got up and pulled off his sweatshirt. He is trim and narrow, and his body doesn't show his years. He is famous for never doing conditioning sprints, never running at all, and when I mentioned this he smiled and said, "I've never run the ball across the plate yet." An old joke. "I stretch and I do just about ever'thing else," he said, "but I don't do weights. It's just that much more muscle to tighten up when you've finished for the day. Maybe those big boys can throw the ball harder, but when the game's over you see them iced down from their wrists to their hips. I never ice. Well, maybe I did about four times in my career, but I can't exactly remember the last time. Maybe I'm getting old."

○

GRUMPY: Some of us were eating our cold-cuts lunch off paper plates in the Cardinals' pressroom before a Cards–Blue Jays game in Al Lang Stadium, when I noticed that the small, snub-nosed man sitting next to me was Birdie Tebbetts, the old-time Tiger catcher; he also managed the Reds, the Braves, and the Indians. Tebbetts is seventy-four years old, and scouts for the Indians. He listened to our conversation about pitches and pitchers, and muttered, "Sometimes I watch one of these young pitchers we've got, and I tell my club, 'This man needs another pitch. By which I mean a strike.' "

○

There is a lot to this game. As my spring trip began to run out, I realized how many aspects of pitching I hadn't gone into yet, or hadn't asked enough about—what it takes to break in as a major-league pitcher, and how great a part luck plays in the kind of pitching roster and the kind of club a rookie is headed for, for instance. Pete Rose said that it was often easier for a youngster to make it up to the majors in the middle of a season, if the chance came, because his control would be better than it was in the spring. What about bum steers—poor advice from a pitching coach, or the wrong advice for that particular pitcher? Charlie Leibrandt, a first-rate left-hander with the Royals, told me that the Cincinnati coaches had insisted that he was a power pitcher, a fastballer, when he tried to catch on with the Reds some years ago, because they were a team that specialized in big hard throwers. He had four scattered, so-so seasons with the team, then went back down to the minors, and when he came back, with the Royals, it was as a breaking-ball, control sort of pitcher, and he felt at home at last. "I remember being on the mound at Riverfront Stadium and hearing the ball popping over the sidelines while the relief pitchers warmed up to come in for me," he said cheerfully. "I was about to be gone again, and somebody in the dugout would be yelling 'Throw strikes!' and I'd think, Oh, *strikes*—so *that's* what you want! Why didn't you say so?" I also wanted to talk with the Mets about how they bring along *their* young pitchers, because they seem to be so good at it. And someday I want to sit down with a first-class control pitcher and go over a video of a game he has just pitched, and make him tell me why he chose each pitch to each batter, in every situation, and how it related to what patterns he had thrown before that.

The business of strength came up a lot in my conversations, I noticed—

which pitchers lasted, and why, and whether young pitchers today were in better shape than their predecessors twenty or thirty years ago. Almost everybody said yes, they *were* in better shape today, and probably stronger, too. Aerobics and weight work and a much better understanding of nutrition came into that, of course, and so did plain genetics; ballplayers are all noticeably bigger and taller than they used to be—you can see it. But I heard some interesting opinions to the contrary.

Jim Kaat, the deep-chested left-hander who pitched twenty-five years in the majors (he is one of the few players at any position who have performed in the big leagues in four calendar decades), told me that he'd been wondering about the decline of the fastball pitchers—the burners—and about why so many pitchers of his generation, like Gaylord Perry, Nolan Ryan, and Phil Niekro, had lasted so long. "One of my theories is that we did a lot of work by hand when we were kids," he said. "Mowed the lawn, washed the car, shovelled snow, and walked. I used to walk everywhere." (Kaat grew up in Zeeland, Michigan, on the western edge of the Michigan peninsula.) "Now you see kids who haven't logged as many sandlot innings as I did, and when they come into baseball you don't know how big they're going to be. When I was eighteen, my body was developed."

Mel Stottlemyre, the old Yankee wizard who is now the pitching coach for the Mets, said, "There's no doubt that there are fewer good arms than there used to be. For one thing, a lot of young pitchers start throwing breaking balls when they're too young, and they don't develop their bodies the way they could have. That's going to take a toll. I think there's less plain throwing than there used to be—just throwing the ball back and forth with your neighbor or your brother. There are more things for kids to do now, so they end up not playing catch. You see kids in Little League who aren't strong enough to pitch at all, hardly, and there they are, throwing breaking balls. There's nothing I hate worse than to see a Little Leaguer with his arm in ice—but I've seen that a lot." (Mel Stottlemyre's twenty-one-year-old son Todd, by the way—or perhaps *not* by the way—is a pitcher with the Toronto organization; he is still a year or two away from the majors but is considered one of the great young prospects in the country.)

Other pitching people I talked to did not quite agree. Dave Duncan, the pitching coach for the Athletics, said, "I'm sorry, but I just don't go along with that idea about the old days. Oh, young players and pitchers may have lost some of that sandlot toughness, but baseball is taught so much better now, with all that work on body strengthening and conditioning, that I think skill and muscular development are way ahead of what they were when I first came along."

I put this question to Tex Hughson, the commanding old Red Sox righty of the nineteen-forties—he is seventy-one now, but still long and cowboy-lean; he used to raise quarter horses near San Marcos, Texas—and at first he went along with Duncan and that group. He was sure that young players at the college and minor-league levels were far stronger and better developed than they had been in his time. But then I mentioned what Jim Kaat had said—what I think of as the Walk-to-School Factor—and he did a turnabout. "Why, that's so," he said cheerfully. "Course it is. I walked to school every day—three miles on a gravel road in Kyle, Texas, throwin' rocks the whole way. Maybe I picked up some control that way, and developed my arm. Chunked at everything. But if it was bad weather my mother would drive us in our old Model A Ford." And I'd heard somewhere that Roger Clemens also walked three miles to school—it's always three miles, never two or three and a half—when he was a kid.

I didn't know what to think, but in time it came to me that, of course, it is mental toughness that matters most of all to a pitcher: nobody would disagree about that. I was strengthened in this conviction by a talk I had with Bob Ojeda, the left-hander picked up by the Mets in a trade with the Red Sox, who played such a sizable part in his team's triumphs last summer and last fall. Ojeda is midsize and tightly put together. His uniform fits him perfectly— not a rumple or a wrinkle on the man or his clothes. He looks dry-cleaned.

When I asked how he would describe himself, he said that he was a man who had to work at his work—think ahead of the hitters, concentrate on control, and come inside on the batters. This last can be a long lesson for lefties at Fenway Park, where Ojeda first came to full command, because of its horribly proximate left-field wall. He told me that he had talked to Roger Craig over the winter (not about the split-finger, for Ojeda already possessed a peerless changeup, which he throws by choking the ball back in his hand), and Craig had said to him at one point, "You're a *pitcher*."

"That meant a lot to me," Bobby O. said. "If I hadn't learned some things over the years, I wouldn't be here. When I say I'm a pitcher, I'm thinking of guys like Mike Flanagan and Scott McGregor, of the Orioles. I always tried to watch how they worked, how they set up the hitters. Or Steve Carlton, if he was on TV. I remembered how they pitched in certain situations, how they changed from what they'd done before, because of what the game situation was—man on first, men on first and second, and the rest. To me, it doesn't matter if you strike out ten guys in a game. But if you've got the bases loaded and nobody out, and then you get your first strikeout and then a ground ball, how big was that strikeout? That's the kind of stat players notice. Tommy John sometimes gives up six, seven, eight hits in a game, but only one run, and that is the number that counts."

I told Ojeda that his victory over the Astros in the second game of the playoffs had been the sort of game I enjoy most—a first-class ten-hitter—and he grinned. "That's right—it was," he said. "There are always days when every ground ball is going to find a hole. Days when you have to reach back a little. It all comes down to how many runs you give up. I look at the runs—not whether they're earned or not. You look in the paper, and if you've lost it'll say 'Larry Ojeda.' " ("Larry" for "loser," as in a line score or box score: "L: Ojeda.") "A run is a run, and you try to prevent those. There's *so* much strategy that goes into that. Each day is different. Each day, you're a different pitcher. Consistency is the thing, even if it's one of those scuffle days. When I've started, I've been very consistent, and that's something I'm proud of. I led the league in quality starts last year—you know, pitching into the seventh inning while giving up three runs or less. That means something to me."

He said that breaking into a new league, with unknown batters, hadn't been especially difficult for him. "I was as new to them as they were to me," he said. He doesn't believe in extended studies of the opposing team's batters before the game. "I see them up at bat—where they are in the box, how they stand—and it clicks into place: Oh, yeah—you're *that* one. It's the situation that matters more than the batter—there's always the situation. Maybe this particular batter doesn't like to pop people in—maybe he bats .300 but only has fifty runs batted in. Then there are the guys who bat .260 unless there are men on base. Then they're much, much tougher up at the plate. Those are the guys I respect."

Like who, I asked, and Ojeda said, "I don't want to name them—I don't want to *think* about them—but I know who they are, and they know who they are. No, there really are some great, famous hitters that I don't mind seeing up at bat in certain situations, because I know those are the situations they don't like."

Ojeda relishes being on a World Champion team. "I can't get over what we did last fall," he said seriously. "When you grow up in this sport, all you hear is people talking about what they're going to do if they ever get into a World Series. But that's just talk—we went out and did it. I like the chance to do things. It's 'This *happened*,' and then there's no more talk. Back when I was a kid, I had those dreams of playing in a World Series someday, but so what? Every player in this clubhouse and every player in all the twenty-five other camps right now had those same dreams. But those other guys don't know how they'd do, and we know. To get there *and then win it*—that's the thing. Because who knows if you'll ever have another shot? If I'd still been with the Red Sox— If you'd gotten there and then you didn't win it, if you'd made some bad mistakes like some of their guys did—*major mistakes!*—and then you began to think you'd never get that chance back, because you'd never be there again . . . I don't think I could stand that."

Celebration

We were driving through East Harlem, heading for a ballgame. "Where does 'bullpen' come from?" my companion said. "I heard Ralph Kiner talking about it the other night, and he said it was from those Bull Durham tobacco billboards on the outfield fences, back in the old days. The pitchers warmed up out there, so the name carried over. That sounds logical, but it's almost too neat, don't you think? Now I suppose it's all going to get mixed up with this movie *Bull Durham*. But it would be good to know. And where does 'home plate' come from? That's a better question. I keep coming back to it, because it says so much about baseball and about other things. About ourselves. Home—'Safe at home,' 'Home is the sailor, home from sea,' and the rest of it. I make a lot of that *nostos*. But who gave it the name 'home' in baseball? It's never called 'fourth base,' you know. It must go way back to the beginnings of the game."

The light changed, and we crossed Second Avenue and swung up onto the Triborough ramp. We were on our way to Shea, and the Mets against the Reds.

"Well, there's 'Home' in Parcheesi, isn't there?" I said, digging out change for the toll. "Isn't it printed out there in the middle of the board, in that funny lettering? That's an old game, too."

"I guess so," he said.

"And what about that eighteenth-century nursery quatrain they keep reprinting in all the baseball anthologies?" I said. "You know—'The ball once struck, off speeds the boy' . . . something, something . . . 'then home with joy'?"

"Yes, I know it," he said. "That must have been about rounders, or some other children's game. So the usage was there before there was any baseball. Sometimes I think baseball was invented just to remind us of things. It's a living memory, and it has an epic quality—you can't get away from it. Think of the man at the plate and what he wants to do up there—travel that long way around, and all just to get back where he started from, back home. He's a pioneer. He has to wander and explore, but it's dangerous out there, and he remembers the other need as well—the need to get back home. You can die at second base."

"Base runners die at third, too," I said. "Look at the Yankees lately."

"Yes, but mostly you die at second, don't you?" he went on. "I don't know why, except that it's the farthest place from home. And if you forget the home place you're lost."

"You're out," I said.

"You've got it," he said. We laughed.

"But then you have to do it again and again, and then again, no matter how hard it is," he said, not quite as an afterthought. "It's the eternal return. It's that repetition and impediment that are so much a part of the game and the legend."

"Even talking about it, it's O.K. to repeat ourselves," I said.

"Absolutely," he said with satisfaction. "We participate in the epic by talking about it while it's in progress. It's a celebration."

For me, the ideal seatmate at a game should verge upon the taciturn, reserving comments or curses (or screamings, of course) for the serious business at hand, but I am prepared to make exceptions. The gent sitting to my right in the front seat of my Shea-ward Volvo on this steamy evening early in July looked stubbornly ill-prepared for our outing, in his buttoned-up shirt, striped tie, and rumpled navy blazer. He was solid and shaggy, with a noble beard, a seafaring complexion, a Homeric brow, a lidded but burning outbound-inbound gaze, a rumbling laugh, and a smile by turns gentle and razory. As exceptions are measured, he belonged on Mt. Rushmore: A. Bartlett Giamatti, president of the National League, who came to the post two years ago fresh from an eight-year term as president of Yale. A scholar in Renaissance literature, he had served twenty previous years on the Yale faculty, in the Department of English and Comparative Literature, picking up a burry assortment of honors and memberships and titles along the way (John Hay Whitney Professor of English and Comparative Literature, director of the Division of Humanities, Guggenheim Fellow, Woodrow Wilson Fellow, Fellow of the American Academy of Arts and Sciences, member of the American Philosophical Society, the Dante Society, etc., etc.), and writing such books as "The Earthly Paradise and the Renaissance Epic," "Play of Double Senses: Spenser's 'Faerie Queene,'" and "The University and the Public Interest." Baseball, for all its ordered paths, is a game of constant surprises, but its choice of a bearded Ivy League scholar-prexy, easily capable of turning the full mid-title colon, as the twelfth president of the senior circuit was a startler unmatched in the pastime since Al Weis's home run for the Mets in the fifth game of the 1969 World Series.

Giamatti's turn at the helm of Yale produced warmer relations between the university and its alumni and between town and gown, and, academically, a firming up of traditional standards; he brought in a succession of balanced budgets and, while expressing distaste for the role of "professional mendicant," achieved a handsome bulge in the endowment. Giamatti in person was candid, energetic, and, of course, splendidly voluble (he once referred to old-grad William F. Buckley, Jr., as a "limousine Luddite")—a nice range afield that certainly did not escape the notice of the baseball old boys who hired him. As expected, he has fitted smoothly and happily into his new command, and has acquired friends and devotees among the serried keepers of the game, including owners, general managers, front-office people, field managers, umpires, and (some, at least) writers. Last June, Peter Ueberroth announced that he would not be a candidate to succeed himself as commissioner of baseball when his five-year term expires at the end of 1989, and although no one has officially approached Bart Giamatti about the matter, he is, by consensus, the man most likely to take on the job.

As luck would have it, Giamatti and I kept running into each other at spring-training games in Florida and Arizona last March, and somewhere along the line we made a date to go to a game together during the regular season. Giamatti, by the time we met, had had a bumpy trip through the first couple of months of the season, thanks to the extended fuss over the new "discernible stop" clause in the enforcement of the balk rules (six hundred and forty-five balks had been called by the time of the midseason All-Star game, as against three hundred and fifty-six in the full 1987 season), and, more particularly, because of his almost unprecedented (for its severity) thirty-day suspension of Cincinnati manager Pete Rose after an umpire-shoving incident and an ugly near-riot during a Mets-Reds game at Riverfront Stadium on April 30th. However, my wish to spend a couple of hours with Giamatti at the park came not from any desire to ferret out his views on the late news or the smoldering issues of the game or to quiz him about the commissionership (by unspoken agreement, we never discussed it at all) but from the prospect of listening to a lifetime .400 talker strut his stuff in the proper setting. Giamatti's gab, I had already realized, is stylistically unique, displaying education and natural brilliance simultaneously, just as George Brett's swing says Charley Lau and *Watch out*. Standing beside the batting cage one evening at the Mets' spring-training camp at Port St. Lucie, he and I had watched Darryl Strawberry uncoil on a pitch and waft the ball lengthily into some mid-distant pine barrens. "Ah," breathed Giamatti, "that was *echt* Straw."

○

As we drove along the Grand Central Parkway and inserted ourselves into the pre-game lines of traffic headed for the Shea parking lots, Giamatti told me a little about his job. He said that a surprising amount of his time—part of almost every day, right through the season—is given to reviewing disputed plays and field incidents and rules infractions from games around the league. There is a prescribed process of evidence-gathering, assessment and argument, judgment, notice of fines and suspensions, appeal hearings, and so forth, which begins with an umpire's telephone call to the league office after the game in question, followed by his written report within the next twenty-four hours. Videotapes of the game are consulted in most cases, and Giamatti discusses the reports and the tapes with Phyllis Collins, the National League vice-president, and Ed Vargo, chief of umpires. "The actual rules don't come into these cases very often, except perhaps on questions of interference," Giamatti told me. "More often we're assessing the severity or the length of an argument on the field. Did the player have to be restrained? Did he precipitate fan reaction? Did he throw his helmet down in anger or did he just flip it? And so on. And, of course, it can be marvellous, because the *Rashomon* questions are always there. Does anyone know what *really* happened? You may want to go back and hear from the crew chief again, or even from the manager. Then, there's the telling and the retelling. The tape can be very helpful if there's been a brawl. You can slow it down to see who was doing what. You look and look, and then you say, 'Ooo—what was *that*? Go back, go back, go back! There! Who's that 29, and why did he do that?' Even so, you may learn something later on that changes your mind. Last year, I watched a tape of a melee involving the Braves and the Reds, and I decided that Mr. Ozzie Virgil"—Virgil is a catcher with the Braves—"had played a less than useful role in it all, and I wrote him a letter to remonstrate with him. Well, Mr. Virgil, to his credit, picked up the phone and called me and said, 'But you've got this exactly wrong. You misunderstood what you saw. I swung my arm like that because I was trying to get their guy off the pile.' A few weeks after that, there was another mass misunderstanding, in another park, in which Mr. Virgil featured prominently as a peacemaker, and I called him and said I'd seen this, and that I appreciated it. After that, Mr. Virgil and I became more than nodding acquaintances, and that was nice."

I asked whether baseball people had found it odd to hear themselves addressed as "Mister," for a change.

"That implacable first-naming seems to go way back," Giamatti said. "I think it's built in—a holdover from all those years when the players were the hired help, back before we got rid of the reserve clause. But they're grown men, not boys. In my first months on the job, when Chub Feeney, my predecessor, was staying around to show me the ropes, he saw a letter about an infraction I was about to send off to Dave Parker, and he advised against my

'Dear Mr. Parker.' But I didn't agree. I still like formality—it comes naturally to me—and these are grown men. Nowadays I call Pete Rose Pete, but when I first met him I called him Mr. Rose. I think you have to earn that intimacy. Baseball people are very *intime*, but there's also a reticence, a family dignity, that comes along with it. Bob Fishel, the wonderful American League executive who died the other day, personified that. So did Dick Howser." He paused and then said, "Well, owners tend to be about the age of the players' fathers, so maybe first-naming comes naturally."

I asked if there were some people in baseball who had been particularly helpful or welcoming when he first came into their special world.

"Chub was the premier," he said. "And, of course, he's a man who was born into baseball and has given his entire life to the game. He took me up in that wonderfully friendly way of his, and he was sterling. Now Ed Vargo is my standby, my buddy. But there were so many others. Pope Owens, of the Phillies. Chuck Tanner, Whitey Herzog, Al Rosen, Dallas Green. Bobby Brown, my opposite number in the American League. Frank Cashen has become a good friend, and so has Syd Thrift, of the Pirates. Some of them were interested in what I'd been doing before I came into baseball, and some less so. If there's one thing I'm an expert on, it's athletic stereotypes about academe and academic stereotypes about athletics, but it's easy to say that the baseball world showed much less prejudice about me, an academic, taking this job than the other way around. It was simply no contest."

Giamatti is close to his umpires, although the relationship is clearly a boss-employees one. The players are more distant, of course. "They think of me as a faceless bureaucrat in a suit, who can never know what it's like being out there at a particular moment in a particular game," he said. "What they do remember is being fined. Even now, a couple of years later, one of them may come up to me and say, 'Hey, you're the one who hit me for two hundred.' They don't like authority, and I admire that. I try to avoid the clubhouse. That's their workplace, their office, and they're in a hard line of work. Anyway, I'm one person who didn't come into baseball in order to make friends with the stars. I'd already known a whole lot of guys that age."

I said I'd sometimes wondered whether he wished, in retrospect, that he'd had his present power to fine and suspend back when he was running Yale, and his face lit up like a scoreboard.

"Well, maybe not with the students," he said when he'd thought about it for a minute. "There's almost no way to bargain in good faith with a student. But with the faculty—oh, would I have put it to good use!"

Did he mean there were more rules infractions among the Yale faculty than he'd found in the pastime?

"Are you kidding?" he cried. "Of course there were more! These guys, these players, are pretty good most of the time. They try to do the right thing.

But in my old job—" He shook his head. "Come to think of it, the number of people on the Faculty of Arts and Sciences at Yale and the number of ballplayers in the major leagues are almost the same—somewhere around six hundred and thirty. And if we're making analogies, the umpires would be the deans. And tenure? Well, I guess even Mike Schmidt doesn't have tenure. Put the two bodies together, and what you have is one vast, unstable company of prima donnas. Skilled, yes, but oh, brother!"

○

We got to Shea and parked at last—it was another full house for the Mets— and as we walked to our gate several fans recognized Giamatti and waved to him or greeted him by name. He waved back. He was talking about the daily and weekly procession of administrative detail that marches across his desk: changes in ownership, partnership alterations, season schedules, game reschedulings, television relations and revenues, scoreboard designs, ballpark music, ballpark leases, uniforms and uniform-lettering, umpire performance, umpire morale, umpire avoirdupois, spring-training sites and schedules, and—a very large detail indeed—dealings with the press. Each year, the National League issues forty or fifty bulletins to its clubs, and there is always something left over to deal with, or something unexpected happening in another part of what he called "the submerged subcontinent of administration." The week before, he had spent hours on the telephone in the course of dampening an "I Hate New York" campaign of baseball television ads in Pittsburgh—a very popular campaign, let it be said. A week or two before that, he had held extended discussions with Molly Yard, the president of the National Organization for Women, in the wake of some ill-considered remarks about NOW by Mr. Bob Knepper, the free-form Houston left-hander. "That was *exactly* like a Yale issue," Giamatti said cheerfully. "Last year, I worked as hard on my response to the Kevin Gross appeal as I worked on anything I did while I was in New Haven. It was challenging to try to be clear about cheating and what it meant, and to be fair at the same time." (Kevin Gross, a pitcher with the Phillies, was ejected from a game last year, and subsequently suspended for ten days, for affixing sandpaper to his glove, presumably in order to scuff the ball and alter its flight. Later on, I looked up the Giamatti opinion on the Gross appeal. Its ten pages of resonant text shone forth like Cardozo: "Acts of cheating are . . . secretive, covert acts that strike at and seek to undermine the basic foundation of any contest declaring the winner—that all participants play under identical rules and conditions. . . . They destroy faith in the game's integrity and fairness; if participants and spectators alike cannot assume integrity and fairness, and proceed from there, the contest cannot in its essence exist." Etc.)

All this and the rulebook, too. "When I first read through the rulebook, it seemed interesting but fairly simple," Giamatti told me. "But that was like buzzing a field from a low-flying plane—it all looked green and smooth and inviting. When I went back and walked over that same terrain on foot, so to speak, I began to find the holes and stumps and hollows and gnarled roots and treacherous washes in it. Thank God for Eddie Vargo, who annotated the book for me, and even added some cross-references—'See 7.04 and 4.10(d),' and so on. Now I've begun to learn some parts of it by heart. But there's no real end to it, because it's another wonderful compound of old law and accrued opinion, with a few passages where the intention is beyond clear interpretation. There's a sentence, part of 8.05—about what happens to the base runners when there's a hit or an error or a hit batsman or something else on a pitch that has just been called a balk—that Eddie and I have been talking about all year. I find all this pleasurably difficult. It may not be intellectual, but the intellectual quality of university life isn't very high, either, once you get into the administrative side. There are deeper implications, of course. The question of how a society goes about its recreation isn't inconsequential—not to me, at least. How human beings choose to recreate came up in my first book, 'The Earthly Paradise.' I think I've been involved in the same issues all along.

"There are people who insist that my going from my old job to this one was as if I'd suddenly taken up being a dogsled driver or something, but I don't agree. Both jobs involve historically oriented, retrospective cultures, very slow to change. They're closed in—not hermetically, but they're very conscious within themselves of who you are and of the kind of apprenticeship it takes to become whatever you're going to be. They're medieval cultures. My friends say it tells a lot about me that I was drawn to such things. There's even more, if you think about it. You're administering nonprofit organizations—the league is nonprofit—which means you have to work by suasion. You have multiple constituencies, equally intent on collaborating and competing. The departments are the teams, of course. Guilds and chivalric codes—medieval!"

O

Baseball first came looking for Bart Giamatti back in 1983, when an owners' search committee (with Bud Selig, of the Brewers, at its head) was seeking a replacement for Bowie Kuhn as commissioner and sensed the need to explore outside the immediate community of the sport. Peter Ueberroth, then engaged in administering the financing and mountainous details of the 1984 Olympic Games, in Los Angeles—he did it brilliantly—was the ultimate choice, but along the way the committee also interviewed the young president of Yale, who not only was showing a firm hand (some said more than firm) in dealing with a very difficult and divisive labor situation at Yale that year but also had written about the game of baseball with knowledge and feeling. Perhaps the best of his baseball pieces was a 1977 *Harper's* article, "Tom Seaver's Farewell," which flayed the Mets' ownership of that period for trading away a player of Seaver's ability, high principle, and clearly articulated sense of self-worth. The Mets, he concluded, had not perceived that "among all the men who play baseball there is, very occasionally, a man of such qualities of heart and mind and body that he transcends even the great and glorious game, and that such a man is to be cherished, not sold." Though Giamatti, it turned out, was not free to leave Yale just then, the combination of a strong-minded, loquacious administrator and a learned fan was hard to forget, and when the National League presidency became vacant in 1986 Peter O'Malley, of the Dodgers, came calling in New Haven.

Giamatti, in truth, knew more about the other league. He grew up in South Hadley, Massachusetts—in his words, "a place with an A. & P., a drugstore, a Filene's, and a college." His father, Valentine Giamatti, was a second-generation American, a professor of Italian language and literature at Mount Holyoke, and a Red Sox fan. With no movies and no television to distract him, young Bart grew up reading books and listening to Curt Gowdy doing the Bosox games from Fenway Park. His father took him to his first game there in 1946; Boo Ferriss was pitching for the good guys, and Bart recalls asking his old man why the fans kept booing. His father had been a graduate student at Yale some years before, and Giamatti can recall his talking about one shining day when the lordly Yankees came to New Haven to play an exhibition game and he saw Babe Ruth and Lou Gehrig playing catch on Yale Green. "Those *enormous* throws," Giamatti said softly. "My father's gone now," he went on, "and I've come to realize that I never did ask him what baseball had meant to him—whether it had helped him to become American or feel American, the way it did in so many immigrant families."

We went back to the Red Sox, an infirmity we held in common (we were having supper in the Shea press lounge by this time), and he recalled a long-ago day when a car with New Hampshire plates stopped at this particular gas station in South Hadley, near his house, and the driver got no service at all: "He got out and stomped around and stared at us—ten or twenty men and boys, just standing there in the service bay. He thought he'd come to a place where he could get gas, but he was wrong. The purpose was to let us stand in the shade of the bay and listen to the Red Sox. It was like that all over New England then, of course. The Sox were the lingua franca."

I said I'd found that some of that Red Sox fervor had dimmed in recent summers in New England, perhaps beginning after Carlton Fisk's heroic twelfth-inning home run in Game Six of the 1975 World Series. (The Bosox lost the seventh game and the Series the next evening.)

"Or even after Bernie Carbo's homer," Giamatti said. "Everybody forgets that Bernie had to tie up the game first. Maybe his was the highwater mark, because it made the next one possible."

We had somehow skipped over Game Six of the 1986 World Series, when the Mets (representing President Giamatti's own league, of course) survived defeat at the last possible instant, thanks to Bill Buckner's horrendous muff of a tenth-inning grounder at first base, and went on to seize a world championship that the Red Sox had held within their grasp. I had seen the miserably victorious Giamatti just after that game, and he had looked worn and wan, like Odysseus thrown up on still another beach: a man wrung dry by the gods.

"Everyone in America remembers where he was when Fisk hit his home run," Giamatti was saying. "My wife, Toni, and I were home in bed on Central Avenue, in New Haven, with the set on—it was after midnight, of course—and our three kids were supposed to be asleep, but, of course, they were outside, prowling around. Then they heard us yelling, and they came rushing in pretending they didn't know what was happening. We all ended up jumping up and down on the bed together."

We talked a little about baseball's power to act as a clear-amber preservative of long-gone innings and instants, and Giamatti said he was constantly surprised at the way old pitchers could recall an entire sequence of pitches they had thrown to a particular batter in a particular at-bat thirty or forty years ago.

I asked if he ever got back to Fenway these days, and he hunched his shoulders conspiratorially and whispered, "Now and then. Once this year, once last year. I make official visits to all the National League parks every season, of course—or try to—but this is off-duty. I even saw part of a Yale game this spring, too. I was back in New Haven on a weekend—my family still lives there, and I sort of camp out in New York during the week—and the coach, wonderful Joe Benanto, let me come and sit in the dugout for a couple of innings."

The Yale connection will not quite go away. I said I had noticed that a few baseball writers and columnists still tended to mention his professorial background and Ivy League roots whenever they disagreed with some edict of his. (This had come up in force at the time of the Pete Rose suspension, when a Philadelphia columnist, Peter Pascarelli—among many others, to the same general effect—complained in *The Sporting News*, "The ludicrously lengthy 30-day sentence dealt to Rose by a league president whose baseball credentials consist of waxing poetic about the beauties of Fenway Park . . . " and "To make Rose the guilty party . . . is to ignore significant evidence you'd think a Yale professor would weigh.")

Giamatti shrugged. "I don't want to be viewed as commenting on these people, but I have a very clear taxonomy in my head about who these particular writers are," he said. "There are about three of them who still like to go on about my background, but it's strange that when they want to take me to task they've never called me up to ask 'Why did you do that insane thing?' or 'What foolishness did you have in mind there?' Not once. Other writers and broadcasters are much better about that, but sometimes when one of them has slipped in some mention of me and Yale or me and Dante I tell the little story about when Pat Moynihan was campaigning for the Senate for the first time, and his opponent, early in some television debate, called him 'Professor.' Pat threw up his hands and said, 'Uh-oh—the mud-slinging starts!' "

The academic community and Yale itself can't quite shed the old connections, either. A number of people within the temple simply couldn't believe that Giamatti would move along into something like baseball, and there were scandalized late-night telephone calls and murmurous dining-hall conversations that came down to "He's *kidding*—he can't be serious!" Giamatti told me that his taking the job had seemed the ultimate *trahison des clercs* to some but that there had been divisions of opinion about it. "Historians and littérateurs tended to find it logical," he said. "Mathematicians and scientists were not happy. Philosophers almost enjoyed the idea. Some friends—I realized that I knew a lot of baseball fans on the faculty—even said, 'Great! Good for you!' For these valiant few I'd worked up a line that went 'I'm almost fifty years old and I've just fallen in love and run away with a beautiful redhead with flashing eyes whose name is baseball.' My wife, who's a blonde, said to me, 'Why did she have to be a redhead?' But, seriously, what you need to remember is that my taking the league president's job caused much less of a shock and seemed much less of a sellout to the academic community than my previous move, from teaching to administration—to being a college president. That was considered infinitely worse—it was as if I'd joined the Vietcong. There's a distinguished professor of literature at Columbia who stopped speaking to me the day I did that, but now that I'm in baseball we're friends again. It was that first move that was outré. Well, I'm not High Church anymore. It's as though I became a Quaker first and then an Anabaptist."

He laughed, and we got up and headed down for the game. Looking at him, I had the impression that he was still going over his last turn of phrase in his mind, like a brilliant painter stepping back from his canvas for an instant to see what he had just put up there.

○

It was a good night to be at the park—warm and muggy, but with a little edge to the occasion. This was the eighty-fourth game for the Mets, just past the midpoint of the long season, and although they held a six-and-a-half-game lead in the NL East over the second-place Pirates, the famous and favored locals had shown some recent vapory spells and still gave the impression that they hadn't quite taken firm hold on their fortunes. Just the night before, Cincinnati's Tom Browning and John Franco had held them to four hits in the course of a 3–1 shellacking. We were in Mets courtesy seats, directly behind home plate and ten or twelve rows up from the screen. During the evening, various members of Giamatti's *cuadrilla* at the league office turned up to join us, including Cathy Davis, who is housemother, travel agent, and big sister to the league's twenty-seven umpires; and, for a few outs or innings at a time, Ed Vargo. The Papa Ump whispered something to Giamatti at one point, and when Bart let out a laugh Vargo told me about it, too. "It was nothing," he said. "Only, just now in the umpires' room Frank Pulli was saying he's decided he's going to start calling the boss Angelo from now on." (*Angelo* Bartlett Giamatti—I'd never asked.) "He said he knew it'd probably cost him two hundred, but he didn't care. 'He's *paisan*, isn't he?' he said. I said, 'Make that four hundred.' "

"Frank Pulli is a strong character, with whom I've had a few moderate run-ins," Giamatti said. "He's also a fine umpire. You know, there's almost nothing like sitting with scouts at a game, because that's where you learn how this game is played. But I've learned that the umpires have a detailed, precise knowledge of baseball and what it takes to play it and win it. But, of course, all that is bottled up in them. They don't let it out."

The Mets' starter on this evening was Ron Darling, who had pitched for Yale in his day—pitched for Bart Giamatti, you might say—but I noticed that my companion didn't say much about the coincidence once we'd noticed it. Then I remembered that he, too, had to keep baseball bottled up now.

"I'm still a fan, but an entirely different kind of fan now," Giamatti said a bit later. "Not rooting is a deprivation. You're not just watching the game, you're trying to get the feel of the game—the umpires, the crowd, the ushers, the drinking. It's entirely different. You feel responsible for what's happening, and with the umpires you *are* responsible. It's like loving the theatre all your life and then becoming a producer. You still get that thrill, except you know more about the sets and the flats and the lighting board and what the unions are asking for today."

Darling finally set down the Reds in the first, after giving up a walk and a single, and as the teams were changing sides a fan came down the aisle and introduced himself to Giamatti. "Izzy Padula," he said, seizing the presidential paw. "Look, I didn't want to bother you, but my cousin is Joe Padula, who was a student of yours once, and he'd want me to say hello. He lives out in Brielle now and has a medical practice in Point Pleasant."

"Joe Padula!" Giamatti cried. "My God! Joe Padula was a student of mine for first-year Italian, back when I was an instructor at Princeton. Of *course* I remember him, but that must have been—it must have been 1964, and the class met on the second floor of East Pyne. Up the stairs and to your left. I can't believe it."

After Padula had taken his leave, carrying warm greetings to his cousin from his old teacher and invitations for him to call up when he was next in New York, I started to remind Giamatti about something, but he beat me to it, of course. "That's *exactly* what we were talking about!" he said. "That's like an old pitcher remembering a slider he threw back in 1950. Joe Padula—isn't that amazing! I think it must have something to do with remembering times when you were really focussed. It's about intensity."

There was a short, explosive noise on the field before us, and Giamatti and I shifted focus to the upper and outer right-field sector, where the ball, having encountered the bat of Darryl Strawberry, was now disappearing into the darkness behind the Met bullpen. Straw eased around the bases and accepted a low five from Wally Backman, who had come to the home place just in front of him. "Where did that *go!*" Giamatti said, his pleasure safely unnoticed in the forty-thousand-tonsils din. (Later we learned that the ball had bounced off the Reds' team bus, peacefully parked out in the lot.)

Jack Armstrong, the eponymous—*fairly* eponymous—Cincinnati right-hander, kicked the mound a couple of times as he rubbed up the new ball, but before he could deliver a pitch to Howard Johnson, the next Mets batter, home-plate ump Doug Harvey walked a few steps toward the mound, asking for the ball. He examined it for a moment, and then flipped it back to Armstrong, and the game went on.

"Did you see that?" Giamatti said. "That's not about scuffing the ball—no way. That's Doug Harvey letting the pitcher know he wants no response from out there. It's a little message. Doug Harvey is a master at running a game. His games move right along—you'll see."

The game—both games, in fact: the baseball and the baseball talk—flew along, almost too quickly and pleasurably for recapitulation. I did my best to keep up, and my scorecard still preserves some vivid Giamatti at-bats:

On inside pitches: "The umpire is caught in the middle—as usual. Because of some recent changes, he has to issue warnings from time to time, not because he thinks anything is going on but only because the batter is upset. It's a general warning—to keep order, but not as the result of any infraction or intention. And that's too bad: it's a misuse. The batters have the upper hand just now, and they're much less inclined to put up with something that was once accepted as a normal part of the game. That inside pitch used to be thrown to reëstablish the pitcher's part of the plate. There's a general effort to sanitize the game right now, and I don't care for it. I think a batter who crowds the plate—and more and more of them are doing it—should understand that it's a legitimate strategy in the struggle between him and the pitcher, and he can expect that tight inside pitch in response. And I'm not talking about anybody throwing at a batter intentionally or exacting punishment or paying him back—that's something else altogether. We don't want anybody charging the mound. I think my view about this is probably the umpires' view, too."

On ballparks: "More domes are coming, and I regret it. This game is meant to be played outdoors and on grass, but I don't see how we can expect a city to come up with a hundred-million-dollar stadium-bond issue and not want to amortize that with conventions and car-crushing contests and football and the rest, which call for all-season stadiums. What I don't understand is the lack of imagination in ballpark design. I've gotten fond of this place"— he gestured at the tatty encircling rows and banked levels of Shea—"but that's because I'm used to it. Modern ballparks are the most conventional architecture since Mussolini's social realism. Why can't we build an idiosyncratic, angular park, for a change, with all the amenities and conveniences, and still make it better than anything we have now? I just don't get it. A ballpark should be a box, not a saucer—everybody knows that—but why couldn't we walk *down* to our seats, for a change: dig a stadium, instead of always starting flat and then going up? It might even solve the wind problem in some places. Why can't we think up a stadium that would have some of the virtues of a Fenway Park—a place of weird angles and distances and beautiful ricochets? It could be done."

On instant replay: "We had that moment in Pittsburgh the other day when Paul Runge, who was working the plate, called a wild pitch but then reversed himself when he looked up on the Diamond Vision board and saw that the ball had actually touched the batter's bat and deflected. He called it a foul. There was a terrific stink, but I commended him later for not taking the easy way and denying he'd seen something he saw. A lot of columnists and commentators and media types got on me after that and said that now the instant-replay cameras would descend on baseball and would be used as the determining factor in close decisions, but they were wrong about that—as they could have found out if they'd bothered to give me a call. I don't like the instant replay. We don't need it for decisions, and for fans it damages imagination and diminishes our memories. I was talking with Stan Isaacs, of *Newsday*, about this just this afternoon, and I said that the 'Marseillaise' scene in *Casablanca* has absolutely lost its dramatic force, because we've all seen it so often. We know it by heart. It even occurred to me to make some kind of connection between instant replay and hard-core pornography, but then I decided it wasn't quite the example to give when talking about a family game."

On drunken fans: "The Mets are making a real effort to control drinking here, mostly by persuasion, and I think the situation has already got better. The same thing is happening in other parks, with differing degrees of success. It's something that has to be brought under control; we all have the horrifying example of the British soccer crowds before us. We get more letters and comments on call-in radio shows about the environment and ambience of baseball than about anything else, I think. The ramifications go on and on, sometimes in quite specific form. Beer drinking affects the condition of the rest rooms, and the state of the ladies' rooms is an important matter for baseball and the kinds of audiences and kind of future it will have."

On mascots, ballgirls, pre-game bands, etc.: "It sort of depends on how it's done. We don't have a halftime in this sport, thank God, but in some places I've begun to notice what I think of as the N.F.L.-ization of baseball. This isn't a patriotic-territorial military sport. I've fought against the pre-game parachutists. I think there are a few people in the business who secretly suspect that baseball isn't interesting or entertaining enough on its own. They're like theatrical companies who only want to do Shakespeare in motor-cycle boots and leather jackets. They've given up on the beautiful language."

On labor relations, owners v. players, etc.: "Everything in baseball is a throwback—No, I won't say that, no way! Everything in baseball . . . uh . . . goes back and back, which is why you see the owners acting like nineteenth-century capitalists at times, and the players acting like union members from the late nineteen-thirties. It's a nineteenth-century game, and people in it tend to be strongly individualist. Free agency is only about twelve years old, and baseball has been exempt from monopoly regulation all along. I think it still may feel exempt from a lot of other considerations and patterns of behavior as well. The players were chattels for far too long. I'm convinced that the sudden huge escalation in salaries came in part from a pent-up guilt among the owners about their delay in bringing about what was fair. Now the market has taken over. But it's hard to be an owner, and I trust and admire most of the ones I've come to know. It isn't easy to be a colleague and a competitor at the same time—to help set policy with the commissioner and to remember at the same time that the idea is to have intense competition. Baseball is a small industry—it's about like the paper-box business—but with this intense, worldwide visibility. It's like no other enterprise I've ever heard of."

On the balk rule: "It's beginning to work out. The pitchers have adjusted, by and large, and the media are calming down, too, I hope. Our National League umpires began calling that full stop last year, so it's not all *that* new. I've been kidded for adding the word 'discernible' to the language of base-ball, but there were ten or twelve other people in the room when we agreed on the language, and they all knew what it meant and what we were after. It had got so that the pitchers were just changing direction out there, instead of coming to the stop that the rules called for. Now they understand. What still fries me is the complaint that the balk calls were slowing up the game. Look, the pitcher balks, an umpire puts up his hand and points to the next base, and the base runner walks down there—it all takes less time than a batter stepping out and refastening his batting glove."

○

Giamatti sustained this lecternless flow without pause or visible effort, and kept his full attention on the game and its sideshows as well. He smoked Benson & Hedges cigarettes and drank a soda and chatted amicably with his colleagues and with a party of young men just behind us, whose tickets to the game had been left for them by John Franco, the Cincinnati bullpen ace—a schoolmate of theirs at Lafayette High School, in Brooklyn. "Sandy Koufax's old school," Giamatti said when they told us about this. "Also Fred Wilpon's—you know, the Mets' co-owner. And then Franco went on to pitch at St. John's, didn't he?" And very soon he was discussing which Italian neighborhood and which streets in Brooklyn our neighbors and John Franco had grown up in, and which city parks they had played in there.

"You're a fan," one of the young men said.

"Thank you, sir," Giamatti said.

The names of the National League starters for the All-Star game, less than a week away, went up on the scoreboard, and we discussed the lineup, position by position, and who wasn't there and why. Then the message disappeared, and Giamatti said, "Aw, c'mon! Leave it up there a minute, will you! That's *my* franchise, just for this week."

"I detect a bias," said one of the men behind us.

"Yeah, if you'd been in the other league, you'd have had Billy Martin *shot*—right?" said his companion.

Giamatti was silent, just barely, but he fielded the inevitable next question, about his current relations with Pete Rose, without missing a step. "Pete's a pro," he said. "He doesn't agree about the thirty days, but we've talked about it. He's a great man." To me, he added that he had received unsigned ballots from the twelve league managers listing their choices for the pitchers to be named to the All-Star squad—the league handles that part, not the fans—and that one of the ballots had come in with "Thirty days is still too long!" written across the bottom. "I saw Pete today," Giamatti said, "and the first thing he said was 'You get my ballot?' He was tickled."

I said that thirty days had seemed just about right to *me* (one of the umpires, Dave Pallone, had been pelted with objects thrown from the Cincinnati stands after the argument and the shoving incident, and had actually been forced to leave the field—a first in my baseball recollection), and added that I'd wondered about the kind of complaints that had come into his office after the decision, and their number.

"Well, we didn't keep exact count," Giamatti said, "but there must have been at least five hundred letters, and a few hundred phone calls on top of that. Seventy-five or eighty percent of the mail opposed the decision, and the great majority of those complaints came from Ohio and Kentucky, which is Reds country. And I'm not even talking about the obscene mail and calls—we don't pay attention to those. The letters in support of the suspension came from all over, but there weren't as many, of course. At that, the number of Pete Rose letters didn't approach what came to me in New Haven in 1981 after I made a speech laying into the Moral Majority, and the level of bitterness in this one didn't come close to what I heard after I once refused to let the Yale Glee Club sing the Solidarity anthem in a broadcast for the Voice of America. George Will practically stripped me of my citizenship. I was accustomed to being called a dangerous right-wing radical, but this time the student press began to compare me with General Franco and some other epigones of the right. So I got it in stereo that time. For sheer noise, the Rose thing was probably bigger. This was a more public issue, and Pete just about owns lower Ohio and points east and west. Actually, everybody feels that he or she owns baseball, right across the country, which is one of its incomparable assets."

At about this point, the scoreboard flashed a trivia question, asking us to name the Most Valuable Player of the 1982 All-Star game, in Montreal. Giamatti sat up.

"With these board questions, the answer is always a guy who is here at the park, on one of the two teams," he said. "Only this time I don't think—"

The answer went up a moment or two later: Dave Concepcion, the veteran Cincinnati shortstop.

"I knew it," Giamatti said. "Only, he happens to not be on the premises. Mr. Concepcion threw a base during a game argument a little while ago, and I had to let him know it would cost him a couple of days. He just withdrew his appeal, so he won't be around tonight to read his name up there. But it feels funny that I'm here and he's not. Should that bother me, I wonder."

○

The Mets and the Reds gave us a great show, it turned out. Ron Darling, cruising along on a two-hitter and still ahead by 2–0 in the sixth, suddenly gave up a single and then a low, hurrying two-run home run to Kal Daniels. Then Chris Sabo singled and Paul O'Neill bonked *another* homer: 4–2, Reds. If you had reached under your seat to retrieve a fallen peanut, you would have missed the whole thing. The Mets masses issued a bee-swarm murmur of disbelief, which Kevin McReynolds, in the Mets' half of the same inning, stilled with a leadoff wrong-field double, just fair down the line in right. I was on my feet, yelling, and so was Bart Giamatti: "Great call, Frank! That's staying on the ball out there!" To me, he said, "Did you see him get down that line on that call? Just great." He was talking about his first-base umpire, Frank Pulli.

The Reds changed pitchers, and Strawberry, with the encircling masses screeching and beating their paws in supplication, struck out mightily. But Howard Johnson walked, and Dave Magadan singled in McReynolds, to cut the Reds' lead to one. Gary Carter, up to pinch-hit, mattered in several ways, because Darling, approaching the on-deck circle, was now wavering once again on the edge of invisibility, with another loss or still another no-decision game—his specialty, so to speak—to show for his night's work. Carter bounced a single to left, tying the game. Spared for the moment, Darling was allowed to bat for himself, and stepped up gratefully, waggling his bat like Frank Merriwell.

"You remember how he used to hit at Yale?" said the other Old Blue, and Darling, on the instant, whacked the first pitch on a line into center, putting the Mets in front once again.

"Good call!" I shouted into Giamatti's ear. The noise around us was insupportable.

"I was impressed, myself," he said. We sat down again.

But Darling couldn't quite believe it all, either. With two out in the Cincinnati seventh, he nailed Barry Larkin on the shoulder (it was his second Larkin-plunk of the evening), quickly went to two balls on Daniels, and was gone. Randy Myers, the Mets' hulking left-handed fireballer, stalked to the mound, took a Clint Eastwood gander at the unpromising scene, and blew Daniels away on three straight fastballs.

It was one of those moments when a game fulfills the home crowd's uttermost desires, and even after the teams had changed sides and we had stood and stretched and root-root-rooted for the home team, the party din continued to swell and beat all about us, as bits of paper and peanut shells took wing in the soft summer air. Giamatti stretched his arms out along our seat backs and smiled and said, "Look, just look. Even the weather has changed—it's a great night for baseball. Here's a big, beautiful crowd behaving itself and having the time of its life, and I'm the only guy here in a coat and tie. But I don't care—you can't have everything, can you?"

The game rushed to its ending now, thanks to Randy Myers. He picked up the last six Cincinnati outs with a handful of pitches, fanning another batter and not allowing anything beyond the infield. The crowd ate it up, and for the last couple of outs everybody in the place was up on his feet, chanting and clapping, rocking along on the tremendous sounds from the loudspeakers, yelling for more. Giamatti and I looked around at the exuberant faces near us and stretching away from us and above us in countless rows. We were smiling, too, of course—it was terrific fun—but I think we were watching the crowd as well, perhaps in that self-conscious, smiley way that older people take on when they've been allowed into a kids' party. And, anyway, we'd been talking about baseball crowds. I had remembered some recent remarks of Giamatti's, as quoted by Murray Chass in a *Times* piece, about the possible expansion of the major leagues in the nineteen-nineties, and the current expectations, or demands, of a good many cities around the country that now felt it was their turn to have a big-league team, too. Giamatti had claimed there was an "entitlement mentality" at large among the American people, which said, "I have made my demand, I have made it courteously, I have made it stridently, but I have made my demand and I am entitled to the solution I have demanded." He called this point of view understandable but said that things didn't necessarily happen that way in the real world. Now I asked him if the same notion didn't extend to a lot of fans at the parks these days. Were they perhaps saying that they expected their team always to win when they were there, that they were entitled to a winning team, and that they could protest stridently or violently or drunkenly whenever that didn't happen?

"Could be," he said. "Maybe there's that carryover. But I'm old-fashioned enough to believe that this is a legacy of the sixties—the old conviction that if any private sentiment is strong enough it's entitled to carry the day. It's a form of late romanticism."

"Are you saying that George Steinbrenner is a hippie?" I said.

"I'll pass on that," he said, shooting me a look. "But there's a connection. Let's call the crowd feelings Emersonian. There's this wonderful American sense that if we will it, it will happen, because we're supremely gifted as a people. We have all this space and all this boundless energy. Nothing is beyond our grasp, and if obstacles inevitably do arise—whether technological or ideological or civic or accidental—there still can be no final check to the primacy of the heart. Yes, I believe that fans have come to believe that it's always their turn to win now and that it's not fair when this doesn't happen. That notion prevails in many cities and ballparks, though maybe not in Boston, where there's an older ethos that says you've never been promised *anything*, and that it's good enough for you to be able to get up in the morning and start reading some more. I almost think Boston fans don't want to win it all—they'd rather have winning out there as a shining ideal."

But what about the prevalent nastiness in the stands now, I wanted to know—the heavy drinking, the fistfights breaking out in the late innings, with young fans watching all *that* with such visible pleasure, and seemingly willing to forget the game in the process? What was going on?

"It's that notion that there should be no checks on frustration," Giamatti said. "We're not supposed to block it. We fans are licensed to come here and do virtually anything we want, because this is one of the last places where anything of the sort is allowed. Recreational violence in the stands is the entitlement mentality—not so much because we feel we're entitled to win as because we're convinced that we're entitled to do whatever we feel like. It's the sacramentalizing of the individual, the primacy of *me*."

The Mets took the field for the top of the ninth, and, out of habit, I began to pencil in some totals on the Mets side of my score sheet.

"Look," Giamatti went on, in his alert, cheerful way. "You and I are traditional fans. We come here in a ceremonial fashion. We don't exactly kneel, but we're interested only in that stuff"—he gestured at the diamond and the outspread field before us—"for our basic information. We come to testify. We're not participatory fans. For them, that object"—he pointed to the towering Diamond Vision board in left center—"is more important than anything that happens on the field. For them, it's the videos and the dot races and the commercials, which are probably all connected to rock music in the end. For us, it's still the pitcher and the batter and the score, which are connected to the printed page. This is our text, that's theirs. It differs from stadium to stadium, but there are places where the big board seems to be trying to make sure that the game never interrupts the show. I don't think that the rock connection automatically means violence. But there's a great section of the crowd now that comes to the games in order to move around, to see their friends, to drink, and to wait for the TV camera to point their way. The game is O.K.—they may even like it—but it's mostly an occasion for their privatized pleasures. It's going to be interesting to see how baseball accommodates itself to these two audiences. All of us are adept at reading signals nowadays, and most of the baseball clues are coming from the board and the loudspeakers. What I hear is a lot of Queen and Bruce Springsteen, and not much 'Take Me Out to the Ball Game.' Like it or not, those are the cultural expectations."

○

After the game, Giamatti and I walked down to the umpires' room, in the nether catacombs of Shea, so that he could visit his crew. The four men were sweaty but cheerful, and they greeted Giamatti almost effusively. Umps have a lonely life, and they love company. Giamatti congratulated them on a good game. Frank Pulli was tucking into some cold pasta on a paper plate. Giamatti asked after his wife.

"She's doin' great," Pulli said, "and now the doc says it looks like it's going to be twins."

"Two *more* Frank Pullis!" Giamatti exclaimed.

Doug Harvey, who is tall and white-haired and magisterial, peeled off his blue short-sleeved shirt and a soaked T-shirt and then started unstrapping the hinged plastic upper-body and upper-arm protector that home-plate umps wear as armor. Giamatti asked about the three hit batsmen (Dave Magadan had also taken a pitch to the shoulder, late in the game), and Harvey said, "Darling has that palm-ball, or whatever he calls it—we've seen it before—that backs up a foot or more, it looks like, and that's what gets Larkin the first time. The other time—what was it, the seventh?—the pitch just gets away from Darling. He's trying to hold a one-run lead late in the game—no way he wants to hit anybody. Nobody thought different. The pitch that hit Backman—no, it was Magadan—was just a good close inside pitch. It was legitimate, in the zone, and Magadan was leaning. I told him so and I made the sign. No problems."

"Good game," Giamatti said. "Thank you."

The four umpires were heading off to Atlanta and the Braves–Expos games there over the weekend—their last stop before the All-Star break, the coming week. Frank Pulli was to be one of the umps at the All-Star game, in Cincinnati. (The job is rotated among the umpires in both leagues, like the league-championship games and the World Series.) Harvey told us that his wife was flying in from the West Coast to meet him in Atlanta, and they would take a trip to the Georgia beaches during the short holiday. "I've never been out there," he said. "I'm glad she's coming, because of Lee. I'm taking that hard, I don't mind saying." A few days earlier, Lee Weyer, a veteran National League umpire, had died of a heart attack in San Francisco, where he had been working a Cubs–Giants series. He and Harvey had both come into the league as rookie umpires in 1962. The funeral plans were not yet complete, and Harvey and Giamatti talked a little now about what kind of memorial service might be arranged later on. Then Giamatti and I said our farewells and walked out to the parking lot, back with the crowds again.

"Umpires are a brotherhood," Giamatti said after we got into the car. "Lee Weyer never married, but he was a warm man. One thing I remember about him is the way he dusted off the plate. He'd dust it clean and then he'd make this clear outline around the perimeter of the plate, with his brush. Nobody else did that."

We talked of other things on the slow homeward trip to Manhattan, but now and then in the car, and in the days since that evening, I wondered what other people in the closed, special world of baseball made of Bart Giamatti. I could certainly ask some of them, but not quite in the usual ways—not casually or as a reporter, that is—because of the chance that the owners may choose him to be the next commissioner. This has changed things, and whatever an owner or a manager, or even a player, might say about Giamatti now, good or bad, would have the taste of campaign news. He had already begun to slip away from me a little, and I wanted more, of course. Then I remembered, almost as an afterthought, that he was a writer, and over the next week or two I found some of his books and began to dip into them at odd moments, reading almost at random and looking more for the author than for some new appreciation of bygone prosody or passion. One day, leafing through "Exile and Change in Renaissance Literature," I thought I had a sudden glimpse of him—not with his tie and blazer but in brighter, heraldic colors—in the person of Matteo Boiardo, a fifteenth-century Italian poet, whose great work was "Orlando Innamorato."

"Boiardo's deepest desire is to conserve something of purpose in a world of confusion," Giamatti had written. "He knows that chivalry is an outmoded system, but he wants to keep something of its value, its respect for grace and noble behavior, even while he relinquishes its forms and structures. . . . Boiardo wants to check the urge to dissolution . . . that time seems inevitably to embody. He does not want to turn back the clock and regain the old world, but he does want to recapture the sense of control of oneself, if nothing else, that marked life under the old system. He wants to be able to praise something other than the giddy, headlong rush."

No, But I Saw the Game

— S U M M E R   1 9 8 9

Baseball movies make baseball fans feel good for the wrong reasons. Watching actors taking their Aunt Hattie cuts at the plate, turning the twelve-second double play (was that slo-mo, or what?), or striking out the side with high-parabola fastballs, we smile unpleasantly in the dark, smug in the knowledge that our sport and its practitioners are beyond imitation. This tingle of superiority isn't particularly satisfying, since we fans of the game are there in another capacity, as moviegoers; more than anyone else in the audience, we want the baseball on the screen to work, to sweep us up and make us care about the story, so we can forget how badly these guys on the screen play ball. Sometimes that happens, but more often we can feel the old Susp.-of-Disb. gears creaking and groaning inside, particularly during baseball movies in which the plot depends heavily on stuff that happens on the field. Real baseball drama takes its time, as we know, and its thrilling or melodramatic resolutions tend to be minor events—a misplayed grounder, a little flare that drops in behind second, a hit-and-run bouncer that finds its way through the created aperture in the infield defense—which feel gigantic or explosive because they release us from a debilitating anxiety. All the accumulating and seemingly eventless previous innings have been crammed with news and notices and gnawing concerns for the fan in the stands. Does our pitcher have his good breaking ball today, and (a few minutes later) what's he *doing* nibbling away at this No. 8 hitter? . . . Why is Straw playing so deep? . . . Why does Davey have Keith guarding the line like that, now that Randy's out there firing? . . . Hey, look at this—there's two up-pitches from Browning, he's beginning to lose it for sure, but let's get him before they can bring in Franco, O.K.? . . . Come on now, you guys. C'mon. . . .

Not much of this is translatable into movie language, of course, since it is silent and lengthily ongoing, and since the focus of our concern—the difference of a foot or two in the placement of the infield defense, or of millimeters in or out as the pitched ball flashes across the plate—is daunting for the cinematographer and invisible to the inexpert moviegoer. Movies have to keep moving, and thus can't wait around for the slow, hourglass slippage of baseball time, in a game or in a summer. Baseball is mostly lowlights, but baseball movies must suggest otherwise, often by edited, closeup snatches of bats meeting balls, gloves gobbling up grounders, spiked feet toeing a base, and so on, or by the opposite distortion—the super-slow-motion shot of the batter waiting and tensing as the ball spins in from the mound with all stitches showing, and then, after a flurry of intercut batter movements and grimaces, operatically soars up and away and, most of the time, into the bleachers. Onscreen baseball action leans toward the grotesque: swinging strikes that miss by a mile; wild pitches that hit the screen on the fly or comically nail some bystander on the noggin; and that game- and series- and movie-winning homer into the upper deck, accompanied by rainbow lights, music up, and fan feelings down. Movie baseball is inexorably entertaining, while real baseball, as every fan knows, is too serious, most of the time, to be fun at all.

Moviemakers have tried to patch over some of the built-in hazards of the genre by including segments of actual game footage in their dramas. This does the job well enough in panorama—packed audiences at Wrigley Field or Yankee Stadium rising and roaring in response to some offscreen event, and then a glimpse of some distant but unmistakably authentic player rounding second and just beating the throw in to third—but documentary closeups often work the other way. *Bang the Drum Slowly,* an exemplary (for its time) diamond flick made in 1973, has several authenticating shots of big-leaguers presumably in action against the movie's home team, the New York Mammoths, but when I watched it again on my homescreen video the other day, a sudden vision of Tony Perez swinging massively at an upper-level fastball and then a glimpse of Brooks Robinson batting (and wearing that peculiar helmet of his, with its almost invisible bill) made me forget all about pitcher Henry Wiggen and catcher Bruce Pearson and the pennant hopes of the Mammoths; I stopped the movie, rewound, and watched the real heroes once more, for the thrill of it. This distraction turns up again and again. A 1933 movie, *Elmer the Great*, which stars Joe E. Brown as a comical rube phenom, has a riveting black-and-white flash of Lou Gehrig and Tony Lazzeri warming up on the sidelines of Wrigley Field before one of the games of the 1932 Yankees–Cubs World Series. *Field of Dreams*, the baseball tearjerker now in the theatres, includes a lovely middle-distance shot of a night game at Fenway Park, but I was snatched away from the view and the story when I noticed that the batter was Ron Hassey, the Oakland catcher, who popped out to short right field; the next time I saw the movie, I got the same little start when I saw that the pitcher working to Hassey was Oil Can Boyd. (A friend of mine, commenting on this unsettling phenomenon in baseball movies, said that it reminded him of reading along in a so-so literary biography and suddenly coming on a quoted passage by the biographee, put there by the author to prove his scholarship but now, alas, serving only to prove which writer was really worth reading.)

Old-time baseball-movie producers used to go further in the authentication dodge by giving real major-leaguers walk-on parts in their baseball epics. Babe Ruth, Bill Dickey, and Mark Koenig play themselves during some Yankee-clubhouse scenes in the wheelhorse *The Pride of the Yankees*, which starred Gary Cooper as Lou Gehrig; and Dickey turned up again, along with Jimmy Dykes, in *The Stratton Story*, in which Jimmy Stewart, as Monty Stratton, a White Sox pitcher of the nineteen-thirties, loses a leg in a hunting accident but makes it back to the bigs again, thanks to prosthesis and June Allyson. There's a bit of interest in watching Ruth swing at a couple of pitches in *The Pride of the Yankees*, even in contrived studio shots, but the kick for us *(My God, there he is! There's the Babe!)* is exactly the same as it must have been for movie audiences back when the picture first appeared, as we hear him talk and watch him sort of act, big as life. Celebrity turns don't do the trick anymore, now that television has made us intimately aware of every athlete's looks and mannerisms and self-assured or mumbly interview style, so I was startled when Pete Vuckovich, the stalwart, recently retired Brewer right-hander, showed up in a new baseball flick, *Major League*. He was playing a cameo role as a menacing Yankee slugger named Clu Haywood, but the pinstripes didn't fool me: unshaven face, slitty eyes, Fu Manchu mustache—it was Vuke all right, and for a while there I happily forgot the movie and worried again about his torn rotator cuff and his long struggle to come back and be a great money pitcher, as before. Early in the movie, though, Vuckovich whacked a grand slam against Charlie Sheen, and I was tickled for him. Pitchers love to hit.

○

There have been so many new baseball movies in the past couple of years that it has seemed at times that filmmakers were taking on the form as a kind of penance. Some of the results have been pretty good, or partly good, and some god-awful; one of the movies is just about perfect, to my way of thinking. (It's *Bull Durham*, which offers almost the first evidence that the phrase "baseball movie" is not an oxymoron.) As must be clear by now, I put in a lot of time this spring and early summer catching up on the new stuff in the theatres and also hunting down oldies in the video stores and playing them at home. My purpose, I hope, was something more than snickering about movie baseball. I am a fan of both of the celebrated indigenous art forms, and I wanted to try to figure out for myself why they have had such a famously hard time getting together. It also occurred to me that by thinking about the most popular of the recent offerings I might have a fresh notion of what it is that American audiences look for or long for in the sport—catch a glimpse of our baseball unconscious, so to speak, which may affect the game and its future in ways we don't always understand. More than once, I was tempted to abandon this lightsome task, because the glaring technical drawbacks—the flubs and misplays I have just mentioned—seemed to be telling me to leave the two national pastimes alone, safely tucked away in separate quarters in my head. I hung in there, though, persisting even after I unexpectedly remembered *The Bob Lemon Story*—no, no: a Bob Lemon story—about his own very brief career in the movies. Call it a parable. Lemon, then the incumbent Yankee manager, was talking in the home dugout one night before a game up at the Stadium, back in the early nineteen-eighties, when somebody asked him about the time he'd been hired to do a little stand-in pitching for Ronald Reagan. The movie was a sub-epochal film bio called *The Winning Team*, in which Reagan played Grover Cleveland Alexander, the alcoholic but justly acclaimed Hall of Fame pitcher, who won three hundred and seventy-three games over the course of a twenty-year career in the National League. It was shot back in the early nineteen-fifties, when Lemon himself was at the peak of his form as a right-handed starter in the awesome Feller-Wynn-Lemon-Garcia rotation of the Cleveland Indians; he was, in fact, hurrying to Cooperstown himself (he knocked off a hundred and eighty-six victories during one nine-year stretch in here), and it could be argued that he was more famous at the moment than the star he briefly replaced. He told us he had been called out to Hollywood to add verisimilitude to a few Reagan-for-Alexander pitching sequences—in particular, for an early scene in which the budding immortal, then a gangling Nebraska farm boy, learns control by throwing again and again at a catcher's mitt he has nailed up on a barn door. As Lemon recalled it, he was nervous about being asked to perform on cue before the customary assemblage of floodlights and cameras and grips and studio technicians, but he went at it bravely. "My first pitch was a strike," he said. "It hit the side of the pocket, just up on the thumb a dab. I was at the full distance, so I thought it was a hell of a pitch, but then the man in charge—the director or whoever the hell it was—goes 'Cut! Cut! Hold it!' and he comes over and tells me I've got to hit the *middle* of the pocket with the pitch. He told me to wake up and do better, and they started the cameras again—they were shooting sort of from behind, so you couldn't tell it was me pitching—but of course I just got worse after that." The takes and retakes went on, and in the end the movie people said, well, they guessed they could piece something together out of it all, but the whole thing was a disaster. At one point, the unit director lost his temper with Lemon and barked, "I thought you guys were professionals!"

○

I didn't get to *The Winning Team* in my recent swing around the flick-leagues, but dim recollection tells me that it included a few songs by Doris Day, conveniently cast as Alexander's wife; the movie omitted his epilepsy, and attributed his boozing bouts to dizziness (Reagan frowning and shaking his head on the mound) brought on by a prior beaning. I also skipped a good many other baseball bios and dramas of the forties and fifties, including *The Babe Ruth Story* (William Bendix as a bumbling, cleaned-up Bambino), *Fear Strikes Out* (Tony Perkins, in a warmup for *Psycho*, playing Jimmy Piersall), *Take Me Out to the Ball Game* (Gene Kelly and Frank Sinatra as hoofers in spiked shoes), *The Pride of St. Louis* (Dan Dailey as Dizzy Dean), *It Happens Every Spring* (Ray Milland as a nutty perfesser who invents a substance that causes pitched balls to dodge bats), *The Kid from Left Field* (never saw it), *Rhubarb* (a cat inherits a major-league team), *Angels in the Outfield* (seraphic tamperings liven up a pennant race), and *Damn Yankees* (the dandy musical, with Ray Walston wearing red socks because he's the Devil). I have more recent and more cheerful memories of *The Bad News Bears*, in which Walter Matthau winced and groaned as the manager of a hapless Little League team, and of *The Bingo Long Traveling All-Stars and Motor Kings*, about a team of black barnstormers, but I didn't check them out again. Nor did I find time to look up some movies I recall as including some lively little baseball sidebars in the middle of the story: Clark Gable, down from the skies in *Test Pilot*, taking Myrna Loy (here a Kansas farm girl) to a game in Wichita; Spencer Tracy as a sportswriter bringing his political-pundit girlfriend, Katharine Hepburn, into the press box at Yankee Stadium in *Woman of the Year*. There are probably more of these, but I couldn't think of them, perhaps because I was still in trembling remission from my revisit with *The Pride of the Yankees*.*

*After this piece ran in *The New Yorker* in the summer of 1989, I had a lively letter from Ron Shelton, the screenwriter and director of *Bull Durham*, in which he made passing reference to his 1983 action film, *Under Fire*, and its brief but riveting baseball scene, which I instantly recalled, once Shelton had nudged me. In the movie (Shelton wrote the screenplay, and Roger Spottiswoode was the director), a young rebel with the Sandinistas during the 1979 revolution in Nicaragua is summoned to fling a grenade into a distant belfry where some Somoza snipers have taken refuge. He is wearing an old Baltimore Orioles cap, and when Nick Nolte, who plays an American television journalist, begins to talk baseball with him, the kid says, "Koufax is good, but Dennis Martinez is better. He's from Nicaragua." Later, he says, "You see Dennis Martinez, you tell him my curveball is better and I have a good scroogie."

He goes to his fastball when flinging the grenade, however—a terrific peg that brought

It's my theory that a good many senior baseball people—coaches and managers and writers, and front-office people in particular—never got over *The Pride of the Yankees*, a major Hollywood effort that parlayed a strong original news peg (Lou Gehrig's courage in the face of his fatal illness, which struck him down at the age of thirty-seven) into an all-purpose foldout valentine to filial duty, faithful marriage, uncomplaining loyalty to the boss, the rewards of athletic persistence, and the efficacy of good deeds for shut-ins. Its producer, Sam Goldwyn (the director was Sam Wood), was never one to stint on high-cholesterol family values, but we should also remind ourselves that the movie came out in 1942, when Hollywood had just begun fighting a war. The opening dedication presents the movie as the "story of a hero of the peaceful paths of everyday life" who "faced death with that same valor and fortitude that has been displayed by thousands of young Americans on far-flung fields of battle." It's a recruiting poster, then, and perhaps also a warning that we shouldn't complain when bad things happen to nice guys.

The persistent joke about *The Pride of the Yankees* has been that its star, Gary Cooper, who plays Gehrig, couldn't run or throw or bat at *all*, and that Goldwyn, having failed in his plan to convert Cooper to a southpaw (Gehrig was left all the way), had to outfit him with a uniform with a reversed Yankee logo and No. 4 (and reversed pinstripes, too, I guess), and then flipped the negative in the developing room. Nothing helped, and subsequent viewings only reawaken the embarrassment we felt back then when we saw Gary Cooper (as much a hero to us, of course, as Lou Gehrig) doing something awkward on the screen for the very first time—except for trying to act, I mean. But there was something palpably wrong about this reflexive one-star-for-another setup, which seemed to degrade Lou Gehrig a little, even in the stagey, overlit movie footage. Gehrig was immensely strong, and he left a strong impression on anyone who ever saw him play. He was thick-legged and heavyset, with sloping shoulders; he had dimples, which showed up startlingly in black-and-white closeups of his rounded, unemotional face; and he waggled the top of his bat around in a brief circle before taking that great smooth swing—nothing at all like the cowboyish, lank-handed, nose-rubbing, gawky-sweet Cooper. I was a wise-guy college senior when *The Pride of the Yankees* came out, and I certainly didn't have much of this clear in my head, but I can recall the way my friends and I went around making fun of its heartwarming family scenes, imitating the German-immigrant Mom Gehrig as

me straight up in my seat in the theatre when I first saw the movie. A minute later, he is shot dead. The actor, Eloy Ray Casados, was a three-sport high-school star in New Mexico, and he can *throw*. As Shelton says in his letter, "Verisimilitude in this area is very important."

NO, BUT I SAW THE GAME

she rebuked Lou, as a lad, after he defied her no-ballplaying rule and, natch, busted a grocery-store window ("It isn't chust the money—it's the time you vaste") and the moment when she learned that he hasn't been studying engineering at Harvard but playing minor-league ball at *Hartford* ("Lou—to giff up everyting ve had planned! For vat? Baseballers are güt-for-nutting!"). But she forgiffs him:

LOU: Are you still my best gal, Mom?
MOM: Alvays.

(Pop Gehrig, I should add, was on Lou's side. He was played by Ludwig Stossel, who would shortly take his own useful Bierstube accent into *Casablanca* and its immortal "What watch?" . . . "Such much?" lines.) I'm afraid we also made fun of the big scene near the end of the movie when Lou gets the very bad news from the medics at the Scripps Clinic: "I'm a man who likes to know his batting average. Is it three strikes, Doc?"

I had hoped that the passage of almost fifty years might have made me a kindlier fellow, but on my latest go-round the mawkishness of *The Pride of the Yankees* seemed even more difficult to endure—particularly in its depiction of the affectionate but apparently eventless married life of the Iron Horse and his missus (Teresa Wright), which lingers over footage of Eleanor G. pasting up Lou's clipbooks, to the strains of Irving Berlin's "Always," with Lou (I'm eliding a bit here) suddenly exclaiming, "Holy mackerel—I'll miss *batting practice*!" Well, even Noël Coward might have had a hard time sustaining dialogue over a span of two thousand one hundred and thirty consecutive games. Dan Duryea plays a cynical newspaperman, who says of Gehrig, "A guy like that is a detriment to any sport" (how or why is never quite explained), to which Walter Brennan, the good-guy scribe, responds, "Let me tell you about heroes. . . . Lou Gehrig is a guy who does his job." Nothing doing, no edge anywhere, then, until the sad and sudden end. There's a nice shot of Cooper coming onto the field for the farewell tribute, with the sunlight moving up from his feet to cover his entire body as he emerges from the dark tunnel, and the picture ends with the "Today I consider myself the luckiest man on the face of the earth" speech, complete with the Stadium echoes—the best thing in it, but a pale patch on that famous newsreel shot of the great man at his greatest moment.

Watching *The Pride of the Yankees* again, I found myself trying to forgive its excesses, perhaps because I had heard so many old baseball writers and coaches and executives (by "old" I mean people of my own age) speak of it with great fondness, or perhaps just because it was made so long ago. The latter impulse, I suspect, should be rejected. The movie presents a baseball world (and a human world) that never existed, and Hollywood in 1942 was in fact at the apex of the big-studio era, and had almost unlimited capabilities for muscle, sophistication, and intelligence. *Ninotchka*, *The Maltese Falcon*, *The Grapes of Wrath*, *The Lady Eve*, *The Long Voyage Home*, and Goldwyn's own *The Little Foxes*—to name but a few beauties—had all preceded *The Pride of the Yankees* by a year or two or three, and the movie's co-writer, Herman Mankiewicz, came to the job shortly after finishing his script for *Citizen Kane*. The syrup wasn't innocent, then, but Goldwyn thought nothing better suited a dying hero and poor old baseball, and he had the old Log Cabin poured on by the bucketful.

○

Bang the Drum Slowly felt fresh and smart and different from its predecessors when it came along in 1973. It was the first one that seemed to be a movie about baseball instead of another baseball movie, a form by then as fixed and familiar as the Mickey Rooney kid musical. The script, by Mark Harris, was based on his own novel (the second volume in a series of four about Henry Wiggen, a fictional big-league southpaw), and it preserved some of the wit and zing of the original. The lore and language in the movie sound convincing and insidy, although in fact they include a good many deft Harris inventions, such as the fish-catching hotel-lobby card game TEGWAR ("the exciting game without any rules"). They have the *flavor* of baseball, which is almost all that matters. There's another dying ballplayer at the center of things—a second-string catcher, Bruce Pearson, played by Robert De Niro—but the movie, despite some damp-hankie moments near the end, is lightly ironic in tone, since it shows how shabbily all the Mammoths treat the dumb clod Bruce when they don't know he's "doomded" (in his words) and how they pull together and briefly pay attention to him (and start to win) when the news about his condition gets out. There's a funny, dark little moment when the manager, Dutch Schnell (Vincent Gardenia), startles Bruce by unexpectedly addressing him during a clubhouse speech: "I know that you know, personally, I never had anything but the greatest respect for you as a human being." The movie was made by a young director, John Hancock, and features young actors (including Michael Moriarty, as Henry Wiggen, and Danny Aiello as the first baseman, Horse) who were allowed to run and throw and bat for themselves in most of the baseball scenes. Moriarty shows a commanding, Seaverlike repose on the mound (he'd done his homework), and his off-field Wiggen is handsome, smart, unruffled, and a little sleek: a winner to the life. De Niro doesn't throw or hit or run very convincingly, but his awkwardness fits into his restrained depiction of a poor schlunk; he never goes for the heartache in the role. The baseball in *Bang the Drum Slowly* was shot mostly at Shea Stadium, which looks great in its pristine, green-walled, pre-Diamond Vision, pre-Big Apple Hat youth. The movie feels so young that

I wanted to forgive it. On my revisit, much of the indoor plot action seemed stiff and talky, but the story picks up some confidence and style as it goes along. This was the first baseball movie that included action shots and ball-park shots that seemed to be there for their own sakes: a view of the Shea grounds crew rolling out the tarps during a shower, for instance, and then the rain falling on the soaking, beautifully green field. The last baseball in the movie is in slow motion—Bruce Pearson circling helplessly under a foul pop near the plate (he doesn't know where the ball is and he doesn't know where *he* is), and then the first baseman, drifting in from screen left to glove the easy chance as the Mammoths clinch. It gets you (it got me all over again), and you even come out of the movie remembering its little tag line: "It's sad—it makes you want to cry. It's sad—it makes you want to laugh."*

○

I think Bernard Malamud had a lot more fun writing *The Natural* than Robert Redford and the director, Barry Levinson, and the scriptwriters, Roger Towne and Phil Dusenberry, had making the movie, five years ago. Malamud had come up with a rousing idea for the novel (it was his first, and came out in 1952), which was to weave together the legends of baseball and the thick, misty tangle of Arthurian fable—chivalry and single combat, blood and be-trayal and loss—into a tale about a magically talented country-boy pitcher (later, like Babe Ruth, a mighty slugger) who falls and rises again but suc-cumbs at last to the envious wiles of the unheroic. But "weave" is the wrong word; Malamud was a fan as well as a scholar, and the yellowing sports-page stuff fell into place in the book almost more easily than the Malory. Roy Hobbs, the hero, becomes the young king of baseball (for a while, at least) thanks to Wonderboy, his magical bat—fashioned from a lightning-struck tree but plainly the "Excalibur"-model Louisville Slugger—and the big-league team he plays for is the Knights, whose fortunes are meddled with by the wily Merlinesque sportswriter Max Mercy (in the movie, Robert Duvall). Iris is Roy's Guinevere-Iseult, and she restores him, late in the season, after his old wounds have reopened in battle (sort of like Tristram going on the D.L. after the Palamedes series). The movie's baseball echoes were always clearer. Whammer Wambold is the Babe, of course, and when Bump Bailey, the star outfielder for the Knights, runs into a fence and dies, Roy replaces him in the fans' hearts almost overnight, just like Mickey Mantle taking over center field from Joe DiMaggio. Early on, when Roy is shot in a hotel room by a deranged

---

*Some readers with long memories wrote me after this piece appeared, to recommend an earlier televised version of *Bang the Drum Slowly,* which was presented on the "U.S. Steel Hour" back in 1956, with Paul Newman, Albert Salmi, and George Peppard in the leading roles.

young woman, fan-readers instantly recalled Eddie Waitkus, the Phillies' first baseman, who suffered the same near-fatal wound at the hands of a psychopathic Baseball Annie back in 1949. The gamblers in the novel and the foul owner, Judge Goodwill Banner, who together try to fix the big game, are wraiths from the Black Sox Series, and so on. Sometimes these invisibly footnoted references in the twin tales felt scholar-strained or showoffy (Pop Fisher, managing the Knights in the wasteland of last place, can't get even a trickle out of the dugout water fountain), but you didn't mind much in the book; you hurried along to the next page. On the screen, however, legends feel heavy, and tend to be underlit and overblown. *The Natural* is plainly about a baseball superhero from the sticks, and I don't think many movie fans cared about most of this, or ever had a clue about why Roy (the knight in banishment) reappears as a much older player to take up his quest, or what the hell the poisoning was all about (Kim Basinger, as the temptress Memo Paris, slips Roy a bad canapé at a party he should have passed up), or what the bleeding wounds and the old-silver-bullet-in-the-gut diagnosis were doing in there, late in a pennant race. Roy's hospital scenes are so murmurous and violet-hued that we think we're in church. Robert Redford, as Roy Hobbs, stalks through all this with a glum rigidity, stunned by meaning and afraid to spit.

The portentous stuffiness of *The Natural* is a shame, because the baseball in it sometimes isn't bad at all, and you keep thinking the whole thing is going to take off and take you with it, like a pennant race that suddenly catches fire along about Labor Day. Redford afield is the most convincing ballplayer yet filmed: runs well, throws well, hits with power (he modelled his swing on Ted Williams', I'm told)—you want to sign him up. I enjoyed the nicely sustained scene, early on, when Roy, the rookie pitcher, strikes out Whammer Wambold in an impromptu railroad-siding matchup beside a waiting, huffing steam engine. Joe Don Baker is the Ruthian slugger who calls his shot and then fans, and you almost cheer when Roy, in a lozenge-design sleeveless sweater, fires strike three past him in the golden, buggy country twilight. There's a funny, quick bit later on, when Roy literally knocks the cover off a baseball, and there's comfort in the easy, wide-bottom performances of Wilford Brimley, as Pop, and Richard Farnsworth, as a worn-out, white-haired coach. (I'll bet my old Virgil Trucks autograph ball that stacks of film-school master's theses are already piling up at U.C.L.A. or Columbia tracing the long line of fat roles as movie-baseball managers or coaches or good guys which have brought employment to notable character actors like Frank Morgan, Charles Bickford, Walter Brennan, Paul Douglas, Frank Lovejoy, John Mahoney, and more: "Third Billings in the Stengel Strain," or some such.) The old-timey, steeply tiered, steel-post ballpark—it was the old Buffalo Bisons' stadium—has the proper angles and shadows, and you can sense that some real money and real efforts to get things right went into the movie. Fans I know (and some players as well) still put *The Natural* at the top of their list of movies about the pastime.

My own hopes gathered themselves about midway through the movie (I felt the same way on later viewings), when it suddenly seemed that it had a chance to seize on a legitimate variant of the Arthurian bushwa—something to the effect that extraordinary athletic ability is untouchable and beyond explanation, truly magical, and that when it goes you die. But *The Natural* drops this more often than it picks it up, and gives us easier and dumber chords instead: expiation by true love (Glenn Close, as Iris, appearing in the stands with a heavenly halo of light around her head); redemption by cuteness (Wonderboy splits apart, but Roy accepts a fresh bat fashioned by the fat, smiling batboy); and generational rebirth (Roy and Iris had a son, it suddenly turns out, and we take our leave after a final, sun-filled shot of dad and kid throwing the old pill around in a wheatfield). There was never much chance that *The Natural* could resist stuff like this, given the prior absence of anything like everyday ball and everyday life—any quickness on the base paths or in the dialogue. The last mistake, and the fatal one for all meaning, is that Hobbs-Redford cannot be allowed to fail and fall, as he does in the book (which ends, "He lifted his hands to his face and wept many bitter tears"), since movie heroes, unlike ballplayers, don't *really* get old. Roy, with blood oozing through his pinstripes, wafts the game-winning, pennant-winning homer into the arcs, and circles the bases in slow (very slow) motion as showers of light fall about his golden locks. It's a good thing for him that the game and the season are over; the first pitch of his next at-bat would have been in his ear.

o

John Sayles' *Eight Men Out*, which came out last year, should be anti-myth—it's based on Eliot Asinof's workmanlike, unsentimental 1963 account of the Black Sox scandal—but sometimes it slips and seems to encourage our unmelting conviction (the old lollipop in the national phiz) that there was something innocent about our American past. Modern baseball scholarship—for example, Charles Alexander's recent *John McGraw*, a first-class biography—has made it clear that early big-league ball was commonly accompanied by fisticuffs, the whiff of bribery, the intimidation of umpires, and endemic drunkenness in the stands and on the field, but not much of this message has reached us. I got the feeling that *Eight Men Out* wasn't going to be able to help itself once I saw the opening shot, of some Chicago street kids in knee pants and little cloth caps hanging around Comiskey Park and talking excitedly about their White Sox heroes—the bought-off, degraded stars who would hand over the 1919 Series to the Cincinnati Reds and eventually get themselves thrown out of baseball. We know what's ahead, because the story has to come down to the engraved, Insta-Sob punchline, "Say it ain't so, Joe." By the time the motto and its moment arrive, well along in the picture, we've learned a good deal about the various lunkheaded or aggrieved or gullible or mixed-up White Sox players and their braggart, miserly owner, Charlie Comiskey, and the double-dealing underworld creeps and bullies who helped Arnold Rothstein put in the fix, but the line (it's delivered by a kid in the crowd outside the Cook County Criminal Courts Building, and goes unanswered by Shoeless Joe Jackson, the beclouded nonpareil) empties our heads and swells up our hearts: kids were good back there before the fall, and so were ballplayers—hell, *America* was good. Sayles tried to be cool and documentary about his material, but the movie colorings and costumes—straw hats and cigars, dark old saloons—and the Chicago-Dixieland background music and the rotogravure groupings lay a waxy, museum-exhibit sheen on the enterprise. It feels educational. Asinof's book was sharper and more intelligently cynical, because he didn't have to mess around with authenticity. But there's a lugubriousness about the Sayles *Eight Men Out* that's hard to account for. It's almost as if we had grown more, instead of less, oppressed by the Black Sox scandal as it recedes in history— as if we wanted to get it back and rewrite it, to see if it won't come out better. (In *Field of Dreams*, which we will get around to shortly, this revisionism floats down from Heaven, and is played out by ghosts.) *Elmer the Great* culminates in an attempted fix of the World Series, too, but the 1933 script, which was based on the play by Ring Lardner and George M. Cohan, is lighthearted about it. Joe E. Brown's Elmer Kane, the "miracle hitter and run-getter," piles up a gambling debt with some gangsters (led by the perdurable slime Douglass Dumbrille), because he's too innocent to understand that the games at their casino are played for money. Finally cleared, he smacks a ball off the wall in a rainstorm at Wrigley Field and slides home on his face in a mud puddle to win the World Series. Nothing to it.

The story line in *Eight Men Out* is more difficult, and by the end of the picture we're worn out, like Louvre visitors, because we've lost our concentration. The picture makes it tough for anybody to focus on a particular player, or even on two or three among the infamous eight. Nicknames and attributes and identifying scraps of dialogue fly about in the early ballpark, clubhouse, parlor-car, and hotel scenes, but we're almost at the grand-jury inquest before we can tell Lefty Williams from Chick Gandil or Swede Risberg for sure; we want a scorecard. (I thought *Eight Men Out* was better on a second viewing, and others who went back again or took home the video have told me the same thing.) Sayles has to hurry over the hearings in the end, and we never quite know whether the jury was also fixed when it voted to acquit the accused players. (The newly appointed first commissioner,

Kenesaw Mountain Landis, banned them all for life just the same, because they hadn't reported the bribes.) The picture is vague because history is vague here, but after reconsulting Asinof I realized that the movie had done a little fixing of its own, by shining up its portraits of Buck Weaver and Shoeless Joe. Baseball scholars still don't know for sure what happened in that Series, in which Weaver batted .324 and Jackson .375, with a homer as well, even with the fixers' loot in their pockets. This year, there's been a fresh campaign in the sporting press to forgive and forget Jackson's misdeeds and wheel him into the Hall of Fame, where he'd certainly belong if he'd stayed clean: his lifetime .356 is the third-best average in the annals of the game.

Sayles, to his credit, has stayed his hand in other ways. There's no faked-up *Pride of the Yankees* domestic drama that would have pushed our sympathy and attention toward some center-stage actor, although you keep thinking that's about to happen. Eddie Cicotte (David Strathairn), the classy senior pitching ace who's been gypped out of a bonus by the odious Comiskey, agonizes with his innocent wife about his part in the fix, but only for a moment or two. We glimpse Mrs. Joe Jackson reading aloud to her illiterate husband (D. B. Sweeney), and hear the hard-burning third baseman, Buck Weaver (John Cusack), telling some street kids—a little mawkishly, perhaps—that his mistake was that he never grew up out there, but then the flash or the scene mercifully ends. Almost reluctantly, Sayles has to settle for a team photo, but the movie shows its class by never quite patronizing its foolish victim-heroes, and when the sweet sadness creeps in at the close— the exiled Shoeless Joe is playing under an alias for a New Jersey semi-pro team in 1925, and Weaver, in the stands, murmurs, "I saw him play . . . he was the best"—you don't mind much, because it feels earned.

There are strong faces and several brusque, satisfying portrait-performances in *Eight Men Out*, and some pleasing work by celebrity non-actors, as well—Studs Terkel as the sportswriter Hughie Fullerton, John Sayles himself as Ring Lardner (an amazing likeness), and even a glimpse of Eliot Asinof, the original author, here elevated to league president. Charlie Sheen is wonderfully vapid as the brainless Hap Felsch, and Strathairn is tight-faced and withdrawn as the wronged Cicotte: there's a remarkable shot of him sitting alone in a marble courthouse corridor, with his folded, too neat topcoat alongside him, as he awaits his call to testify. But Sayles' feat in this flawed, almost impressive movie is to make some of his players recognizable in the end not by their acting but by the way they look on the field. Cicotte's smooth, effortless windup and delivery tell us in a minute how tough and expert he was out there, and Joe Jackson has a loping way of running the bases and an open-stance flat-bat, left-handed cut at the ball (D. B. Sweeney worked at this for many months before the shooting started, beginning by learning how to swing from the other side), which you pick up with an inner thrill each time you see it: you remember it as a fan, I mean. I can't think of any other baseball film or cast of baseball actors that pulls this off. The best shot in the picture is the last one, behind the final credits, when we see the eight players, not yet the Black Sox, cheerfully flinging the ball around on the sidelines in some pregame warmup, long before their troubles began. There's style and ease and skill in their playful, offhand movements—the stuff that great athletes toss off without effort—and the moment conveys their pleasure in the game and ours in watching them.

○

Now and then when I emerged from the dark this spring, I asked some baseball people and some players which baseball movies they preferred, and it came as a shock to me that some of them disliked *Bull Durham*. They thought that there was too much sex in it, and that it was bad for the image of the game. But I shouldn't have been surprised. I always have to keep reminding myself that there is as much variety of opinion and taste and private preference among sports people as there is in any other profession; we fans must give the players the last word about baseball authenticity, to be sure, but an opinion poll of their favorite baseball movies wouldn't tell us much. One doesn't need Bat Masterson to make up one's mind about *Red River* or *Shane*. But I don't care what anyone else says about *Bull Durham*, which is a comic delight and maybe a miracle. It's the first baseball movie that gets things right without trying; there isn't a line in it that feels reverent or fake-tough or hurriedly explanatory, or that tries to fill in the uninitiated about what's going on out there. It assumes you're going to stay with the game, even in its dreariest, dusty middle innings, when the handful of folks in the stands are slumped down on their spines waiting for something to happen, even a base on balls. It's an adult's homage to the game ("There's no guilt in baseball, and it's never boring," Susan Sarandon says in her now celebrated "Church of Baseball" voice-over), and it's about people who have been around and have come back to baseball as grownups, willing to strip away the clichés and the uplift and the mystical crap to find how strong and funny and rich the sport remains at its center. Its characters talk about the game lightly but with avid pleasure, and they back away a little after they've said something sharp or freshly appreciative about it, as if they were asking themselves if it's really true—is baseball really this great? This is the way a few friends of mine talk about baseball at times—not idle sometime fans, or macho males who are simply sustaining their year-round sports guff, but men and women who have suddenly or slowly attached themselves to the game, usually through some particular team, and then can't quite believe how wonderful baseball can be, how baffling and heartbreaking, and how rewarding.

Bull Durham came out last year, but it feels like a classic already, and probably needs little recapitulation here. The story—Crash Davis (Kevin Costner), an experienced but beaten-down catcher, a career minor-leaguer, is brought down to the Class A Durham Bulls in order to educate and smooth up a great young scatter-arm pitching prospect, Nuke LaLoosh (Tim Robbins), who's headed for the majors if he can only get his stuff and his head together—has a nice balance to it, because it allows its veteran hero to show us, along with Nuke, how the game should be approached and held in mind as well as how it should be played. "Don't hold the ball so hard," Crash says to his crazily impatient kid battery-mate. "It's an egg." In a later scene, Crash says, "You gotta play this game with fear and arrogance"; Nuke murmurs "Fear and ignorance," and of course Crash loses his temper again. But Nuke isn't really dumb—just careless and in a hurry. He doesn't have a clue when Crash tells him that strikeouts are Fascist and to throw ground balls because they're more democratic, but in time he begins to pitch better, and slowly he begins to get it, too. Near the end, he listens with sad affection when Crash drunkenly expatiates about the trifling one extra hit per week—a flare, a ground ball with eyes, a dying quail—that separates a major-league hitter from a lifelong minor-leaguer: the edge of talent that he will never possess.

The movie's writer and director, Ron Shelton, played minor-league ball for five years, so none of this feels worked up or literary. He's found actors who can run and throw a little, and who can go through the movements of a double play, but he doesn't keep cutting away from them in an attempt to jack up the look of the baseball. The pegs and pitches here are probably only a hair above half speed by pro standards (although Nuke does let fly with one fastball that seems to have some pop on it), but the flow is there, and that's good enough. Shelton's skills aren't limited to the diamond. He's drawn exceptional performances from his three leads, of which the most surprising is Tim Robbins as Nuke (he's ridiculous and charming on the mound, with his overconfident stare and a hotdog, Valenzuela roll of his eyes in mid-windup), who actually does seem a little smarter and more thoughtful, against all odds, by the time he's called up to the big show. As Annie, Susan Sarandon is a grownup, too—beautiful and sexual and sure of herself, kooky and literate at the same time. She picks out Nuke as her summer bedmate, but you know that Crash will get there in the end, because he and Annie are so alike; they're old enough to know there's no big hurry. Kevin Costner's Crash Davis is worn down and beat up but always in charge of things: an old catcher if there ever was one. He looks right not just throwing and swinging the bat but in the way he trudges out to the mound, carrying his mask in his hand and wondering how the hell he got here and what he can say to this boob to make him pay attention, so we can all get back in the shade again. He wants things done right, as they should be in baseball—and everywhere else. Nuke, strumming a guitar on the team bus, sings "She may get woolly, young girls, they do get woolly, because of all the stress" to the tune of "Try a Little Tenderness," and Crash goes bonkers and grabs the instrument and tells him how to sing the old lyrics properly. "I hate people who get the words wrong," he says.

Bull Durham is as fresh and funny and surprising about sex as it is about baseball, which is saying a lot. It's certainly the first movie that ever suggested (and enjoyed) the fact that ballplayers are sexual animals, objects of vivid interest to women. They do beautiful things with their bodies, it says, and we watch them not just to see who's going to win. This is the ongoing joke about the movie, and of course it holds up. It's a funny picture, and not only because of its now famous set pieces, like the mound conference during which the players discuss whether to buy silver candlesticks for a teammate who's about to get married (this wasn't in the original script), or Crash teaching Nuke the clichés he's going to need when he deals with the big-city media. A friend of mine went to the picture with a man from Israel who thought he knew baseball and knew America but who was startled by the ongoing flood of light laughs from the audience. "What are they laughing at?" he'd whisper in the dark. "What's funny about *that*?" Some of those jokes are little jabs at orthodoxy and at the family-value glop of other baseball movies. When Nuke gets the word that he's going up to the show, his downhome dad, who's there on a visit, suggests that they all join in a little prayer of thanks, but Annie says, "Oh, let's not." And when Crash needs the pine-tar rag during an at-bat, the smiling young batboy whispers, "Get a hit," but Wonderboy isn't wanted this time. "Shut up," Crash says, and he goes out to take his hacks.

Bull Durham moves along and takes its time, too, just like baseball. There are nicely extended midgame scenes—Crash muttering to himself in voice-over as he works out an at-bat against an enemy pitcher, or worrying about Nuke's head when the busher seems to be closing in on a shutout. Most plans and hopes fail, just as they do in the real game, and when Crash does hit a homer (he's called it in advance) he makes a mock bow and a "woo woo" gesture to his laughing teammates in the dugout as he heads on down to first. He knows how lucky he's been, and so do we.

o

Bull Durham was a big hit when it came out, and its first inevitable spinoff was *Major League*, a comedy still in the theatres here and there, which also has a retread old catcher, here played by Tom Berenger, as its hero. The movie has a rushed, corner-cutting feel to it, though, and the jokes are so broad and dim-witted that we groan to ourselves for laughing at them. There's a lot of dirty-mouth cursing, which takes the place of repartee, and we get the little slapstick joke about each of the different players in the first nanosecond—a quick black outfielder who is named Willy Mays Hayes; a voodoo-afflicted Hispanic slugger who shaves his head with a machete; an overpaid sissy third baseman (Corbin Bernsen) who has yuppie plans for his life. Bernsen is the least convincing major-leaguer since Gary Cooper. The rookie pitcher, Wild Thing Ricky Vaughn (it's Charlie Sheen again: he must have got traded), can't get the ball over the plate until somebody persuades him to wear glasses, and then he's Bob Feller; the whole problem takes about two minutes. The plot involves another fix—the showgirl owner of the Cleveland Indians wants them to finish last, so she can move the franchise to Miami, but when the assorted losers who have been chosen to pad the roster find out, they decide to win instead—and it's no more demanding than I've made it sound here, and most of the other twists are so feeble that they're given up in mid-progress. A lot of actual big-league players loved this movie, I'm told, and I can't help thinking that it may have been because nobody was expecting them or us to believe it. It's a goof.

In the second half of *Major League*—along about the seventh inning, let's say—there's a rally that makes you sit up and cheer up. The movie suddenly throws away its soapy little turns of plot and stays with the crowds as they watch the Indians start to pick up momentum. There are bopping bar scenes, with the fan-patrons yelling about game stuff on the television screen, and we see Wild Thing T-shirts beginning to turn up on downtown street corners. The people who made the movie—it was written and directed by David S. Ward—somehow manage some convincingly exultant crowd scenes in nice old Milwaukee County Stadium, and the sign-waving, screeching, dugout-dancing throngs during the Indians' one-game divisional playoff with the Yankees reminded me of the game-long celebrations at Three Rivers Stadium in 1979, when the "We Are Family" Pirates were winning and sweeping us up in their wonderful party. Fan excitement hasn't been done much in baseball movies, and it gives this flick an unexpected whiff of freshness and fun. There's a happy small scene in which the players make a rap-song American Express Card commercial, with Willy Mays Hayes sliding in at the last minute to say "Don't Steal Home Without It," and the Indians do win in the end, of course—on a bunt, of all things. You can't believe the movie wins in the end, either: it may be only a little single, but it's a hit.

o

I didn't entirely abandon baseball—the real thing instead of its depiction—during my film festival, and I never found any problems in adjustment whenever I went out to Shea or up to Yankee Stadium, for the two entertainments are nothing alike. Now and then, however, I'd finish a baseball rerun on my home set and flip over to a televised ballgame: an amazing shift, almost a revelation, in spite of the familiarity of what I found there. Games in progress, I realized, contained not just a sports story in the making but swift, onflowing catch-up on a couple of dozen stories and characters I already knew and remembered and cared about. It was like picking up an enormous novel (to change forms, for a moment) that I had been immersed in for days or weeks, which would then swiftly bring back old friends and enemies and crotchety neighbors, now all caught up in fresh difficulties. I think we fans sometimes forget how much we know, or can be quickly reminded of, about a couple of hundred ballplayers and their teams and managers, wounds, and hopes: know *well*, I mean, to the degree that a player's smallest gesture—a fiddled-with batting glove, a distinctive cap angle, the way he grinds his back foot in the batter's box just before the pitch—can please and comfort us like the face and tone of voice of a cheerful acquaintance or an old friend unexpect-edly encountered on the street. Baseball seems to have more of this built-in fiction or family history to it than other sports, and television can sometimes bring us the attribute more clearly than a seat at the park, if only because of the medium's sophisticated use of closeup—that sharp little dig in the ribs for our attention. Baseball is a great storyteller, better than Scheherazade, and effortlessly spins its whodunits and sentimental novels, shootouts and comedies, and high or low operas, game after game and week after week, for its casual or attentive devotees. One afternoon, I finished another baseball rerun on my video—I think it was *Bang the Drum Slowly*—punched REW on my wand, flipped over to Channel 4 of the TV, and was instantly transported into the midst of a rowdy Cubs–Cardinals encounter at Busch Stadium, brought to me by NBC's "Game of the Week." Pitchers pitched, groaning with the effort, batters banged away, and the cameras sailed and flew and zoomed down close to a batter, over to some fan faces, up and away to deep center field, in tight on the umpire's hand holding his indicator, staring over the pitcher's shoulder at the catcher's waggling fingers semaphoring a sign, while the announcers, Vin Scully and Tom Seaver, murmured and speculated and filled us in. There was Whitey Herzog mumbling something and chewing on something and resettling his cap over his scrub-brush coiffure after a homer by the Cubs' Mitch Webster; here was Don Zimmer stumping out to the mound, with his thick, short Brian Donlevy arms making a parenthesis around his middle; here was Calvin Schiraldi's unhappy stare, sadder and more soulful as he fell behind in the count. Ozzie Smith, blank-faced under his cap, glided, pirouetted, and flipped, and went back to his post with the same unsurprised "What did you expect?" look on him as the cheering and applause fell about him once again. Mitch Williams, the Cubs' madman new reliever, flung the ball and then hilariously flung himself after it, finishing with his back to the batter and himself peering over his own left shoulder in case of accident—in case anybody somehow made contact. Here came Dan Quisenberry, still pinkly quizzing away—go, Quis!—lobbing his up-and-down sinkers from his shoe tops and then half falling down himself, but with a more thoughtful, more gentlemanly mien. Commercials crossed my screen, cloud shadows crossed the bright field, the lead changed hands and then changed back, and the crowd roused itself and sank back again in despair. Somebody won—I forget who—but the announcers reminded us it was early yet in the summer and to wait and see. It was a good game, and, watching it, I understood once again what a daunting job it must be to make a decent baseball movie, and how tough the competition really is. Baseball games and baseball movies aren't after the same thing, to be sure, but they both want our attention. Ballgames win us without effort, like genius authors or dazzling athletes—like Dickens or Ozzie Smith—while the guys with scripts and cameras must think and confer and strain over the same stuff, and hope for our forgiveness when they're done. It's amazing that movie baseball works at all, considering the odds.

o

Just when *Eight Men Out* and *Bull Durham* and parts of *Major League* made me think the movies had finally started to get the hang of baseball, along came *Field of Dreams*. America has squeezed this picture to its bosom like Mom Gehrig, and I sense there's not much point in my carrying on here for too long about how much I didn't care for it. In the reviews it's been likened to a Capra movie or to a Disney World attraction, but for me it was a Sara Lee chocolate layer cake, with icing so thick that I could feel it dripping onto my shoes. Kevin Costner—a gentler, kindlier Costner—is back again, here as Ray Kinsella, an ex-hippie who's doing O.K. as an Iowa farmer (Amy Madigan is his smart, upbeat wife, and Gaby Hoffman is their young daughter) until a voice (or a Voice: it's the Big Fellow Upstairs) tells him to build a ballfield right in the middle of his corn crop. Ray obliges, single-handedly laying down a floodlit diamond of such opulence that you think he's hoping for an expansion franchise, and his vaguely promised reward is the arrival onfield of Shoeless Joe Jackson (Ray Liotta), limned in white light, who looks a little slack-jawed but seems to have picked up the sounds of literacy, or the sounds of writing, during his stopover in the Sweet By-and-By: "I'd wake up at night with the smell of the ballpark in my nose and the cool of the grass on my feet . . . the thrill of the grass." Jackson has also been reversed in the Darkroom Up There, for he now throws left and bats right (like Rickey Henderson and Cleon Jones), instead of the other way around, as he did in life. Kinsella—it's the last name of the author of the originating novel, *Shoeless Joe*, who gave it to the hero—responds to further instructions over the Vox Dei and so travels to Boston and to Minnesota to collect a disillusioned leftish novelist, Terence Mann (in the book, it was J. D. Salinger), played by

/

James Earl Jones, and the ghost of a dead country doctor (Burt Lancaster), who once played half an inning for John McGraw's Giants. By the time they get back to Iowa, the creditors are snapping at the Kinsella mortgage, but Shoeless Joe has picked up a few more illustrious major-league deads, including (we're told) Smokey Joe Wood and Mel Ott and Gil Hodges; we don't know what league they're in or who's playing whom, but, to their credit, they don't seem to mind the endless batting practice or the sounds of snuffling in the theatre.

Field of Dreams is a little smarter and more fun than I'm making it sound here. It skips along in its own sunshine, and there are some small jokes to make you feel less sentimental and less used (one of the spectral Black Sox, slipping back into invisibility in the center-field corn rows, kids around by yelling "I'm melting! I'm mel-l-ting!" like the Wicked Witch of the West in The Wizard of Oz), but its Hallmarky messages are a caution. The dreamy field, it turns out, is needed so that Ray can be reconciled with his late father, a fan and would-be pro player who idolized Shoeless Joe; there was a falling-out ("When I was fourteen, I started to refuse," Ray says. "Can you imagine an American boy refusing to play catch with his father?"), but the two make it up onscreen by T.-ing the old P. around in the gloaming (Dad can't throw for beans, but never mind), and Terence, Darth Vadering the moral for us in his suspenders, says that the one American constant through all the years has been baseball: "This field, this game, is part of our past. It reminds us of all that once was good and could be again."

The goo of goodness lies so thick over Field of Dreams that I probably shouldn't have been bothered by its dopiness or its wacky baseball, but its dreams kept waking me up. I liked being at Fenway Park with Ray and Terence until they suddenly walked out on me in the fourth inning—"Hey, guys, I thought you said you were fans!"—after spotting a mystical message on the scoreboard, and when Ray asked what American boy wouldn't want to play catch with his pop, I quickly thought of Ty Cobb and Ted Williams and Joe DiMaggio and, yes, Lou Gehrig, and a million more who never did and (sorry) who never said they'd missed it. More things seemed wrong with the actor-players and the baseball action in Field of Dreams than I could quite account for, in fact, and it took a smart friend (Bill James, the eagle-eyed baseball historian) to point out to me that, for one thing, it looked like they'd made the ball bigger in the flick—made it dreamier, I guess. The movie ends with a long, ascending night shot of the car headlights of arriving fan families, who are coming in countless numbers to watch the Spooks play and thus to save the farm for the Kinsellas. (Wise old Terence has told Ray to charge twenty bucks a pop for admission, which is eight-fifty more than the going rate for box seats at Wrigley Field, but maybe this is going to be more of a theme park.) All I could think of as the lights came on and the smiling

344

folks around me began gathering up their wadded Kleenexes was the inexorably arriving parking crunch at the Kinsella place (the rest of the cornfield would go to blacktop), the Port-o-Sans, the uniformed security goons, the Doppelfranks concession, and the blazered lawyers and agents. In dreams begin cable rights.

There may be a point here beyond jokes or some fresh concern about our national hyperglycemia readings. Organized baseball loves its image as a family-centered, nonviolent, tradition-based entertainment, but I wonder at times if any of that matters much. Maybe it's a load. Other sports get along well, or well enough, without this old heavy-mohair mantle of goodness, and maybe the commissioner or somebody else could arrange to loan it out to one of them—to basketball or stock-car racing or croquet—for a season or two and see if our game didn't feel lighter and quicker on its feet without it. I like baseball, the game and the games, but I can't always understand why it's so hard to look at the pastime with a clear gaze. We seem to want to go on sweetening it up, frosting the flakes, because we want it to say things about ourselves that probably aren't true. We don't have to go to the movies to find this out, either; we can just look at the TV news and the newspapers. All this spring and summer, I've been reading about Pete Rose, and wishing—with decreasing hope lately; say it ain't so, Pete—that the stories about his gambling and his foolishness were wrong. But the home Cincinnati fans—great numbers of them, at least—aren't waiting for the facts about Rose's betting to come out, one way or the other, after the legal squabbles are resolved; they believe in Pete. It's an article of faith, and they want the truth about him to be their truth, nothing else. I think it will be a sad day if Rose ends up being exiled from the game he illuminated and made joyful with his play. That would be a tragedy for him, but something less, surely, for the rest of us, unless we go on insisting, against all evidence, that our sports heroes must all be as good at life as they were at their games. That doesn't feel like a useful dream to hang on to. I'm told that Rose has received an offer for the film rights to his story, but I don't expect that a film bio would mean much. It's strange, because I've been seeing moving pictures of Pete Rose for weeks now—Pete up at bat, glaring out at the man on the mound and then leaning over the plate like a surveyor to follow the flight of the ball past his knees and into the catcher's mitt, and then flicking his gaze back at the home-plate ump, fighting for the call. I can see him waggling his fat-barrelled bat and fouling off pitches, and then, with the odds somehow mastered and turned his way, putting the bat on the ball once again and serving it smartly into left-center field; he sees a chance for two—and so do I, in the same half instant, and I jump to my feet, even though I know the outcome already, as he piston-thumps around first, spraying dirt and excitement along his bending path. Pete bangs into the base—safe by inches, safe by a mile—and pops up on his feet again, slaps his gloved hands together, settles his helmet with a fist-rap, and stares down at third now, ready for the next thing. These are memories, but they're crisp and clear, and I don't think they'll ever go away. They make a great movie.

The Interior Stadium

S ports are too much with us. Late and soon, sitting and watching— mostly watching on television—we lay waste our powers of identification and enthusiasm and, in time, attention as more and more closing rallies and crucial putts and late field goals and final playoffs and sudden deaths and world records and world championships unreel themselves ceaselessly before our half-lidded eyes. Professional leagues expand like bubble gum, ever larger and thinner, and the extended sporting seasons, now bunching and overlapping at the ends, conclude in exhaustion and the wrong weather. So, too, goes the secondary business of sports—the news or non-news off the field. Sports announcers (ex-halfbacks in Mod hairdos) bring us another live, exclusive interview in depth with the twitchy coach of some as yet undefeated basketball team, or with a weeping (for joy) fourteen-year-old champion female backstroker, and the sports pages, now almost the largest single part of the newspaper, brim with salary disputes, medical bulletins, franchise maneuverings, all-star ballots, drug scandals, close-up biogs, after-dinner tributes, union tactics, weekend wrapups, wire-service polls, draft-choice trades, clubhouse gossip, and the latest odds. The American obsession with sports is not a new phenomenon, of course, except in its current dimensions, its excessive excessiveness. What *is* new, and what must at times unsettle even the most devout and unselective fan, is a curious sense of loss. In the midst of all these successive spectacles and instant replays and endless reportings and recapitulations, we seem to have forgotten what we came for. More and more, each sport resembles all sports; the flavor, the special joys of place and season, the unique displays of courage and strength and style that once isolated each game and fixed it in our affections have disappeared somewhere in the noise and crush.

Of all sports, none has been so buffeted about by this unselective prolif-

347

eration, so maligned by contemporary cant, or so indifferently defended as baseball. Yet the game somehow remains the same, obdurately unaltered and comparable only with itself. Baseball has one saving grace that distinguishes it—for me, at any rate—from every other sport. Because of its pace, and thus the perfectly observed balance, both physical and psychological, between opposing forces, its clean lines can be restored in retrospect. This inner game—baseball in the mind—has no season, but it is best played in the winter, without the distraction of other baseball news. At first, it is a game of recollections, recapturings, and visions. Figures and occasions return, enormous sounds rise and swell, and the interior stadium fills with light and yields up the sight of a young ballplayer—some hero perfectly memorized— just completing his own unique swing and now racing toward first. See the way he runs? Yes, that's him! Unmistakable, he leans in, still following the distant flight of the ball with his eyes, and takes his big turn at the base. Yet this is only the beginning, for baseball in the mind is not a mere returning. In time, this easy summoning up of restored players, winning hits, and famous rallies gives way to reconsiderations and reflections about the sport itself. By thinking about baseball like this—by playing it over, keeping it warm in a cold season—we begin to make discoveries. With luck, we may even penetrate some of its mysteries. One of those mysteries is its vividness—the absolutely distinct inner vision we retain of that hitter, that eager base-runner, of however long ago. My father was talking the other day about some of the ballplayers he remembered. He grew up in Cleveland, and the Indians were his team. Still are. "We had Nap Lajoie at second," he said. "You've heard of him. A great big broad-shouldered fellow, but a beautiful fielder. He was a rough customer. If he didn't like an umpire's call, he'd give him a faceful of tobacco juice. The shortstop was Terry Turner—a smaller man, and blond. I can still see Lajoie picking up a grounder and wheeling and floating the ball over to Turner. Oh, he was quick on his feet! In right field we had Elmer Flick, now in the Hall of Fame. I liked the center fielder, too. His name was Harry Bay, and he wasn't a heavy hitter, but he was very fast and covered a lot of ground. They said he could circle the bases in twelve seconds flat. I saw him get a home run inside the park—the ball hit on the infield and went right past the second baseman and out to the wall, and Bay beat the relay. I remember Addie Joss, our great right-hander. Tall, and an elegant pitcher. I once saw him pitch a perfect game. He died young."

My father has been a fan all his life, and he has pretty well seen them all. He has told me about the famous last game of the 1912 World Series, in Boston, and seeing Fred Snodgrass drop that fly ball in the tenth inning, when the Red Sox scored twice and beat the Giants. I looked up Harry Bay and those other Indians in the *Baseball Encyclopedia*, and I think my father must have seen that inside-the-park homer in the summer of 1904. Lajoie batted

.376 that year, and Addie Joss led the American League with an earned-run average of 1.59, but the Indians finished in fourth place. 1904. . . . Sixty-seven years have gone by, yet Nap Lajoie is in plain view, and the ball still floats over to Terry Turner. Well, my father is eighty-one now, and old men are great rememberers of the distant past. But I am fifty, and I can also bring things back: Lefty Gomez, skinny-necked and frighteningly wild, pitching his first game at Yankee Stadium, against the White Sox and Red Faber in 1930. Old John McGraw, in a business suit and a white fedora, sitting lumpily in a dark corner of the dugout at the Polo Grounds and glowering out at the field. Babe Ruth, wearing a new, bright yellow glove, trotting out to right field—a swollen ballet dancer, with those delicate, almost feminine feet and ankles. Ruth at the plate, uppercutting and missing, staggering with the force of his swing. Ruth and Gehrig hitting back-to-back homers. Gehrig, in the summer of 1933, running bases with a bad leg in a key game against the Senators; hobbling, he rounds third, closely followed by young Dixie Walker, then a Yankee. The throw comes in to the plate, and the Washington catcher—it must have been Luke Sewell—tags out the sliding Gehrig and, in the same motion, the sliding Dixie Walker. A double play at the plate. The Yankees lose the game; the Senators go on to a pennant. And, back across the river again, Carl Hubbell. My own great pitcher, a southpaw, tall and elegant. Hub pitching: the loose motion; too slow, formal bows from the waist, glove and hands held almost in front of his face as he pivots, the long right leg (in long, peculiar pants) striding; and the ball, angling oddly, shooting past the batter. Hubbell walks gravely back to the bench, his pitching arm, as always, turned the wrong way round, with the palm out. Screwballer.

Any fan, as I say, can play this private game, extending it to extraordinary varieties and possibilities in his mind. Ruth bats against Sandy Koufax or Sam McDowell. . . . Hubbell pitches to Ted Williams, and the Kid, grinding the bat in his fist, twitches and blocks his hips with the pitch; he holds off but still follows the ball, leaning over and studying it like some curator as it leaps in just under his hands. Why this vividness, even from an imaginary confrontation? I have watched many other sports, and I have followed some—football, hockey, tennis—with eagerness, but none of them yields these permanent interior pictures, these ancient and precise excitements. Baseball, I must conclude, is intensely remembered because only baseball is so intensely watched. The game forces intensity upon us. In the ballpark, scattered across an immense green, each player is isolated in our attention, utterly visible. Watch that fielder just below us. Little seems to be expected of him. He waits in easy composure, his hands on his knees; when the ball at last soars or bounces out to him, he seizes it and dispatches it with swift, haughty ease. It all looks easy, slow, and, above all, safe. Yet we know better, for what is certain in baseball is that someone, perhaps several people, will

349

fail. They will be searched out, caught in the open, and defeated, and there will be no confusion about it or sharing of the blame. This is sure to happen, because what baseball requires of its athletes, of course, is nothing less than perfection, and perfection cannot be eased or divided. Every movement of every game, from first pitch to last out, is measured and recorded against an absolute standard, and thus each success is also a failure. Credit that strike-out to the pitcher, but also count it against the batter's average; mark this run unearned, because the left fielder bobbled the ball for an instant and a runner moved up. Yet, faced with this sudden and repeated presence of danger, the big-league player defends himself with such courage and skill that the illusion of safety is sustained. Tension is screwed tighter and tighter as the certain downfall is postponed again and again, so that when disaster does come—a half-topped infield hit, a walk on a close three-and-two call, a low drive up the middle that just eludes the diving shortstop—we rise and cry out. It is a spontaneous, inevitable, irresistible reaction.

○

Always, it seems, there is something more to be discovered about this game. Sit quietly in the upper stand and look at the field. Half close your eyes against the sun, so that the players recede a little, and watch the movements of baseball. The pitcher, immobile on the mound, holds the inert white ball, his little lump of physics. Now, with abrupt gestures, he gives it enormous speed and direction, converting it suddenly into a line, a moving line. The batter, wielding a plane, attempts to intercept the line and acutely alter it, but he fails; the ball, a line again, is redrawn to the pitcher, in the center of this square, the diamond. Again the pitcher studies his task—the projection of his next line through the smallest possible segment of an invisible seven-sided solid (the strike zone has depth as well as height and width) sixty feet and six inches away; again the batter considers his even more difficult proposition, which is to reverse this imminent white speck, to redirect its energy not in a soft parabola or a series of diminishing squiggles but into a beautiful and dangerous new force, of perfect straightness and immense distance. In time, these and other lines are drawn on the field; the batter and the fielders are also transformed into fluidity, moving and converging, and we see now that all movement in baseball is a convergence toward fixed points—the pitched ball toward the plate, the thrown ball toward the right angles of the bases, the batted ball toward the as yet undrawn but already visible point of congruence with either the ground or a glove. Simultaneously, the fielders hasten toward that same point of meeting with the ball, and both the base-runner and the ball, now redirected, toward their encounter at the base. From our perch, we can sometimes see three or four or more such geometries appearing at the same instant on the green board below us, and, mathematicians

350

that we are, can sense their solution even before they are fully drawn. It is neat, it is pretty, it is satisfying. Scientists speak of the profoundly moving aesthetic beauty of mathematics, and perhaps the baseball field is one of the few places where the rest of us can glimpse this mystery.

The last dimension is time. Within the ballpark, time moves differently, marked by no clock except the events of the game. This is the unique, unchangeable feature of baseball, and perhaps explains why this sport, for all the enormous changes it has undergone in the past decade or two, remains somehow rustic, unviolent, and introspective. Baseball's time is seamless and invisible, a bubble within which players move at exactly the same pace and rhythms as all their predecessors. This is the way the game was played in our youth and in our fathers' youth, and even back then—back in the country days—there must have been the same feeling that time could be stopped. Since baseball time is measured only in outs, all you have to do is succeed utterly; keep hitting, keep the rally alive, and you have defeated time. You remain forever young. Sitting in the stands, we sense this, if only dimly. The players below us—Mays, DiMaggio, Ruth, Snodgrass—swim and blur in memory, the ball floats over to Terry Turner, and the end of this game may never come.

ABOUT THE AUTHOR

Roger Angell has also written *The Stone Arbor, A Day in the Life of Roger Angell, The Summer Game, Five Seasons, Late Innings,* and *Season Ticket.* He is senior fiction editor of the *New Yorker* magazine and lives in New York City with his wife and son.

IVAN R. DEE PAPERBACKS

Literature, Arts, and Letters
Roger Angell, *Once More Around the Park*
Walter Bagehot, *Physics and Politics*
Stephen Vincent Benét, *John Brown's Body*
Isaiah Berlin, *The Hedgehog and the Fox*
F. Bordewijk, *Character*
Robert Brustein, *Cultural Calisthenics*
Robert Brustein, *Dumbocracy in America*
Anthony Burgess, *Shakespeare*
Philip Callow, *From Noon to Starry Night*
Philip Callow, *Son and Lover: The Young D. H. Lawrence*
Philip Callow, *Vincent Van Gogh*
Anton Chekhov, *The Comic Stories*
Bruce Cole, *The Informed Eye*
James Gould Cozzens, *Castaway*
James Gould Cozzens, *Men and Brethren*
Clarence Darrow, *Verdicts Out of Court*
Floyd Dell, *Intellectual Vagabondage*
Theodore Dreiser, *Best Short Stories*
Joseph Epstein, *Ambition*
André Gide, *Madeleine*
Gerald Graff, *Literature Against Itself*
John Gross, *The Rise and Fall of the Man of Letters*
Olivia Gude and Jeff Huebner, *Urban Art Chicago*
Irving Howe, *William Faulkner*
Aldous Huxley, *After Many a Summer Dies the Swan*
Aldous Huxley, *Ape and Essence*
Aldous Huxley, *Collected Short Stories*
Roger Kimball, *Tenured Radicals*
Hilton Kramer, *The Twilight of the Intellectuals*
Hilton Kramer and Roger Kimball, eds., *Against the Grain*
F. R. Leavis, *Revaluation*
F. R. Leavis, *The Living Principle*
F. R. Leavis, *The Critic as Anti-Philosopher*
Marie-Anne Lescourret, *Rubens: A Double Life*
Sinclair Lewis, *Selected Short Stories*
William L. O'Neill, ed., *Echoes of Revolt: The Masses, 1911–1917*
Budd Schulberg, *The Harder They Fall*
Ramón J. Sender, *Seven Red Sundays*
Peter Shaw, *Recovering American Literature*
James B. Simpson, ed., *Veil and Cowl*
Tess Slesinger, *On Being Told That Her Second Husband Has Taken His First Lover, and Other Stories*
Donald Thomas, *Swinburne*
B. Traven, *The Bridge in the Jungle*
B. Traven, *The Carreta*
B. Traven, *The Cotton-Pickers*
B. Traven, *General from the Jungle*
B. Traven, *Government*
B. Traven, *March to the Montería*
B. Traven, *The Night Visitor and Other Stories*
B. Traven, *The Rebellion of the Hanged*
B. Traven, *Trozas*
Anthony Trollope, *Trollope the Traveller*
Rex Warner, *The Aerodrome*
Rebecca West, *A Train of Powder*
Thomas Wolfe, *The Hills Beyond*
Wilhelm Worringer, *Abstraction and Empathy*

The Shakespeare Handbooks by Alistair McCallum
   Hamlet
   King Lear
   Macbeth
   Romeo and Juliet

Theatre and Drama
Linda Apperson, *Stage Managing and Theatre Etiquette*
Robert Brustein, *Cultural Calisthenics*
Robert Brustein, *Dumbocracy in America*
Robert Brustein, *Reimagining American Theatre*
Robert Brustein, *The Theatre of Revolt*
Stephen Citron, *The Musical from the Inside Out*
Irina and Igor Levin, *Working on the Play and the Role*
Keith Newlin, ed., *American Plays of the New Woman*
Louis Rosen, *The South Side*
David Wood, with Janet Grant, *Theatre for Children*
Plays for Performance:
   Aristophanes, *Lysistrata*
   Pierre Augustin de Beaumarchais, *The Barber of Seville*
   Pierre Augustin de Beaumarchais, *The Marriage of Figaro*
   Anton Chekhov, *The Cherry Orchard*
   Anton Chekhov, *The Seagull*
   Euripides, *The Bacchae*
   Euripides, *Iphigenia in Aulis*
   Euripides, *Iphigenia Among the Taurians*
   Euripides, *Medea*
   Euripides, *The Trojan Women*
   Georges Feydeau, *Paradise Hotel*
   Henrik Ibsen, *A Doll's House*
   Henrik Ibsen, *Ghosts*
   Henrik Ibsen, *Hedda Gabler*
   Henrik Ibsen, *The Master Builder*
   Henrik Ibsen, *When We Dead Awaken*
   Henrik Ibsen, *The Wild Duck*
   Heinrich von Kleist, *The Prince of Homburg*
   Christopher Marlowe, *Doctor Faustus*
   Molière, *The Bourgeois Gentleman*
   The Mysteries: Creation
   The Mysteries: The Passion
   Luigi Pirandello, *Six Characters in Search of an Author*
   Budd Schulberg, with Stan Silverman, *On the Waterfront* (the play)
   Sophocles, *Antigone*
   Sophocles, *Electra*
   Sophocles, *Oedipus the King*
   August Strindberg, *The Father*
   August Strindberg, *Miss Julie*
The Shakespeare Handbooks by Alistair McCallum
   Hamlet
   King Lear
   Macbeth
   Romeo and Juliet

American History and American Studies
Stephen Vincent Benét, *John Brown's Body*
Henry W. Berger, ed., *A William Appleman Williams Reader*
Andrew Bergman, *We're in the Money*
Paul Boyer, ed., *Reagan as President*
William Brashler, *Josh Gibson*
Robert V. Bruce, *1877: Year of Violence*
Douglas Bukowski, *Navy Pier*
Philip Callow, *From Noon to Starry Night*
Laurie Winn Carlson, *A Fever in Salem*
Kendrick A. Clements, *Woodrow Wilson*
Richard E. Cohen, *Rostenkowski*
David Cowan and John Kuenster, *To Sleep with the Angels*
George Dangerfield, *The Era of Good Feelings*
Clarence Darrow, *Verdicts Out of Court*
Allen F. Davis, *American Heroine*
Floyd Dell, *Intellectual Vagabondage*
Elisha P. Douglass, *Rebels and Democrats*

Theodore Draper, *The Roots of American Communism*
Edward Jay Epstein, *News from Nowhere*
Joseph Epstein, *Ambition*
Peter G. Filene, *In the Arms of Others*
Richard Fried, ed., Bruce Barton's *The Man Nobody Knows*
Lloyd C. Gardner, *Pay Any Price*
Lloyd C. Gardner, *Spheres of Influence*
Paul W. Glad, *McKinley, Bryan, and the People*
Eric F. Goldman, *Rendezvous with Destiny*
Sarah H. Gordon, *Passage to Union*
Daniel Horowitz, *The Morality of Spending*
Kenneth T. Jackson, *The Ku Klux Klan in the City, 1915–1930*
Edward Chase Kirkland, *Dream and Thought in the Business
    Community, 1860–1900*
Herbert S Klein, *Slavery in the Americas*
Aileen S. Kraditor, *Means and Ends in American Abolitionism*
Hilton Kramer, *The Twilight of the Intellectuals*
Hilton Kramer and Roger Kimball, eds., *The Betrayal of Liberalism*
Irving Kristol, *Neoconservatism*
Leonard W. Levy, *Jefferson and Civil Liberties: The Darker Side*
Leonard W. Levy, *Original Intent and the Framers' Constitution*
Leonard W. Levy, *Origins of the Fifth Amendment*
Leonard W. Levy, *The Palladium of Justice*
Seymour J. Mandelbaum, *Boss Tweed's New York*
Thomas J. McCormick, *China Market*
John Harmon McElroy, *American Beliefs*
Gerald W. McFarland, *A Scattered People*
Walter Millis, *The Martial Spirit*
Nicolaus Mills, ed., *Culture in an Age of Money*
Nicolaus Mills, *Like a Holy Crusade*
Roderick Nash, *The Nervous Generation*
Keith Newlin, ed., *American Plays of the New Woman*
William L. O'Neill, ed., *Echoes of Revolt: The Masses, 1911–1917*
Gilbert Osofsky, *Harlem: The Making of a Ghetto*
Edward Pessen, *Losing Our Souls*
Glenn Porter and Harold C. Livesay, *Merchants and Manufacturers*
John Prados, *The Hidden History of the Vietnam War*
John Prados, *Presidents' Secret Wars*
Patrick Renshaw, *The Wobblies*
Edward Reynolds, *Stand the Storm*
Louis Rosen, *The South Side*
Richard Schickel, *The Disney Version*
Richard Schickel, *Intimate Strangers*
Richard Schickel, *Matinee Idylls*
Richard Schickel, *The Men Who Made the Movies*
Edward A. Shils, *The Torment of Secrecy*
Geoffrey S. Smith, *To Save a Nation*
Robert W. Snyder, *The Voice of the City*
Bernard Sternsher, ed., *Hitting Home: The Great Depression in Town
    and Country*
Bernard Sternsher, ed., *Hope Restored: How the New Deal Worked
    in Town and Country*
Bernard Sternsher and Judith Sealander, eds., *Women of Valor*
Athan Theoharis, *From the Secret Files of J. Edgar Hoover*
Nicholas von Hoffman, *We Are the People Our Parents Warned Us Against*
Norman Ware, *The Industrial Worker, 1840–1860*
Tom Wicker, *JFK and LBJ: The Influence of Personality upon Politics*
Robert H. Wiebe, *Businessmen and Reform*
T. Harry Williams, *McClellan, Sherman and Grant*
Miles Wolff, *Lunch at the 5 & 10*
Randall B. Woods and Howard Jones, *Dawning of the Cold War*
American Ways Series:
    John A. Andrew III, *Lyndon Johnson and the Great Society*
    Roger Daniels, *Not Like Us*
    J. Matthew Gallman, *The North Fights the Civil War: The Home Front*
    Lewis L. Gould, *1968: The Election That Changed America*
    John Earl Haynes, *Red Scare or Red Menace?*
    D. Clayton James and Anne Sharp Wells, *From Pearl Harbor to V-J Day*
    John W. Jeffries, *Wartime America*
    Curtis D. Johnson, *Redeeming America*

Maury Klein, *The Flowering of the Third America*
Larry M. Logue, *To Appomattox and Beyond*
Jean V. Matthews, *Women's Struggle for Equality*
Iwan W. Morgan, *Deficit Government*
Robert Muccigrosso, *Celebrating the New World*
Daniel Nelson, *Shifting Fortunes*
Thomas R. Pegram, *Battling Demon Rum*
Burton W. Peretti, *Jazz in American Culture*
Hal K. Rothman, *Saving the Planet*
John A. Salmond, *"My Mind Set on Freedom"*
William Earl Weeks, *Building the Continental Empire*
Mark J. White, *Missiles in Cuba*

European and World History
John Charmley, *Chamberlain and the Lost Peace*
Lee Feigon, *China Rising*
Lee Feigon, *Demystifying Tibet*
Mark Frankland, *The Patriots' Revolution*
Lloyd C. Gardner, *Spheres of Influence*
David Gilmour, *Cities of Spain*
Raul Hilberg, et al., eds., *The Warsaw Diary of Adam Czerniakow*
Gertrude Himmelfarb, *Darwin and the Darwinian Revolution*
Gertrude Himmelfarb, *Marriage and Morals Among the Victorians*
Gertrude Himmelfarb, *Victorian Minds*
Thomas A. Idinopulos, *Jerusalem*
Thomas A. Idinopulos, *Weathered by Miracles*
Allan Janik and Stephen Toulmin, *Wittgenstein's Vienna*
Hilton Kramer and Roger Kimball, eds., *The Betrayal of Liberalism*
Ronnie S. Landau, *The Nazi Holocaust*
Filip Müller, *Eyewitness Auschwitz*
Clive Ponting, *1940: Myth and Reality*
A.L. Rowse, *The Elizabethan Renaissance: The Life of the Society*
A.L. Rowse, *The Elizabethan Renaissance: The Cultural Achievement*
Scott Shane, *Dismantling Utopia*
Alexis de Tocqueville, *Memoir on Pauperism*
Paul Webster, *Petain's Crime*
John Weiss, *Ideology of Death*

Philosophy
Philosophers in 90 Minutes by Paul Strathern
    Thomas Aquinas in 90 Minutes
    Aristotle in 90 Minutes
    St. Augustine in 90 Minutes
    Berkeley in 90 Minutes
    Confucius in 90 Minutes
    Derrida in 90 Minutes
    Descartes in 90 Minutes
    Foucault in 90 Minutes
    Hegel in 90 Minutes
    Hume in 90 Minutes
    Kant in 90 Minutes
    Kierkegaard in 90 Minutes
    Leibniz in 90 Minutes
    Locke in 90 Minutes
    Machiavelli in 90 Minutes
    Marx in 90 Minutes
    Nietzsche in 90 Minutes
    Plato in 90 Minutes
    Bertrand Russell in 90 Minutes
    Sartre in 90 Minutes
    Schopenhauer in 90 Minutes
    Socrates in 90 Minutes
    Spinoza in 90 Minutes
    Wittgenstein in 90 Minutes